creativity

Other titles in this
series include:

creativity

A READER *for* WRITERS

Ryan G. Van Cleave
Ringling College of Art + Design

New York   Oxford
Oxford University Press

Oxford University Press is a department of the University of Oxford.
It furthers the University's objective of excellence in research,
scholarship, and education by publishing worldwide.

Oxford   New York
Auckland   Cape Town   Dar es Salaam   Hong Kong   Karachi
Kuala Lumpur   Madrid   Melbourne   Mexico City   Nairobi
New Delhi   Shanghai   Taipei   Toronto

With offices in
Argentina   Austria   Brazil   Chile   Czech Republic   France   Greece
Guatemala   Hungary   Italy   Japan   Poland   Portugal   Singapore
South Korea   Switzerland   Thailand   Turkey   Ukraine   Vietnam

For titles covered by Section 112 of the US Higher Education Opportunity Act,
please visit www.oup.com/us/he for the latest information about
pricing and alternate formats.

Published by Oxford University Press
198 Madison Avenue, New York, New York 10016
http://www.oup.com

Library of Congress Cataloging-in-Publication Data
Names: Cleave, Ryan van.
Title: Creativity : a reader for writers / Ryan Van Cleave.
Description: 1 Edition. | New York : Oxford University Press, 2016.
Identifiers: LCCN 2015037612| ISBN 9780190279929 (alk. paper) |
    ISBN 9780190279943 (alk. paper)
Subjects: LCSH: Creative ability.
Classification: LCC BF408 .C7534 2016 | DDC 153.3/5--dc23 LC record available
    at http://lccn.loc.gov/2015037612

Printing number: 9 8 7 6 5 4 3 2 1

Printed in the United States of America
on acid-free paper

brief table of contents

contents

Isaac Asimov, **"How Do People Get New Ideas?"** *MIT Technology Review*   2

"Making the cross-connection requires a certain daring. It must, for any cross-connection that does not require daring is performed at once by many and develops not as a 'new idea,' but as a mere 'corollary of an old idea.'"

Mihaly Csikszentmihalyi, **"The Creative Personality"** Abridged from *Creativity: Flow and the Psychology of Discovery and Invention*   8

"Of all human activities, creativity comes closest to providing the fulfillment we all hope to get in our lives. Call it full-blast living."

Steven Johnson, **"The Adjacent Possible"** *Where Good Ideas Come From: The Natural History of Innovation*   16

"We have a natural tendency to romanticize breakthrough inventions, imagining momentous ideas transcending their surroundings, a gifted mind somehow seeing over the detritus of old ideas and ossified tradition. But ideas are works of bricolage; they're built out of that detritus."

"Essentially, creativity is an endless resource, initiated by your drive to tackle challenges and to seize opportunities. Anything and everything can spark your Innovation Engine—every word, every object, every decision, and every action."

"Innovators seek to do things differently and be radical without a conventional framework. However, adaptors seek to do things better by operating *within* a conventional framework."

"When creativity engages individuals—when it inveigles thoughts, conjoins passions, and enlightens the mind—it begins to alter lives by starting with one's life and then progressing to others. It arrives at a level of maturity that could not be obtained otherwise because creativity requires movement if it is going to thrive."

"Too many people believe creativity is a talent with which some people are born and the rest can only envy. This is a negative attitude that is completely mistaken. Creativity is a skill that can be learned, developed and applied."

2 Creativity Myths   71

"You can't just turn on creativity like a faucet. You have to be in the right mood."

"Wow. I feel sorry for you. It must be hard going through life without any creativity."

"If we weren't naturally creative and couldn't find ideas, humans would have died out long ago."

"While newness seems central to the concept of creativity, by itself it guarantees neither admiration nor acceptance."

"Everyone says they love innovation. Most companies don't. In fact, most of them hate innovation."

"The good news: you get a few good creative ideas each week. The bad news: you have to bite your tongue and only try to act on 2–3 each year."

"The commitment of creative people is highly contingent, and their motivation comes largely from within."

"In a fear-based, failure-averse culture, people will consciously or unconsciously avoid risk. They will seek instead to repeat something safe that's been good enough in the past."

"Space is a key factor in each of our habitats, because it clearly communicates what you should and shouldn't be doing."

will die and never be seen again, people don't hold on out of fear that they'll have nothing to offer at the end."

"Making lists is my way of raking ideas into a critical mass before I work them out. While my pen scribbles and *order* settles in, my imagination runs ahead, anticipating creation."

7 Creativity Strategies and Hacks 365

"If you think some people are just born that way (and you're not one of them), think again. Experts say we all have a wellspring of creative energy. The secret is how to tap it."

"If you want to be a creator instead of a consumer, you must view existing ideas as fuel for your mind. You must stop seeing them as objects of functional things—they are combinations of ingredients waiting to be reused."

"When James Dyson, inventor of the famous Dyson vacuum cleaner, came to speak at Target, someone asked him, 'How do you innovate?' He replied, 'That's easy. Find something that pisses you off and fix the problem.'"

"Spiral Thinking is a process designed to expand the patterns and rigors of our traditional learned linear thinking. It makes every attempt to extend beyond the routine, the obvious and the expected, not to be rebellious, but to become exponentially productive at the speed of the new century."

rhetorical contents

academic writing

argument and persuasion

cause-and-effect analysis

comparison and contrast

definition

example and illustration

Personal

Visual

Creativity is something everybody desires and admires, but ask them to define it and things get murky fast. Over the past two years, I've been asking colleagues, students, neighbors, and even strangers at grocery stores what they think creativity is. Here's a sense of the range of responses I've received.

- Creativity is pure genius.
- Creativity is when your intelligence has fun.
- Creativity is like listening to God.
- Creativity is the sort of thing that only happens when you don't pay attention to it.
- Creativity happens when you make something new.
- Creativity is playing a musical instrument well.
- Creativity is something you're born with.
- Creativity is impossible to define.

The longer the list of answers got, the less sure I was that I was understanding creativity better as a result of asking these questions.

After reading a mountain of work on this topic, speaking to the leading experts, and teaching a new course ("The Creative Imagination: Process and Theory") that I designed at my college, it seems that two things hold true. (1) Creativity is universally believed to be a good thing. (2) We want to know more about it. Need proof? Just Google "creativity" and be prepared for a lifetime's worth of reading. Want to narrow it down some? Here are useful search terms: "creativity definition," "creativity in the classroom," "creativity and the brain," "creativity activities," "creativity and innovation," "creativity and mental illness," "creativity test," "creativity and intelligence," "creativity blog," "creativity quote," "development of creativity," "creativity study," "creativity expert," "creativity genius," "creativity help," "creativity killer," and "creativity and psychology." Perhaps now more than ever, it appears that anything worth doing seems like it can be done better—more powerfully, more efficiently, more excitingly—with creativity.

One challenge in compiling a thematic reader like this is deciding what to include, and how much. I had a sizable handful of much-loved pieces that I felt strongly about including, and then I spent a lot of time looking for topics and categories that I felt should be included. The first gathering of these texts on creativity was unpublishable out of sheer length—think *War and Peace* long! A (much) later incarnation found a far more acceptably sized manuscript that was a mix of industry experts and newer voices, including canonical texts and fresh takes on this age-old topic. The readings in this final version come from a wide range of interests, intellectual vantage points, and moments in time. Taken together, they provide a thoughtful but not exhaustive look at this thing we call creativity. There's enough here to carry a class through an entire year, a single semester, or a powerhouse unit on creativity.

If you skim through the table of contents and don't see a specific name in the world of creativity that you're looking for, rest assured, I read their work, spoke to them on the phone, bought them a Caramel Ribbon Crunch Frappucino blended coffee at Starbucks somewhere while I interviewed them, and/or spoke with their students, and/or watched their videos/e-learning courses. In short, their work is represented in the chapter introductions and the accompanying questions, in one way or another. And it's also worth noting that many of the authors of these texts do directly mention and build upon the work of others, so this text is far more multivocal than a simple scan of the table of contents might suggest.

Of all the things I heard, read, or saw about creativity, here are the two bits of wisdom that I wrote on index cards and taped next to my computer screen. From jazz bassist and bandleader Charles Mingus: "Making the simple complicated is commonplace; making the complicated simple, awesomely simple, that's creativity." And from creativity expert Edward de Bono: "There is no doubt that creativity is the most important human resource of all. Without creativity, there would be no progress, and we would be forever repeating the same patterns." These resonated with me in a powerful way.

Find out which ideas, quotations, and tips in this book speak to you in an equally powerful fashion, and then send me a note via the CONTACT ME page on www.ryangvancleave.com. I want to know! (Why is that professors can't help but keep gathering data and doing research?)

This book challenges readers to investigate what they know—or think they know—about creativity and the creative process. It invites them to be part of the ongoing enterprise of creative self-improvement, which is more and more relevant no matter one's arena of work. Yes, it's messy. Yes, it's elusive. But creativity is also proving to be the cornerstone of our new world economy. Daniel Pink's *A Whole New Mind: Why Right-Brainers Will Rule the Future* isn't a mega-bestseller for nothing! The crux of his argument? Right-brainers—meaning creative people—are going to be in high demand in the twenty-first century. How's that for some encouraging news? So read on and keep this idea in mind: creative people aren't afraid to fail. They aren't afraid of being challenged, either.

Creativity: A Reader for Writers is part of a series of brief single-topic readers from Oxford University Press designed for today's college writing courses. Each reader in this series approaches a topic of contemporary conversation from multiple perspectives.

- **Timely** Most selections were originally published in 2010 or later.
- **Global** Sources and voices from around the world are included.
- **Diverse** Selections come from a range of nontraditional and alternate print and online media, as well as representative mainstream sources.
- **Curated** Every author of a volume in this series is a teacher-scholar whose experience in the writing classroom, as well as expertise in a volume's specific subject area, informs their choices of readings.

In addition to the rich array of perspectives on topical (even urgent) issues addressed in each reader, each volume features an abundance of different genres and styles—from the academic research to the pithy Twitter argument. Useful but nonintrusive pedagogy includes the following:

- **Chapter introductions** that provide a brief overview of the chapter's theme and a sense of how the chapter's selections relate to both the overarching theme and each other.
- **Headnotes** introduce each reading by providing concise information about its original publication and the author's background.

- **"Analyze" and "Explore" questions** after each reading scaffold and support student reading for comprehension, as well as rhetorical considerations, providing prompts for reflection, classroom discussion, suggestions and brief writing assignments.
- **"Forging Connections" and "Looking Further"** prompts after each chapter encourage critical thinking by asking students to compare perspectives and strategies among readings both within the chapter and with readings in other chapters, suggesting writing assignments (many of which are multimodal) that encourage students to engage with larger conversations in the academy, the community, and the media.
- **An appendix on "Researching and Writing About Creativity"** guides student inquiry and research in a digital environment. Co-authored by a research librarian and a writing program director, this appendix provides real-world, transferable strategies for locating, assessing, synthesizing, and citing sources in support of an argument.

about the author

Ryan G. Van Cleave is an author, writing coach, keynote speaker, and liberal arts professor who reads, studies, teaches, and writes in nearly every genre. The author of more than twenty books, his own writing has appeared in *The Christian Science Monitor, Harvard Review, The Missouri Review, Ploughshares*, and *The Writer*, among other venues. He holds an MA in English (American Literature/Creative Writing-Fiction) and PhD in English (American Literature/Creative Writing-Poetry) from Florida State University, where he was an Edward H. and Marie C. Kingsbury Fellow. His honors also include a gold medal from the Florida Book Awards, a Florida Individual Artist Fellowship, and a residency at The Hermitage Artist Retreat, plus he was a Jenny McKean Moore Writer-in-Washington at George Washington University and the only Anastasia C. Hoffman Poetry Fellow at the University of Wisconsin–Madison's Institute for Creative Writing. Currently, he runs the Creative Writing B.F.A. program at the Ringling College of Art + Design in Sarasota, Florida.

For more information, see www.ryangvancleave.com.

acknowledgments

My dearest thanks to the contributors in this volume whose work was selected from a host of compelling pieces. Thank you for agreeing to be part of this book.

Special thanks go to the Ringling College of Art + Design, whose students field-tested the bulk of the texts, writing prompts, and discussion questions included in this book. The students who helped are too many to name, but know that their contributions and feedback were greatly appreciated and exceedingly helpful. (Rest assured, they received ample reward by way of brownie points, extra Halloween/Easter candy, and, occasionally, gluten-free baked goods that my wife sent along in huge Tupperware containers.)

I also extend my heartfelt thanks to Carrie Brandon and Garon Scott, who have both shown incredible interest, support, and enthusiasm in my Oxford University Press projects. Thanks, too, is due to Christian Holdener and S4Carlisle Publishing Services for their incredible work in the editing stage. And, as always, I thank my wife and daughters, who offer unwavering support, patience, and good spirit.

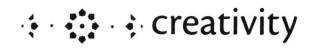 creativity

The Creative Process

"Creativity about life in all of its aspects, I think, is still the secret of great creative people."

—Leo Burnett, American advertising executive

We all know about creativity. But ask someone to pin down exactly what it is—what the process is and how it actually works—and you get enough answers to fill the Grand Canyon. Artists, inventors, businesspeople, teachers, authors, psychologists, and philosophers alike yearn to more fully understand the powerful force of creativity. American philosopher and psychologist John Dewey claims it's all about hunches. World-class poet T. S. Eliot believes in the incubation of ideas. Scott Barry Kaufman, scientific director of The Imagination Institute in the

Positive Psychology Center at the University of Pennsylvania, believes it's far more than the left brain/right brain distinction and that a four-stage process is really what's happening in terms of the neuroscience of creativity. English author Neil Gaiman adds that it's about "desperation and deadlines," and "most of all, ideas come from confluence—they come from two things flowing together. They come, essentially, from dreaming."

What's clear is that it's not clear. Not at all. We know creativity is good. We know creativity is something that's demonstrated more often in certain individuals than others. We know it's elusive and (seemingly) not always available when we wish it to be. We know there is some kind of process or methodology to it.

Taken together, the following pieces work to zero in on some core ideas at the heart of the creative enterprise. Understand that while these blueprints, these understandings, might work for some people, they might not all work as well for all people. So find the ones that speak most directly to your own creative process, but don't forget that the other pieces aren't therefore wrong, invalid, or un-useful, either.

So read on with an open mind and fuel yourself with some wisdom from one of the most prolific writers of his generation, Jack London, who said: "You can't wait for inspiration, you have to go after it with a club." Get your club ready!

Isaac Asimov
"How Do People Get New Ideas?"

Author of more than five hundred books on a wide range of subjects, Russian-born **Isaac Asimov** (1920–1992) was a professor of biochemistry at Boston University School of Medicine. His *Foundation* series and the novel *I, Robot* are considered two of the most influential science fiction works of all time. "How Do People Get New Ideas?" first appeared in the October 2014 issue of *MIT Technology Review.*

N ote from Arthur Obermayer, friend of the author:
In 1959, I worked as a scientist at Allied Research Associates in Boston. The company was an MIT spinoff that originally focused on the effects of nuclear weapons on aircraft structures. The company received a contract with the acronym GLIPAR (Guide Line Identification Program for Antimissile Research) from the Advanced Research Projects Agency to elicit the most creative approaches possible for a ballistic missile defense system. The government recognized that no matter how much was spent on improving and expanding current technology, it would remain inadequate. They wanted us and a few other contractors to think "out of the box."

When I first became involved in the project, I suggested that Isaac Asimov, who was a good friend of mine, would be an appropriate person to participate. He expressed his willingness and came to a few meetings. He eventually decided not to continue, because he did not want to have access to any secret classified information; it would limit his freedom of expression. Before he left, however, he wrote this essay on creativity as his single formal input. This essay was never published or used beyond our small group. When I recently rediscovered it while cleaning out some old files, I recognized that its contents are as broadly relevant today as when he wrote it. It describes not only the creative process and the nature of creative people but also the kind of environment that promotes creativity.

On Creativity

H ow do people get new ideas?
Presumably, the process of creativity, whatever it is, is essentially the same in all its branches and varieties, so that the evolution of a new art form, a new gadget, a new scientific principle, all involve common factors. We are most interested in the "creation" of a new scientific principle or a new application of an old one, but we can be general here.

One way of investigating the problem is to consider the great ideas of the past and see just how they were generated. Unfortunately, the method of generation is never clear even to the "generators" themselves.

But what if the same earth-shaking idea occurred to two men, simultaneously and independently? Perhaps, the common factors involved would be illuminating. Consider the theory of evolution by natural selection, independently created by Charles Darwin and Alfred Wallace.

There is a great deal in common there. Both traveled to far places, observing strange species of plants and animals and the manner in which they varied from place to place. Both were keenly interested in finding an explanation for this, and both failed until each happened to read Malthus's "Essay on Population."

Both then saw how the notion of overpopulation and weeding out (which Malthus had applied to human beings) would fit into the doctrine of evolution by natural selection (if applied to species generally).

Obviously, then, what is needed is not only people with a good background in a particular field, but also people capable of making a connection between item 1 and item 2 which might not ordinarily seem connected.

Undoubtedly in the first half of the 19th century, a great many naturalists had studied the manner in which species were differentiated among themselves. A great many people had read Malthus. Perhaps some both studied species and read Malthus. But what you needed was someone who studied species, read Malthus, and had the ability to make a cross-connection.

That is the crucial point that is the rare characteristic that must be found. Once the cross-connection is made, it becomes obvious. Thomas H. Huxley is supposed to have exclaimed after reading *On the Origin of Species*, "How stupid of me not to have thought of this."

But why didn't he think of it? The history of human thought would make it seem that there is difficulty in thinking of an idea even when all the facts are on the table. Making the cross-connection requires a certain daring. It must, for any cross-connection that does not require daring is performed at once by many and develops not as a "new idea," but as a mere "corollary of an old idea."

It is only afterward that a new idea seems reasonable. To begin with, it usually seems unreasonable. It seems the height of unreason to suppose the earth was round instead of flat, or that it moved instead of the sun, or that objects required a force to stop them when in motion, instead of a force to keep them moving, and so on.

A person willing to fly in the face of reason, authority, and common sense must be a person of considerable self-assurance. Since he occurs only rarely, he must seem eccentric (in at least that respect) to the rest of us. A person eccentric in one respect is often eccentric in others.

Consequently, the person who is most likely to get new ideas is a person of good background in the field of interest and one who is unconventional in his habits. (To be a crackpot is not, however, enough in itself.)

Once you have the people you want, the next question is: Do you want to bring them together so that they may discuss the problem mutually, or should you inform each of the problem and allow them to work in isolation?

My feeling is that as far as creativity is concerned, isolation is required. The creative person is, in any case, continually working at it. His mind is shuffling his information at all times, even when he is not conscious of it. (The famous example of Kekulé working out the structure of benzene in his sleep is well-known.)

The presence of others can only inhibit this process, since creation is embarrassing. For every new good idea you have, there are a hundred, ten thousand foolish ones, which you naturally do not care to display.

Nevertheless, a meeting of such people may be desirable for reasons other than the act of creation itself.

No two people exactly duplicate each other's mental stores of items. One person may know A and not B, another may know B and not A, and either knowing A and B, both may get the idea—though not necessarily at once or even soon.

Furthermore, the information may not only be of individual items A and B, but even of combinations such as A-B, which in themselves are not significant. However, if one person mentions the unusual combination of A-B and another the unusual combination A-C, it may well be that the combination A-B-C, which neither has thought of separately, may yield an answer.

It seems to me then that the purpose of cerebration sessions is not to think up new ideas but to educate the participants in facts and fact-combinations, in theories and vagrant thoughts.

But how to persuade creative people to do so? First and foremost, there must be ease, relaxation, and a general sense of permissiveness. The world in general disapproves of creativity, and to be creative in public is particularly bad. Even to speculate in public is rather worrisome. The individuals must, therefore, have the feeling that the others won't object.

If a single individual present is unsympathetic to the foolishness that would be bound to go on at such a session, the others would freeze. The unsympathetic individual may be a gold mine of information, but the harm he does will more than compensate for that. It seems necessary to me, then, that all people at a session be willing to sound foolish and listen to others sound foolish.

If a single individual present has a much greater reputation than the others, or is more articulate, or has a distinctly more commanding personality, he may well take over the conference and reduce the rest to little more than passive obedience. The individual may himself be extremely useful, but he might as well be put to work solo, for he is neutralizing the rest.

The optimum number of the group would probably not be very high. I should guess that no more than five would be wanted. A larger group might have a larger total supply of information, but there would be the tension of waiting to speak, which can be very frustrating. It would probably be better to have a number of sessions at which the people attending would vary, rather than one session including them all. (This would involve a certain repetition, but even repetition is not in itself undesirable. It is not what people say at these conferences, but what they inspire in each other later on.)

For best purposes, there should be a feeling of informality. Joviality, the use of first names, joking, relaxed kidding are, I think, of the essence—not in themselves, but because they encourage a willingness to be involved in the folly of creativeness. For this purpose I think a meeting in someone's home or over a dinner table at some restaurant is perhaps more useful than one in a conference room.

Probably more inhibiting than anything else is a feeling of responsibility. The great ideas of the ages have come from people who weren't paid to have great ideas, but were paid to be teachers or patent clerks or petty officials, or were not paid at all. The great ideas came as side issues.

To feel guilty because one has not earned one's salary because one has not had a great idea is the surest way, it seems to me, of making it certain that no great idea will come in the next time either.

Yet your company is conducting this cerebration program on government money. To think of congressmen or the general public hearing about scientists fooling around, boondoggling, telling dirty jokes, perhaps, at government expense, is to break into a cold sweat. In fact, the average scientist has enough public conscience not to want to feel he is doing this even if no one finds out.

I would suggest that members at a cerebration session be given sinecure tasks to do—short reports to write, or summaries of their conclusions, or brief answers to suggested problems—and be paid for that, the payment being the fee that would ordinarily be paid for the cerebration session.

The cerebration session would then be officially unpaid-for and that, too, would allow considerable relaxation.

I do not think that cerebration sessions can be left unguided. There must be someone in charge who plays a role equivalent to that of a psychoanalyst. A psychoanalyst, as I understand it, by asking the right questions (and except for that interfering as little as possible), gets the patient himself to discuss his past life in such a way as to elicit new understanding of it in his own eyes.

In the same way, a session-arbiter will have to sit there, stirring up the animals, asking the shrewd question, making the necessary comment, bringing them gently back to the point. Since the arbiter will not know which question is shrewd, which comment necessary, and what the point is, his will not be an easy job.

As for "gadgets" designed to elicit creativity, I think these should arise out of the bull sessions themselves. If thoroughly relaxed, free of responsibility, discussing something of interest, and being by nature unconventional, the participants themselves will create devices to stimulate discussion.

Analyze

1. Why does Asimov feel that isolation is a prerequisite for the creative process? What do you think about the role of isolation in the creative process?

2. In his example on how Charles Darwin and Alfred Wallace were the only ones to create a theory of evolution via natural selection despite the fact that "a great many naturalists had studied the manner in which species were differentiated among themselves," he uses the term "cross-connection." What does that term mean? What does cross-connection require? What examples of cross-connection can you draw from your own life?

3. What does Asimov mean when he says "to think of congressmen or the general public hearing about scientists fooling around, boondoggling, telling dirty jokes, perhaps, at the government expense, is to break into a cold sweat"? Do you think he really means it? In what ways might that fear seem true today?

4. The piece ends with a mention of "'gadgets' designed to elicit creativity." What are some examples of these gadgets, then and now?

Explore

1. In his preface note, Arthur Obermayer says about finding this long-misplaced writing by Asimov that "I recognized that its contents are as broadly relevant today as when he wrote it." In what way(s) might one view Asimov's ideas to be as relevant today as they were in 1959?

2. Asimov mentions how the scientist August Kekulé worked out the structure of benzene in his sleep. Use the Internet to find out the facts of this story. What role do you think dreams play in creativity and breakthroughs such as this?

3. A Russian-born American writer and biochemist, Asimov was one of the most prolific writers of the last century—he wrote or edited more than 500 books and close to 100,000 postcards/letters. More surprisingly, his books have been published in nine of the ten major categories of the Dewey Decimal system, which is to say he wrote about a wide variety of subjects from Christianity to humor to science fiction to history to a guide to Shakespeare to biology. Write something outside of your own comfort zone. Use your creativity to push beyond your perceived limits.

4. Write your own essay entitled "How Do People Get New Ideas?" What type of examples, considerations, and processes should you include? What can you do to make it relevant for readers a half-century into the future?

Mihaly Csikszentmihalyi
"The Creative Personality"

Born in Italy in 1934, **Mihaly Csikszentmihalyi** (pronounced me-HIGH chick-sent-me-HIGH-ee) immigrated to the United States at age twenty-two to study psychology. The author of numerous books on creativity and psychology, he serves as the Distinguished Professor of Psychology and Management at Claremont Graduate University. He is also the founding co-director of the Quality of Life Research Center, a nonprofit research institute that studies positive psychology, such as optimism, creativity, intrinsic motivation, and responsibility. "The Creative Personality" comes from his book *Creativity: Flow and the Psychology of Discovery and Invention.*

O f all human activities, creativity comes closest to providing the fulfillment we all hope to get in our lives. Call it full-blast living.

Creativity is a central source of meaning in our lives. Most of the things that are interesting, important, and human are the result of creativity. What makes us different from apes—our language, values, artistic expression, scientific understanding, and technology—is the result of individual ingenuity that was recognized, rewarded, and transmitted through learning.

When we're creative, we feel we are living more fully than during the rest of life. The excitement of the artist at the easel or the scientist in the lab comes close to the ideal fulfillment we all hope to get from life, and so rarely do. Perhaps only sex, sports, music, and religious ecstasy—even when these experiences remain fleeting and leave no trace—provide a profound sense of being part of an entity greater than ourselves. But creativity also leaves an outcome that adds to the richness and complexity of the future.

I have devoted 30 years of research to how creative people live and work, to make more understandable the mysterious process by which they come up with new ideas and new things. Creative individuals are remarkable for their ability to adapt to almost any situation and to make do with whatever is at hand to reach their goals. If I had to express in one word what makes their personalities different from others, it's complexity. They show tendencies of thought and action that in most people are segregated. They contain contradictory extremes; instead of being an "individual," each of them is a "multitude."

Here are the 10 antithetical traits often present in creative people that are integrated with each other in a dialectical tension.

1. Creative people have a great deal of physical energy, but they're also often quiet and at rest. They work long hours, with great concentration, while projecting an aura of freshness and enthusiasm. This suggests a superior physical endowment, a genetic advantage. Yet it is surprising how often individuals who in their seventies and eighties exude energy and health remember childhoods plagued by illness. It seems that their energy is internally generated, due more to their focused minds than to the superiority of their genes.

This does not mean that creative people are hyperactive, always "on." In fact, they rest often and sleep a lot. The important thing is that they control their energy; it's not ruled by the calendar, the dock, an external schedule. When necessary, they can focus it like a laser beam; when not, creative types immediately recharge their batteries. They consider the rhythm of activity followed by idleness or reflection very important for the success of their work. This is not a bio-rhythm inherited with their genes; it was learned by trial and error as a strategy for achieving their goals.

One manifestation of energy is sexuality. Creative people are paradoxical in this respect also. They seem to have quite a strong dose of eros, or generalized libidinal energy, which some express directly into sexuality. At the same time, a certain spartan celibacy is also a part of their makeup; continence tends to accompany superior achievement. Without eros, it would be difficult to take life on with vigor; without restraint, the energy could easily dissipate.

2. Creative people tend to be smart yet naive at the same time. How smart they actually are is open to question. It is probably true that what psychologists call the "g factor," meaning a core of general intelligence, is high among people who make important creative contributions.

The earliest longitudinal study of superior mental abilities, initiated at Stanford University by the psychologist Lewis Terman in 1921, shows rather conclusively that children with very high IQs do well in life, but after a certain point IQ does not seem to be correlated any longer with superior performance in real life. Later studies suggest that the cutoff point is around 120; it might be difficult to do creative work with a lower IQ, but an IQ beyond 120 does not necessarily imply higher creativity.

Another way of expressing this dialectic is the contrasting poles of wisdom and childishness. As Howard Gardner remarked in his study of the major creative geniuses of this century, a certain immaturity, both emotional and mental, can go hand in hand with deepest insights. Mozart comes immediately to mind.

Furthermore, people who bring about an acceptable novelty in a domain seem able to use well two opposite ways of thinking: the convergent and the divergent. Convergent thinking is measured by IQ tests, and it involves solving well-defined, rational problems that have one correct answer. Divergent thinking leads to no agreed-upon solution. It involves fluency, or the ability to generate a great quantity of ideas; flexibility, or the ability to switch from one perspective to another; and originality in picking unusual associations of ideas. These are the dimensions of thinking that most creativity tests measure and that most workshops try to enhance.

Yet there remains the nagging suspicion that at the highest levels of creative achievement the generation of novelty is not the main issue. People often claimed to have had only two or three good ideas in their entire career, but each idea was so generative that it kept them busy for a lifetime of testing, filling out, elaborating, and applying.

Divergent thinking is not much use without the ability to tell a good idea from a bad one, and this selectivity involves convergent thinking.

3. Creative people combine playfulness and discipline, or responsibility and irresponsibility. There is no question that a playfully light attitude is typical of creative individuals. But this playfulness doesn't go very far without its antithesis, a quality of doggedness, endurance, perseverance.

Nina Holton, whose playfully wild germs of ideas are the genesis of her sculpture, is very firm about the importance of hard work: "Tell anybody you're a sculptor and they'll say, 'Oh, how exciting, how wonderful.' And I tend to say, 'What's so wonderful?' It's like being a mason, or a carpenter, half the time. But they don't wish to hear that because they really only imagine the first part, the exciting part. But, as Khrushchev once said, that doesn't fry pancakes, you see. That germ of an idea does not make a sculpture which stands up. It just sits there. So the next stage is the hard work. Can you really translate it into a piece of sculpture?"

Jacob Rabinow, an electrical engineer, uses an interesting mental technique to slow himself down when work on an invention requires more endurance than intuition: "When I have a job that takes a lot of effort, slowly, I pretend I'm in jail. If I'm in jail, time is of no consequence. In other words, if it takes a week to cut this, it'll take a week. What else have I got to do? I'm going to be here for twenty years. See? This is a kind of mental trick. Otherwise you say, 'My God, it's not working,' and then you make mistakes. My way, you say time is of absolutely no consequence."

Despite the carefree air that many creative people affect, most of them work late into the night and persist when less driven individuals would not. Vasari wrote in 1550 that when Renaissance painter Paolo Uccello was working out the laws of visual perspective, he would walk back and forth all night, muttering to himself: "What a beautiful thing is this perspective!" while his wife called him back to bed with no success.

4. Creative people alternate between imagination and fantasy, and a rooted sense of reality. Great art and great science involve a leap of imagination into a world that is different from the present. The rest of society often views these new ideas as fantasies without relevance to current reality. And they are right. But the whole point of art and science is to go beyond what we now consider real and create a new reality. At the same time, this "escape" is not into a never-never land. What makes a novel idea creative is that once we see it, sooner or later we recognize that, strange as it is, it is true.

Most of us assume that artists—musicians, writers, poets, painters—are strong on the fantasy side, whereas scientists, politicians, and businesspeople are realists. This may be true in terms of day-to-day routine activities. But when a person begins to work creatively, all bets are off.

5. Creative people tend to be both extroverted and introverted. We're usually one or the other, either preferring to be in the thick of crowds or sitting on the sidelines and observing the passing show. In fact, in psychological research, extroversion and introversion are considered the most stable personality traits that differentiate people from each other and that can be reliably measured. Creative individuals, on the other hand, seem to exhibit both traits simultaneously.

6. Creative people are humble and proud at the same time. It is remarkable to meet a famous person who you expect to be arrogant or supercilious, only to encounter self-deprecation and shyness instead. Yet there are good reasons why this should be so. These individuals are well aware that they stand, in Newton's words, "on the shoulders of giants." Their respect for the area in which they work makes them aware of the long line of previous contributions to it, putting their own in perspective. They're also aware of the role that luck played in their own achievements. And they're usually so focused on future projects and current challenges that past accomplishments, no matter how outstanding, are no longer very interesting to them. At the same time, they know that in comparison with others, they have accomplished a great deal. And this knowledge provides a sense of security, even pride.

7. Creative people, to an extent, escape rigid gender role stereotyping. When tests of masculinity/femininity are given to young people, over and over one finds that creative and talented girls are more dominant and tough than other girls, and creative boys are more sensitive and less aggressive than their male peers.

This tendency toward androgyny is sometimes understood in purely sexual terms, and therefore it gets confused with homosexuality. But psychological androgyny is a much wider concept referring to a person's ability to be at the same time aggressive and nurturant, sensitive and rigid, dominant and submissive, regardless of gender. A psychologically androgynous person in effect doubles his or her repertoire of responses. Creative individuals are more likely to have not only the strengths of their own gender but those of the other one, too.

8. Creative people are both rebellious and conservative. It is impossible to be creative without having first internalized an area of culture. So it's difficult to see how a person can be creative without being both traditional and conservative and at the same time rebellious and iconoclastic. Being only traditional leaves an area unchanged; constantly taking chances without regard to what has been valued in the past rarely leads to novelty that is accepted as an improvement. The artist Eva Zeisel, who says that the folk tradition in which she works is "her home," nevertheless produces ceramics that were recognized by the Museum of Modern Art as masterpieces of contemporary design. This is what she says about innovation for its own sake:

"This idea to create something is not my aim. To be different is a negative motive, and no creative thought or created thing grows out of a negative impulse. A negative impulse is always frustrating. And to be different means 'not like this' and 'not like that.' And the 'not like'—that's why postmodernism, with the prefix of 'post,' couldn't work. No negative impulse can work, can produce any happy creation. Only a positive one."

But the willingness to take risks, to break with the safety of tradition, is also necessary. The economist George Stigler is very emphatic in this regard: "I'd say one of the most common failures of able people is a lack of nerve. They'll play safe games. In innovation, you have to play a less safe game, if it's going to be interesting. It's not predictable that it'll go well."

9. Most creative people are very passionate about their work, yet they can be extremely objective about it as well. Without the passion, we soon lose interest in a difficult task. Yet without being objective about it, our work is not very good and lacks credibility. Here is how the historian Natalie Davis puts it:

"I think it is very important to find a way to be detached from what you write, so that you can't be so identified with your work that you can't accept criticism and response, and that is the danger of having as much affect as I do. But I am aware of that and of when I think it is particularly important to detach oneself from the work, and that is something where age really does help."

10. Creative people's openness and sensitivity often exposes them to suffering and pain, yet also to a great deal of enjoyment. Most would agree with Rabinow's words: "Inventors have a low threshold of pain. Things bother them." A badly designed machine causes pain to an inventive engineer, just as the creative writer is hurt when reading bad prose.

Being alone at the forefront of a discipline also leaves you exposed and vulnerable. Eminence invites criticism and often vicious attacks. When an artist has invested years in making a sculpture, or a scientist in developing a theory, it is devastating if nobody cares.

Deep interest and involvement in obscure subjects often goes unrewarded, or even brings on ridicule. Divergent thinking is often perceived as deviant by the majority, and so the creative person may feel isolated and misunderstood.

Perhaps the most difficult thing for creative individuals to bear is the sense of loss and emptiness they experience when, for some reason, they cannot work. This is especially painful when a person feels his or her creativity drying out.

Yet when a person is working in the area of his or her expertise, worries and cares fall away, replaced by a sense of bliss. Perhaps the most important quality, the one that is most consistently present in all creative individuals, is the ability to enjoy the process of creation for its own sake. Without this trait, poets would give up striving for perfection and would write commercial jingles, economists would work for banks where they would earn at least twice as much as they do at universities, and physicists would stop doing basic research and join industrial laboratories where the conditions are better and the expectations more predictable.

Analyze

1. According to Csikszentmihalyi, what is the one thing that makes the personality of creative individuals different than others? What does he mean by this?
2. What is the "g factor"? What is the relationship between it and creative people?
3. How does Csikszentmihalyi differentiate between convergent thinking and divergent thinking? Which seems most useful to people wanting to be more creative? Why?
4. Why is it important for creative people to have an internalized sense of culture? Do you agree with artist Eva Zeisel's explanation of this idea? Why or why not?

Explore

1. Which of the examples from point 3 regarding playfulness and discipline speak to you most clearly, Nina Holton's or Jacob Rabinow's? Why? Where else have you encountered a creative individual who combines responsibility and irresponsibility?
2. Csikszentmihalyi mentions Gardner's study on major creative geniuses in which "a certain immaturity, both emotional and mental, can go hand in hand with deepest insights." He then mentions Mozart as a prime example. Research Mozart online or view the award-winning movie *Amadeus*. Where do you most see the "contrasting poles of wisdom and childishness"? Do you think Mozart would have been more productive, effective, or creative without such childishness? Why or why not?
3. Csikszentmihalyi offers reasons why creative people "escape rigid gender role stereotyping." What does he mean by this? In your own experience, what truth(s) do you find in his claim?
4. Write a poem, story, or essay that deeply explores one or more of the "10 antithetical traits often present in creative people that are integrated with each other in dialectical tension." What insights does your writing bring about for you? For others?

Steven Johnson
"The Adjacent Possible"

The author of nine books, **Steven Johnson** (1968–) is an American popular science author and media theorist. *Newsweek* named him one of the "Fifty People Who Matter Most on the Internet." He is a regular contributor to *Wired, The New York Times, The Wall Street Journal,* and other periodicals. Johnson is a Distinguished Writer in Residence at the New York University Department of Journalism. "The Adjacent Possible" comes from his book *Where Good Ideas Come From: The Natural History of Innovation.*

Sometime in the late 1870s, a Parisian obstetrician named Stephane Tarnier took a day off from his work at Maternité de Paris, the lying-in hospital for the city's poor women, and paid a visit to the nearby Paris Zoo. Wandering past the elephants and reptiles and classical gardens of the zoo's home inside the Jardin des Plantes, Tarnier stumbled across an exhibit of chicken incubators. Seeing the hatchlings totter about in the incubator's warm enclosure triggered an association in his head, and before long he had hired Odile Martin, the zoo's poultry raiser, to construct a device that would perform a similar function for human newborns. By modern standards, infant mortality was staggeringly high in the late nineteenth century, even in a city as sophisticated as Paris. One in five babies died before learning to crawl, and the odds were far worse for premature babies born with low birth weights. Tarnier knew that temperature regulation was critical for keeping these infants alive, and he knew that the French medical establishment had a deep-seated obsession with statistics. And so as soon as his newborn incubator had been installed at Maternité, the fragile infants warmed by hot water bottles below the wooden boxes, Tarnier embarked on a quick study of five hundred babies. The results shocked the Parisian medical establishment: while 66 percent of low-weight babies died within weeks of birth, only 38 percent died if they were housed in Tarnier's incubating box. You could effectively halve the mortality rate for premature babies simply by treating them like hatchlings in a zoo.

Tarnier's incubator was not the first device employed for warming newborns, and the contraption he built with Martin would be improved upon significantly in the subsequent decades. But Tarnier's statistical analysis gave newborn incubation the push that it needed: within a few years, the Paris municipal board required that incubators be installed in all the city's maternity hospitals. In 1896, an enterprising physician named Alexandre Lion set up a display of incubators—with live newborns—at the Berlin Exposition. Dubbed the *Kinderbrutenstalt*, or "child hatchery," Lion's exhibit turned out to be the sleeper hit of the exposition, and launched a bizarre tradition of incubator sideshows that persisted well into the twentieth century. (Coney Island had a permanent baby incubator show until the early 1940s.) Modern incubators, supplemented with high-oxygen therapy and other advances, became standard equipment in all American hospitals after the end of World War II, triggering a spectacular 75 percent decline in infant mortality rates between 1950 and 1998. Because incubators focus exclusively on the beginning of life, their benefit to public health—measured by the sheer number of extra years they provide—rivals any medical advance of the twentieth century. Radiation therapy or a double bypass might give you another decade or two, but an incubator gives you an entire lifetime.

In the developing world, however, the infant mortality story remains bleak. Whereas infant deaths are below ten per thousand births throughout Europe and the United States, over a hundred infants die per thousand in countries like Liberia and Ethiopia, many of them premature babies that would have survived with access to incubators. But modern incubators are complex, expensive things. A standard incubator in an American hospital might cost more than $40,000. But the expense is arguably the smaller hurdle to overcome. Complex equipment breaks, and when it breaks you need the technical expertise to fix it, and you need replacement parts. In the year that followed the 2004 Indian Ocean tsunami, the Indonesian city of Meulaboh received eight incubators from a range of international relief organizations. By late 2008, when an MIT professor named Timothy Prestero visited the hospital, all eight were out of order, the victims of power surges and tropical humidity, along with the hospital staff's inability to read the English repair manual. The Meulaboh incubators were a representative sample: some studies suggest that as much as 95 percent of medical technology donated to developing countries breaks within the first five years of use.

Prestero had a vested interest in those broken incubators, because the organization he founded, Design that Matters, had been working for several years on a new scheme for a more reliable, and less expensive, incubator, one that recognized complex medical technology was likely to have a very different tenure in a developing world context than it would in an American or European hospital. Designing an incubator for a developing country wasn't just a matter of creating something that worked; it was also a matter of designing something that would break in a non-catastrophic way. You couldn't guarantee a steady supply of spare parts, or trained repair technicians. So instead, Prestero and his team decided to build an incubator out of parts that were already abundant in the developing world. The idea had originated with a Boston doctor named Jonathan Rosen, who had observed that even the smaller towns of the developing world seemed to be able to keep automobiles in working order. The towns might have lacked air conditioning and laptops and cable television, but they managed to keep their Toyota 4Runners on the road. So Rosen approached Prestero with an idea: What if you made an incubator out of automobile parts?

Three years after Rosen suggested the idea, the Design that Matters team introduced a prototype device called the NeoNurture. From the outside, it looked like a streamlined modern incubator, but its guts were automotive. Sealed-beam headlights supplied the crucial warmth; dashboard fans provided filtered air circulation; door chimes sounded alarms. You could power the device via an adapted cigarette lighter, or a standard-issue motorcycle battery. Building the NeoNurture out of car parts was doubly efficient, because it tapped both the local supply of parts themselves and the local knowledge of automobile repair. These were both abundant resources in the developing world context, as Rosen liked to say. You didn't have to be a trained medical technician to fix the NeoNurture; you didn't even have to read the manual. You just needed to know how to replace a broken headlight.

Good ideas are like the NeoNurture device. They are, inevitably, constrained by the parts and skills that surround them. We have a natural tendency to romanticize breakthrough innovations, imagining momentous ideas transcending their surroundings, a gifted mind somehow seeing over the detritus of old ideas and ossified tradition. But ideas are works of bricolage; they're built out of that detritus. We take the ideas we've inherited or that we've stumbled across, and we jigger them together into some new shape. We like to think of our ideas as $40,000 incubators, shipped direct from the factory, but in reality they've been cobbled together with spare parts that happened to be sitting in the garage.

Before his untimely death in 2002, the evolutionary biologist Stephen Jay Gould maintained an odd collection of footware that he had purchased during his travels through the developing world, in open-air markets in Quito, Nairobi, and Delhi. They were sandals made from recycled automobile tires. As a fashion statement, they may not have amounted to much, but Gould treasured his tire sandals as a testimony to "human ingenuity." But he also saw them as a metaphor for the patterns of innovation in the biological world. Nature's innovations, too, rely on spare parts. Evolution advances by taking available resources and cobbling them together to create new uses. The evolutionary theorist Francois Jacob captured this in his concept of evolution as a "tinkerer," not an engineer; our bodies are also works of bricolage, old parts strung together to form something radically new. "The tires-to-sandals principle works at all scales and times," Gould wrote, "permitting odd and unpredictable initiatives at any moment—to make nature as inventive as the cleverest person who ever pondered the potential of a junkyard in Nairobi."

You can see this process at work in the primordial innovation of life itself. We do not yet have scientific consensus on the specifics of life's origins. Some believe life originated in the boiling, metallic vents of undersea volcanoes; others suspect the open oceans; others point to the tidal ponds where Darwin believed life first took hold. Many respected scientists think that life may have arrived from outer space, embedded in a meteor. But we have a much clearer picture of the composition of earth's atmosphere before life emerged, thanks to a field known as prebiotic chemistry. The lifeless earth was dominated by a handful of basic molecules: ammonia, methane, water, carbon dioxide, a smattering of amino acids, and other simple organic compounds. Each of these molecules was capable of a finite series of transformations and exchanges with other molecules in the primordial soup: methane and oxygen recombining to form formaldehyde and water, for instance.

Think of all those initial molecules, and then imagine all the potential new combinations that they could form spontaneously, simply by colliding with each other (or perhaps prodded along by the extra energy of a propitious lightning strike). If you could play God and trigger all those combinations, you would end up with most of the building blocks of life: the proteins that form the boundaries of cells; sugar molecules crucial to the nucleic acids of our DNA. But you would not be able to trigger chemical reactions that would build a mosquito, or a sunflower, or a human brain. Formaldehyde is a first-order combination: you can create it directly from the molecules in the primordial soup. The atomic elements that make up a sunflower are the very same ones available on earth before the emergence of life, but you can't spontaneously create a sunflower in that environment, because it relies on a whole series of subsequent innovations that wouldn't evolve on earth for billions of years: chloroplasts to capture the sun's energy, vascular tissues to circulate resources through the plant, DNA molecules to pass on sunflower-building instructions to the next generation.

The scientist Stuart Kauffman has a suggestive name for the set of all those first-order combinations: "the adjacent possible." The phrase captures both the limits and the creative potential of change and innovation. In the case of prebiotic chemistry, the adjacent possible defines all those molecular reactions that were directly achievable in the primordial soup. Sunflowers and mosquitoes and brains exist outside that circle of possibility. The adjacent possible is a kind of shadow future, hovering on the edges of the present state of things, a map of all the ways in which the present can reinvent itself. Yet is it not an infinite space, or a totally open playing field. The number of potential first-order reactions is vast, but it is a finite number, and it excludes most of the forms that now populate the biosphere. What the adjacent possible tells us is that at any moment the world is capable of extraordinary change, but only *certain* changes can happen.

The strange and beautiful truth about the adjacent possible is that its boundaries grow as you explore those boundaries. Each new combination ushers new combinations into the adjacent possible. Think of it as a house that magically expands with each door you open. You begin in a room with four doors, each leading to a new room that you haven't visited yet. Those four rooms are the adjacent possible. But once you open one of those doors and stroll into that room, three new doors appear, each leading to a brand-new room that you couldn't have reached from your original starting point. Keep opening new doors and eventually you'll have built a palace.

Basic fatty acids will naturally self-organize into spheres lined with a dual layer of molecules, very similar to the membranes that define the boundaries of modern cells. Once the fatty acids combine to form those bounded spheres, a new wing of the adjacent possible opens up, because those molecules implicitly create a fundamental division between the inside and outside of the sphere. This division is the very essence of a cell. Once you have an "inside," you can put things there: food, organelles, genetic code. Small molecules can pass through the membrane and then combine with other molecules to form larger entities too big to escape back through the boundaries of the proto-cell. When the first fatty acids spontaneously formed those dual-layered membranes, they opened a door into the adjacent possible that would ultimately lead to nucleotide-based genetic code, and the power plants of the chloroplasts and mitochondria—the primary "inhabitants" of all modern cells.

The same pattern appears again and again throughout the evolution of life. Indeed, one way to think about the path of evolution is as a continual exploration of the adjacent possible. When dinosaurs such as the velociraptor evolved a new bone called the semilunate carpal (the name comes from its half-moon shape), it enabled them to swivel their wrists with far more flexibility. In the short term, this gave them more dexterity as predators, but it also opened a door in the adjacent possible that would eventually lead, many millions of years later, to the evolution of wings and flight. When our ancestors evolved opposable thumbs, they opened up a whole new cultural branch of the adjacent possible: the creation and use of finely crafted tools and weapons.

One of the things that I find so inspiring in Kauffman's notion of the adjacent possible is the continuum it suggests between natural and man-made systems. He introduced the concept in part to illustrate a fascinating secular trend shared by both natural and human history: this relentless pushing back against the barricades of the adjacent possible. "Something has obviously happened in the past 4.8 billion years," he writes. "The biosphere has expanded, indeed, more or less persistently exploded, into the ever-expanding adjacent possible. . . . It is more than slightly interesting that this fact is clearly true, that it is rarely remarked upon, and that we have no particular theory for this expansion." Four billion years ago, if you were a carbon atom, there were a few hundred molecular configurations you could stumble into. Today that same carbon atom, whose atomic properties haven't changed one single nanogram, can help build a sperm whale or a giant redwood or an H1N1 virus, along with a near-infinite list of other carbon-based life forms that were not part of the adjacent possible of prebiotic earth. Add to that an equally formidable list of human concoctions that rely on carbon—every single object on the planet made of plastic, for instance—and you can see how far the kingdom of the adjacent possible has expanded since those fatty acids self-assembled into the first membrane.

The history of life and human culture, then, can be told as the story of a gradual but relentless probing of the adjacent possible, each new innovation opening up new paths to explore. But some systems are more adept than others at exploring those possibility spaces. The mystery of Darwin's paradox that we began with ultimately revolves around the question of why a coral reef ecosystem should be so adventurous in its exploration of the adjacent possible—so many different life forms sharing such a small space—while the surrounding waters of the ocean lack that same marvelous diversity. Similarly, the environments of big cities allow far more commercial exploration of the adjacent possible than towns or villages, allowing tradesmen and entrepreneurs to specialize in fields that would be unsustainable in smaller population centers. The Web has explored the adjacent possible of its medium far faster than any other communications technology in history. In early 1994, the Web was a text-only medium, pages of words connected by hyperlinks. But within a few years, the possibility space began to expand. It became a medium that let you do financial transactions, which turned it into a shopping mall and an auction house and a casino. Shortly afterward, it became a true two-way medium where it was as easy to publish your own writing as it was to read other people's, which engendered forms that the world had never seen before: user-authored encyclopedias, the blogosphere, social network sites. YouTube made the Web one of the most influential video delivery mechanisms on the planet. And now digital maps are unleashing their own cartographic revolutions.

You can see the fingerprints of the adjacent possible in one of the most remarkable patterns in all of intellectual history, what scholars now call "the multiple": A brilliant idea occurs to a scientist or inventor somewhere in the world, and he goes public with his remarkable finding, only to discover that three other minds had independently come up with the same idea in the past year. Sun-spots were simultaneously discovered in 1611 by four scientists living in four different countries. The first electrical battery was invented separately by Dean Von Kleist and Cuneus of Leyden in 1745 and 1746. Joseph Priestley and Carl Wilhelm Scheele independently isolated oxygen between 1772 and 1774. The law of the conservation of energy was formulated separately four times in the late 1840s. The evolutionary importance of genetic mutation was proposed by S. Korschinsky in 1899 and then by Hugo de Vries in 1901, while the impact of X-rays on mutation rates was independently uncovered by two scholars in 1927. The telephone, telegraph, steam engine, photograph vacuum tube, radio—just about every essential technological advance of modern life has a multiple lurking somewhere in its origin story.

In the early 1920s, two Columbia University scholars named William Ogburn and Dorothy Thomas decided to track down as many multiples as they could find, eventually publishing their survey in an influential essay with the delightful title "Are Inventions Inevitable?" Ogburn and Thomas found 148 instances of independent innovation, most them occurring within the same decade. Reading the list now, one is struck not just by the sheer number of cases, but how indistinguishable the list is from an unfiltered history of big ideas. Multiples have been invoked to support hazy theories about the "zeitgeist," but they have a much more grounded explanation. Good ideas are not conjured out of thin air; they are built out of a collection of existing parts, the composition of which expands (and, occasionally, contracts) over time. Some of those parts are conceptual: ways of solving problems, or new definitions of what constitutes a problem in the first place. Some of them are, literally, mechanical parts. To go looking for oxygen, Priestley and Scheele needed the conceptual framework that the air was itself something worth studying and that it was made up of distinct gases; neither of these ideas became widely accepted until the second half of the eighteenth century. But they also needed the advanced scales that enabled them to measure the minuscule changes in weight triggered by oxidation, technology that was itself only a few decades old in 1774. When those parts became available, the discovery of oxygen entered the realm of the adjacent possible. Isolating oxygen was, as the saying goes, "in the air," but only because a specific set of prior discoveries and inventions had made that experiment thinkable.

· ✦ ·

The adjacent possible is as much about limits as it is about openings. At every moment in the timeline of an expanding biosphere, there are doors that cannot be unlocked yet. In human culture, we like to think of breakthrough ideas as sudden accelerations on the timeline, where a genius jumps ahead fifty years and invents something that normal minds, trapped in the present moment, couldn't possibly have come up with. But the truth is that technological (and scientific) advances rarely break out of the adjacent possible; the history of cultural progress is, almost without exception, a story of one door leading to another door, exploring the palace one room at a time. But of course, human minds are not bound by the finite laws of molecule formation, and so every now and then an idea does occur to someone that teleports us forward a few rooms, skipping some exploratory steps in the adjacent possible. But those ideas almost always end up being short-term failures, precisely because they have skipped ahead. We have a phrase for those ideas: we call them "ahead of their time."

Consider the legendary Analytical Engine designed by nineteenth-century British inventor Charles Babbage, who is considered by most technology historians to be the father of modern computing, though he should probably be called the great-grandfather of modern computing, because it took several generations for the world to catch up to his idea. Babbage is actually in the pantheon for two inventions, neither of which he managed to build during his lifetime. The first was his Difference Engine, a fantastically complex fifteen-ton contraption, with over 25,000 mechanical parts, designed to calculate polynomial functions that were essential to creating the trigonometric tables crucial to navigation. Had Babbage actually completed his project, the Difference Engine would have been the world's most advanced mechanical calculator. When the London Science Museum constructed one from Babbage's plans to commemorate the centennial of his death, the machine returned accurate results to thirty-one places in a matter of seconds. Both the speed and precision of the device would have exceeded anything else possible in Babbage's time by several orders of magnitude.

For all its complexity, however, the Difference Engine was well within the adjacent possible of Victorian technology. The second half of the nineteenth century saw a steady stream of improvements to mechanical calculation, many of them building on Babbage's architecture. The Swiss inventor Per Georg Scheutz constructed a working Difference Engine that debuted at the Exposition Universelle of 1855; within two decades the piano-sized Scheutz design had been reduced to the size of a sewing machine. In 1884, an American inventor named William S. Burroughs founded the American Arithmometer Company to sell mass-produced calculators to businesses around the country. (The fortune generated by those machines would help fund his namesake grandson's writing career, not to mention his drug habit, almost a century later.) Babbage's design for the Difference Engine was a work of genius, no doubt, but it did not transcend the adjacent possible of its day.

The same cannot be said of Babbage's other brilliant idea: the Analytical Engine, the great unfulfilled project of Babbage's career, which he toiled on for the last thirty years of his life. The machine was so complicated that it never got past the blueprint stage, save a small portion that Babbage built shortly before his death in 1871. The Analytical Engine was—on paper, at least—the world's first programmable computer. Being programmable meant that the machine was fundamentally open-ended; it wasn't designed for a specific set of tasks, the way the Difference Engine had been optimized for polynomial equations. The Analytical Engine was, like all modern computers, a shape-shifter, capable of reinventing itself based on the instructions conjured by its programmers. (The brilliant mathematician Ada Lovelace, the only daughter of Lord Byron, wrote several sets of instructions for Babbage's still-vaporware Analytical Engine, earning her the title of the world's first programmer.) Babbage's design for the engine anticipated the basic structure of all contemporary computers: "programs" were to be inputted via punch cards, which had been invented decades before to control textile looms; instructions and data were captured in a "store," the equivalent of what we now call random access memory, or RAM; and calculations were executed via a system that Babbage called "the mill," using industrial-era language to describe what we now call the central processing unit, or CPU.

Babbage had most of this system sketched out by 1837, but the first true computer to use this programmable architecture didn't appear for more than a hundred years. While the Difference Engine engendered an immediate series of refinements and practical applications, the Analytical Engine effectively disappeared from the map. Many of the pioneering insights that Babbage had hit upon in the 1830s had to be independently rediscovered by the visionaries of World War II–era computer science.

Why did the Analytical Engine prove to be such a short-term dead end, given the brilliance of Babbage's ideas? The fancy way to say it is that his ideas had escaped the bounds of the adjacent possible. But it is perhaps better put in more prosaic terms: Babbage simply didn't have the right spare parts. Even if Babbage had built a machine to his specs, it is unclear whether it would have worked, because Babbage was effectively sketching out a machine for the electronic age during the middle of the steam-powered mechanical revolution. Unlike all modern computers, Babbage's machine was to be composed entirely of mechanical gears and switches, staggering in their number and in the intricacy of their design. Information flowed through the system as a constant ballet of metal objects shifting positions in carefully choreographed movements. It was a maintenance nightmare, but more than that, it was bound to be hopelessly slow. Babbage bragged to Ada Lovelace that he believed the machine would be able to multiply two twenty-digit numbers in three minutes. Even if he was right—Babbage wouldn't have been the first tech entrepreneur to exaggerate his product's performance—that kind of processing time would have made executing more complicated programs torturously slow. The first computers of the digital age could perform the same calculation in a matter of seconds. An iPhone completes millions of such calculations in the same amount of time. Programmable computers needed vacuum tubes, or, even better, integrated circuits, where information flows as tiny pulses of electrical activity, instead of clanking, rusting, steam-powered metal gears.

You can see a comparable pattern—on a vastly accelerated timetable—in the story of YouTube. Had Hurley, Chen, and Karim tried to execute the exact same idea for YouTube ten years earlier, in 1995, it would have been a spectacular flop, because a site for sharing video was not within the adjacent possible of the early Web. For starters, the vast majority of Web users were on painfully slow dial-up connections that could sometimes take minutes to download a small image. (The average two-minute-long YouTube clip would have taken as much as an hour to download on the then-standard 14.4 bps modems.) Another key to YouTube's early success is that its developers were able to base the video serving on Adobe's Flash platform, which meant that they could focus on the ease of sharing and discussing clips, and not spend millions of dollars developing a whole new video standard from scratch. But Flash itself wasn't released until late 1996, and didn't even support video until 2002.

To use our microbiology analogy, having the idea for a Difference Engine in the 1830s was like a bunch of fatty acids trying to form a cell membrane. Babbage's calculating machine was a leap forward, to be sure, but as advanced as it was, the Difference Engine was still within the bounds of the adjacent possible, which is precisely why so many practical iterations of Babbage's design emerged in the subsequent decades. But trying to create an Analytical Engine in 1850—or YouTube in 1995—was the equivalent of those fatty acids trying to self-organize into a sea urchin. The idea was right, but the environment wasn't ready for it yet.

All of us live inside our own private versions of the adjacent possible. In our work lives, in our creative pursuits, in the organizations that employ us, in the communities we inhabit—in all these different environments, we are surrounded by potential new configurations, new ways of breaking out of our standard routines. We are, each of us, surrounded by the conceptual equivalent of those Toyota spare parts, all waiting to be recombined into something magical, something new. It need not be the epic advances of biological diversity, or the invention of programmable computing. Unlocking a new door can lead to a world-changing scientific breakthrough, but it can also lead to a more effective strategy for teaching second graders, or a novel marketing idea for the vacuum cleaner your company's about to release. The trick is to figure out ways to explore the edges of possibility that surround you. This can be as simple as changing the physical environment you work in, or cultivating a specific kind of social network, or maintaining certain habits in the way you seek out and store information.

Recall the question we began with: What kind of environment creates good ideas? The simplest way to answer it is this: innovative environments are better at helping their inhabitants explore the adjacent possible, because they expose a wide and diverse sample of spare parts—mechanical or conceptual—and they encourage novel ways of recombining those parts. Environments that block or limit those new combinations—by punishing experimentation, by obscuring certain branches of possibility, by making the current state so satisfying that no one bothers to explore the edges—will, on average, generate and circulate fewer innovations than environments that encourage exploration. The infinite variety of life that so impressed Darwin, standing in the calm waters of the Keeling Islands, exists because the coral reef is supremely gifted at recycling and reinventing the spare parts of its ecosystem.

There's a famous moment in the story of the near-catastrophic *Apollo 13* mission—wonderfully captured in the Ron Howard film—where the mission control engineers realize they need to create an improvised carbon dioxide filter, or the astronauts will poison the lunar module atmosphere with their own exhalations before they return to Earth. The astronauts have plenty of carbon "scrubbers" on board, but these filters were designed for the original, damaged spacecraft, and don't fit the air ventilation system of the lunar module they are using as a lifeboat to return home. Mission Control quickly assembles what it calls a "tiger team" of engineers to hack their way through the problem, and creates a rapid-fire inventory of all the available equipment currently on the lunar module. In the movie, Deke Slayton, head of Flight Crew Operations, tosses a jumbled pile of gear on a conference table: suit hoses, canisters, stowage bags, duct tape, and other assorted gadgets. He holds up the carbon scrubbers. "We gotta find a way to make this fit into a hole for this," he says, and then points to the spare parts on the table, "using nothing but *that.*"

The space gear on the table defines the adjacent possible for the problem of building a working carbon scrubber on a lunar module. The device they eventually concoct, dubbed the "mailbox," performs beautifully. The canisters and nozzles are like the ammonia and methane molecules of the early earth, or Babbage's mechanical gears, or those Toyota parts heating an incubator: they are the building blocks that create—and limit—the space of possibility for a specific problem. In a way, the engineers at Mission Control had it easier than most. Challenging problems don't usually define their adjacent possible in such a clear, tangible way. Part of coming up with a good idea is discovering what those spare parts are, and ensuring that you're not just recycling the same old ingredients. This, then, is where the next six patterns of innovation will take us, because they all involve, in one way or another, tactics for assembling a more eclectic collection of building block ideas, spare parts that can be reassembled into useful new configurations. The trick to having good ideas is not to sit around in glorious isolation and try to think big thoughts. The trick is to get more parts on the table.

Analyze

1. In what ways are good ideas like the NeoNurture device the inexpensive solution to the lack of working infant incubators in developing countries?

2. The scientist Stuart Kauffman uses the term "the adjacent possible." What does this term mean in the world of science? In the world of creativity?

3. Johnson points out patterns of simultaneous discovery in intellectual history such as the impact of X-rays on mutation rates in 1927 or the invention of the telephone, radio, or steam engine. Why does this—called "the multiple"—seem to happen so often? What did the two Columbia University scholars who studied it in the 1920s uncover?

4. What does Johnson mean by calling nineteenth-century British inventor Charles Babbage's Analytical Engine an idea that were ahead of its time? How does this relate to the idea of the adjacent possible?

5. What kind of environment creates good ideas? Why? How?

Explore

1. The NeoNurture device is an example of how creative thinking—and a proper environment—can lead to big innovations. What other important innovations are the result of creative thinking and a proper

environment? Brainstorm with classmates or use online sources for examples. What similarities do you find between these innovations and the NeoNurture? What differences?

2. Johnson writes: "But trying to create an Analytical Engine in 1850— or YouTube in 1995—was the equivalent of those fatty acids trying to self-organize into a sea urchin. The idea was right but the environment wasn't ready for it yet." Think of a time where you've had a good idea but the environment wasn't ready for it yet. What did you do? What new options do you now see for handling a similar situation in the future?

3. Create your own version of the *Apollo 13* movie crisis by dividing into groups of two or three, then distributing to each group a set of six items that might reasonably be found on a space ship: duct tape, cans, and so on. While it might be asking a bit much to create carbon scrubbers the way they did in the movie, you can still challenge each team to use the exact same materials to create useful items for the astronauts to use. After a set amount of time, share your results and discuss the effectiveness of the items/tools you've created.

4. Draw up the plan for a device that is—as much as you are able to make it so—way ahead of its time. Then draw up one for a device that builds on existing technologies, ideas, and/or products. Which was easier to create? Which one is the "better" idea? Why?

Tina Seelig
"Inside Out and Outside In"

Tina Seelig (1957–) is a Professor of the Practice in the Department of Management Science and Engineering at Stanford University as well as the Executive Director of the Stanford Technology Ventures Program. She has authored seventeen popular science books and education games. "Inside Out and Outside In" comes from her book *inGenius: A Crash Course on Creativity.*

Sangduen Chailert, known as Lek, has always loved elephants. She grew up in the small rural village of Baan Lao in a remote part of northern Thailand and became passionate about elephants as a youngster when her family cared for one. As she grew older she saw how terribly most elephants in captivity are treated, and saving elephants became her mission in life. Her passion led her to learn as much as she could about these endangered animals. She found that the elephant habitats in Thailand are shrinking quickly and that as few as five hundred wild elephants remain in the country. In addition, most of the two thousand domestic elephants that entertain tourists have a grim future. Lek decided that she had to do something meaningful to protect them.

In the early 1990s, Lek founded the Elephant Nature Park near Chiang Mai, Thailand. She struggled desperately to raise the funds needed to take care of the elephants and to fight against fierce local critics who tried to prevent her from doing this work. Despite these obstacles, Lek came up with an innovative way to rescue and protect elephants that have been injured by land mines and excessive work in the logging industry and that have been mistreated as circus entertainers. The Elephant Nature Park is now home to thirty-five elephants and is open to visitors and volunteers who are transformed by their experience with these amazing animals.

Essentially, Lek's *attitude* about elephants motivated her to gain *knowledge* about these magnificent animals—a rich *resource* in Thailand. Her knowledge became a toolbox for her *imagination*, which she drew upon to create a *habitat* where she could protect the animals and share her passion and knowledge with others. The visitors' new knowledge and appreciation changes their *attitudes* about elephants and is slowly changing the *cultural* response to these creatures. This is an example of the Innovation Engine at work! The Innovation Engine captures the relationship between the factors that influence your creativity, both *inside* your mind and in the *outside* world.

On the inside, your creativity is influenced by your knowledge, imagination, and attitude. These factors are inspired by Benjamin Bloom's original work in the 1950s on learning. He focused on what you *know*, what you *do*, and how you *feel*, which are generally known as knowledge, skills, and attitude. Since we're focused specifically on creativity, I've changed "skills" to "imagination," as imagination captures the specific skills needed for creativity. Let's look at the three factors on the inside of the Innovation Engine in more detail.

Knowledge

Knowledge in any domain, from minerals to music to mushrooms to math, is the fuel for your imagination. That is, the more you know about a particular topic, the more raw materials you have to work with. For example, if you want to design an inventive solar car or find a cure for cancer, you need to begin with a base of knowledge about engineering or biology, respectively.

Some people argue the contrary—that there is a benefit to having a "beginner's mind," so that you come at challenges without established knowledge or entrenched beliefs. There are examples that bear this out. However, if you look closely, you will see that in most of these cases these folks have expertise in a related or tangential field upon which they can draw. Successful entrepreneurs often come from outside the domain of their new venture, and their unorthodox ideas aren't inhibited by industry doctrine. They dominate the field, because they don't know what can't be done. As Mark Twain famously said, "The best swordsman in the world doesn't need to fear the second best swordsman in the world; no, the person for him to be afraid of is some ignorant antagonist who has never had a sword in his hand before; he doesn't do the thing he ought to do, and so the expert isn't prepared for him; he does the thing he ought not to do; and often it catches the expert out and ends him on the spot."

Serial entrepreneurs, who start companies in diverse fields, are masters at building on their accumulated knowledge from past ventures as they move fluidly from one endeavor to another. They don't initially have expertise in the new domain, but quickly come up to speed using past knowledge to propel them forward. A compelling example comes from a new company called the Climate Corporation, which makes sophisticated software that enables it to offer weather insurance to farmers. In this fast-growing firm, not a single person in the company, including David Friedberg, the founder, has any formal training in meteorology or agriculture. David was trained as an astrophysicist, spent time as an investment banker, and worked on strategy at Google. Other members of the company also bring a deep knowledge in diverse fields, each of which sheds a fresh light on the problems they are trying to solve. Team members include mathematicians, engineers, and even a neuroscientist. The neuroscientist, for example, was trained to analyze complicated, quickly changing data and is using that knowledge to analyze weather patterns. Over time they are each building an expertise in agriculture and meteorology, which they will bring to their subsequent endeavors.

Imagination

Your imagination—the ability to create something new—is a powerful force. It is the catalyst required for creative combustion. Without it, new ideas are impossible to generate. There are specific skills and approaches you can hone to unleash your imagination. These include connecting and combining ideas, reframing problems, and challenging assumptions. These tools allow you to use what you know to generate fresh ideas.

Karl Szpunar and Kathleen McDermott have examined the literature on how our imagination is deeply connected to memory. They cite a wide range of psychology and neuroscience research that reinforces the hypothesis that the same parts of our brain are invoked when we remember and when we imagine, including evidence that those who don't have the ability to remember the past are unable to conjure up a vision of the future. Our imagination essentially transforms what we know—our memories—into new ideas. For example, we remember a car and a bird, and our imagination connects those concepts into new ideas, including a flying car and a mechanical bird.

Using your knowledge about the world as fuel, your imagination is an endless renewable resource. To demonstrate this point, I ask students in my classes to do a warm-up exercise inspired by Patricia Ryan Madson in her book, *Improv Wisdom*. I tell them there is an imaginary present sitting on their desk and ask them to pick it up and feel how heavy it is, how big it is, and to imagine how beautifully it is wrapped. Without opening it, they are to imagine what's in the box. Once they have that in mind, they are to open the box slowly to see what is inside. I tell them that they will be surprised to find that the present *isn't* what they expected. We go around the room and each person says what they thought was in the box and what they actually found. Everyone names different things, from books and chocolate to airplane tickets for an around-the-world adventure. I then ask them to look into the box to find yet another present, and another, and another. Each time they bring out something new and surprising. The key is that this "box"—your imagination—is bottomless. If you dig down, you will always find something new.

Attitude

Your attitude is the spark that jump-starts your creativity, and without the attitude that you can come up with breakthrough ideas, your Innovation Engine comes to a standstill. Your attitude, or mind-set, determines how you interpret and respond to situations, and it has deep neurological underpinnings.

A new study, to be published in *Psychological Science*, found that those people who believe they can learn from their errors have different activity in their brains in response to mistakes than people who think intelligence is fixed. Jason Moser and his colleagues at Michigan State found that those individuals who think intelligence is malleable say things such as "When the going gets tough, I put in more effort" or "If I make a mistake, I try to learn and figure it out." However, those who think that their intelligence is fixed don't take opportunities to learn from their mistakes.

While measuring their subjects' brain activity (EEG), Moser and his colleagues gave them a simple task that is easy to mess up. Subjects were asked to identify the middle letter of a five-letter series such as "MMMMM" or "NNMNN." Sometimes the middle letter was the same as the other four letters, and sometimes it wasn't. Moser says, "It's pretty simple, doing the same thing over and over, but the mind can't help it; it just kind of zones out from time to time." That's when people make mistakes—and they notice it immediately.

When a subject made an error, the researchers saw two quick signals on the EEG: an initial response that indicated something had gone awry—Moser calls it the "'Oh, crap' response"—and a second signal that indicated the person was consciously aware of the error and was trying to figure out what went wrong. Both signals occurred within a quarter of a second of the mistake. After the experiment, the researchers asked the subjects if they believed they could learn from mistakes. Those who said yes turned out to be the ones for whom there was a larger second signal; it was as if their brains were saying, "I see that I've made a mistake, and I will learn from that error."

It is important to note that our mind-sets are malleable. Carol Dweck of the Stanford School of Education has done a tremendous amount of work on this topic and has shown how the messages that others tell us and that we tell ourselves dramatically influence how we see our place in the world. Compelling proof comes from a study by Dweck and Lisa Sorich Blackwell on low-achieving seventh graders. All of the students had a study skills workshop. Half of the group attended a general session on memory, while the other half learned that the brain, like a muscle, grows stronger through exercise. The group that was told that the brain is like a muscle showed much more motivation and had significantly improved grades in math, while the control group showed no improvement. This study is supported by extensive research and demonstrates that your mind-set and attitude are within your own control.

No matter how much we improve our knowledge, imagination, and attitude, we are embedded in a world that has a huge influence on us. I remember clearly when my son, Josh, was four years old, and he had never seen commercial TV before, which meant that he had never seen a commercial. One day, to keep him safely occupied while I took a shower, I turned on the TV and told Josh to come get me if there was any problem. Within two minutes Josh started shouting, "Mommy, Mommy, Mommy!" With soap running down my face, I quickly grabbed a towel and ran to see what was wrong. Josh exclaimed, "Mommy, we *have* to buy Pop-Tarts!" This story is a reminder that we are swimming in a cultural soup that profoundly influences our attitudes and our actions. No matter how much we try to control our environment, the outside world always leaks in and influences how we think, feel, and act.

There are three important factors in the outside world that contribute to your Innovation Engine: the resources in your environment, your local habitat, and the surrounding culture. These environmental factors can either stimulate or inhibit your creativity. Let's look at each of them more closely.

Resources

Resources are all the things of value in your environment. They come in all different forms, including funds that can be invested in new

companies and natural resources such as fish, flowers, copper, diamonds, beaches, and waterfalls. They include individuals with knowledge and expertise who can serve as guides, role models, and mentors as well as organizations such as universities and local firms that foster innovation.

The more knowledge you have, the more resources you can mobilize. For example, the more you know about fishing, the more fish you can catch; the more you know about copper, the more you can mine; and the more you know about venture capital, the more likely you are to get funding. Of course, if you live somewhere with a lot of fish, you learn about fishing; if you live somewhere where there is an abundance of copper, you learn about mining; and if you live in a place with a wealth of venture capitalists, you learn about venture capital. As such, the resources in your environment influence your knowledge, and your knowledge allows you to access the resources. This is why resources are right outside knowledge in the Innovation Engine.

It is important to note that some of the resources in your environment are easy to spot, while others require physical or mental mining. It is up to you to recognize the unique resources in your environment and to gain the knowledge to utilize them. Unfortunately, in some parts of the world people don't recognize the assets in their environment. They are so focused on trying to replicate the assets in other parts of the world that they don't see the value in their own resources.

For example, I was recently in northern Chile, which is one of the most magical places on earth. The country is essentially a tiny strip of land with a three-thousand-mile beach on one side and the magnificent Andes on the other. I was talking with local residents in Antofagasto and asked what was getting in the way of their economic prosperity. A man turned to me and

said, "Our unattractive environment." I looked at him with surprise. Outside the window was a stunning view of the ocean. He literally didn't see the beauty and potential right in front of him.

Habitat

Habitat is placed right outside Imagination on the Innovation Engine because the habitats we create are essentially an external manifestation of our imagination. We create physical spaces that reflect the way we think, and in turn, those habitats influence our imagination. We need to think carefully about the spaces we design, the incentives we put in place, the rules we enforce, the constraints we impose, and the people with whom we work, because each of these factors contributes to our ability to generate new ideas. Managers, educators, parents, and community leaders play a big role in creating habitats that foster imagination in their employees, students, and children. Small changes in the environment have a big influence on creative output.

Culture

Culture captures the ways in which groups of people perceive, interpret, and understand the world around them. We are each extremely sensitive to our culture, including stories about local heroes, gossip about those who are doing things that don't fit the cultural norms, laws that determine

what is considered acceptable behavior, and advertisements that directly tell us what to do. From the moment we wake up until the moment we go to sleep, we are immersed in a cultural stew that deeply influences our thoughts and actions. As we all know, someone who grows up in San Francisco is surrounded by a completely different culture from someone who grows up in suburban New Jersey, rural India, or downtown London. These cultures communicate directives that have a profound influence on how we think, what we believe, and how we act.

Each person, family, school, and organization contributes to the culture, and therefore the culture in any community is essentially the collective attitudes of all those who live there. This is why culture sits right outside attitude in the Innovation Engine. If even a small number of individuals change their attitude, then the ambient culture naturally changes. Consider how cultural norms about throwing trash on the ground, recycling cans and bottles, smoking cigarettes, and saving energy have changed over the years. Each of these waves of change started when a few people modified their attitudes and behaviors. Over time these ideas became contagious and were eventually supported by laws that reinforce those collective attitudes. Therefore, we all have an important role in cultivating the culture in our communities.

All the parts of your Innovation Engine are inexorably connected and deeply influence one another.

- Your *attitude* sparks your curiosity to acquire related *knowledge*.
- Your *knowledge* fuels your *imagination*, allowing you to generate innovative ideas.

- Your *imagination* catalyzes the creation of stimulating *habitats*, leveraging the *resources* in your environment.
- These *habitats*, along with your *attitude*, influence the *culture* in your community.

Below is the fully functional Innovation Engine, showing how all the parts are braided together. The inside of the engine is intertwined with the outside; and the factors on the inside and outside mirror each other. By engaging all the parts of this engine, creativity is unleashed, leading to transformative changes in individuals, teams, and organizations.

There are great examples of this type of transformation all over the world, where individual entrepreneurs draw upon their drive and imagination to create new hubs of innovation in unlikely places. Daniel Isenberg, of

Babson College, describes this beautifully in "How to Start an Entrepreneurial Revolution":

> It has become clear in recent years that even one success can have a surprisingly stimulating effect on an entrepreneurial ecosystem— by igniting the imagination of the public and inspiring imitators. I call this effect the "law of small numbers." Skype's adoption by millions and eventual $2.6 billion sale to eBay reverberated throughout the small country of Estonia, encouraging highly trained technical people to start their own companies. In China, Baidu's market share and worldwide recognition have inspired an entire generation of new entrepreneurs.

Isenberg goes on to tell a wonderful story of a young man in Saudi Arabia, Abdulla Al-Munif, who broke through traditional expectations to launch a business making chocolate-covered dates, which he sold in kiosks inside other stores. His business, Anoosh, eventually grew into a national chain of stores, and Abdulla Al-Munif became a local hero, admired and then emulated by other young people in Saudi Arabia.

This philosophy is embraced by Endeavor, an organization with the goal of identifying and empowering high-potential entrepreneurs in the developing world. With branches throughout Latin America, the Middle East, and Africa, Endeavor successfully creates local role models in each region. These entrepreneurs, who boldly and creatively start ventures in their communities, become icons of success and change the landscape of what can be accomplished in each region. Essentially, as individuals, they change the entire culture in their communities, making them more open, accepting, and supportive of future innovators. The key, as Isenberg states, is to "foster homegrown solutions—ones based on the realities of their own circumstances, be they natural resources, geographic location, or culture."

There are several remarkable cases from Endeavor entrepreneurs. For example, Wenceslao Casares (Wences), who was born in a remote part of Patagonia, along with Meyer Malka (Micky) from Caracas, Venezuela, decided to start the first online brokerage site in Argentina. The company, called Patagon, quickly expanded to serve all of Latin America and was ultimately purchased by Banco Santander in Spain. Wences and Micky become role models across Latin America as well as investors and mentors. As a result, dozens of companies have been started with their help, and hundreds have been inspired by their success. Their venture literally sparked an entrepreneurial revolution in the region, which has had far-reaching effects on the economy and quality of life for tens of thousands of people.

This story is played out over and over again in other regions of the world. David Wachtel of Endeavor shared the story of Fadi Ghandour in Jordan, who founded a company called Aramex, a package-delivery business. This venture grew in size and became the first company in the Middle East to be traded on NASDAQ. Fadi became a local role model and investor and is active in promoting entrepreneurship as an Endeavor Jordan board member. He is helping to spark the evolution of many other ventures, including Maktoob, an Arab-language Internet portal that was sold to Yahoo. That sale led to another large pool of investors and mentors who, in turn, triggered the founding of additional ventures.

Many inspiring stories from Endeavor don't involve high-technology businesses. For example, in Egypt two sisters, Hind and Nadia Wassef, started a chain of bookstores in Cairo. Not only has their business thrived, but these stores have also become cultural centers within the community, creating an ecosystem for sharing ideas. And in South Africa, Cynthia Mkhomba started a contract cleaning business. She now employs nearly one thousand people and has helped them escape poverty. The important thing to keep in mind is that each of these ventures is a virtual engine for the creation of ideas that, in turn, spawn new ventures.

To give students the experience of seeing opportunities where others don't, at STVP we launched a Global Innovation Tournament five years ago, in which students were given either five dollars or a simple object, such as a water bottle or a handful of rubber bands, and asked to create as much value as they could from these objects. The results of this project, described in detail in *What I Wish I Knew When I Was 20,* point to the fact that everything, even a handful of rubber bands, can be turned into something of greater value. In fact, several of these weeklong projects turned into companies that have been growing for several years now.

I have received messages from people from around the world who have run the five-dollar project—changing the currency, but not the concept—including the United States, India, Korea, Kenya, Thailand, Canada, and Japan. For example, in Kenya, an organization named LivelyHoods, founded by Maria Springer, used this project to select homeless youth to participate in a new program designed to get them off the streets and into real jobs. LivelyHoods was created to help unemployed young people in the slums who barely survive by collecting plastic, washing cars, or turning to prostitution. Its goal is to create a way for these young people to earn a proper living.

When candidates arrive at the LivelyHoods offices to apply for the program, the LivelyHoods team puts them into pairs and gives them two hours to earn as much as possible, starting with a tiny amount of money. In one instance, as soon as the teams started, rain began to pour down. One pair bought tomatoes and tried to resell them on the street corner, and another did the same with lollipops. However, a third team looked around and decided to use the rain to their advantage. Instead of using the money they had been given, they used the rain. They dashed to the water station on the outskirts of the town, where the women go to fetch water for their families, and offered to carry the heavy ten-liter jugs. The women were delighted not to have to walk home with the large jug of water in the pouring rain and agreed to pay the equivalent of twelve cents for this service. The young men ran back and forth to the water station and returned to the LivelyHoods offices, sopping wet, at the end of two hours. They realized that the most valuable assets they had at that moment were the rain and their strength. By leveraging both of those, they created more value than their compatriots who were selling tomatoes or candy.

I just returned from Japan, where I gave an even more challenging assignment to a group of forty students at Osaka University. Instead of starting with something of small value, such as five dollars or a handful of rubber bands, I challenged the participants to create as much value as possible from the contents of a single trash can in only two hours. While there, I sent a note to several colleagues around the world and asked them to invite their students to participate as well. As a result, we had teams from Thailand, Korea, Ireland, Ecuador, and Taiwan taking part in this challenge at the same time.

At first the students thought this assignment was crazy. How could they create something from trash?! But this challenge prompted them to contemplate the meaning of "value." They spent hours discussing what value meant to each of them, coming up with such things as health, happiness, community, knowledge, and financial security. These insights led them to look at the contents of each trash can in a new light.

The results from this assignment were fascinating and remarkably diverse. One team from Japan took old hangers and plastic garment covers from a local dry cleaner and created mats that can be used for sitting on damp grass on their campus. They painted game boards on the mats so that students can play with one another while they enjoy time together. A team from Ecuador created a beautiful sculpture of a bird using organic yard waste, and a team from Thailand made a spectacular carved elephant out of a used coconut shell. A team from Ireland turned a bunch of old socks into a fabulous sweater. And a team from Taiwan made a collection of toys for children using the contents of a single trash can. One of the participating students remarked afterward, "I had no idea that we are so creative!"

These interactive projects are designed to demonstrate that starting with essentially nothing, you can create remarkable innovations. In the trash-can challenge, the students used their own knowledge, imagination, and attitude to create something from nothing, and I provided the habitat, culture, and resources to stimulate that process. This is important. The students already had the innate skills they needed, but the habitat created by our classroom environment and the rules of the assignment triggered their motivation and unleashed their creativity. The Innovation Engine captures the relationship between all these factors:

- Your *knowledge* provides the fuel for your imagination.
- Your *imagination* is a catalyst for the transformation of knowledge into ideas.
- This process is influenced by a myriad of factors in your environment, including your *resources*, *habitat*, and *culture*.
- Your *attitude* is a powerful spark that sets the Innovation Engine in motion.

Essentially, creativity is an endless resource, initiated by your drive to tackle challenges and to seize opportunities. Anything and everything can spark your Innovation Engine—every word, every object, every decision, and every action. Creativity can be enhanced by honing your ability to observe and learn, by connecting and combining ideas, by reframing problems, and by moving beyond the first right answers. You can boost your creative output by building habitats that foster problem solving, crafting environments that support the generation of new ideas, building teams that are optimized for innovation, and contributing to a culture that encourages experimentation.

You hold the keys to your Innovation Engine and have creative genius waiting to be unleashed. By tapping into this natural resource, you have the power to overcome challenges and generate opportunities of all dimensions. Your ideas—big and small—are the critical starting point for innovations that propel us forward. Without creativity, you are trapped in a world that is not just stagnant, but one that slips backward. As such, we are each responsible for inventing the future. Turn the key.

Analyze

1. What is the relationship of knowledge, attitude, and imagination to creativity?
2. Why do some people argue that a beginner's mind is a useful way to approach a challenge? What do you think?
3. How does imagination connect with memory? What does the work of Karl Szpunar and Kathleen McDermott have to say about this connection?
4. What is the relationship of culture, habits, and resources? How do these environmental factors relate to creativity?

Explore

1. The research by Carol Dweck at the Stanford School of Education tells us that a good attitude—like believing our brain is a muscle—can have a huge impact in terms of our ability to learn and stay motivated. The next time you experience your own "Oh, crap!" moment when you know you've made a mistake, take the time to explore what went wrong. How might you improve in the future? Your brain will respond accordingly.
2. Throughout Seelig's book, she emphasizes that "small changes in the environment have a big influence on creative output." What small changes can you do to the environment in which you handle your homework? What small changes can be made in the classroom to increase motivation, attention, or retention of ideas? Share your thoughts with others. Consider acting upon the best of them.
3. As Seelig challenged others to do, have your class create as much value as possible from the contents of a single trash can in only two hours. What type of value can you create? Think broadly about what the word "value" means. Consider challenging other classes on campus or

at other schools to take on the same task. Strive every day to keep the mind-set of finding value in what previously seemed valueless.

4. At the end of her piece, Seelig claims, "without creativity, you are trapped in a world that is not just stagnant, but one that slips backward." What do you believe she means by this? Do you agree? Why or why not?

D. Anthony Miles
"Creativity Theory"

D. Anthony Miles (1963–) is an entrepreneur, researcher, legal expert witness, and best-selling author. He is CEO and founder of Miles Development Industries Corporation, a consulting practice and venture capital firm. This is the first publication of "Creativity Theory."

Creativity Theory: The Two Types of Creativity

The literature on creativity has been varied and interesting to say the least. There is still somewhat a mystery as to what creativity is exactly and how to recognize it. Recognizing creativity is not an infallible task. The first theory of creativity is based on two concepts: *Innovation* and *Adaptation*. Both of these concepts have distinct differences. This concept was developed from Kirton's *Adaptive-Innovative Theory* (1976). This theory was originally developed in order to explain cognitive tendencies and problem-solving styles. Since the inception of this theory, both constructs have evolved and have taken new meanings in the understanding of the phenomenon of creativity.

The first construct of Creativity Theory is *Innovation*. Innovation is defined as creating something new (Merriam-Webster, 2015). This means a new idea or process is introduced. This consists of something which never existed before or never tried and tested before. For example, creating a new product, or starting a new company. Innovation also involves taking risks and challenges to creating a new product or service. Innovation is the act of introducing something new.

The second construct of Creativity Theory is *Adaptation*. Adaptation is defined as the process of changing to fit some purpose or situation; the process of adapting (Merriam-Webster, 2015). This involves adapting a preexisting object, concept and new idea or shaping in a new way. For example, this could mean taking an existing product, modifying it and creating a new product. Adaptation is the act of modifying and shaping a preexisting object into something new. Some companies are better at innovation and other companies are better at adaptation.

Most notably, innovators seek to do things *differently* and be radical, without a conventional framework. However, *adaptors* seek to do things *better,* operate *within* a conventional framework (Kirton, 1976; Strum, 2009). Innovators tend to find solutions to problems that do not exist. Adaptors tend to find improvement solutions to existing product problems that already exist. One cannot argue that one creativity strategy is better. However it would be a better argument to say each strategy must be adapted to the situation.

Creativity Theory: The Tale of Two Companies?

The two types of creativity are most applicable in the business environment and marketplace. In discussing the two constructs of this theory, we can examine companies' product launch strategy. This can be key in understanding how creativity works in the marketplace. A perfect example of applying Creativity Theory to the business environment would be to study Apple Computers and Microsoft Corporation. This is a classic case of an *innovation*-driven strategy versus an *adaptation*-driven strategy. These two companies could not be any more polar opposites in their product strategies.

Apple's core philosophy is to be radical and think differently. Apple has an innovation-strategy that is a derivative of their company philosophy. For example, Apple challenged the personal computer market by introducing such unconventional devices such as the mouse and a user-friendly icon platform which consisted of a menu on the computer monitor for the user. At the time, this was a radical departure from the conventional personal computers at the time. To Apple, IBM computers were the enemy. Years later, Apple continued to be a radical innovator by introducing new products and disrupting the marketplace with product innovations such as the iPhone, iPad, iTunes, and lately the Apple Watch (or iWatch). Apple may have saved the record business and record companies with the platform of iTunes. Apple can also be viewed as a disruptor in the marketplace: they disrupt the marketplace by introducing new products that are a radical departure from the conventional thinking.

The downside of this type of creativity strategy is that sometimes products can be ahead of their time and the marketplace is not receptive to these products. Remember Newton? Innovation strategy does not work all of the time. It has its place. This leads us to the *Product/Time Theory* (Miles, 2011), which illustrates Creativity Theory, new products, and the possibility of market acceptance. There are four components to this theory. Product position and dilemmas: (a) Right product, *Right time*: product meets a market need; possesses a competitive advantage (iTunes; iPod); (b) Wrong product, *Right time*: product does not meet a market need but consumers want something just not this (e.g., New Coke!); (c) Right product, *Wrong time*: product is good, but it tends to be ahead of its time (e.g., remember the Zip Disk?); and (d) Wrong product, *Wrong time*: There is no hope for this product. Product does not meet a need. It tends to be either before its time or after its time (e.g., remember DIVX? PalmPilot?).

Microsoft, on the other hand, tends to be an adaptation-driven company and their products are a derivative of their philosophy. Microsoft *rarely* introduces innovative products to the marketplace. However, they are a master at adaptive products. They tend to introduce products that are an improvement to preexisting products in the marketplace. For example, Microsoft builds software for computers. They did not create DOS. However, they developed Windows that made computing easier for pc users. Before Windows, individual software packages were often developed by different companies and they were not integrated. Windows allowed pc users to multitask functions. However, Windows was *adapted* from Apple's original platform for Apple Computers. Windows was developed for IBM personal computers. Windows also allowed pc users to use a mouse and eliminated the use of F-function keys to issue commands to the computer. The cornerstone of Microsoft's creativity is use an *adaptor strategy*. Microsoft created Windows, Office, Xbox, Windows Phone and lately the Surface. Most of their products and product lines are *adaptations* rather than *innovations*. Microsoft has the tendency to make improvements or innovations to existing products in the marketplace. For example, Microsoft Office was created after the emergence of software packages such as WordPerfect (*Word*), Harvard Graphics (*PowerPoint*), Lotus 1-2-3 (*Excel*), and dBase (*Access*).

The downside of this type of creativity strategy is that sometimes it works and sometimes it does not work. Adaptation can be too late or can be a Herculean effort to change the mind of the consumer. When they introduce new products, they often fail. Sometimes their adaptation strategy does not work. Remember Zune Tunes? This is a classic example of an innovator-driven company versus an adaptor-driven company. This illustrates the Creativity Theory in the business environment and marketplace.

REFERENCES

Kirton, M. (1976). Adaptors and innovators: A description and measure. *Journal of Applied Psychology*, 61 (5), 622–629.

Merriam-Webster, 2015. Retrieved from http://www.merriam-webster.com/dictionary/innovation

Miles, 2011. "The Product/Time Theory" *The Product Launch Matrix*.

Strum, J. (2009). Kirton's Adaption-Innovation Theory: Managing Cognitive Styles in Times of Diversity and Change. *Emerging Leadership Journeys*, *1*(1), pp. 66–78.

Analyze

1. In your own words, explain what innovation is. What are examples of innovation?
2. In your own words, explain what adaptation is. What are examples of adaptation?
3. What are the key creative differences between Apple and Microsoft? In your opinion, which company is more creative? Why?

Explore

1. Make a list of the most innovative companies you—or a small group of students—can think of. In what ways are these companies similar to Apple? What differences do you see?
2. Put on your Innovator's Hat. Write up the details for a new, innovative way for college teachers (in a class just like you're in now) to teach students. Once you've got that one written, switch to your Adaptor's hat.

Write up the details for an effective adaptation for a college class. Share your results with classmates. Discuss the merits of innovations versus adaptations. Ask your teacher which option(s) seem most useful.

3. What of the following quotations do you like most? Why? Debate the merits of each with classmates.

   a. "Failure is a part of innovation—perhaps the most important part."—Curt Richardson, founder and chairman of Otter Products

   b. "An idea that is not dangerous is unworthy of being called an idea at all."—Oscar Wilde, Irish author, playwright, and poet

   c. "If you think of it [resilience] in terms of the Gold Rush, then you'd be pretty depressed right now because the last nugget of gold would be gone. But the good thing is, with innovation, there isn't a last nugget. Every new thing creates two new questions and two new opportunities."—Jeff Bezos, founder and CEO of Amazon

Stephanie Freeman and Wendy Rountree
"Creativity from Beyond One's Natural Grasp: Finding Your Most Creative Ideas through Spirituality"

The author of two books, **Stephanie Freeman** (1970–) has contributed to numerous articles, including ones published in *The Huffington Post*, *The Wall Street Journal*, *Essence Magazine*, and *Redbook*. She is currently the program director for Arts and Humanities at North Carolina Central University in Durham, North Carolina. This is the first publication of this essay.

Wendy Rountree (1972–) has published scholarly articles, book chapters, book reviews, two academic books—*Just Us Girls: The Contemporary African-American Young Adult Novel* and *The Boys Club: Male Protagonists in Contemporary African-American Literature*—and a young adult novel, *Lost Soul*. She is a Professor of English at North Carolina Central University in Durham, North Carolina. This is the first publication of this essay.

What is called the imagination (from image, magi, magic, magician, etc.) is a practical vector from the soul. It stores all data, and can be called on to solve all our "problems." The imagination is the projection of ourselves past our sense of ourselves as "things." Imagination (Image) is all possibility, because from the image, the initial circumscribed energy, any use (idea) is possible. And so begins that image's use in the world. Possibility is what moves us.

—Amiri Baraka, "The Revolutionary Theatre"

Introduction

Amiri Baraka's sentiments in the above epigraph illustrate the many aspects of the connections between creativity and spirituality within the human spirit and soul. Creativity is the backbone of human existence. It is the force that drives humankind forward and keeps human beings mentally balanced. It is, therefore, worthy of cultivating. It is worthy of examination and must be held in high regard in each individual's life as well as society at large. Otherwise, what is mundane and stagnant will become normalized. In order to allow one's creativity to reach into the highest realm—into the spiritual depths from which comes the most life-altering ideas—one must procure and then engage it. Then, from that nebulous of spiritual oases (the place where ideas, dreams, and thoughts originate) will come the skeletal structure—the part that awaits infusion with one's passions and other people's energies to fashion the highest form of imagination—engaged creativity.

When creativity engages individuals—when it inveigles thoughts, conjoins passions, and enlightens the mind—it begins to alter lives by starting with one's own life and then progressing to others. It arrives at a level of maturity that could not be obtained otherwise because creativity requires movement if it is going to thrive. Engaged creativity moves beyond a single person; it must if it is going to become its most potent. Engaged creativity must have time to develop in singularity, but during that process and afterward, it must begin its reach beyond isolated walls and into some communal setting. The process is layered and starts with a spiritual connection—the place from which the structural pieces begin to form. "While there are no empirical studies to date concerning an association between creativity and spirituality, an increasing number of publications [discuss] a proposed link between creativity and spirituality from a theoretical perspective. There is a very clear consensus in the literature with regard to the mutual interaction between creativity and spirituality, whereby creativity is most often regarded as an aspect of spirituality" (Corry, Mallet, Lewis, and Abdel-Khalek 980). The process of engaged creativity continues with personalized growth and then matures with communal engagement—and becomes a "cord of three strands [that] is not quickly broken" (*New International Version, Ecclesiastes* 4:12).

The spiritual connection needed to provide creativity's structure is, perhaps, the most difficult stage. What constitutes spirituality can often fluctuate in both depth and understanding, so the structure itself may lack density. If this foundation is too weak, it may not be able to support or sustain creative growth. Fortunately, the spiritual bones can be fortified and the creative process strengthened if aided by tenacity and resilience. I must note here that I do not believe that creativity can exist without spirituality, and for that reason, I will give a definition of spirituality that most fits this premise. It is "a quality that goes beyond religious affiliation, that strives for inspiration, reverence, awe, meaning and purpose" (qtd. in website "National Center for Cultural Competence," def. *spirituality*). And, I am not alone; Karen Buckenham in "Creativity and Spirituality: Two Threads of the Same Cloth" states, "Spirituality and creativity are experienced by many people as inseparable. In the process of creating, they feel there is something bigger going on that speaks of God" (56). Spirituality, therefore, is the striving that becomes the impetus so prevalent in narratives about the creative process.

One such narrative about the creative process that shows the powerful quality of this spiritual connection/striving can be found in Alice Walker's seminal, womanist book entitled *In Search of Our Mothers' Gardens*. The womanist examinations come from a more racially and feminist-infused tapestry of various forms of prose. She posits that African American ancestors, especially grandmothers and mothers, as artists were spiritual vessels that needed to express their creativity through their various cultural products (i.e., quilts, cooking, gardening) in spite of and to counteract racism and discrimination. She writes:

> For these grandmothers and mothers of ours were not Saints, but Artists; driven to a numb and bleeding madness by the springs of creativity in them for which there was no release. There were Creators, who lived lives of spiritual waste, because they were so

rich in spirituality—which is the basis of Art—that the strain of enduring their unused and unwanted talent drove them insane. Throwing away this spirituality was their pathetic attempt to lighten the soul to a weight their work-worn, sexually abused bodies could bear. (233)

Walker emphasizes the importance of reaching beyond oneself into a "larger perspective," and embracing that perspective with fearless abandonment. She says, "What is always needed in the appreciation of art, or life, is the larger perspective. Connections made, or at least attempted, where none existed before, the straining to encompass in one's glance at the varied world the common thread, the unifying theme through immense diversity, a fearlessness of growth, of search, of looking, that enlarges the private and the public world" (5). Thus, both spirituality and creativity have the potential to intellectual and socially elevate the individual and society.

Walker's words provide the landscape for the spiritual connection about which I speak. In an interview with Wendy Rountree, Professor of English and Literature, she says, "In Walker's work *In Search of Our Mothers' Gardens*, we see the struggle for true creativity to emerge and rise powerfully in all people. She uses the metaphor of the garden to show how varied and beautiful each person's creative endeavors can be, especially if the soil is fertile and the water supply unhindered." Rountree correctly assesses Walker's skillful use of this metaphor to elaborate on the beauty of a creative mind and soul.

Freeman's Spiritual Connection Makes Its Debut and Tinder Awaits a Spark

Over the course of twenty-six years, I have had much time to examine various modes of creativity and their catalysts. Over two decades ago, I was a naïve nineteen-year-old college senior who felt a compelling call into the ministry. I was anxious to the point of being terrified because my youthful co-ed days were coming to a sudden close. I was going to graduate early, and my real life (as I had been told countless times) was about to begin. I was not ready for that life or the responsibilities therein, but I did feel ready for some sort of ministry. Later, I realized the absurdity of that very thought—that I could feel ready for some sort of ministry but not for "real" life (as if ministry and real life were separable parts).

In hindsight, what I was really ready for was authenticity. I wanted to be the person I had once dreamed I would be—someone who did more than write papers or decode information. I wanted to be a woman who created poems, sang, acted, and preached—all at once if the spirit so hit me. In three years of college life, I had not tapped into any of those creative parts in a significant way. I had performed in talent shows here and there to tweak my creative flare, but I engaged in no formalized development of the components that felt the most real in my life. Ministry, at the time, seemed to be more open to the possibility of "me," as it seemed the less structured. "Real life" meant a job at some company and the accompanying paycheck that would confine me to a lifetime of "chattel for hire" positions.

The woman that I wanted to be, that I thought ministry would allow me to be, connected with me as a pre-teen. At that time, I was also longing for creative outlets that school (middle school) lacked. I had been pegged as a math and science scholar, so much of my days were spent solving equations and memorizing formulas and elements. I was bored beyond comprehension, so I created songs to help myself remember information. One night, as I prayed to God to help me like school (or at least tolerate it), I fell asleep in the midst of the prayer and of crying. That night, from the creative depths of my soul, came a dream that would serve to guide me through my post-Baccalaureate period. A radiant woman appeared to me in that dream. At the time I was about twelve years old, and she had been waiting for several years (I believe) for my creativity and maturity (such as it can be at twelve years old) to reach her. By now, I had enough vocabulary so that she could speak and enough life experience so that she could dance and sing and move about in an appropriate setting—all enhanced by my budding imagination.

In that dream, the woman (whom I later identified as myself) danced and sang while moving up and down the aisles filled with people. Then, as if she were suddenly overcome with joy and excitement, she lifted her head high and started proclaiming scriptures in an alternating songlike and preaching fashion. She was dressed in a beautiful white gown that flowed effortlessly around her body. She was free in every sense of the word, and the smile on her face reflected that freedom. That smile branded itself upon my mind and was the tinder upon which my creative fires would later ignite.

At twelve years old, I had become astute enough to know that a lifetime of solving equations and memorizing formulas was not for me. I still held a great appreciation for those fields, but I was not going to be their champion. My migration to high school was coming quickly, and my career path would be more set. If a transition in my concentration was going to occur, it needed to occur now. Consequently, I needed a spiritual connection at that point to start changing the trajectory of my life toward the creative channels that were lying dormant inside. That desire, laden with creative passion, was what allowed the dream to come forth from the spiritual beyond and to give me hope that one day I would find my path.

The Creative Structure Takes Shape and Self-Development Starts Quickly

Through that dream, I realized that I had obtained the pieces by which my creative backbone would be formed. However, my formative, creative years did not start in earnest until, as I mentioned earlier, I was about to graduate from college. It was then that I felt the woman in my dream breathing inside my very soul—my spirit's expressive component. She was growing larger and more potent with every breath she took. One day, as I listened to Maya Angelou's words set to Branford Marsalis's music—music emanating from a cheap cassette tape playing in a friend's worn-out boom box—I felt the fullness of her strength. The spiritually-charged tone on that tape had emboldened me and my creative path was set in motion.

I borrowed that cassette tape, which was a copy of a copy, and listened to it for hours. I did not care about the poor sound quality or the parts that skipped because the tape was worn. I was determined to learn that creative vibe. The only thing that mattered was the woman's voice that I heard on the tape and the way she connected it to the music—jazz music (a spiritual music in its own right). She was a poet, a songstress, and, I thought, a preacher. She reminded me of the woman in my dream, and I imagined that she too wore a flowing gown and a big smile. Her voice was authoritative and fearless—like she knew what she was doing *and* what she was born to do. Her words spoke to me and called me into action. I had to be, as Angelou says in her poem "Phenomenal Woman," a phenomenal woman who was "just as cool as [I] please" (15). The coolness that I needed, if I could obtain it, would come from confidence—confidence in knowing that I was doing what I was born to do and doing it in the most creative way possible.

Later, I found out that the tape was called *Branford Marsalis and Buckshot—LaFonque: "I Know Why the Caged Bird Sings."* Angelou combined her autobiographical "life sermons" (as I called them) and her poetry to create song and spoken word sequences. That tape sparked the fire of creativity within me that burned hotter and hotter throughout my time in undergraduate and graduate school. It was the catalyst that birthed a small montage of poems, songs, and stories of my own that I kept safeguarded in college-ruled notebooks.

My once dormant spiritual enlightenment had a role model to emulate, and I had a hope for a brighter, more creative future. I was still confined to the rigidity of academic programs/curricula, but I had a goal—to create my own mixture of spoken word, sermons, and songs and to give them my personal bend (which was yet to be discovered).

My Formative Creative Years Include Shame and Harsh Judgments

One reason the formative creative years must start in isolation and be shaped in the midst of personal growth is that the person needs to develop fearlessness and tenacity. These "twins" work in tandem so that the structure they help build will be strong enough to sustain communal engagement. People who dare to assert their creativity with or for other people risk rejection, harsh judgments, and at times, failure. In fact,

> The creative process is paradoxical, leading to personal and spiritual growth partly because it involves both facing one's own fears, and the experience of great joy. There are tensions and internal struggles of trying to put down what is envisioned, or what is inside, or letting it unfold. Through the creative process, courage and trust is required, trust that the artist and the artwork will emerge out of the depths that feel out of control. (Buckenham 64)

The final stage of creative development is the messiest because it requires implementation and it adds an additional element to a very controlled environment. That element could be volatile, unstable, weak, or a host of other things that could curtail the formation of engaged creativity. Those pitfalls are the reason I suggest taking the formative years seriously and developing the strength of character, the fortitude, to handle what may lie ahead.

My formative years included mostly informal observations (though in too few places) and limited, extremely awkward mentoring sessions (with people who could not or would not embrace who I wanted to be or why I wanted to be that person). My disastrous, nearly-fatal creative downfall came when I tried to implement my hybridized self into ministerial form and present that new creation into a rigidly traditional environment.

My Journey into Ministry Begins . . .

At age nineteen, I had no idea what aspect of ministry I would undertake or what a "calling" entailed, but I knew that I wanted to do something profound with my life—something that only a pursuit of God and spirituality could fulfill. In my pursuit of this calling, I started studying people who were already in the ministry. I still had the awakened passion brought on by the Angelou/Marsalis tape, but I wanted to see if I could find some touchable examples of this same model—someone who would mentor me. I did not know what he or she would be called or in what ministerial capacity he/she would operate, but I told myself, "You will know it when you see it."

During this informal study, I thought everyone in ministry fell into one of four categories—a pastor, deacon, minister, or evangelist. Ministers, I thought, were all of the other people who did something for God but were not pastors or deacons, and evangelists were just traveling ministers. I was not obsessed with having a title; I wanted to know which title would be most compatible with the freedom I needed. My experiences had taught me that I would need to be called something if ever I received the opportunity to minister. I knew that in order for the ministerial doors to open, I had to be more than "Miss So-and-So." I surmised: my ministry may not be traditional, but my title better be (especially given my age and youthfulness).

I searched and searched within the limited confines of my area, my knowledge base, and the few churches that I was able to visit for a mentor and a place of comfort. I started with the church and not the stage because I felt my creative bend/platform would be bringing my talents into the church. I thought, "Angelou used jazz and a stage as part of her platform, so I will use gospel music and the pulpit as part of mine." With that conclusion, I was ready to conjure the smiling and dancing from my dreams.

What I found was not comforting—no one seemed to be doing what I thought I wanted to do—not even anything close. I saw bits and pieces of what I wanted to be—some bits of spoken word added to a sermon; a praise dance during praise and worship; or a sermonic song—but I saw none of those things combined. The woman in my dream did all of them simultaneously, and that was the flow that I wanted. I felt stifled. I longed to have all of my creative "selves" merged into one human/spiritual being. Doubt crept in and then fear, and I asked myself, "What if I am being heathenish trying to combine ministry and performance—light and darkness—sacred and secular?" I had, unknowingly, introduced shame and harsh judgments into my own creative/spiritual equation.

Throughout the days and into the nights, I questioned myself. "Are you just trying to be different to be different (i.e., not traditional), or do you really want to create and minister in this way?" My conclusion—I did not hate traditional ministers or ministering; I just did not seem to fit those boxes. Here, in this temple of my unfamiliar (to revise the title of one of Alice Walker's books), I found a temporary solace. I shed the shame and judgment that I had heaped upon myself, and I decided to press onward toward the creativity I knew lay within me. After all, I reasoned, I would not have had the dream if I were not meant to embody it someday. In order to solidify that summation, however, I decided to test my conclusion by accepting that speaking engagement at a friend's church. The invitation called for a speaker, but I decided to engage the congregation with my new brand of speaking/ministering. Here, in my first attempt to break with tradition and to step (unknowingly) into engaged creativity, I encountered the circumstances that led to my aforementioned, creative downfall. When I stepped before the audience, I lost my nerve and fear took over. What I planned to do that day had been honed, polished, and practiced, but what I did instead was cave into the traditional—to let prudish-looking faces and hushed comments about my age strip me of my creativity. I gave a traditional speech peppered with all the enthusiasm that I could muster. It was a grammatically correct and theologically sound speech, but it lacked the dynamism I had so desperately wanted.

The Shame and Harsh Judgments Come

"While many artists see the source and inspiration of their creativity as Divine, and feel that they are participating in something sacred," I discovered the dynamics of creativity and spirituality are not always as clear or clean as one might desire (Buckenham 58). When one reaches into his/ her consciousness and pulls out something creative that originated from deep within the spiritual beyond, one must be prepared to face ridicule, rejection, or even mistrust. The known and the unknown may collide and leave harsh looks and reactions in the wake. I faced the backlash of many and the acceptance of few.

Once I accepted the speaking engagement at my friend's church, I thought the hardest part of my journey was over. I had made the decision to move forward. I had taken a leap of faith and set out on my creative path. I was twenty-three years old at the time—past my teenage years, done with my graduate degree, and teaching at a university. I had learned more, written more, and practiced more. I was as ready as I could get—at least in exhibiting my craft. What I was not ready for was the reaction I would get once my craft was engaged—once it had reached an audience. I was not ready for the lack of acceptance, the stares, the whispers, and the rejection.

Before I faced opposition, I thought I was brilliant—my face all aglow with the joy that one's authentic creativity can bring. Yet, "Overcoming fear in the creating of an artwork has implications for moving one out of self-imposed limits. It contributes to a way of approaching life that takes courage and risk, inspiring confidence in oneself" (Bukenham 64). I was determined not to hide my gift and to exude excellence in whatever I did. I was letting my light shine so that all the world could see it (*New International Version*, Matt. 5:16). I would fulfil this scriptural mandate with near-flawless execution. Before I fell prey to rejection, I had a defiant attitude similar to the persona in Langston Hughes's poem "I, Too." He had awaited the day when he would be grown (mentally and physically) and independent from his oppressors. When that day came, he jubilantly and defiantly stated that his oppressors would have to take note of him because they would see him in all his true glory. He says, "They'll see how beautiful I am/And be ashamed," for he knew his authenticity would bring a change in heart (16–17).

Hughes's persona had weathered the trials of oppression and had emerged strong enough to engage with anyone without needing his/her reinforcement. I, however, bent and then crumbled beneath the weight of judgment (whether presumed or real). I had engaged too soon—before my emotions could be checked and my resilience built. I needed acceptance in order to progress, and when that acceptance did not come, I could no longer unleash all of the creative forces within. I put my creative forces away and for fifteen years settled for an alternate path—a job and more graduate school. I reasoned, "One day, some day, my creativity will emerge." In those years, I read and prayed and studied my own fundamental nature. I faced my frustrations and made changes. Although Atuolu Omalu, an African scholar, is discussing a movement among African philosophers, the process he describes was one I too endured. He says in his book *Some Unanswered Questions in Contemporary African Philosophy*: "The history of African philosophy began with 'frustration' (and not with wonder as it was in Western philosophy) that generated angry questions and then responses and reactions. These reactions led to the nationalist movements. . ." (9). My cyclical, philosophical thinking did not lead to a national movement, but it did toughen my demeanor and create resilience.

The Mask Comes Off and the Pioneers of Faith Give Comfort

After years of reconstruction, I needed to shed the self-inflicted and other hurts that had contributed to my original deconstruction. Initially, to use a phrase from Paul Laurence Dunbar's poem "We Wear the Mask," I proceeded with a "torn and bleeding heart" (4). I understood too well what Dunbar meant when he penned, *We smile, but, O great Christ, our cries/To thee from tortured souls arise* (10–11).

However, that mask of indecision and fear was even more stifling than not seeing a place for my creativity to blossom. The mask had molded itself to me and would not allow me to see my way clearly to higher levels of creativity—that is until I ripped it off and replaced it with my spiritual and creative glasses. As the process to engagement continued, I turned to a virtual community before returning to a live one. I read blogs and posts and followed people in social media until finally, I had built a modern-day "Hall of Faith"—a list of people (both alive and dead) who would inspire me to engage once again in a live community.

I learned, for example, how certain people, usually referred to as pioneers of the faith, found their way into their callings after much perseverance and turmoil. That turmoil came with a lifetime of difficulties and more than its own share of tears, and I wondered if I would ever be ready for such an endeavor. I decided that I had to be ready because I too could not separate my uniqueness from my spirituality—and thus, my creativity was going to have its day, once again, to shine. I garnered hope from the likes of Ida B. Wells (defiant activist); Charlotte Hawkins Brown (preparatory school founder); John Chavis (free black educator); and Sally Ride (astronaut and futurist).

I might join those pioneers one day and be shunned, but on a bright note, I might also be the inspiration someone might need to go beyond the ordinary . . . and going beyond the ordinary is where creativity thrives. It soars to its highest levels when humans loose the chains of the mundane and allow the freedom of creativity to straighten itself.

Jean Toomer's character King Barlo, depicted in his lyrical book *Cane*, epitomizes this righted posture when he rises from the critical chains brought on by poverty and creates a new socio-economic paradigm for himself—that of prophet and historian. Toomer writes: "Barlo rises to his full height. He is immense. To his people he assumes the outlines of his visioned African" (*Cane*, "Esther," 31).

Barlo seizes the opportunity to let creativity and spirituality unite, and the result is a sermon so powerful that it causes a racially divided community to become humane toward one another. The result is nothing less than phenomenal because it also leads to creativity in other people who had beforehand been too bogged down in the routine to create. That creativity, which the town had never before witnessed, included paintings of a black Jesus on the courthouse wall and dreams of creative, immaculate conceptions—creations that would come from the spiritual beyond.

My Students Help Me Find the Way Back

My personal journey is not unique as I have learned. I have been teaching on a collegiate level for over twenty years now, and I often hear students discussing ways to express their creativity. Many times, they have ideas but are not sure from whence those ideas came. They ask where I think their thoughts about this or that originated. More often, they feel an urge to be more creative in their lives, and they are searching for ways to tap into the creativity that they sense is within. They speak in excited tones and use grand gestures to tell stories of their triumphs and failures as they tried something new. They share the emotional battle scars they obtained while they struggled to introduce creativity into whatever field that had aroused their passion. Musicians, for example, try to compose new songs—sometimes hiding themselves in obscure band rooms or closets in case they produce more noise than music or more dissonance than melody. Poets reach into their deepest, most-impactful emotions to create phrases and sentences that convey the pain or joy of events shared by millions. Then, they leave those poems in notebooks until someone (like me) compels them to open them (usually for some group project or extra credit points). I encourage engaged creativity in the classroom because it is a controlled environment geared toward learning and exploration. That way, their engagement has a safety net. It also has an exhorter, for I will applaud and praise the effort and the creation no matter how it sounds. Its birth is what is beautiful to me.

I recognize in my students what I once grappled with myself—how to take one's creativity to yet-unattained levels without being singled out as strange or silly. They too struggle with how much creativity will be accepted and how much of themselves they are willing to hold up for ridicule as they try to obtain that creativity. Creativity, as I explain to them, can be "a very messy process, full of mistakes and misgivings and frustrated pauses, but it is worth the struggle." I developed those words to comfort them in this journey. Then, I tell them, "Remember, your journey will not be complete until you seek the unknown realms of spirituality and supersede regular commonalities." They may never be free of ridicule, but they can get beyond both it and the feeling of silliness it fosters.

The Questions Come and I Expose My Journey

When my students ask how I stepped into my current creativity and overcame the initial fears it fostered, I have an answer. With every passing year, I became more and more determined to live as creatively and authentically as possible. I became less afraid of being ostracized or sounding passé than I was of being bored (or worst still—of being boring). I let a lesser fear (of being rejected) be overshadowed by a greater one (of living in the mundane) until the lesser fear disappeared entirely. I knew that if the lesser fear was gone, the bigger one would soon follow—and it did. I also decided that I could not do any great or enduring calling for humankind until I honored the spiritual forces that made me who I am. I had a debt yet unpaid, and I knew that my creativity would be stifled and then die if I did not fulfil my obligation to create. I had a debt to pay to "human guile"—to outsmart the creative haters out to squelch my flow (Dunbar, *We Wear the Mask*, 3).

Inspiration Comes from a Master, Self-Help Guru

One need not agree with Napoleon Hill's philosophies or life affirmations to see the power in some of the statements he makes. In his classic book *Think and Grow Rich*, Hill summarizes the longing that so many people finally replace with satisfaction. Through multiple real-life examples, he shows the power of creativity put in motion. Furthermore, he shows, and my own life attests, that over time, a strong enough desire will forge its way into existence—despite any hesitancies or resistance it may have faced. Hill states: "I had learned from years of experience with men, that when a man really desires a thing so deeply that he is willing to stake his entire future on a single turn of the wheel in order to get it, he is sure to win" (*Introduction*). Creativity is great whenever and wherever it comes, but it is magnificent when it comes with spiritual awakening. When one acknowledges the spiritual forces that made creativity possible, the creativity gets a boost that propels ordinary humans into pioneers/icons of their field. Creativity takes passion and makes it better, more intense. It makes the pragmatic and the procedural rise to the historical and legendary. However, as great as one's creativity may become, it is incomplete until it engages with other human beings. That audience may be hostile, but it is necessary for both the creator and the created product's full maturation. Consequently, when one is involved in engaged creativity, one must be prepared to lay one's emotions at the altar of judgment, as heightened creativity often becomes entangled with criticism. If one can endure, however, one can mitigate the criticism and be fulfilled by a spiritual awakening.

Analyze

1. In the essay, Freeman and Rountree offer an example of spirituality from Alice Walker's *In Search of Our Mother's Gardens*. Why is the garden an appropriate metaphor here? How does the garden relate to creativity?
2. In what way did Freeman see ministry as a path to "the possibility of 'me'"? In what ways might ministry offer new outlets for creativity?
3. What does Freeman see as the final stage of creative development? How does she describe it? What pitfalls are inherent in it?
4. What role do students play in Freeman's work and life? What type of teacher do you imagine her to be? Why?

Explore

1. How do you define spirituality? Explain the various components of your definition. What role do you think spirituality has in the creative

process, and how aware of it are you in your own creative process? Have you ever had a teacher who emphasized the spiritual versus the verbal or analytic? How so?

2. Many authors use spirituality in their creative process and in their writings. Name a writer or two who incorporates spirituality directly into their work. What extra dimensions/elements does the spiritual aspect provide? Is there a connection to artistic expression and a sense of mystery? How might the word *transformation* come into play?

3. Freeman discusses her struggles to cultivate her creativity on her own terms. Write a paragraph or two about a time when you had to be creative on your own terms. Share your writing with a classmate and compare points of contrast and comparison with his or her own experiences.

4. Do you believe that dreams can lead to creative expression? Why or why not? Has a dream ever helped you overcome a creative challenge? How? Why?

WORKS CITED

Angelou, Maya. *Phenomenal Woman*. Family Friends Poems. Web. 22 May 2015. http://www.familyfriendpoems.com/poem/phenomenal-woman-by-maya-angelou. Web.

Baraka, Amiri. "The Revolutionary Theatre." *The Norton Anthology of African American Literature*. Eds. Henry Louis Gates, Jr and Valerie A. Smith. 3rd ed. 2 vols. New York: W. W. Norton & Company, 2014. 688–691. Print.

Bukenham, Karen. "Creativity and Spirituality: Two Threads of the Same Cloth." *Religion & Theology* 18 (2011). 56–76. Print.

Corry, Dagmar Anna Susanne, John Mallett, Christopher Alan Lewis, and Ahmed M. Abdel-Khalek. "The Creativity-Spirituality Construct and Its Role in Transforming Coping." *Mental Health, Religion & Culture* 16:10 (2013). 979–990. Print.

Dunbar, Paul Laurence. *We Wear the Mask*. Poetry Foundation. Web. 22 May 2015. www.poetryfoundation.org/poem/173467. Web.

Hill, Napoleon. *Think and Grow Rich*. Introduction. Start Publishing, LLC. First Start Publishing eBook edition. 2013 October. Web. 22 May 2015.

Hughes, Langston. *I, Too*. Poetry Foundation. Web. 22 May 2015.http://www.poetryfoundation.org/poem/177020 Web.

Murray and Zentner. 1989: 259. qtd. by website "National Center for Cultural Competence." "Body/Mind/Spirit: Toward a Biopsychosocial-Spiritual Model of Health." Georgetown University Center for Child and Human Development. 29 May 2015. Print.

New International Version. Bible Gateway. Web. 29. May. 2015. Print.

Omalu, Atuolu. Some Unanswered Questions in Contemporary African Philosophy. Ed. By Jonathan O. Chimakonnam. University Press of America, Inc., Lanham, Maryland, 2015. Print.

Rountree, Wendy. Personal Interview. 1 June 2015.

Toomer, Jean. *Cane*. Reprinted. Elizabeth Alexander and Graywolf Press, Minneapolis, Minnesota, www.graywolfpress.org. Web. 22 May 2015.

Walker, Alice. *In Search of Our Mothers' Gardens*. Harcourt, Inc. Orlando, Florida. 1983. Print.

Edward de Bono
"Creativity Workout"

Born in Malta, **Edward de Bono** (1933–) is a physician, inventor, consultant, and writer of more than eighty books. He created the term "lateral thinking" and was the first person to propose that the human brain was a self-organizing system. In 1988, de Bono was awarded the first Capire prize in Madrid, Spain, for a "significant contribution to humankind." He is regarded as one of the foremost experts in the field of creativity. "Creativity Workout" first appeared in his book *Creativity Workout: 62 Exercises to Unlock Your Most Creative Ideas*.

E veryone wants to be creative.

Everyone should want to be creative. Creativity makes life more fun, more interesting and more full of achievement.

Research shows that 94 percent of youngsters rate "achievement" as the most important thing in their lives. Creativity is the key skill needed for achievement.

Without creativity there is only repetition and routine. These are highly valuable and provide the bulk of our behavior—but creativity is needed for change, improvement and new directions.

In business, creativity has become essential. This is because everything else has become a commodity available to everyone.

If your only hope of survival is that your organization will continue to be more competent than your competitors, that is a weak position. There is nothing you can do to prevent your competitors also becoming competent.

Information has become a commodity available to everyone. Current technology has become a commodity, with a few exceptions—where a 16-year patent life offers some protection.

Imagine a cooking competition with several chefs at a long table. Each chef has the same ingredients and the same cooking facility. Who wins that competition?

At a lower level the chef with the highest quality wins. But at the higher level all chefs have excellent quality. So who wins? The chef who can turn the same ingredients into superior quality.

In business, competing with India and China on a price basis is impossible. That leaves creating new value as the basis for competition. And that needs a more serious commitment to creativity than is the case at the moment.

Creativity as Talent

Too many people believe that creativity is a talent with which some people are born and the rest can only envy. This is a negative attitude that is completely mistaken.

Creativity is a skill that can be learned, developed and applied.

I have been teaching creative thinking for over 30 years to a wide variety of people:

. . . from four-year-olds to 90-year-olds

. . . from Down's syndrome children to Nobel laureates

. . . from illiterate miners in Africa to top executives

Using just one of the techniques of *"lateral thinking,"* a group of workshops generated 21,000 ideas for a steel company in one afternoon.

Uninhibited

An ordinary man is walking down the road. A group of people seize him and tie him up with a rope. Then a violin is produced. Obviously, the man tied up with the rope cannot play the violin. So what do we say?

We claim that if the rope was cut the man would play the violin. This is clearly nonsense. Cutting the rope does not make the man a violinist.

Unfortunately we have the same attitude towards creativity. If you are inhibited it is difficult to be creative. Therefore if we make you uninhibited you will be creative!

This is the basis of "brainstorming" and other popular techniques. There is some merit in these systems but the approach is a very weak one. The formal and deliberate "tools" of lateral thinking are much more powerful.

The brain is designed to be "non-creative." If the brain were creative, life would be impossible. With 11 pieces of clothing to put on in the morning there are 39,916,800 ways of getting dressed. If you tried one way every minute you would need to live to be 76 years old, using your entire waking life trying ways of getting dressed.

Fortunately for us, the brain is designed to form stable patterns for dealing with a stable universe. That is the excellence of the brain and for that we should be very grateful.

So removing inhibition is of value, but only a weak way of developing creativity.

Creativity as Skill

Creativity is a skill that everyone can learn, practice and use.
It is as much a skill as skiing, playing tennis, cooking or learning mathematics.

Everyone can learn such skills. In the end not everyone is going to be equally good at these skills. Some people cook better than others. Some people play tennis better than others. But everyone can learn the skill. And everyone can seek to get better through practice.

Creativity Is Not a Mystery

For the first time in history we can now look at creativity as the "logical" behavior of a certain type of information system. The mystery and mystique can be removed from creativity.

1. We need to look at the human brain as a "self-organizing information system."
2. Self-organizing information systems form patterns.

3. All pattern-making systems are "asymmetric."
4. This is the basis of humor and of creativity. Humor is by far the most significant behavior of the human brain because it indicates the nature of the underlying system. Reason tells us very little because any "sorting system" run backwards is a reasoning system. Humor indicates asymmetric patterns. This means that the route from A to B is not the same as the route from B to A.

"Lateral thinking" is the creativity concerned with changing ideas, perceptions and concepts. Instead of working harder with the same ideas, perceptions and concepts, we seek to change them. This "idea creativity" is not the same as "artistic creativity," which is why a new term was needed.

All these things are explained in my books on lateral thinking; an understanding of such systems is the logical basis for the practical tools of lateral thinking.

The Word "Creative"

In the English language, the word "create" means to bring into being something that was not there before.

So someone can "create a mess." That means bringing into existence a mess that did not exist before. Is that person "creative"?

We hasten to add that what has been brought into existence must have "value." So creativity is bringing into existence something that has value.

There is, of course, the element of "newness" because repetition—no matter how valuable—is not seen as creative.

The word "creative" has largely been taken over by the arts, because in the arts all the work is new and has value. It is true that the value is not always recognized at first. For example, the Impressionist painters were not fully appreciated in their time.

In the English language there does not exist a separate word to distinguish the creativity of new ideas from the creativity of art. So when I claim that "creativity" can indeed be taught, I am asked if Beethoven could be produced in this way. The answer is "no," but "idea creativity" can be taught, learned and developed in a formal way. The purpose of the exercises in this book is to help develop creative habits of mind.

The "creativity" of the art world includes a large element of "aesthetic judgement." The artist judges that something is "right." This is quite different from the ability to produce new ideas. While artists may be excellent in their field, they are not especially good at changing ideas and creating new ideas.

This language problem has two very serious consequences.

The first consequence is that education authorities believe that they are "teaching creativity" by encouraging dancing and music-playing. This is totally wrong. These activities are of value in themselves but they are not teaching creativity.

The second consequence is that people say that if you cannot produce a Beethoven to order, then creativity cannot really be taught. This is also garbage. Idea creativity can be taught.

As a matter of interest, my work is used quite widely in the arts world, particularly in music. Because music does not represent existing sounds, there is a great need for creativity rather than just expression.

Habits of Mind

There is no sharp distinction between a mental skill and a mental habit. The two overlap and blend into each other. The purpose of this book is to provide opportunity for practising the mental skill of creativity and developing the habits of mind that make creativity happen.

Suppose you developed the habit of mind of trying to find alternative meanings for well-known acronyms.

So when you looked at NASA, you did not only think of the North American Space Agency, but of other possibilities:

Not Always Same Astronaut

Not Always Same Ascent

Not Always Same Ambition

Or:

New Adventures Splendid Achievements

New Ambitions Serious Attainments

As with a joke, the new explanation is more powerful if it links in with existing knowledge, or even prejudice, about the organization.

Possibility

Educational establishments totally underestimate the importance of "possibility."

Two thousand years ago, China was far ahead of the West in science and technology. They had rockets and gunpowder. Had China continued at the same rate of progress, then today China would easily have been the dominant power in the world.

What happened? What brought progress to a halt?

The Chinese scholars started to believe you could move from "fact to fact." So they never developed the messy business of possibility (hypothesis, etc.). As a result, progress came to a dead end.

Exactly the same sort of thing is happening in the world today. Because of the excellence of computers, people are starting to believe that all you need to do is to collect data and analyze it. This will give you your decisions, your policies and your strategies. It is an extremely dangerous situation, which will bring progress to a halt. There is a huge need for creativity to interpret data in different ways; to combine data to design value delivery; to know where to look for data; to form hypotheses and speculations, etc., etc.

I have held academic positions at the universities of Oxford, Cambridge, London and Harvard. I have to say that at each of these wonderful institutions the amount of time spent on the fundamental importance of possibility was zero.

Our culture and habits of thinking insist that we always move towards certainty. We need to pay equal attention to possibility.

Peptic ulcer (stomach or duodenal ulcer) is a serious condition that affects many people. Sufferers used to be on antacids for 20 years or more. There were major operations to remove part or all of the stomach. A large number of beds were occupied by patients under treatment or diagnosis of the condition. Hundreds of people were researching this serious condition.

Then a young doctor, Barry J. Marshall, in Perth, Western Australia, suggested that peptic ulcer might be an infection. Everyone laughed, because the hydrochloric acid in the stomach would surely kill any bacteria. No one took the possibility seriously. Many, many years later it turned out that he was right. Instead of antacids for 20 years and losing some or all of your stomach, you simply take antibiotics for one week!

Possibility is very important. And possibility is the key to creativity.

Analyze

1. De Bono says that research shows 94% of youngsters rate what as the most important thing in their lives? What does de Bono think is the key skill to help them achieve that goal?
2. Why does de Bono claim that the brain is noncreative? Why is this ultimately a good thing?
3. What does de Bono believe is the most significant behavior of the human brain because it indicates the nature of the underlying systems?
4. What is the distinction between "idea creativity" and "artistic creativity"? Why does de Bono make that distinction?

Explore

1. One of de Bono's key concepts is lateral thinking, which is a way to solve problems not by thinking/working harder, but rather by circumventing step-by-step reasoning and logic to come at an answer from an indirect and creative approach. Here are two puzzles that are not easily solved without using lateral thinking. Try to come up with the answers on your own (though the answers are listed in Appendix B, if you need them).
   a. A baby fell out of a forty-story building and lived. How is this possible?
   b. There are five loaves of bread in a basket. Five people each take one of the loaves. How is it that one loaf of bread is still left in the basket?
2. De Bono writes "Our culture and habits of thinking insist that we always move towards certainty. We need to pay equal attention to possibility." What do you imagine he means by that? Why is possibility so important? How often are you truly open to possibility in your own life?
3. In what ways to mental habits and mental skills overlap? What is their relationship? What specifically can you do to improve your mental habits and mental skills?
4. There are many freely available videos online of de Bono sharing his ideas on creativity, lateral thinking, and humor in lectures, classes, and interviews. Watch at least one video and then strive to implement his ideas into your daily life for a week. What effect do his ideas have? What changes do you see in your mental habits?

Forging Connections

1. This chapter has a range of ideas on the creative process. Select three of the included authors from this chapter and create a multimedia presentation—or write an essay—that identifies the points of connection and differences in their included pieces. Share your results with the class and discuss your ideas.

2. How is creativity related to the work of being a college student? What areas of your life as a student would benefit most from an increased level of creativity? Consider options beyond homework and studying— think about your health, your living environment, your mental and emotional well-being, your identity, your relationships. Develop an essay that forges a connection between creativity and your world of being a student. Also, you might borrow insights from writers in Chapter 3: The Creative Workplace. For instance, Ed Catmull's selection "Fear and Failure" may shed light on these connections.

Looking Further

1. One of the challenges a thematic reader like this creates is that including a book chapter, an essay, or an article only offers a limited take on someone's life work. Other than Isaac Asimov, these authors have delved deeply into the subject of creativity in their research and writing. How can three, eight, or eighteen pages encapsulate all they know? Overcome this challenge by finding one of their books on creativity and read it deeply. Get a fuller grasp on what they have to offer. How do they expand or extend the ideas from this chapter's selections?

2. Construct an infographic that shows your own creative process. Be thorough and specific. Include whatever stages, ideas, actions, and processes that are part of what you do when you're being creative. If you're not particularly artistic, handle this challenge creatively and have some fun with it.

Creativity
Myths

"Many highly talented, brilliant, creative people think they're not—because the thing they were good at at school wasn't valued, or was actually stigmatized."

—Sir Ken Robinson, English creativity expert

What do you envision when someone says, "Picture a creative person"? Is it a lonely, angst-ridden poet sitting on a bridge at night, her Birkenstocked feet dangling over the slow-moving water below? Is it some Stanford professor in a lab coat, armed with enough Ph.D.s to choke a mule? Is it some special spiritual person who has a rare connection to God, the divine, the universe, or the Powers That Be? Is it someone whose name everyone knows is synonymous with a Big Idea (or two or three)?

Here's the truth. Talk with ten strangers about creativity and you'll quickly see that the myths of creativity—like these—are everywhere, like crabgrass choking out an untended lawn. These myths serve to create elitism and ultimately keep people from achieving their potential. Which of these sound familiar?

- Only right-brained people are creative.
- Creativity should be fun.
- Creativity can't be taught.
- Creativity just happens.
- Great creative moments will be instantly recognized. ("Eureka!")
- Mozart/Shakespeare/Picasso never needed a second draft.
- Creative people never struggle.
- I'm not creative.
- You're either born with creativity or you're not.

One major goal of this book is to demystify the creative process for readers and, in so doing, make creativity something they can add to their arsenal. If someone repeats any of these myths of creativity, like any repeated lie, it starts to manifest into a reality. For instance, one doesn't need to be crazy to be creative. Creativity researcher Dr. Dean Keith Simonton reports that "few creative individuals can be considered truly mentally ill. Indeed, outright disorder usually inhibits rather than helps the creative process. Furthermore, a large proportion of creators exhibit no symptoms, at least not to any measurable degree." So why then do so many people we consider creative—comic Robin Williams who committed suicide, musician Sting who was "the King of Pain," and Mr. Morose himself, Edgar Allen Poe, who suffered a lifetime of torment and emotional anguish—seem mentally ill, at least from our general, albeit distant perspective?

Perhaps one reason many feel they aren't creative is that despite sometimes Herculean effort, there isn't any transformative, tangible end result. Would a truly creative person squander such serious time and effort on something that ended up so poorly? Would Stephen Hawking have come up with a better result? Would Beyoncé? Would Andy Warhol? Thinking like this leads one to quickly conclude: "I must not be that creative." Studies show, however, that creativity can be learned, fostered, and strengthened through practice. Just like trying to swing a golf club the first time doesn't usually go well, neither might one's creative efforts.

See what the experts in this chapter have to say about the myths of creativity.

Bill Watterson
"Do You Have an Idea for a Story Yet?"

Bill Waterson (1958–) is one of the most successful newspaper cartoonists of the twentieth century. His critically acclaimed comic, *Calvin and Hobbes*, ran from November 18, 1985, until December 31, 1995. In 1986, Watterson was the youngest person to win the Reuben Award for Outstanding Cartoonist of the Year. He won the award again in 1988. This comic first ran on May 24, 1992.

Analyze

1. How prevalent is Calvin's idea on inspiration in the lives of people you know? Your classmates? Yourself?
2. Is "last-minute panic" likely going to work as a motivator for Calvin? Why or why not?
3. What comment does Bill Watterson seem to be making about idea generation?

Explore

1. Calvin is a precocious six year old who has said such lucid things as "Nothing spoils fun like finding out it builds character" and "Life is full of surprise, but never when you need one." What do you imagine Calvin would say about innovation? Geniuses? Thinking?

2. Part of the meaning of a comic strip comes from things beyond the text itself. What nontextual elements contribute to this comic's meaning?

3. When others are around, Hobbes is just a stuffed tiger. When it's just Calvin, Hobbes is alive and kicking, portraying the much-needed straight man to Calvin's own brand of wisdom. What does this situation say about the creativity of children? What other instances of creativity have you witnessed firsthand in children?

Scott Adams
"I'm Looking for an Employee Who Is Creative"

Scott Adams (1957–) is the creator of *Dilbert*, the "most photocopied, pinned-up, downloaded, faxed, and e-mailed comic strip in the world." More than 20 million *Dilbert* books and calendars have been sold, and more than half of his books were *New York Times* bestsellers.

Analyze

1. What comment does Scott Adams seem to be making about creativity in the corporate world?
2. Why is this comic in the chapter on creativity myths? What other chapters might it fit in?
3. What point is made here about *having* information and *understanding* information? How does finding that information on the Internet add to Scott Adams point?

Explore

1. Create your own comic about the myth of creativity. If you're not particularly artistic, embrace that fact and just have fun with it. Share your results with the class.
2. Part of the meaning of a comic strip comes from things beyond the text itself. What nontextual elements contribute to this comic's meaning? How do Adams' nontextual elements differ than those Wattersonused in the included *Calvin* and *Hobbes* comic?
3. Compare this take on corporate creativity to Todd Dewett's in "Long Live the Organizational Deviant" in Chapter 3: The Creative Workplace. How aligned are they? What differences do you see? Is Dilbert an organizational deviant or does he take an alternate path?

Scott Berkun
"Good Ideas Are Hard to Find"

The author of six books, **Scott Berkun** (1961–) is a popular speaker on culture, business, philosophy, and creativity. He has been a regular commentator on CNBC, MSNBC, and National Public Radio. Berkun is also the director of the film project *We Make Seattle*. "Good Ideas Are Hard to Find" first appeared in his book *The Myths of Innovation*.

While I was waiting in a city park to interview someone for this book, a nearby child played with Silly Putty and Legos at the same time. In my notepad I listed how many ideas the young boy, not more than five years old, came up with in 10 minutes. Sitting in the grass, he combined, modified, enhanced, tore apart, chewed on, licked, and buried various creations I'd never have imagined. His young mother, chatting on a phone while resting her morning coffee on the park bench, barely noticed the inventive creations her kid unleashed on the world. After being chased away for making her nervous (an occupational risk for writers in parks), I wondered what happens to us—and what will happen to this boy—in adulthood. Why, as is popularly believed, do our creative abilities decline, making ideas harder to find? Why aren't our conference rooms and board meetings as vibrant as childhood playgrounds and sandboxes?

If you ask psychologists and creativity researchers, they'll tell you that it's a myth: humans, young and old, are built for creative thinking. We've yet to find special creativity brain cells that die when you hit 35, or hidden organs only the gifted are born with that pass ideas to their minds. Many experts even discount genius, claiming that the amazing works by Mozart or Picasso, for example, were created through ordinary means, exercising similar thinking processes to what we use to escape shopping mall parking lot mazes or improvise excuses when late for dinner.[1] Much like children, the people who earn the label *creative* are, as Howard Gardner explains in *Frames of Mind*,[2] "not bothered by inconsistencies, departures from convention, non-literalness. . .", and run with unusual ideas that most adults are too rigid, too arrogant, or too afraid to entertain.

The difference between creatives and others is more attitude and experience than nature. We survived hundreds of thousands of years not because of our sharp claws, teleportive talents, or regenerative limbs, but because our oversized brains adapt, adopt, and make use of what we have. If we weren't naturally creative and couldn't find ideas, humans would have died out long ago. A sufficiently motivated bear or lion can easily kill any man—even the meanest all-pro NFL linebacker. However, given creative problems to solve, an average human being is hard to beat. We make tools, split atoms, and have more patents than the world's species combined (but please don't tell the bears—they get pissy about patents). Our unique advantage on this planet is the inventive capacity of our minds. We even make tools for thought, like writing, so that when we find good ideas—such as how to tame and cage lions—we can pass that knowledge to future generations, giving them a head start.

But with the advance of civilization, creativity may have moved, for many, to the sidelines. Idea reuse is so easy—in the form of products, machines, websites, and services—that people are enabled to go for years without finding ideas on their own. Modern businesses thrive on selling prepackaged meals, clothes, holidays, entertainments, and experiences, tempting people to buy convenience rather than make things themselves. I don't believe everyone should make everything themselves, or even most things. But I do believe everyone has the capacity to enjoy creating something, and the temptation for convenience inhibits many people from discovering what it is they'd like to make. Passive consumption of television and the Web has absorbed time we could be using for active hobbies and pastimes, age-old places for nurturing our creative selves. The need for craftsmen and artists, professional idea finders, has thus faded; more people than ever make livings in careers Lloyd Dobler would hate: selling, buying, and processing other things.[3] Even when charged to work with ideas, few adults can do so as easily as they could in their youth.

Einstein said, "Imagination is more important than knowledge," but you'd be hard-pressed to find schools or corporations that invest in people with those priorities. The systems of education and professional life, similar by design, push the idea-finding habits of fun and play to the corners of our minds, training us out of our creativity.[4] We reward conformance of mind, not independent thought, in our systems—from school to college to the workplace to the home—yet we wonder why so few are willing to take creative risks. The truth is that we all have innate skills for solving problems and finding ideas: we've just lost our way.

The Dangerous Life of Ideas

Quick test: Name five new ways to change the world, or you'll die! Sorry, time's up. Fortunately, I can't kill anyone from this side of the book, and writers killing readers is bad business. But if I did honor the threat, you'd be dead. No one can come up with one big idea, much less five, that fast. As absurd as this paragraph is so far, it mirrors how adults often manage creative thinking: "be creative, and perfect, right now." Whenever ideas are needed because of a crisis or a change, there's a fire-drill call, an immediate demand. But rarely is the call met with sufficient resources— namely time—to mine those ideas. The bigger the challenge, the more time it will take to find ideas, but few remember this when criticizing ideas to death moments after they've been born.

Cynical idea-killing phrases like "that never works," "we don't do that here," or "we tried that already" are common and can easily make idea-finding environments more like slaughterhouses than gardens. It's as if an idea knocks on the door, and someone answers, waving his fist: "Go away! I'm looking for ideas." Ideas need nurturing and are grown, not manufactured, which suggests that idea shortages are self-inflicted. It doesn't take a genius to recognize that ideas will always be easier to find if they're not shot down on sight.

The myth that leads to this idea-destroying behavior is that good ideas will look the part when found. When Henry Ford made his first automobiles—awkward, smelly machines that stalled, broke down, and failed even the most generous comparisons to horses—people judged the superficial aspects, not the potential (see Figure 2.1). Everyone believes the future will come all at once in a neatly gift-wrapped package, as if Horse 2.0, whatever its incarnation, would make its first appearance with trumpets blaring and angels hovering above. The future never enters the present as a finished product, but that doesn't stop people from expecting it to arrive that way.

The idea of the computer mouse (see Figure 2.2) was equivalently weird and uninspiring to pre-PC-age eyes ("Wow, a block of wood on a cord! The future is here!"). Evaluating new ideas flat out against the status quo is pointless.

Figure 2.1 Would you see this idea—a flimsy gas-powered cart called the quadcycle—as the future of transportation in 1898? Most people then didn't either. This is one of Henry Ford's first automobiles.

Figure 2.2 The superficials of innovation are rarely impressive. This is a version of the first computer mouse.

New ideas demand new perspectives, and it takes time to understand, much less judge, a point of view. Flip a world map or this book upside down, and at first it will feel bizarre. But wait. Observe for a few moments, and soon the new perspective will make sense, and might even be useful. However, that bizarre initial feeling tells you nothing about the value of the idea—it's an artifact of newness, not goodness or badness. This means using statements like "this hasn't been done before" or "that's too weird" alone to kill ideas is creative suicide: no new idea can pass that bar.

How to Find Good Ideas

To open minds and find good ideas, return to the kid in the park. What is it about his attitude that allows fearless idea exploration? Linus Pauling, the only winner of two solo Nobel Prize awards in history, had this to say about finding ideas: "The best way to have a good idea is to have lots of ideas." This sounds idiotic to most ears because it cuts against the systematic, formulaic, efficiency-centric perspective worshiped in schools and professions. It seems wasteful to follow Pauling's advice. Can't we just skip to the good ideas? Optimize the process? Memorize a formula to plug stuff into? Well, you can't.

The dirty little secret—the fact often denied—is that unlike the mythical epiphany, real creation is sloppy. Discovery is messy; exploration is dangerous. No one knows what she's going to get when she's being creative. Filmmakers, painters, inventors, and entrepreneurs describe their work as a search: they explore the unknown hoping to find new things worth bringing to the world. And just like with other kinds of explorers, their search for ideas demands risk: much of what's found won't be satisfactory. Therefore, creative work cannot fit neatly into plans, budgets, and schedules. Magellan, Lewis and Clark, and Captain Kirk were all sent on missions into the unknown with clear understanding that they might not return with anything, or even return at all.

The lives of well-known creative thinkers were filled with compulsions for playing with ideas: they wanted wide landscapes to explore. Beethoven obsessively documented every idea he had, madly scribbling them on tree trunks or on the manuscript paper he had jammed into his clothing, even interrupting meals and conversations to scratch them down.[5] Ted Hoff, the inventor of the first microprocessor (Intel 4004) used to tell his team that ideas were a dime a dozen, encouraging them not to obsess or fixate on any particular one until a wide range of ideas had been explored. Hemingway made dozens of rewrites and drafts, changing plots, characters, and themes before he published his novels. WD-40 is named because of the 40 attempts it took to get it right (Dr. Ehrlich's cure for syphilis, called Salvarsan 606, was similarly named). Picasso used eight notebooks to explore the ideas for just one of his paintings (*Guernica*); if you watch the film *The Mystery of Picasso,* you can watch the master exploring ideas, good and bad, in real time as he creates dozens of paintings.[6] See Figure 2.3.

Figure 2.3　Many artists use canvases to try out ideas as they paint—they're not painting by numbers, but exploring and making mistakes.

Idea Killers

These are phrases for thoughtless idea rejection. They're used by people who are too lazy to give useful criticism or direction, who fail to ask idea-provoking response questions, or who dismiss others not believed to have the potential for good ideas. Phrases like "it's not in our budget" or "we don't have time" are half-truths, as budgets and schedules can be changed for a sufficiently good idea. Others are idiotic, such as "we've never done that before," a condition of any new idea, good or bad.

- We tried that already.
- We've never done that before.
- We don't do it that way here.
- That never works.
- Not in our budget.
- Not an interesting problem.
- We don't have time.
- Executives will never go for it.
- It's out of scope.
- People won't like it.
- It won't make enough money.
- How stupid are you?
- You're smarter with your mouth shut.

A complete list of idea killers is at *http://www.scottberkun.com/blog/?p=492.*

In any field, creatives are those who dedicate themselves to generating, working, and playing with ideas. Pattie Maes, director of MIT Media Lab's Fluid Interfaces group, explains:

> Most of the work that we do is like this. We start with a half-baked idea, which most people—especially critical people—would just shoot down right away or find uninteresting. But when we start working on it and start building, the ideas evolve. That's really the method that we use at the Media Lab . . . in the process of building something we often discover the interesting problems and the interesting things . . . that lead to interesting discoveries.

There is further support for an innovator's desire to seek out new ideas. In a recent survey, innovative people—from inventors to scientists, writers to

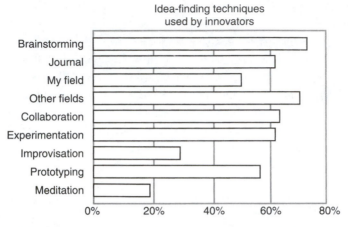

Figure 2.4   Based on a recent online survey of over 100 self-identified innovators in various fields.

programmers—were asked what techniques they used. Over 70% believed they got their best ideas by exploring areas they were not experts in (see Figure 2.4).[7] The ideas found during these explorations often sparked new ways to think about the work in their own domain. And since they didn't have as many preconceptions as the people in that field, they could find new uses for what were seen as old ideas. Doctors studied film production; writers read biographies of painters. Any pool of ideas, no matter how foreign, could become a new area of discovery for an open mind.

As we saw with the child in the park, creativity is intertwined with the ability to see ideas as fluid, free things. Ideas come, they go, and that's OK; to an open mind, ideas are everywhere (something I'll prove shortly). It's the willingness to explore, experiment, and play, to invest energy, hit a dead end, and then chase a new direction that allows minds to find good ideas. All of our notions of play, and its freedoms from formal judgment, are inexplicably linked to finding good ideas.

Ideas and Filters

For all my trumpeting of open-minded thinking, it's true that wandering the Library of Congress looking at random ideas won't result in the Nobel Prize. We're asked to find ideas to solve problems, and even if idea finding approximates explorative play, it has to eventually wander back into something resembling work.

The secret to balancing work and play is thinking of the mind as a filter. Instead of binary switches—open vs. closed, creative vs. routine—we need a sliding scale of openness we can control. If you want new ideas, you have to slide toward openness, turning some filters off, exploring thoughts you'd ordinarily reject offhand. Do this until some interesting ideas are found; then, gradually turn more filters on until you're left with a handful that are both good and practical for the problem at hand. Choosing which filters to apply when has much to do with successful innovation; it's not just having an open mind, it's also knowing when to postpone certain judgments, and then when to bring them back in. If a mind is always open, it never finishes anything; if a mind is never open, it never starts.

Our brains and senses are designed, in part, to filter things out. Consider eyesight: at best we see 160 degrees around us, less than 50% of the visual information nearby. Dogs hear more sounds and cats smell more odors than we do. Even as children, we learn rules of conduct and behavior, both to be safe and to fit into society, filtering out possibilities. And, perhaps worse for creativity, as adults we aim for efficiency in our time, shortcutting through days, looking for fast tracks and power tools. The trap of efficiency is that it's not how explorers or inventors do their jobs: they turn their filters off for long stretches of time, trying to go where others haven't been. They wander into inconvenience, and danger, purposefully. Even when tasked with being creative, most people most of the time apply filters too soon.

The History and Misuse of Brainstorming

The term *brainstorm* has been abused and bastardized in the 50 years since its coinage. The concept originates with Alex F. Osborn, whose excellent book *Applied Imagination* launched the industry of business creativity hooks.[8] Its rise to popularity led to the quick misuse of the technique as a panacea for every conceivable business problem. When it failed to do the impossible of tripling people's IQs, reversing executive stupidity, or instantly transforming dysfunctional teams, the business world turned against it, despite its fundamental goodness. Those who still use the term apply it trivially to refer to any thinking activity they might need to do. The true essence of brainstorming as a method is well described in *Applied Imagination,* a fantastic read and a forgotten classic. The core message is simple:

- You have three things: facts, ideas, and solutions.
- You need to spend quality time with each individually.

The great mistake is leaping from facts to solutions, skipping over the play and exploration at the heart of finding new ideas. Most of us are experienced with finding facts—they're beaten into us throughout our education, and modern media pummels us with more. We're also familiar with solutions, which are the end results that pay the bills and explain why we've survived in the world. But idea finding? What's that? It's what few adults are patient enough to do, yet it's at the heart of creativity (the child in the park) and brainstorming (as defined by Osborn).

- **Fact finding.** The work of collecting data, information, and piles of research about whatever it is that needs to be done.
- **Idea finding.** The exploration of possibilities—free from as many constraints as possible—and using or ignoring facts as needed to find more ideas.
- **Solution finding.** The development of promising ideas into solutions that can be applied to the world.

Finding Ideas and Turning Off Filters

Osborn researched which environments stimulated people's creativity, and this study led to the following four idea-finding (aka brainstorming) rules:

1. Produce as many ideas as possible.
2. Produce ideas as wild as possible.
3. Build upon each other's ideas.
4. Avoid passing judgment.

Rule #1 sets the goal on volume, not quality (think Beethoven, Hoff, and Pauling). Since we don't know which ideas have value until we've explored them, spliced them together, or played with their many combinations, we need a big landscape. According to Osborn, a group of four or five properly led people can continually find new ideas for anything for a half-hour to an hour, producing 50 or 100 ideas before running out of steam (see his book *Applied Imagination*).

Rule #2 encourages crossing boundaries and saying illogical, unexpected, and unpredictable things. Since we naturally inhibit what we say for fear of embarrassment, if you set outrageousness as a goal and reward it, you help turn that filter off, opening up the chance to find interesting ideas. Sometimes asking for the worst ideas for a particular problem can take you in entertaining directions, leading to places you'd never otherwise go. Have you ever been lost in a bad neighborhood in a new city, only to find a fantastic shop or restaurant? Discovery can have any origin, and Rule #2 forces exploration. If nothing controversial, weird, or embarrassing is said in a brainstorming session, you've violated Rule #2.

Rule #3, like Dan Bricklin's combination of innovations to invent VisiCalc, encourages the combination of ideas to force creative thinking through hybrids and idea breeding. All ideas are made from other ideas. Making this explicit prevents people from suppressing ideas for fear of stepping on, or changing, an idea mentioned by someone else. NIH (Not Invented Here) syndrome, where ideas from others are rejected, is a clear violation of Rule #3.[9]

Finally, Rule #4 takes us back to the secret of the kid in the park. Judgment isn't necessary during exploration; we don't know enough about the possibilities, so why would we reject or accept any idea? Would you buy the first car you sat in? Marry the first sexy person you met? When finding ideas, everyone needs to know his ideas won't be judged until later. And if the goal is volume (Rule #1), there's no need to evaluate the initial thought, only to write it down so it can be explored later. Judgment is all too easy, and there's no harm in holding it back a while to give those ideas a fighting chance.

However, there are limitations. When done in groups, the human dynamics of social situations come into play. Is everyone trying to kiss up to the boss? Does Fred always hog the floor? Is Jack afraid to say anything? Designating a skilled facilitator keeps things flowing and fair, and ensures that the rules are followed and that the meeting runs only as long as needed. The vibe should approximate the playful environment of a park: a fun, low-stress, free time to try things out, awaken dormant imaginations, and take pleasure in chasing new ideas.

Proof That Ideas Are Everywhere

One game, famous in improvisation, is called "What Is This?" Look at any object around you: a pen, a cup, this book. Ask yourself, "What else can it be used for?" Take, for starters, this book in your hand: it's a doorstop, a weapon, a plate, a way to get your boss to be less of an idiot, a waste of $20, and on it goes. Play this game with a friend and see who can come up with more ideas.

The point is that anything can be used for things other than its intended purpose. We assume everything has one function, but that's wrong: you can use anything for anything (although it might not work well, you can try). There's nothing stopping you from using this book as underwear or to paper your walls. The game forces you to turn your filters off.

Many great ideas come from the repurposing of one thing for something else. Laser beams were used to make CD players and supermarket checkout scanners. Even attempting to reuse something in a novel way, and failing, can lead to ideas no one else has thought of before. Play the game with items you use in your work or with failed projects just asking for reuse, and you'll soon find yourself off and running with an abundance of good ideas.

NOTES

1 Robert W. Weisberg, *Creativity: Beyond the Myth of Genius* (W. H. Freeman, 1993).

2 Howard Gardner, *Frames of Mind: The Theory of Multiple Intelligences* (Basic Books, 1993).

3 Lloyd Dobler, played by John Cusack, is the main character in the film *Say Anything*. "I don't want to sell anything, buy anything, or process anything as a career. I don't want to sell anything bought or processed, or buy anything sold or processed, or process anything sold, bought, or processed, or repair anything sold, bought, or processed. You know, as a career, I don't want to do that." See *http://www.imdb.com/title/tt0098258/quotes*.

4 See Neil Postman, *The End of Education: Redefining the Value of School* (Vintage, 1994), and Ken Robinson, *Out of Our Minds: Learning to Be Creative* (Capstone, 2001).

5 Edmund Morris, *Beethoven: The Universal Composer* (HarperCollins, 2005).

6 The film *The Mystery of Picasso* (Dir. Henri-Georges Clouzot, Image Entertainment) is a classic of art schools everywhere. Few artists, much less legends, were as open to documenting their process as Picasso, as demonstrated by this film. Make sure to listen to the DVD commentaries, as they provide more insight than the sparse soundtrack. See *http://www.imdb.com/title/tt0049531/*.

7 http://www.scottberkun.com/blog/?p=422.

8 Alex F. Osborn, *Applied Imagination* (Charles Scribner's Sons, 1957).

9 A good review of NIH syndrome and approaches to avoiding it at the organizational level can be found in *Open Business Models*, by Henry Chesbrough (Harvard Business Press, 2006).

Analyze

1. In this reading, what answers do you find to Berkun's own question "Why aren't our conference rooms and board meetings as vibrant as childhood playgrounds and sandboxes?" What answers do you come up with in response?
2. Using the chart on "Idea-Finding Techniques Used by Innovators," what are the three most popular techniques? Which of these surprise you? Which do you think would be most effective for you to use? Which do you actually use?
3. What is the role of filters in the creative process?
4. What does Alex F. Osborn's study show are the four key idea-finding/brainstorming rules? Which of these do you suspect is least used? Why?

Explore

1. Berkun mentions this quotation by Albert Einstein: "Imagination is more important than knowledge." What does that mean to you? And do you find support for this idea at schools? Businesses? Your own life? What do you think about your answers?
2. In the section entitled "Proof that ideas are everywhere," Berkun mentions the famous improvisation game called "What Is This?" Use this book as the subject of that game—he gives you a few of his uses in the text. Give yourself three minutes to write down as many other alternative uses for this book as you can. Check your ideas against the list in Appendix B. How did you fare?
3. On Berkun's website, www.scottberkun.com, he offers a free article entitled "The 177 Myths of Innovation & Creativity: Mega Summary." Which of these popular misconceptions about how creative work is done surprise you? Which do you encounter most often? Which do you find yourself doing/thinking/believing from time to time?
4. Berkun's quick test asking readers to name five new ways to change the world "or you'll die!" is, as he admits, an absurd expectation. But try this: come up with one. On your own, throw wide the doors of creativity within you and create something wonderful. Ignore those "we don't do that here!" or "that never works!" thoughts in your own mind. Write down the details of your world-changing idea. Share it with the class and applaud each other's efforts.

Judith Schlesinger
"Blind Men and Elephant Parts"

Judith Schlesinger, Ph.D. (1961–), is a psychologist, educator, jazz critic, musician, and author of *The Insanity Hoax: Exposing the Myth of the Mad Genius*. For ten years, she wrote the "Shrinktunes" column about the intersection of psychology and music. "Blind Men and Elephant Parts" first appeared in her book *The Insanity Hoax*.

> "Before I came here, I was confused about this subject. Having listened to your lecture, I am still confused—but on a higher level."
>
> —Enrico Fermi

According to some accounts, Beethoven liked to pour water over his head and sing, becoming literally so immersed that he kept flooding his apartments and getting evicted. Did that reflect his madness, his genius, or his attempt to drown out the ominous buzz in his ears that began at age thirty? Jazz pianist Thelonious Monk would abruptly stop playing during performances and whirl like a dervish. Was his bizarre behavior proof of craziness or part of the showmanship he learned early on, while playing for a traveling tent show?

Creativity and madness are slippery things, hard to describe and impossible to quantify. Like pornography, we know them when we see them, but despite years of trying to wrestle them to the mat, there's still no universal definition or test for either one—and when they collide, they raise a whole new cloud of questions.

Which experts are correct: the ones who insist that "manic depression is almost indispensable to genius"[1], or those who claim that "we haven't found compelling evidence of a connection between mental illness and creativity"?[2] Like debates over the existence of God, this field offers more passion than proof; much of its certainty gleams with promise from a distance, but tends to vanish on approach.

For example, because nobody has pinpointed the wiring that enhances creativity, we can't know for certain whether it also increases the risk of pathology. These two variables are so enigmatic that each requires its own chapter (creativity first, madness next). Even then, this book will not explicate all their facets—just what happens when they are thrown together. And jazz, that wonderfully living and changing art form, will not be defined at all—there is too much ongoing fulmination about what it is, or isn't, which is beyond the scope of this enterprise.

Creative Components

Most good dictionaries echo the grand *Oxford English*, which reveals that the word "creativity" didn't actually appear in print until 1875. Its relative recency is one small reason for all the confusion.

When creativity is confined to the ability to bring something new into being, it covers everything from concertos to childbirth. But go just one step further and the squabbling begins: team A argues that creativity stems from environmental factors, team B believes that the key is tucked deep inside the brain, while team C claims that they must interact in some mysterious way. It's that old blind-men-and-elephant thing where each person is firmly convinced that the pachyderm part he's holding is the entire truth.

The whole beast can be embraced at once with the "confluence" model, which acknowledges the convergence of numerous different elements[3]. Psychologist Dean Simonton borrowed the term "stochastic process" from probability theory to characterize this interaction as mysterious.[4] If it were only up to me, I'd stop right there and go out for coffee, but most readers might want a bit more than that. Be warned, however: if you go a'Googling for the definition of creativity, you'll get over nineteen million hits.

What follows are just two of the good ones:

1. Creativity is the ability to produce work that is both novel (original, unexpected) and appropriate (it works: it is useful or meets task constraints).[5]
2. Creativity is the interaction among aptitude, process, and environment by which an individual or group produces a perceptible product that is both novel and useful as defined within a social context.[6]

Unfortunately, such abstractions raise more questions than they answer. For instance, how do you define and measure these abilities, aptitudes, and processes? Does everyone agree on what they look like? And what does "useful" mean, anyway? Useful to whom? For what? And, who says?

"Novelty" is only part of the story, since creativity is far more than newness. So if we consider "quality" as well, who gets to judge that? Experts? Teachers? Peers? And by what criteria? Are there reliable assessments of artistic quality, and if so, can they ever calibrate the essence of beauty?

And while we're at it, who decides what's "appropriate" in a creative domain? Is "meeting task constraints" the best yardstick for that brilliant trumpet solo that just ignited the room? Shouldn't some intrinsic factors be considered as well? And if so, can we specify what they are, and how to identify them as they're flying by?

This is only some of the static on this channel, which also includes the paradox that successful creativity requires both nonconformity and social acceptance at the same time. Genius adds its own dynamic, because achievements at that level create "propulsive moments" that can smash through traditional boundaries to change a domain.[7] But even that isn't reliable, since their progress may be blocked by the self-appointed guardians of a domain's "purity" who refuse to move it away from its past.

Here's another conundrum to consider: do people qualify as creative if nobody likes what they create? History's graveyard is full of artists celebrated for being "ahead of their time"—but only retroactively, since they died poor and unappreciated before they could get there. Van Gogh made no money from his paintings, and even Bach's music was dismissed as being "over-elaborate and old fashioned" during his lifetime.[8]

But if the public is the ultimate judge of creative value, how do you calculate the fleeting impact of fads? Or of influential critics who get excited about something that puts everyone else to sleep (and vice versa)? Many times in my two decades of jazz writing, a colleague's review has made me wonder if we heard the same music. Then there's the frequent disconnect between critical praise and public favor that can churn up great stress in a creative life. One famous example is Stephen Sondheim's musical *Follies,* which won seven Tony Awards in 1971 but lost its entire investment ($800,000) because of poor attendance.

"Originality" is yet another lump in the sauce. While newness seems central to the concept of creativity, by itself it guarantees neither admiration nor acceptance. In an ingenious study, Simonton fed 15,618 classical melodies into a computer that evaluated the originality of their first six notes. When he plotted the results against the frequency of performance, he discovered that the most original pieces were not the most popular. The favorite music actually sat somewhere between "hackneyed" and "aggravating," nestled in the sweet spot between familiar and boring.[9]

Even if you doubt that six notes are enough to evaluate originality, and dismiss the musical judgment of computers, this study was a bold attempt to hoist something quantifiable out of the creative morass. I can also offer some anecdotal support for the idea that a mix of the known and the new is most appealing. In the song "Don't Know Why," the monster debut for singer Norah Jones in 2002, the first five notes are identical to those of Vince Guaraldi's beloved "Charlie Brown's Christmas" and lead right into an unmistakable quote from Paul McCartney's "Yesterday." These subliminal echoes of cherished anthems helped propel the song to number one, providing just enough nostalgia to soothe the listener without waking the beast of copyright infringement.

"Talent" is yet another concept that's easier to recognize than define. At least "productivity" has tangible units of measurement, but it's more relevant in business than art—after all, it only took a handful of stories to vault Franz Kafka and J. D. Salinger into the permanent pantheon of great writers.

Even premature death affects creativity by enhancing our view of how great someone *might* have been. Jazz has a long list of such tragic icons, including saxophonist Charlie "Bird" Parker and bassist Paul Chambers, both of whom died at thirty-four, and bassist Jaco Pastorius, whose stormy life ended at thirty-six. Their brilliance is undisputed, but their legends—like those of Judy Garland, James Dean, Otis Redding, and Heath Ledger—draw additional voltage from our communal sense of bafflement and loss.

Today creativity has come to encompass so much that it hardly means anything at all. In the ivory tower, whole careers are built on identifying its components and their interactions, and there are many excellent books to explore for those who want to wade further in. But it's also possible to detour around the confusion by leaving creativity undefined.

Now and then writers are so impatient with square one that they leap right over it, and nobody seems to mind. Researchers have made real scientific progress in understanding creativity without even mentioning the concept—as when mapping the brains of people playing music.

Big Bad C

For all the hoopla about cultivating creativity, it also has a negative side, even when it falls short of genius level. Psychologist Hans Eysenck puts it this way:

> Creativity, solemnly praised, is in fact anathema. It threatens the structure and cannot be tolerated—the creative person is willy nilly turned into a rebel, an outcast, a maverick [. . . or diagnosed as bipolar?].[10]

Although creativity can be a kind of life-enhancing filigree, like a gift for languages or a knack for soufflés, turning it into a livelihood is something else altogether. Many parents who value creativity mistrust the creative life, recognizing the vast difference between funding their future lawyer's sax lessons and coaxing her into a jazz career. But this paradox is easily resolved by a gesture worthy of Solomon: whacking creativity into two types, the ordinary (little c) and the great (Big C).

Popular for more than six decades, this distinction separates the cozy creativity—the domesticated companion who solves daily problems and tosses off witty remarks—from the scary kind, the mystical midwife of humanity's greatest art and ideas. Unlike little c, which is a universal plug-in, Big C requires a specific human vessel in which to flourish; it is sadistically elusive, despite the most urgent of invitations. It is also where the greatest madness supposedly lies.

Much of the Big C research has focused on people who are considered "eminent," which presumes that public acclaim comes only to the talented (for an alternate view, see Hilton, Paris, and Kardashians, Any). Some scholars file all their subjects in the same drawer, despite the obvious differences in achievements and domains. For example, in Arnold Ludwig's widely cited *The Price of Greatness* (1995), the same factors that elevated Ernest Hemingway and George Gershwin in their respective fields are supposed to boost Henry Ford, Albert Einstein, and Martin Luther King in theirs. This seems reductionistic, at best. As psychiatrist William Frosch suggests in his discussion of creativity research,

> The impulse to create and the skills necessary to each of the tasks are likely to differ. It may be that we are linking many kinds of acts

because they are special and mystifying, not because they are the same.[11]

Big C was a major interest for Freud, who painted it with his usual limited palette of depression and discontent. His philosophy was basically this: once parents pour your mold and it sets, life becomes a constant struggle against its (always) uncomfortable fit. And so the very best that people can expect, even those who faithfully undergo the treatment he invented, is to replace their aberrant "hysterical misery" with the "common unhappiness" suffered by everyone else. In a universe that runs on pain, Freud reduces creativity to a consolation prize for the frustrated:

> [The artist] is one who is urged on by instinctual needs which are too clamorous; he longs to attain honour, power, riches, fame, and the love of women; but he lacks the means for achieving these gratifications. So, like any other with an unsatisfied longing, he turns away from reality and transfers all his interest, and his libido [sex drive] too, on to the creation of his wishes in the life of phantasy . . . every hungry soul looks to it for comfort and consolation.[12]

Even the creative explorations of Leonardo da Vinci, whom Freud greatly admired, were propelled by his frustrated homosexuality: "He has investigated instead of loving," said Sigmund, who would know about that, reportedly giving up sex himself at the age of forty-one.[13]

In any event, whenever the tired old notion of creative personality drags itself along, there are all kinds of rusty clichés clanking behind it. At best, Big C people are moody, self-centered, high-strung, and unreliable; at worst, they are wildly emotional and teeter on the verge of psychosis and suicidal despair. Or they're absent-minded buffoons, since people with their heads in the clouds tend to stumble over things on the ground. Even the great cultural sage Ann Landers weighed in on this one, suggesting that "all families should have three children; in case one turns out to be a genius, there will be two others to support him".[14]

People who buy this whole piñata are convinced that Big C's hover so close to meltdown that they desperately lunge at poetry or music just to vent their emotional pressure cookers. For some, art is the mental prophylactic that prevents dangerous leakage; for others, it's a buildup that must be released: "If I don't write to empty my mind, I go mad," said Byron, in his usual understated way.[15] He would surely appreciate the French poet and playwright Antonin Artaud's take on it:

> There is in every madman a misunderstood genius, whose idea, shining in his head, frightened people, and for whom delirium is the only solution to the strangulation that life had prepared for him.[16]

Such effusions are seen as solid empirical proof for those who believe in creative fragility, since the myth dictates that Big C's are either inflamed by mania, frozen in despair, or endlessly whiplashed between the two. But it's just as easy—and much better documented—to view the creative process as healthy and life-affirming. In fact,

> psychological studies have shown again and again that, however much we want to romanticize [genius], it is typified by qualities that are disappointingly opposite of psychotic: self-discipline, tenacity, organization, calmness, and strong self-image.[17]

There is extensive research to support this positive view and bring the genius out of the shadows. Here comes some of the best.

The Sunny Side

Harvard psychiatrist Albert Rothenberg and his team conducted a great deal of the authoritative research on the creative mind. Rather than making athletic inferential leaps from centuries of gossip, they gathered firsthand data from people they could speak to without a Ouija board. These were living artists and scientists who had won prestigious awards, such as the Nobel and Pulitzer Prizes, National Gold Medal and Poet Laureate designations, or had been elected to such elite organizations as the National Academy of Sciences and the Royal Academy of London.

The achievers were interviewed at different stages of their creative projects—from the initial idea to its ultimate realization—in order to shed light on the process. Rothenberg's team also spoke to family members and conducted controlled psychological experiments that were designed to identify characteristic creative thinking. After *twenty-five* years of this, they concluded that

> first, contrary to popular as well as professional belief, there is no specific personality type associated with outstanding creativity. Creative people are not necessarily childish and erratic in human relationships, as is often thought, nor are they necessarily extraordinarily egotistic or rebellious or eccentric.

And here's the kicker:

> Only one characteristic of personality and orientation to life and work is absolutely across the board, present in ALL creative people: motivation. They want specifically to create and be creative, [which requires] direct, intense, and intentional effort.[18]

Unfortunately, hard work will never be as thrilling as drowning, whether in the white waters of ecstasy or the sludge of despair. This helps explain why Rothenberg's crucial work is only a small, dry footnote in a world full of frenetic splashing.

Also on creativity's hopeful side is the experience of "flow," that delicious moment when ability and challenge are perfectly balanced to produce an exhilarating rush of mastery. (Athletes know it as "being in the zone.") Similar to psychologist Abraham Maslow's notion of "peak experiences," flow also resembles the joyful ecstasy of successful creative inspiration.

Flow was popularized by psychologist Mihaly Csikszentmihalyi, who comes from a uniquely positive perspective. Having survived the Holocaust, he became interested in how people find meaning and happiness in life, not how they cope with their misery. Flow has nothing to do with psychopathology—it's just the opposite, providing the serene timelessness that many seek through yoga and other meditative practices. And while flow is theoretically accessible to everyone, it seems that the greater openness and flexibility of creatives enable them to get there more easily and more often.[19]

Psychiatrist and pianist Denny Zeitlin refers to this feeling as "the purity of the merger state," which is "the prerequisite for true creativity"; and speaking of mergers, vocalist Sara Krieger calls it "having sex with music."[20] Pianist Monty Alexander uses "chasing the moment" to describe the ongoing pursuit of this bliss, which makes the hassles and heartbreaks of the music business disappear, at least while it's happening.

The World Out There

Now the searchlight leaves the creative mind to illuminate the environmental influences around it. There's no guarantee that a fortunate setting will spark creativity—or that a barren one will quash it. But adding social variables to the mix is more realistic than treating creatives as if they lived in bubbles, propelled only by their own quirkiness and a splash or two from the family gene pool.

Many researchers have wondered how various aspects of the real world impinge on the creative person. One ongoing debate is whether creativity is a delicate thing, requiring a kind of hothouse nurturing to bloom, or if it's essentially hardy and resilient, able to thrive despite environmental obstacles and personal adversity.[21] As with most of these arguments, there are strong points to be made on both sides.

Either way, it's undeniably useful to have someone run interference for people who are trying to create, taking care of external concerns on their behalf.[22] There's a common perception that no one can be exceptionally artistic and good at business at the same time, as if these skills are mutually exclusive (many use a simplistic right- versus left-brain dichotomy for this one). However, the notion that creatives are constitutionally incapable of taking out the garbage and showing up on time may well have originated with the creatives themselves.

There is a long list of environmental factors to consider, including childhood exposure to a creative domain, type and duration of training and support (or lack thereof), and the relative power of assorted incentives and rewards. Early parental loss keeps showing up in artistic biographies; so do firstborn or only children, although the implications of birth order are still being argued. What is clear is that the right mentor can launch the right trainee into the orbit of genius. I've often wondered what Stephen Sondheim might have been if he hadn't grown up so close to the great songwriter Oscar Hammerstein (and so, repeatedly, has he).

Other variables that have been examined include the impact of class,[23] culture,[24] and color.[25] There's also the famous "Ten-Year Rule," which predicts that creative people need a full decade of experience, exposure, and skill acquisition before they can begin to make lasting contributions to their

field. This was supported by a study of seventy-six composers that calculated
the time between their first musical instruction and their first masterwork.
Out of five hundred notable compositions produced by this sample, only
three were composed before year 10 of the composer's career (and these were
in years 8 and 9).[26]

Despite the classic image of the self-contained genius, common sense
dictates that the environment has a powerful impact. As far back as the
1950s, humanistic psychologist Carl Rogers noted that creativity blooms
best when people feel psychologically safe and free. Researchers have also
identified specific creativity "killers," like the quest for external reward and
competition—being judged in relation to others—which encourages
people to "play it safe."[27]

Teresa Amabile, author of *Creativity in Context* (1996), is a pioneer of
this reality-based approach. An MBA and professor at Harvard Business
School, Amabile has always taken a refreshingly pragmatic and nonpatho-
logical view of creativity. In her study of what she calls "creativity in the
wild," Amabile and her team analyzed 12,000 journal entries by over two
hundred people who were doing creative projects at work. They found that
creativity is clearly connected to joy and love, and negatively associated with
anger, fear, and anxiety—and the evidence, Amabile reports, is "consistent."[28] (That small whirring sound you hear is Freud, spinning in his grave.)

Here's more good news about creative people: they are actually complicated, not crazy; they are disciplined and committed, happy to take on hard
projects and work hard at them; and they are intensely focused, with a "rage
to master" their chosen domain.[29] Amabile suggests that this "passionate
craft of creativity"—the discipline and perseverance—is at least as important as talent.[30] But she also notes that "scholars' understanding of the creative process and the factors influencing it is still quite limited."[31] And she's
not even touching on Big C.

Low-Hanging Fruit

One way to demystify the whole process is to pull creativity down from
the stars and designate it as an ordinary thing that's accessible to
anyone who wants to learn and practice it. Equal opportunity is the
promise of the genius-making industry that peddles recipes from eager
self-help gurus (*The Genius in All of Us*) as well as books by accomplished
artists like choreographer Twyla Tharp (2003). You can even buy *How to*

Think Like Leonardo: Seven Steps to Genius Every Day, although you could probably step for many years without coming any closer.[32]

The commercializing of creativity undermines its position as an objective, legitimate research question. This has already been "tainted" by its mystical beginnings—all those divine visitations and fluttering Muses—which can make it appear too frivolous for serious scientific study.[33] Here's what psychologist Howard Gardner says about the "nonsense" that is marketed to the public about the ease of acquiring creativity:

> "Come for a weekend, learn to brainstorm, learn to free-associate, we'll make you a creative individual." That just doesn't work. It's a serious business for serious people. Creative work requires, I think, being a certain kind of person, which includes being able to work on things for years, a drive not likely to come to people who paid five hundred dollars for a weekend under a tent.[34]

In any event, given the jumble of variables and viewpoints high and low, it's impossible to construct a universal concept of creativity, let alone pinpoint its precise connection to anything else—particularly madness, which also changes shape depending on who's describing it. It's like trying to lasso a cloud.

Creativity and the Musical Mind

Some Freudy cats (sorry, irresistible) have applied his gloomy principles to music. Psychiatrist Anthony Storr declared that "Freud was right in supposing that [creativity] originates in dissatisfaction." Equating music with self-medication, Storr considers it the perfect refuge for people who don't like people:

> Being the most abstract of the arts, and the least obviously connected directly with human experience, [music] is often the passion of schizoid people, who delight in discovering that there is a way of experiencing and expressing emotion which is impersonal.[35]

Yet even these emotions can be dangerous, especially when listening alone, since they might lead to "a loss of self-identity."[36] Although Freud admitted that explaining creativity was beyond him—"psychoanalysis can do nothing toward elucidating the nature of the artistic gift"[37]—that doesn't keep his fans from squinting at it through his myopic and grimy lens.

Sometimes this psychoanalytic approach gets downright silly—like the notion that the wistful minor key has something to do with oral dependency—thumb-sucking, perhaps.[38] Then there's the bizarre claim that the minor triad evokes sadness because lowering the middle note to create it "clearly represents the castration complex, and hence arouses feelings of anxiety."[39] Since no one explained how this dynamic applies to women, we can only assume they must be worried for their men.

Most Big C researchers wander in the territory of writers, because their GPS rarely includes musical psyches. For one thing, the invisible nature of their art makes its creative process harder to track; for another, as Frank Zappa famously said, "Talking about music is like dancing about architecture." But if its message could be verbalized, it would destroy its uniqueness and defeat its purpose. There's even recent evidence that talking about music can diminish one's memory of it.[40]

Because writers provide the best quotes about their moods and behaviors, they tend to dominate the inquiries into Big C. When musicians want to reveal something personal, they do it in a language that science doesn't speak. Composers Leonard Bernstein, Aaron Copland, and Mickey Hart all wrote excellent books about music, but in general musicians are conspicuously absent from discussions of creativity and madness—unless, centuries after death, someone has gathered up their life bits into "evidence" of how crazy they were.

The most famous exception is composer Robert Schumann, whose leap into the Rhine and asylum death two years later were both recorded at the time. What remains in dispute is the cause. As usual, bipolar disorder is the default diagnosis, but newly translated medical records suggest late stage syphilis instead, which can produce bizarre and delusional behavior for a full twenty years before it causes death.[41] There will be further discussion of Schumann and the pox as we proceed.

Reports from the Front

The above comparison of writers and musicians is not just theoretical. In my own hobnobbing with such creative folk, I've never met a writer who hesitated to discuss inspiration—most are happy to expound on it in some detail and at considerable length. In contrast, many musicians are reluctant to say anything at all, as if analyzing their talent would somehow make it disappear. One composer calls it "meddling with a natural function":

> There is prevalent the superstition that if a composer devotes too much attention to the analysis of the creative process, a catastrophe results in which his inspiration is destroyed and his art rendered meaningless.[42]

Such hesitation makes musicians useless to researchers who are seeking dramatic affirmations of madness. This would not surprise Carl Seashore, the first music psychologist, who wrote that "the normal musical mind is first of all a normal mind" over seven decades ago.[43] More recently, Anthony Kemp observes that musicians are simply more independent and introverted than the average person.[44] But then Kemp is a musician as well as a psychologist, a combination that offers a unique advantage. As Seashore (also an organist and choir director) explains it,

> While the cold details of musical facts can be recorded and organized by **a mere psychologist,** validity and interpretation depend upon an intimate knowledge of music and feeling for it.[45]

Unfortunately, this background doesn't always guarantee superior understanding: psychologist Geoffrey Wills was a drummer and still jumped on the "all beboppers are crazy" train.[46]

Meanwhile, Kemp explains how musicians may feel isolated from a world busy with facts and objects: "Their job is to play upon feeling, to appreciate, to interpret, and to create the beautiful." Some manage their exile with a superior pose, emphasizing their role as "keeper and master of great artistic truths."[47] This outsider attitude becomes a popular shelter for both creatives and those who want to look like them. This too will be described later on.

Understanding musician psychology is difficult when there are more psychology books about the cognitive processing of music than about the people who make it;[48] there was no anthology about musical emotion until several generations after Seashore pioneered the field. That book suffers from the same problem as creativity: lack of clear definition and measurement. But at least it says nothing about inherent creative pathology, and has just one reference to depression: "music as treatment of."[49] Refreshing.

Aaron Copland is one of the great musicians who provided useful reports from the front. Although undeniably a Big C, Copland spent little time bemoaning its burdens; instead, he considered creativity to be a valuable tool for self-knowledge, since it helped "make evident one's deepest feelings about life":

> But why is the job never done? Why must one always begin again? . . . I must create in order to know myself, and since self-knowledge is a never-ending search, each new work is only a part-answer to the question "Who am I?" and brings with it the need to go on to other and different part-answers.[50]

Such confessional disclosure abounds in autobiographies and interviews, but is hard to find in academic writings. In 2002, when I created a university course in the psychology of music, I found that the textbooks were more focused on the laboratory processing of musical snippets than on how people listen in real life. So I gathered up some of my own publications into a collection called *Thought Food: Readings in the Psychology of Music* and used that, along with the one text that offered a whole section on "real world applications."[51] This was a rare find.

Faces in a Cloud

Constructing psychological theory can be just as subjective as lying on your back in a summer meadow and finding faces in the shifting shapes above. It's a widely accepted principle that in order to make sense out of ambiguous stimuli, people must dip into their private mental vaults, using their own experiences to project meaning where none exists.

This is the rationale behind the Rorschach (ink blot) test and other such "projective" measures. Because the images you perceive are constructed from pieces of yourself, they can reveal deep truths about what makes you tick—revelations that emerge without your awareness or permission, and may even be news to you. This principle applies to all humans, even the most venerated of psychologists, and helps explain why virtually every theory sits on a subjective foundation.

The brilliant *Faces in a Cloud* (1979) demonstrates how this works with four of the founding fathers: Sigmund Freud, Carl Jung, Wilhelm Reich, and Otto Rank. Comparing their writing to their personal histories, the authors show how these so-called universal theories were actually invented to explain their own lives:

> No theorist offers definitive statements on the meaning of being human unless he feels those statements constitute a framework within which he can comprehend his own experience.[52]

This applies to creativity theories too, especially since they contain more debate than data. The truth is that, apart from the neuroscientists who can directly image the brain, every psychological doctrine springs from its author's perspective, and its continued health depends on successful consensus and defense (the process is virtually Talmudic).

For example, when Anthony Storr died, the *U.K. Independent* and *The New York Times* described him as being depressed from an early age. "He was no stranger to suffering," wrote Christopher Lehman-Haupt, blaming the fact that his parents were first cousins.[53] But whatever the source of his own pain, Storr projects it onto creatives by painting them as desperate people who cling to art for their emotional salvation. Those were the faces he saw in the cloud, and those were the theories that informed his books, influencing both the public and professional views of creativity.

Similarly, psychologist Alfred Adler invented "the inferiority complex" to explain his childhood misery as the sickly brother of a star athlete; not surprisingly, Adler claimed that people produce art and music "out of their own inadequacies, much as an oyster reacts to the irritation of sand by producing a pearl."[54]

It's easy to see why subjectivity drives the research engine: you do need a strong personal investment to dedicate your life to one particular area. I first learned this during my PhD studies, when the time came to pick a dissertation topic. Knowing that years of slog and sacrifice lay ahead, we all went for something with powerful private resonance, hoping this would carry us through.

My friend Charlie, the Star Trek fan who glued on Spock ears every Halloween, decided to study the shared time perception between therapist and client and how it "warps" as treatment continues. Mark had recently welcomed his first child, so he chose fatherhood. I tested whether musicians' preference for improvisation also shows in the rest of their lives (short answer: pretty much), while another alumna who became a famous sexpert spent her time on inorgasmic women. (Draw your own conclusions.)

The same challenge applies after graduation in choosing academic careers. I know that many creativity researchers are habitual dabblers in the stuff—either accomplished or wannabe painters and pianists, playwrights, and assemblers of collages. Sometimes the link is clear, as when psychologist Ruth Richards, editor of *Everyday Creativity*, describes herself on the book jacket as someone who "draws, writes, and plays three instruments badly."[55] It doesn't take a psychic to understand why Richards studies the kind of creativity that's accessible to everyone. And given that no creative goes home without a diagnosis, little c's get little "mental illnesses" like cyclothymia, a mild cycling of ups and downs that used to be called "moody."[56]

One last observation on the link between professionals and their theories. I have noticed that most of the experts who regularly pass along the mad genius doctrine—and with so little attention to its flaws—are not psychotherapists. With doctorates in social or educational psychology, and careers spent in academic rather than clinical settings, they miss out on the regular, intimate revelations of living creative people.

As such, they may lack firsthand knowledge of what these people are actually tackling, and what they themselves view as their primary problems. In addition, as theorists and not therapists, these academics do not witness, assist in, or clinically evaluate the many solutions that creatives may attempt. Please note: this lack of experience doesn't imply any lack of sincerity or compassion. But the fact is that supporting and guiding graduate students, however kindly or effectively, will never be the same thing as engaging in psychotherapy, with its unique depth of connection and insight.

Moreover, without such ongoing, intimate encounters, it's likely that these scholars are less familiar with the myriad daily repercussions of a bipolar diagnosis. For some, it's even possible—dare I say it?—that Big C people are not quite real: they are abstractions, impersonal and remote. This makes it easier to toss serious psychiatric labels around and consign the genius to a lifetime of serious pathology. Certainly, their guessing from a distance could make them tone-deaf to the quiet creative struggles in real life, and more susceptible to the hyperbolic claims of the flamboyant.

The Non-Theory Theories

A final word on defining creativity (or the impossibility of doing so) comes from psychologist Sigmund Koch, one of the pioneers of this research. From the early 1980s to the mid-1990s, as director of the Boston University Aesthetics Research Project, Koch conducted intensive conversations with eminent artists; alas for us, this work generated no published studies.

But while interviewing the celebrated playwright Arthur Miller, Koch was able to expound on his doubt that creativity will ever be fully understood:

> We're in a scientistic society . . . that presumes you can find some kind of simplistic, or in some sense, complete explanation of everything. There are still many people in my field . . . who would tend to think in these terms: why shouldn't a theory of creativity be possible? This is gibberish. It's very important to establish exactly the senses and the boundaries in which one has simply to stand in awe of the ineffable.[57]

There are almost as many definitions as there are definers. Well, here's mine: I believe that creativity is too individualized for any one-size-fits-all packaging, no matter how logical, just as no single explanation covers anything else that humans aspire to, enjoy, or suffer. Of course, this never discourages psychologists from trying to find one, and the chances are excellent that they will stay on this quest as well.

It's not out of the question that psychic pain can increase the depth to an artist's work, adding wisdom and empathy to her perspective. But is true madness really a prerequisite for great art? And how will we ever know for sure? Here's a radical thought: perhaps we don't need to. It's a safe bet that however it works, creative people will keep producing things that others cannot, despite every attempt to demystify the process and capture its magic with words. It's even possible that explaining it will destroy it; as Leonard Bernstein wrote,

> Please, God, leave us this one mystery, unsolved: why man creates. The minute that one is solved, I fear art will cease to be.[58]

And so the searchlight glides past creativity to the next mystery. As we will see, "madness" is every bit as hard to define as "creativity." Unfortunately, the stakes are much higher.

Analyze

1. When does the word *creativity* first appear in the *Oxford English Dictionary*? Why is that important to note?
2. Schlesinger writes about the possible disconnect between critical praise and public favor, citing the example of Stephen Sondheim's

musical *Follies*, which "won seven Tony Awards in 1971 but lost its entire investment ($800,000) because of poor attendance." What other examples can you think of that were critical successes albeit commercial flops? Do these examples suggest this is a frequent phenomenon? How is it possible to be both creative and unpopular?

3. What is the difference between little c and Big C?
4. What is "flow," the term popularized by Mihaly Csikszentmihalyi? When have you experienced flow in your own life? What was it like?

Explore

1. Schlesinger notes that if you "go a'Googling for the definition of creativity, you'll get over nineteen million hits." Try it yourself. How many results do you get? Why are people so interested in trying to pin down the definition?

2. In this selection, we learn that "Van Gogh made no money from his paintings, and even Bach's music was dismissed as being 'over-elaborate and old fashioned' during his lifetime." What other creative people were similarly unsuccessful in their own times but were later discovered and appreciated more richly? What similarities do you see between these ahead-of-their-times people?

3. Musician Frank Zappa famously said, "Talking about music is like dancing about architecture." Could the same be said about writing/reading about creativity? Why/why not? How else might one come to a better understanding of creativity?

4. Composer Leonard Bernstein once wrote, "Please, God, leave us this one mystery, unsolved: why man creates. The minute that one is solved, I fear art will cease to be." Why do some creative people like Bernstein fear that solving this mystery would be disastrous? What do you think?

REFERENCES

1. Hershman, D. Jablow, and Julian Lieb. 1988. *The Key to Genius: Manic-Depression and the Creative Life*. New York: Prometheus Books.
2. Sawyer, R. Keith. 2006. *Explaining Creativity: The Science of Human Innovation*. New York: Oxford University Press.
3. Sternberg, Robert J., and Todd I. Lubart. 1995. *Defying the Crowd: Cultivating Creativity in a Culture of Conformity*. New York: The Free Press.

4. Simonton, Dean Keith. 2004. "Creativity as a Constrained Stochastic Process." In *Creativity: From Potential to Realization,* edited by Robert J. Sternberg et al., 83–101. Washington, DC: American Psychological Association.

5. Sternberg, Robert J., and Todd I. Lubart. 1996. "Investing in Creativity." *American Psychologist* 51 (7): 677–688.

6. Plucker, Jonathan A., Ronald A. Beghetto, and Gayle T. Dow. 2004. "Why Isn't Creativity More Important to Educational Psychologists?" *Educational Psychology* 39: 83–96.

7. Sternberg, Robert J., James C. Kaufman, and Jean E. Pretz. 2002. *The Creativity Conundrum: A Propulsion Model of Kinds of Creative Contributions.* New York: Psychology Press.

8. Westrup, Sir Jack, and F. Ll. Harrison. 1985. *Collins Encyclopedia of Music.* Revised by Conrad Wilson. London: William Collins & Sons.

9. Simonton, Dean Keith. 1994. *Greatness: Who Makes History and Why.* New York: The Guilford Press.

10. Eysenck, Hans. 1995. *Genius: the Natural History of Creativity.* New York: Cambridge University Press.

11. Frosch, William A. 1987. "Moods, Madness, and Music: 1. Major Affective Disease and Musical Creativity." *Comprehensive Psychiatry* 28 (4): 315–322.

12. Freud, Sigmund. (1922) 1965. *A General Introduction to Psychoanalysis.* Authorized English translation of the revised edition by Joan Riviere. New York: Washington Square Press.

13. Freud, Sigmund. (1910) 1964. *Leonardo da Vinci and a Memory of His Childhood.* Translated by Alan Tyson. New York: W. W. Norton.

14. Landers, Ann. 2000. "Gem of the Day." *Journal News,* September 22, 6E.

15. Marchand, Leslie A. 1957. *Byron: A Biography.* Vol. 2. New York: Alfred A. Knopf.

16. Artaud, Antonin. (1947) 1976. *Van Gogh, the Man Suicided by Society.* Selected Writings. Edited and with an introduction by Susan Sontag. Berkeley, CA: University of California Press. 483–512.

17. Nettle, Daniel. 2001. *Strong Imagination: Madness, Creativity, and Human Nature.* London: Oxford University Press.

18. Rothenberg, Albert. 1990. *Creativity and Madness: New Findings and Old Stereotypes.* Baltimore, MD: Johns Hopkins University Press.

19. Czikszentmihalyi, Mihaly. 1990. *Flow: The Psychology of Optimal Experience: Steps Toward Enhancing the Quality of Life.* New York: Harper & Row.; Czikszentmihalyi, Mihaly. 1996. *Creativity: Flow and the Psychology of Discovery and Invention.* New York: HarperCollins; Czikszentmihalyi, Mihaly. 1997. *Finding Flow: The Psychology of Engagement with Everyday Life.* New York: Basic Books.

20. Sidran, Ben. 1995. *Talking Jazz: An Oral History.* New York: Da Capo Press; Krieger, Sarah. 1994. Personal communication, March 15.

21. Sternberg, Robert J., and Todd I. Lubart. 1995. *Defying the Crowd: Cultivating Creativity in a Culture of Conformity.* New York: The Free Press.

22. Gardner, Howard. 1993. *Creating Minds: An Anatomy of Creativity Seen through the Lives of Freud, Einstein, Picasso, Stravinsky, Eliot, Graham, and Gandhi.* New York: Basic Books.

23. Sawyer, R. Keith. 2006. *Explaining Creativity: The Science of Human Innovation.* New York: Oxford University Press.

24. Sundararajan, Louise, and Averill, James R. 2006. "Creativity in the Everyday Culture, Self, and Emotions." In *Everyday Creativity and New Views of Human Nature: Psychological, Social, and Spiritual Perspectives,* edited by Ruth Richards, 195–220. Washington, DC: American Psychological Association.

25. Gordon, Edmund W., and Bridglall, Beatrice L. 2005. "Nurturing Talent in Gifted Students of Color." In *Conceptions of Giftedness,* 2nd ed., edited by Robert J. Sternberg and Janet E. Davidson, 120–146. New York: Cambridge University Press.

26. Hayes, John R. 1989. "Cognitive Processes in Creativity." In *Handbook of Creativity,* edited by John A. Glover, Royce R. Ronning, and Cecil R. Reynolds, 135–145. New York: Plenum.

27. Hennessey, Beth A., and Teresa M. Amabile. 1998. "Reward, Intrinsic Motivation, and Creativity." *American Psychologist 53* (June): 674–675.

28. Breen, Bill. 2004. "The 6 Myths of Creativity." Interview with Teresa Amabile. FastCompany.com. (89), December 19. www.fastcompany.com/magazine.

29. Winner, Ellen. 2004. "Musical Giftedness." In *Bulletin of Psychology and the Arts Special Issue: Psychology of Music.* American Psychological Association Division 10 4 (1): 2-5.

30. Czikszentmihalyi, Mihaly. 1996. *Creativity: Flow and the Psychology of Discovery and Invention.* New York: HarperCollins; Wallace, Doris B., and Howard E. Gruber. 1989. *Creative People at Work: Twelve Cognitive Case Studies.* New York: Oxford University Press; Von Karolyi, Catya, and Ellen Winner. 2005. "Extreme Giftedness." In *Conceptions of Giftedness,* 2nd ed., edited by Robert J. Sternberg and Janet Davidson, 377–394. New York: Cambridge University Press; Amabile, Teresa M. 2001. "Beyond Talent: John Irving and the Passionate Craft of Creativity," *American* Psychologist 56 (5): 333–336.

31. Amabile, Teresa M., Sigal G. Barsade, Jennifer S. Mueller, and Barry M. Shaw. 2005. "Affect and Creativity at Work," *Administrative Science Quarterly* 50: 367–403.

32. Gelb, Michael J. 1998. *How to Think Like Leonardo da Vinci: Seven Steps to Genius Every Day.* New York: Dell.

33. Richards, Ruth, ed. 2009. *Everyday Creativity and New Views of Human Nature: Psychological, Social and Spiritual Perspectives.* Washington, DC: American Psychological Association; Weisberg, Robert W. 1993. *Creativity: Beyond the Myth of Genius.* New York: W.H. Freeman & Company; Weisberg, Robert W. 2006. *Creativity: Understanding Innovation in Problem Solving,*

Science, Invention, and the Arts. New York: John Wiley & Sons; Sternberg, Robert, J., Todd I. Lubart, James C. Kaufman, and Jean E. Pretz. 2005. "Creativity." In *The Cambridge Handbook of Thinking and Reasoning,* edited by Keith J. Holyoak and Robert G. Morrisonn, 351–369. New York: Cambridge University Press.

34. Shekerjian, Denise. 1990. *Uncommon Genius: How Great Ideas Are Born.* New York: Penguin Books.

35. Storr, Anthony. 1993. *The Dynamics of Creation.* New York: Ballantine Books. xiii, 93.

36. Storr, Anthony. 1992. *Music and the Mind.* New York: Ballantine Books. 113.

37. Arieti, Silvano. 1976. *Creativity: The Magic of Synthesis.* New York: Basic Books.

38. Juni, Samuel, Susan P. Nelson, and Robert Brannon. 1987. "Minor Tonality Music Preference and Oral Dependency." *Journal of Psychology* 121 (3): 229–236.

39. Meyer, Leonard B. 1956. *Emotion and Meaning in Music.* Chicago: University of Chicago Press.

40. Mitchell, Helen F., and Raymond A.R. MacDonald. 2009. "Linguistic Limitations of Describing Sound: Is Talking about Music like Dancing about Architecture?" In *Proceedings of the International Symposium on Performance Science,* edited by Aaron Williamon, Sharman Pretty, and Ralph Buck, 45–50. Utrecht, The Netherlands: European Association of Conservatoires (AEC).

41. Hayden, Deborah. 2003. *Pox: Genius, Madness, and the Mysteries of Syphilis.* New York: Basic Books; Worthen, John. 2007. *Robert Schumann: Life and Death of a Musician.* New Haven, CT: Yale University Press.

42. Shapero, Harold. 1985. "The Musical Mind." In *The Creative Process: A Symposium,* edited by Brewster Ghiselin, 41–45. Berkeley: University of California Press.

43. Seashore, Carl E. 1938. *Psychology of Music.* New York: Dover Publications.

44. Kemp, Anthony E. 1996. *The Musical Temperament: Psychology and Personality of Musicians.* New York: Oxford University Press.

45. Seashore, Carl E. 1938. *Psychology of Music.* New York: Dover Publications.

46. Derbyshire, David. 2003. "It Helps to Be Mad in the Jazz World." London Daily Telegraph, February 9.

47. Kemp, Anthony E. 1996. *The Musical Temperament: Psychology and Personality of Musicians.* New York: Oxford University Press.

48. Deutsch, Diana, ed. 1982. *The Psychology of Music.* New York: Academic Press; Sloboda, John A. 1985. *The Musical Mind: Cognitive Psychology of Music.* London: Oxford University Press; Aiello, Rita, ed., with John A. Sloboda. 1993. *Musical Perceptions.* New York: Oxford University Press.

49. Juslin, Patrik N., and John A. Sloboda, eds. 2001. *Music and Emotion: Theory and Research.* New York: Oxford University Press.

50. Copland, Aaron. 1952. *Music and Imagination.* Cambridge, MA: Harvard University Press.

51. Hargreaves, David J., and Adrian C. North. 1998. *The Social Psychology of Music.* New York: Oxford University Press.

52. Stolorow, Robert D., and George E. Atwood. 1979. *Faces in a Cloud: Subjectivity in Personality Theory.* New York: Jason Aronson. 18.

53. Lehmann-Haupt, Christopher. 2001. "Anthony Storr, 80, Psychiatrist and Writer" (obituary). *New York Times,* March 28, C21.

54. May, Rollo. 1975. *The Courage to Create.* New York: W. W. Norton.

55. Richards, Ruth, ed. 2009. *Everyday Creativity and New Views of Human Nature: Psychological, Social and Spiritual Perspectives.* Washington, DC: American Psychological Association.

56. Richards, Ruth. 1992. "Mood Swings and Everyday Creativity." *Harvard Mental Health Letter* 8 (10): 4–6.

57. Franklin, Margery B. 2001. "The Artist Speaks: Sigmund Koch on Aesthetics and Creative Work." *American Psychologist* 56 (5): 445–452.

58. Bernstein, Leonard. 1982. *Findings.* New York: Simon and Schuster. 232.

Todd Dewett
"The Five Marks of Real Innovators" and "The Creative Person's Survival Guide"

"Tattoo addict, Harley Davidson nut, and recovering management professor" **Todd Dewett** (1971–) is an entrepreneur and author. His expertise as a leadership and life expert is viewed by millions at Lynda.com. Dewett's clients include TGI Fridays, Cox Media, Emerson, and State Farm. "The Five Marks of Real Innovators" and "The Creative Person's Survival Guide" first appeared on the author's own website.

The Five Marks of Real Innovators

Everyone says they love innovation. Most companies don't. In fact, most of them hate innovation.

They suffer from two major ailments. The first I refer to as the innovation rhetoric syndrome. This is when a company consistently suggests it needs and values innovation through every imaginable outlet (their website, press releases, the shareholders report, etc.) while consistently shunning real innovation. The rhetoric is hot air put forth like great PR because they know they are supposed to say these things. What kind of company could possibly not say they are for change, creativity, and innovation?

In practice they can't stand deviations. The average manager wants tight processes, risk reduction, and predictable outcomes. When someone tries something new, their tolerance is low and critical evaluations are doled out quickly. It takes no time at all for this behavior to create a stuffy culture of status quo.

The other major element is a crippling disease known as incrementalism. Here, the company knows that you must change tomorrow and do something different than today, but not too different. To reduce risks they create and constantly tweak a never-ending series of analysis tools, stage gate models, and layers of well-intension bureaucracy that effectively kills innovation. If your only goal is to create a new flavor of toothpaste next year, this approach works fine. Otherwise, it's time to get serious.

If you aspire to more than mere survival you have to learn to embrace these five philosophies of serious innovators:

Compete on different fronts. There are five major innovation targets: products, services, processes, technologies, and business models. Companies make two huge errors here. They compete almost exclusively on products and services (two top line approaches) and they neglect the less sexy but equally potent possibilities found in process innovation (a bottom line approach). For the truly brave, there are two additional risky approaches that are even more neglected: creating new technologies and creating new business models (both of which are more disruptive approaches to innovation). The point is that over time, you can't be a one-trick pony. Focus on multiple targets.

Dream big or go home. Jack Welch gave us the famous example of tasking his team with being #1 or #2 in every market. Steve Jobs asked John Scully whether he wanted to sell sugar water or change the world. Companies don't create engaging cultures full of motivated employees without having clear purpose. The pundits get lost in arguments about the difference between mission and vision and similar labels. Keep it simple—what's the driving purpose? What's the dream? If you say 15% returns annually, you're destined to be mediocre. Think of it this way—if the dream doesn't make everyone just a little bit nervous, it's not audacious enough.

Reward well-intentioned deviance. This is the antidote to incrementalism. You must realize all great outcomes are preceded by half-baked ideas and complete failures. There are no exceptions. That means you have to love learning. The goal is not risk avoidance. It's smart risk taking, faster and cheaper. The real sin is inaction, not principled attempts at innovation that fail. Historically, my favorite example is the famous Hewlett-Packard tale about Chuck House's Medal of Defiance, given to him by David Packard for "extraordinary contempt and defiance beyond the normal call of engineering duty." When it was not clear a display monitor championed by House was going to pan out, he was told to scrap the project. He did not and with the help of other deviants pushed the project all the way to production. It later became very successful and helped the company rethink its approach to passionate deviants and mavericks.

Empower crazy evangelists—serious innovation is difficult and sometimes takes abnormally dedicated zealots to see things through to the end. One take-a-way from the Chuck House story is the need to find intrinsically motivated people, empower them, and get out of the way. Let's be clear—that does not mean formal leaders only. Evangelists might be found among the rank and file. Hell, they might not even be your employees. Nothing makes this more clear than the Graphing Calculator story (http://www.pacifict.com/Story/). In the early 1990s Ron Avitzur and Greg Robbins, two non-employees who should not have been allowed access to the building, somehow created a revolutionary piece of software and found a way to have it shipped on each Apple computer's hard disk. They did not get paid. They just wanted to do something great. Finding your evangelists is a huge part of making innovation more than incremental.

Know when to let go. This has been referred to as killing the cash cow. Clayton Christensen and others have been big supporters. You can argue about the conditions that make this viable, but the idea is solid. Cash cows slowly kill us by sucking up all the resources to keep the cow alive instead of focusing on finding another great cow. This is another way of saying that success will kill you. That's why at the dawn of the computer age, IBM's Watson once allegedly said "there might be a world market for five computers." Whatever made you great yesterday won't last. Get over it, stop overinvesting in it, and start looking for the next cool cow.

Innovation used to mean something. Today it still does, but the word has been tarnished by hoards of companies that cling to the word but don't walk the talk. Real innovators are brave. They take a varied approach to innovation, they dream big, show some love for the deviants, empower the zealots, and know when to let go. These are not easy philosophies to embrace, but they sure feel better than excessive rhetoric and uninspiring incrementalism.

The Creative Person's Work Survival Guide

The typical work environment is not terribly hospitable to creative people. This is of course odd since businesses always claim to want new ideas, change, progress, and innovation! The truth is most companies and most leaders can't stand creativity. In fact, they have great difficulty even seeing creativity when it sticks its head up. They only see risks, costs, and lost time. There might be a few exceptions. For example, people are used to managing creative employees in advertising, research and development, and so on. However, the typical team at work in operations management, accounts payable, or purchasing isn't always the best place for creative employees. But these are places where creativity is needed, so . . .

Here are the five things the creative professional must do to survive in the typical workplace.

First, attempt to focus your creative powers on the neglected world of processes. Creatives are often viewed as lofty dreamers, and a tendency to focus on top line opportunities enhances this stereotype. Top line innovation (e.g., ways to grow revenue, new products and services, and how to win new customers) is sexy, but fraught with risk and rigidly controlled by those in power. Processes, on the other hand, are about saving time and money as opposed to making money. Few people will see your ideas as risky, fewer people will be competing with you to innovate in this area. Not that process improvement is easy—it's not. I'm just saying that it's a more readily available target for your creativity.

Next, know when to fight. The good news: you get a few good creative ideas each week. The bad news: you have to bite your tongue and only try to act on 2–3 each year. The capacity possessed by others to tolerate your creativity is quite limited, so you have to be thoughtful and pick your battles. Among your best ideas, think about the idea that is most likely to be interesting to others, aligned well with department and organizational goals, and easiest for others to comprehend.

Now think about finding a sponsor. This is a person above you in the leadership hierarchy who is well known and in good standing. Preferably, this is a person who has a few creative wins under their belt. You want to know them for two reasons. First, they might serve as a mentor who can offer sage advice on surviving as a creative professional. Second, to the extent that others know you're associated with this person, you might gain the incremental clout needed to successfully sell your ideas.

It's also useful to try and share your ideas as if they were co-created by you and others, not just you. In general, sharing credit widely is a useful tactic at work for building a positive reputation. Whether for wins achieved or ideas you've come up with, it's a smart move. It helps the boss see you as a team player instead of a maverick and it helps your team see you as a collaborator instead of an overly ambitious idea person.

Finally, remember that it's true what they say—there is strength in numbers. That's why it's always smart when sharing your ideas to bring friends. If you have two or three colleagues who have good reputations and who believe in your idea (whether they helped create it or not), bring them along for the initial informal discussion with your boss. Any idea seems more useful and more possible when being advanced by a group instead of an individual.

Many creative professionals are lonely. They don't feel they're able to scratch their creative itch often enough. That can create a feeling of detachment and dissatisfaction, but it doesn't have to be that way. Remember the advice we just discussed and you just might get away with being creative.

Analyze

1. Why does Dewett believe companies hate innovation?
2. What are the five major innovation targets for companies? Which ones do most companies focus on? Why?
3. What is the antidote to incrementalism? Why?
4. What are the reasons to find a supportive sponsor?

Explore

1. This is the first selection in this book that has two readings paired together. Why are these readings paired together? What points of connection do you see?
2. Chuck House received a Medal of Defiance from David Packard of Hewlett-Packard for sticking with a project he believed in despite being told to scrap it. Where in your life might you have earned a Medal of Defiance? Why? If you haven't yet earned one, why not?

3. Dewett mentions that sharing solely created ideas as cocreated is a good tactic to build a positive reputation. What are the benefits of doing so? Have you ever chained down your ego so you could do this? What happened as a result? Share your experiences with the class.
4. Write your own blog-length piece on the role of creativity and innovation in corporate America. Bring in whatever firsthand knowledge you have, from visiting your dad on Take Your Daughter to Work Day to your days flipping burgers at McDonald's to your experiences as a consumer at the mall, car dealerships, or restaurants. Where is creativity in corporate America? Is it all it could be? Why or why not?

Forging Connections

1. The entire chapter is part of the ongoing attempt to defuse and debunk the existing myths about creativity. Why do these myths continue to persist? Is there something about the idea of creativity that people choose to keep at a distance? Is there some perceived value in keeping Mozart Mozart and the rest of us, well, human? Speculate on the reasons for the continued phenomenon of creativity myths. Compare your findings and ideas with a classmate.
2. Throughout this book, by and large, creativity is taken to be something that all people available to them (whether they opt to use that ability or not). This chapter really gets at the heart of that belief by challenging the nondemocratic ideas of creativity that populate the belief systems of many people of many different countries. Think about creative people you admire and then research the most quotable, bumper-sticker things they've said about it. Which do you buy into? Which do you reject? A few examples:
   - Apple cofounder Steve Jobs: "Creativity is just connecting things. When you ask creative people how they did something, they feel a little guilty because they didn't really do it, they just saw something. It seemed obvious to them after a while. That's because they were able to connect experiences they've had and synthesize new things."
   - Music David Byrne: "I subscribe to the myth that an artist's creativity comes from torment. Once that's fixed, what do you draw on?"
   - German aviator Dieter Uchtdorf: "The desire to create is one of the deepest yearnings of the human soul."
   - Poet Maya Angelou: "You can't use up creativity. The more you use, the more you have."

Looking Further

1. Select one text from this chapter and write a rebuttal. Point by point, work to refute what the author posits. Use humor, anecdotes, evidence, data, or just plain common sense to find whatever validity and value you can in the existing myths of creativity. What does an unexpected assignment such as this do for you? What insights does it bring about? How has this assignment informed your understanding of creativity generally and creativity myths specifically? Consider sharing your results with a classmate.

2. This chapter works well in conjunction with Chapter 6: The Creative Genius. Find one text in each chapter that complements the other and write an essay or response paper that brings out the connections, challenges, and questions of these two texts taken together. If the urge to challenge yourself creatively arises, instead create a mind map outline of the two texts and trace the connections and associations visually on the page.

The Creative Workplace

"The things we fear most in organizations—fluctuations, disturbances, imbalances—are the primary sources of creativity."
—Margaret J. Wheatley, author of
Leadership and the New Science

This chapter was initially conceived to be about "workplace" in the most straightforward sense, meaning cubicles, corporations, and places like the Dunder Mifflin Paper Company from the hit TV show *The Office*. But as the selections came in and recommendations were made by professors engaged in the field of creativity, it quickly became clear that "workplace" also meant one's environment in which work is done as much as dealing with bosses, rules, and regulations. And when you talk about a work environment, this could be a home studio, a desk in a bedroom, or a 24-hour computer lab on campus as easily as a roller chair in a corner office on the 34th floor of a $50 million Manhattan skyscraper.

Wherever you work, whatever type of work you do, creativity is a must. The corporate world is quickly coming to value it. Creativity can equal good ideas, and good ideas can equal big bucks, so sure, nearly everyone in the business world is putting a premium on creativity in their employees. What that premium looks like—and how management supports it—differs from company to company. For example, Google created a 20% time policy, where they wanted and expected employees to spend one-fifth of their workweek on individual projects of interest, which resulted in such innovations as Gmail, Adsense, and Google News. While they've recently moved away from that policy, they're working on new ways to encourage and support creativity from their employees.

Google isn't the first company to try such a tactic, however. 3M did this with a 15% rule back in the 1950s. From it, they got masking tape and Post-it notes. Other companies are trying to spark creativity in different ways. Having meetings outside of an office environment. Rewarding (or at least, not punishing) failure. Keeping a running idea file. Infusing the workplace with color versus sticking with boring, drab hues. Making desks/work stations anything but permanent. Tossing out the old-school dress code.

Richard Florida—who has a reading in this chapter—says, "Access to talented and creative people is to modern business what access to coal and iron ore was to steel-making." And Steve Jobs adds, "You cannot mandate productivity; you must provide the tools to let people become their best."

The following readings all come at the idea of where, how, and why creativity fits into the contemporary workplace from a variety of perspectives. If you've ever worked a 9-to-5 job or expect to do so one day, this chapter is especially for you.

Richard Florida
"Managing Creativity"

Richard Florida (1957–) is the director of the Martin Prosperity Institute at the University of Toronto's Rotman School of Management and Global Research Professor at New York University. He is cofounder and editor at large at CityLab.com and senior editor at *The Atlantic*. He's also the founder of the Creative Class Group whose clients include Audi, Zappos, Air Canada, Kraft, and Cirque de Soleil. "Managing Creativity" comes from his book *The Rise of the Creative Class—Revisited, Revised, and Expanded.*

Exposed brick and Helmut Lang t-shirts, whatever their merit, do not equal an organizational structure designed and actively managed to harness creativity. We come therefore to the deeper issue of workplace culture. Many views exist on how to manage and motivate for creativity. Some firms, even in so-called creative industries, still do it the old-fashioned way. They try to impose order and bureaucracy, and simply tally the returns by counting the time their employees put in. Others seek predictable procedures for eliciting creativity and making it more efficient. Some of these companies, like Motorola, take a page from Japanese-style quality management and actively manage and account for creativity. A system called the Capability Maturity Model (CMM), developed at the Software Engineering Institute at Carnegie Mellon, lays out extensive standards and guidelines for managing software developers, a special class of creative workers. Companies that use CMM march through a series of stages, with a scoring system to rate their productivity and performance as they move up the chart to more mature creative capabilities.

Other firms insist that creativity cannot be managed from above. In a recent interview, managers at Sun Microsystems railed against such attempts to manage or engineer creativity.[1] Their hands-off approach says that all you can do is hire talented people—technological virtuosos so to speak—give them the general outlines of a task, and then leave them alone. Most organizations fall somewhere between the extremes. Microsoft favors a blend of structure, self-motivation and peer pressure (see the following box). Yet far too many companies, particularly innovative ones, try to motivate people by lurching from crisis to crisis, launch to launch. Though this battlefield mentality may produce results for a while, it is not sustainable. It eventually leads to a vicious cycle of frustration, backlash and bitterness. In a 2001 Towers Perrin study, fewer than half of all professionals responded that "my company inspires me to do my best work." This implies we have far to go in both our knowledge and practice of how to manage creative workers. But doing it right can generate considerable efficiencies. Stanford University's Jeffrey Pfeffer estimates a considerable performance payback, saying "all that separates you from your competitors are the skills, knowledge, commitment and abilities of the people who work for you. There is a very compelling business case for this idea: Companies that manage people right will outperform companies that don't by 30 percent to 40 percent."[2]

White-Collar Sweatshop versus Caring Company

There is a highly polarized debate over what exactly is happening inside the creative workplace. Jill Fraser's "white-collar sweatshop" perspective, depicts the workplace as a source of greater stress, escalating time demands and increased insecurity.[3] On the other side is the "caring company" point of view, which contends that the workplace really is becoming a more supportive and nurturing environment for employees, and that it's a good thing. In her book *The Time Bind*, University of California sociologist Arlie Russell Hochschild wrote of a large company known as a leader in programs designed to achieve "work–life balance."[4] After studying the company and interviewing scores of employees, what she found was astounding. The company's practices were not leading to a more effective balance of work and life. Rather, they were making work more attractive than other aspects of life. Hochschild thus concluded that people were coming to work to avoid stress at home and in other parts of their lives.

Another version of the caring-company perspective is Andrew Ross's notion of the "bohemian workplace." After studying several Silicon Valley–style dotcoms in New York City, Ross, the director of American Studies at New York University, argues that the New Economy surge of the late 1990s brought about a sweeping transformation of the workplace as a "giant multipurpose playroom for ever-shifting teams of employees." Picking up

HOW MICROSOFT MANAGES CREATIVITY[5]

According To David Thielen

1. **Hire smart people who think.** The company's interview process is designed to separate the people who think from those who simply perform tasks. . . . At Microsoft, the interviewing and final approval of job candidates is always done by the group that is doing the hiring. The most telling questions that Microsoft managers ask are highly unusual. Why are manholes round? Microsoft isn't actually interested in the correct answers. They want to see how the candidate goes about solving a problem. Example: Manholes are round so the covers cannot fall through the holes and so the covers, which are very heavy, can be rolled aside easily.

2. **Expect employees to fail.** If you work in an environment in which the best route to job security is by working to outdo the company's competition, you focus your energy on developing new products and new ways to solve problems.

3. **Keep repercussions small when conquest-oriented employees make mistakes.** You don't want them to feel as though their careers at the company or that their happiness is riding on just one mistake. At Microsoft, failure is expected. If employees don't fail, they're not taking enough risks. In some cases they've even been promoted because of what they learned from their failures.

4. **Create an us versus them mentality.** Microsoft employees are constantly reminded that their competition is other companies, not colleagues. Emphasize the company's goals, but let each individual figure out how to get there.

5. **Sustain the company's start-up mentality.** In a start-up company, there's an ever-present sense of urgency that the business must succeed. Make it everyone's responsibility to watch costs. There are no secretaries at Microsoft. And if a job needs five people to complete it, four are assigned. Frugality keeps employees from becoming too comfortable or lazy.

6. **Make the office feel like home.** Create a work environment that is as nice or nicer than home, and employees will want to be there. At Microsoft, everyone has his own office, and there's no dress code. Employees can walk around barefoot—except in the cafeteria. There's a big connection between enjoying your work and doing good work.

on David Brooks's cultural dialectic between bourgeoisie and bohemian, Ross says the workplace itself has taken on formerly bohemian elements.

> Traditionally bohemian work styles were visible in everything from casual dress . . . to the endorsement of a kind of general hedonism and party culture in the office. . . . A lot of these companies presented themselves as alternatives to corporate America and took on all things bohemian. What's interesting is that both groups needed the other. The world of the bourgeoisie always needed a bohemian underside, a sort of fantasy demimonde, just as the bohemians always needed the bourgeoisie to define themselves against. . . . The fact that such a familiar dialogue has been played out in the business world is quite extraordinary.[6]

All of these views capture elements of the no-collar workplace discussed in the previous chapter, but miss the essential point. Workplaces are changing because the emphasis today is on creative work. And in the quest to elicit creativity, the typical workplace tends to become both more stressful *and* more caring. Stress increases because the Creative Economy is predicated on change and speed. If a firm is to survive, it must always top what it did yesterday. The employees must be constantly coming up with new ideas; constantly finding faster, cheaper or better ways to do things—and that's not easy. It's brutally stressful. At the same time, the smart firm will do its best to attract valuable creative workers and give them what they need to be creative. The result could be called a "caring sweatshop," but there's not really any contradiction here. It's just the reality of a workplace in a Creative Economy. As for the bohemian playroom: Many of the more frivolous, hedonistic aspects of this culture disappeared with the NASDAQ crash, and any that remained were swept away in the aftermath of September 11. But this does not mean that we are returning to the status quo ante. The no-collar workplace is not and never was just an old-style office hung with bohemian trappings or jazzed up with the thrill of a fantasy underside. The modern world is fusing aspects of bourgeois and bohemian so deeply that those old categories no longer apply. The fundamental fact about this new workplace, again, is that it's geared to harness creativity—and the best ways to do this are still being worked out.

Sculpting, Zen and Common Sense

Two increasingly popular strategies for eliciting creativity in the work-place, touted in publications like the *Harvard Business Review* and *Fast Company,* are "job enrichment" and "job enlargement." More recently, the concept of "job sculpting" has been advanced. According to a 1999 article in the *Harvard Business Review,* "Many talented professionals leave their organizations because senior managers don't understand the psychology of work satisfaction; they assume that people who excel at their work are necessarily happy in their jobs. Sounds logical enough. But the fact is, strong skills don't always lead to job satisfaction."[7] So companies strive to "sculpt" jobs in ways that reflect employees' deeply embedded life interests. It is as if we have discovered the Zen of job design.

This is a noble undertaking, and it certainly makes sense to try to fit each job to what the person does best and likes to do. But job sculpting will work only if it is implemented in a culture that is strong on the fundamentals. As we have seen, most people do not quest after some workplace Zen: They desire challenging work, good pay and reasonably competent management that does not get in their way. There is a vast literature on effective organizational cultures. And despite a lot of academic jargon, this perspective says that creative people and knowledge workers respond well to organizations with solid values, clear rules, open communication, good working conditions and fair treatment. People don't want to be abandoned and they don't want to be micromanaged. They don't want to take orders, but they do want direction.

These are not easy lines to walk. All we know for sure is that creative work cannot be taylorized like rote work in the old factory or office, for several reasons. First, creative work is not repetitive. Second, because a lot of it goes on inside people's heads, you literally cannot see it happening—and you can't taylorize what you can't see. Finally, creative people tend to rebel at efforts to manage them overly systematically. We have seen this all too often in the universities, where many a dean and administrator have learned hard lessons about trying to manage highly independent-minded faculty and researchers.

Peter Drucker captured it best when he said that knowledge workers do not respond to financial incentives, orders or negative sanctions the way blue-collar workers are expected to. I particularly like Drucker's observation that the key to motivating creative people is to treat them as "de facto volunteers," tied to the firm by commitment to its aims and purposes, and often expecting to participate in its administration and its governance. "What motivates knowledge workers," writes Drucker, "is what motivates volunteers. Volunteers, we know, have to get more satisfaction from their work than paid employees precisely because they do not get a paycheck."[8] The commitment of creative people is highly contingent, and their motivation comes largely from within.

Soft Control

The no-collar workplace is not being imposed on us from above; we are bringing it on ourselves. For Jack Beatty of *The Atlantic Monthly*, the legions toiling in the no-collar workplace are not victims of corporate oppression. He dubs this new reality "cannibalistic capitalism,"[9] citing a designer quoted in Fraser's *White-Collar Sweatshop*: "We are all devouring ourselves. . . . We all own stock, and as stockholders, all we care about is profits. So we are the ones who are encouraging the conditions that make our work lives so awful." As one high-tech worker wrote to *Fast Company*: "Nobody held a gun to anyone's head. . . . It seems as if the American work ethic of the New Economy . . . turned us into such whores that it's all for sale if the price is right!"[10] More than four of ten American workers described themselves as workaholics, according to a 1999 Gallup Poll.[11] But the real reasons for our present workplace conditions go deeper. Unlike these two people, most of us are not even doing it for the money. Members of the Creative Class do it for the challenge, the responsibility, for recognition and the respect it brings. We do it because we long to work on exciting projects with exciting people. We do it because as creative people, it is a central part of who we are or want to be.

The no-collar workplace runs on very subtle models of control that rely on people's intrinsic motivations. As companies try to motivate and persuade us rather than boss us or bribe us, they're basically seducing us to work harder—and we are most willing to be seduced. As *Business Week* bluntly put it, "The smartest companies know this. Instead of ensnaring employees with more signing bonuses and huge salaries, they are trying to hook them emotionally."[12] I call this "soft control."

One very effective form of soft control is challenge. Recall that more than two-thirds of workers in the *Information Week* survey report that challenge and responsibility are what matter most to them in their jobs. So the no-collar workplace seeks to act on these motivations by allowing workers to define their tasks, assume greater responsibility and confront ever-greater challenge. There are always new and more advanced products to launch, new deadlines to meet, new competitors to beat back. Another effective form of soft control is peer recognition and the pressure it can bring. Nearly one-fifth of workers in the *Information Week* survey report that "working with talented peers" is among the things that matter most to them at work. The no-collar workplace acts on a complex dynamic of peer recognition and competitive peer pressure to harness the talents of creative people.

A New Employment Contract

For all of these reasons, the nature of the employment contract between firms and people is undergoing dramatic change. The old employment contract was group oriented and emphasized job security. The new one is tailored to the needs and desires of the individual. The old organizational age system was truly a package deal, literally a comprehensive "social contract" in which people traded their working lives for money, security and the sense of identity that came from belonging to the firm. They took their places in the hierarchy, followed bureaucratic rules and worked their way up the ladder. In the words of William Whyte, an "ultimate harmony" developed between the managerial class and the large companies they worked for, causing the members of this class to give themselves over more completely to the organization.[13]

The new employment contract could not be more different. Creative people trade their ideas and creative energy for money. But they also want the flexibility to pursue things that interest them on terms that fit them. Thus they trade security for autonomy, and conformity for the freedom to move from job to job and to pursue interesting projects and activities. The shift to self-motivation and personal autonomy in the workplace is bound up with the fact that we no longer take our identity from the company we work for, but find it in the kind of work we do, our profession, our lifestyle interests and the community we live in.

The new reality turns Whyte's ultimate harmony on its head. Instead of a broad social contract, a key feature of today's employment relationship is that employees are seeking out and getting what my Carnegie Mellon University colleague Denise Rousseau calls "idiosyncratic deals." These deals may include not only a "sculpted" job description, but terms of employment tailored to the individual as well. The aim is to provide the mix of security, flexibility, type of challenge and whatnot that a valued person may be seeking.[14] A 2001 Towers Perrin survey of more than 5,500 professionals strongly advised companies to strike such deals, both to retain key people and to capture "the discretionary effort that produces top performance."

The rise of this new employment contract, according to Rousseau, is the result of two interrelated factors. One is that workers are more likely to look for specific short-term deals. The old long-term employment system gave workers more reason to believe their hard work early on would be rewarded with higher pay later in their careers. With little reason to believe they will be with the company for very long, today's workers want their rewards *now*. The other reason is that creative people typically see themselves as unique individuals with unique skill sets and expect to be rewarded accordingly.

The Open Source Example

Open source software development provides an interesting model of how intrinsic motivation, horizontal structure and voluntary membership can be used to motivate creative people and get work done.[15] Open source developers are not a tight-knit community but a far-flung network of individuals—yet together they have created high-quality products like the Linux operating system and the Apache netserver, which powers the computer networks of many large companies. The open source community uses a subtle discipline and structure to mobilize the creativity of thousands of independent software developers. Eric Raymond, a present-day open source guru, argues that while coding remains a solitary activity, the really great contributions or "hacks" come from harnessing the brain power of many. Open source development, in his view, works less like the orchestrated building of a cathedral and more like the chaotic interplay of a bazaar.

At first glance, the production of open source software appears completely unstructured. It is based on voluntary cooperation of developers in many different locations and organizational affiliations around the world. While a shared "hacker culture" may develop across this diffuse community, it contains none of the formal attributes we associate with productive work—no reporting relationships, assignments or clear responsibilities. But look deeper and a clear structure and discipline emerge. In place of the bureaucratic hierarchy of traditional organizations, the structure here is based on performance, capability and peer review. Yet open source software reflects a distinct division of labor. The software itself is "modular"— composed of many smaller, decomposable and well-defined tasks to which individuals and groups contribute. This allows people with different skill sets and capabilities to work on different elements.

Open source projects are structured around a stable group of core contributors who perform key tasks and play a key role in governance, while harnessing the temporary efforts of a much larger group of volunteers. In his research tracking 13,000 open source developers, the economist Josh Lerner of the Harvard Business School found that less than one-tenth of 1 percent of them contributed nearly three-quarters of all code. Nearly three-fourths made only one contribution.[16]

Members of the core group are typically people with extensive professional credentials—usually individuals who have proven themselves as programmers and have contributed to the original source code, though as the project progresses they may do less and less coding themselves. These core people provide the overall vision for the project and also serve as gatekeepers. They review submissions to decide which contributions will be incorporated into the code, and control their own membership by deciding which volunteers shall be elevated to the core group. Yet in contrast to traditional hierarchies— where those in charge can easily exclude or stifle bright, creative people—the members of the core have a strong incentive to actively recruit and harness the very best programmers, for their control exists only so long as the rest of the community supports them. If they behave unwisely or if their vision fails, "forking" may occur, whereby the disgruntled group takes the project's source code (which of course is not protected by any copyright or patent) and starts a new project with a different vision—as has sometimes happened.

An open source software project takes the form of a voluntary membership organization, but with clear rules governing the behavior of the volunteers. There are clear if unwritten principles for how they can enter the community and remain within it. Membership is fluid but only to some extent, and is contingent on performance of tasks, as well as on adhering to norms of appropriate conduct and fair play.

A complex yet subtle system of monitoring and sanctions reinforces the rules and keeps everyone contributing. Members exert strong pressures against noncompliance, for example through "flaming" (sending someone an angry or hostile e-mail), "spamming" (flooding someone with unsolicited e-mail) or "shunning" (deliberate refusal to respond). Faced with such sanctions, members often leave the community of their own initiative; there is frequently no need to expel them.

Open source software development thus relies on the intrinsic motivations of volunteers. Its structure is horizontal to a certain degree, but organized around a core group that provides direction and review. The work, which is complex and difficult, is rewarded largely by peer recognition as opposed to financial compensation. While the opportunity to gain recognition is an important motivation for joining an open source project, the desire to maintain and enhance one's reputation is the key mechanism for ensuring progress. Performance is always visible and transparent. All members can see whether someone has done a good job. Code is reviewed in ways that resemble scientific peer review, except that the process is completely open: The reviewers' names are public. Despite this, their comments can be nothing short of brutal. Posting bad code can elicit vehemently negative and even career-damaging feedback. Contributors accept this risk in exchange for the challenge and recognition that come from being associated with an elite creative community. And in this sense, the open source model reflects two other core values of the Creative Economy: openness to new ideas and meritocracy.

Where It All Began

The no-collar workplace is not new; rather it is a stage in the ongoing evolution toward more efficient ways of harnessing ideas and creativity. It aims to accomplish what John Seely Brown, the former director of Xerox PARC, called "the ability to leverage the community mind" by providing the physical and social context required for creativity.[17] "This place feels just like my graduate engineering lab," exclaimed one of my Carnegie Mellon colleagues upon entering the offices of one of our university spin-off companies. His comment cuts to the heart of where the no-collar workplace comes from: It is derived from older, more established systems for organizing creative work—the artist's studio and the university lab. Artists have long worked in open studio environments, but they tended to work alone. Andy Warhol's "Factory" transformed the isolated studio into a multidimensional creative laboratory for art. The original Factory was a raw, open space. It was entirely covered in silver foil, including the exposed pipes, to provide a "space age" look. Filling it out was a mélange of equipment for silk-screening, filmmaking and other art forms—and a constant parade of friends and associates trooping in and out at all hours. Floating through it all was Warhol himself, the archetypal modern soft-control manager: sometimes coddling or nudging, sometimes merely observing or recording what was going on, sometimes retreating into his own work. Architects and designers extended the studio environment to creative group work, with open-plan offices to encourage collaboration, peer review and feedback.

The laboratories of university professors were also developed on the open-plan model, where professors could come and go as they pleased, engage their students and colleagues, work could be done on a collaborative basis, and ideas could flow. Even the large mega-corporations of the mid-1900s created a special place for the scientists and engineers who were seen as the source of innovation. Theirs was the space of the research and development laboratory, often at a campus explicitly modeled on that of the university. The R&D lab was far removed from the factory or the downtown headquarters, both to encourage flexibility and openness and to ensure that the eccentric ways of scientists and engineers would not infect the executives and managers or, worse, be seen by customers. A casual dress code was accepted at the R&D labs, too. Yet even here, bureaucracy and micromanagement often crept in. In *The Organization Man,* Whyte noted that few corporate R&D labs were able to be truly creative:

> In the great slough of mediocrity that is most corporation research, what two laboratories are conspicuous exceptions in the rate of discovery? They are General Electric's research department and Bell Labs: exactly the two laboratories most famous for their encouragement of individualism—the most tolerant of individual differences, the most patient with off-tangent ideas, the least given to the immediate, closely supervised team project. By all accounts, the scientists in them get along quite well, but they do not make a business of it, and neither do the people who run the labs. They care not a whit if scientists' eyes fail to grow moist at company anthems; it is enough that the scientists do superbly well what they want to do, for though the consequences of profit for The Organization are secondary to the scientist, eventually there are these consequences, and as long as the interests of the group and the individual touch at this vital point, such questions as belongingness are irrelevant.[18]

What could have motivated the corporate leaders to create such labs in the first place? Simply put, they needed such places to attract top scientific talent from leading academic centers. To get such people they had to establish environments and procedures similar to those in academic settings—allowing scientists to pursue their own lines of interest, host visitors in their labs, and freely publish their results in scientific journals.[19] These labs were incredibly productive and many of them still are, making major advances from the development of nylon (Dupont) and the transistor (Bell Labs) to the flat-panel display (RCA and Westinghouse) and much of modern personal computing (Xerox PARC). It was the culture of the R&D labs, born at laboratories like GE, Bell and many others, that later companies like Fairchild Semiconductor, Digital Equipment and Hewlett-Packard, and even Apple and Microsoft, sought to emulate and build upon.[20] Gradually, these norms and practices began to seep into technical divisions of large companies, their IT staffs, and their engineers. Before long they would penetrate larger and larger segments of the economy.

And these practices offered one great efficiency to firms—and one incredible advantage to capitalism—which ultimately assured their further diffusion. They enabled firms and the economy as a whole to capture the creative talents of people who would have been considered oddballs, eccentrics or worse during the high period of the organizational age. Richard Lloyd quotes the founder of one of the Chicago high-tech firms he studied as saying: "Lots of people who fell between the cracks in another generation and who were more marginalized are [now] highly employable and catered to by businesses that tend to be flexible with their lifestyles and lifecycles."[21]

The Real Legacy of the New Economy

The practices and structures of creativity would have permeated corporate life on their own, but the meteoric rise and equally meteoric decline of the New Economy accelerated their diffusion. The New Economy created an additional social and cultural force that pushed these practices to the fore. As *Business Week* commented in April 2001:

> Far from being fads that will evaporate like so many market caps, many of these workplace revolutions developed to coddle employees and warehouse them in offices for as long as possible might very

well strengthen during the next 15 years. Part of the reason is economic. Even with the slowdown, companies must still compete for valued knowledge workers. And as employees are forced to clock workaholic hours in the global 24/7 economy, companies will have to make offices seem more like home.[22]

Like the early days of Silicon Valley before it, the New Economy unleashed a powerful cultural force for business change, but in an even more pervasive way. The rapid rise of the New Economy uprooted the age-old distinction between appropriate business norms and alternative culture. As Andrew Ross has noted, the New Economy redirected a powerful passion for change away from social and political issues and directly into the business world itself. In those heady days, joining a company became a form of self-expression and self-actualization. Many companies actively embraced this by combining commercial zeal with a mission to transform business culture.[23] A clear distinction was drawn between the outmoded, staid and constricting practices of the "Old" economy and the open, progressive, liberating practice of the "New." In propagating the myth of the New Economy as social force, this period raised people's expectations about what they wanted in a company and a job. As Ross sums it up:

> One of the most interesting stories is about the role of young people. How their passion for change, which is endemic to youth in general, somehow got channeled into a passion for corporate change. Which meant that a lot of activism, or socially productive work that they otherwise might have done, was redirected into a kind of infatuation with changing the shape of corporate America. That could only have happened, of course, because of the particularly bohemian cast—the sort of counterculture cast—of the companies that recruited these employees, for better or worse.[24]

In my view, however, it was mostly worse—amounting, in many cases, to little more than a well-choreographed charade. Many companies merely presented a cheap facade of the "alternative"—a ping-pong table, perhaps an espresso machine. And many otherwise sensible people bought into it because they were starved for something different. It wasn't about the money after all. As countless people in my focus groups and interviews have told me, they made these moves in the hopes of being part of a different, more inclusive, more progressive culture. Most of them, however, were quickly disappointed.

Many of these companies failed to reflect even the most basic elements of good management. These were the sorts of places that eat people alive—beset with near constant stress, continuous uncertainty, chronic management turnover, frequent changes of direction and general chaos. They came to resemble "toxic workplaces," a phrase coined by Jeffrey Pfeffer. According to Pfeffer, a key sign that a company is toxic is that:

> It requires people to choose between having a life and having a career. A toxic company says to people, "We want to own you." . . . A toxic company says, "We're going to put you in a situation where you have to work in a style and on a pace that is not sustainable. We want you to come in here and burn yourself out—and then you can leave."[25]

In 1999 and 2000, there was hardly a day that I did not receive a call or e-mail from an employee at a high-tech company complaining of some sort of organizational dysfunction: "Three of our top people left and nobody said anything." "Our COO contradicted what he said last week." "They let five developers go and people are scared; and we have no clue what's happening." "How can I keep my people motivated and engaged in an environment like this? I'm afraid everybody may just up and leave." Or one of my favorites: "Yesterday I received a Microsoft Project schedule e-mail from 'our leaders' for three projects that I never heard of before that need to be done in a couple of weeks and will easily require 50 to 75 percent of my time. I of course flipped. . . . But what else is new." The once great New Economy migration became a great exodus, captured in the telling epitaph: "I'd rather work at Starbucks."[26]

In the summer of 2000, I was asked to address the top management of a major regional bank on how to attract and retain creative and talented workers. We selected an edgy high-tech company as the venue for our workshop and invited two of their top executives to join in the discussion. Within the first half hour of the meeting, after I had given a short introduction to the subject, discussion began in earnest. The bank managers wanted to know what creative people care about, and seemed particularly interested in younger employees. They asked questions about the role of dress codes, workspace design, perks, compensation, location and the like. It became very clear to me that these people were genuinely concerned with managing and motivating their employees—if truth be told with treating them like human beings.

As we got further into it, the two high-tech executives began to chime in with their views, which essentially amounted to a high-tech version of "management by stress"—working people as long and as hard as they could stand. It quickly became clear to the group that these two did not have the foggiest idea of how to motivate or even treat creative people, let alone build an effective and enduring organizational culture. As the end of the workshop drew near and the clock edged toward 6 P.M., the high-tech pair, seemingly unaware of the time, began an extended harangue. As the rest of us sat uncomfortably in our seats, one of the bank managers interrupted the two: "At our company," he said, "we respect the flexibility and the right of our people to go home, if need be, to their spouses, significant others and families, so I think we should draw this meeting to a close."

The NASDAQ crash and subsequent New Economy collapse were a giant wake-up call for people to look beyond the hype, a point that was reinforced by September 11, 2001, and its repercussions. People got smart quickly, becoming much savvier about what they really require in a workplace and an employer, and no longer being entranced by the myth of striking it big. Young people saw their elder siblings' plight in sharp relief. "Working for a startup has a certain stigma associated with it," said one 2001 graduate from Carnegie Mellon. Added another: "People are attracted to big companies for two reasons: job security and not having to work crazy hours." Like creative workers in general, these younger workers expressed a preference for companies that combine the flexibility and openness of the no-collar workplace with job stability, reasonable expectations about working hours, talented peers and responsible management. "You have to remember I grew up in the most insane job market in recent memory. Now it's just a normal job market," is how a 2001 college graduate summed up the change.[27] The real legacy of the rise and fall of the New Economy is that it recalibrated people's expectations about what really matters about their jobs. For this alone, it was an invaluable collective learning experience.

Here and Now

All of which brings us to the present day. The always silly distinction between the New and Old Economies has collapsed. Different types of workplaces are converging and becoming more similar in their quest to attract talented people and harness creativity. People want to work for a company that values them, provides a challenging yet stable work environment, nurtures and supports their creativity, and allows them to realize their full potential. They desire flexibility on matters such as hours, dress and personal work habits. They seek a workplace that incorporates both the freedom and flexibility of a smaller startup and the stability and direction of a larger firm. But the trajectory is not backward to the boredom and drudgery of a traditional corporate bureaucracy.

People have come to expect the key features of the no-collar workplace and simply won't work in places that don't offer them. And this is part of a broader pattern. Improvements in workplace conditions tend to be sticky. Once instituted, they are not easily reversed, even when the job market is lean. Companies of all types are converging on a new style of managing creative work. If we find this new style more suited to our needs than the old, so much the better.

NOTES

1   Personal interview by author, fall 2001.

2   As quoted in "Danger: Toxic Company." *Fast Company,* November 19, 1998, p. 152.

3   Jill Andresky Fraser, *White-Collar Sweatshop: The Deterioration of Work and Its Rewards in Corporate America.* New York: W. W. Norton, 2001.

4   Arlie Russell Hochschild, *The Time Bind: When Work Becomes Home and Home Becomes Work.* New York: Henry Holt & Company, 2000.

5   David Thielen, "Ultimate Management Secrets from Former Microsoft Superstar." Boardroom, Inc., www.bottomlinesecrets.com, 2001. Also see *The 12 Simple Secrets of Microsoft Management.* New York: McGraw Hill Professional Publishing, 1999; www.12simplesecrets.com. Also see Richard Selby and Michael Cusumano, *Microsoft Secrets: How the World's Most Powerful Software Company Creates Technology, Shapes Markets and Manages People.* New York: The Free Press, 1999.

6   As quoted in Christine Canabou, "The Sun Sets on the Bohemian Workplace." *Fast Company,* August 2001, www.fastcompany.com/learning/bookshel/ross.html, p. 2; David Brooks, *Bobos in Paradise: The New Upper Class and How They Got There.* New York: Simon and Schuster, 2001.

7   Timothy Butler and James Waldroop, "Job Sculpting: The Art of Retaining Your Best People." *Harvard Business Review,* September-October 1999, pp. 144–152.

8 See Peter Drucker, "Management's New Paradigm." *Forbes,* 7, October 5, 1998, pp. 152–177.

9 Jack Beatty, "Cannibalistic Capitalism." *Atlantic Unbound/Atlantic online,* June 7, 2001, www.theatlantic.com/unbound/polipro/pp.2001-06-07.htm, pp. 1–2.

10 *Fast Company* on-line dialogue, www.fastcompany.com.

11 Lydia Saad, "American Workers Generally Satisfied, but Indicate Their Jobs Leave Much To Be Desired." *Gallup News Service,* September 3, 1999, www. gallup.com/poll/releases/pr990903.asp.

12 Michelle Conlin, "Job Security, No. Tall Latte, Yes." *Business Week,* April 2, 2001, p. 63.

13 William H. Whyte, Jr., *The Organization Man.* New York: Simon and Schuster, 1956.

14 Denise Rousseau, "The Idiosyncratic Deal: Flexibility Versus Fairness?" *Organizational Dynamics,* 29(4), Spring 2001, pp. 260–273; "The Boundaryless Human Resource Function: Building Agency and Community in the New Economic Era." *Organizational Dynamics,* 27(4), Spring 1999, pp. 6–18; and *Idiosyncratic Employment Arrangements: When Workers Bargain for Themselves.* Armonk, N.Y.: W. E. Sharpe, 2002.

15 My discussion of open source software development draws heavily from the conversations and insights of my colleagues at the Software Center at Carnegie Mellon, particularly Mary Shaw, Ashish Arora, Timothy Halloran, Guillermo Dabos and Orna Raz. The literature on open source development is abundant, but see, for example, Eric Raymond, *The Cathedral and the Bazaar: Musings on Linux and Open Source by an Accidental Revolutionary.* Sebastopol, Calif.: O'Reilly and Associates, Inc., 1999; Pekka Himanen, with Linus Torvalds and Manuel Castells, *The Hacker Ethic: And the Sprit of the Information Age.* New York: Random House, 2001; Karim Lakhani and Eric Von Hippel, "How Open Source Software Works: Free User-to-User Assistance." Cambridge: MIT, Sloan School of Management, Working Paper No. 4117, May 2000.

16 Josh Lerner and Jean Triole, "The Simple Economics of Open Source Software." Boston: Harvard Business School Working Paper No. 00–059, and National Bureau of Economic Research Working Paper No. 7600, December 2000.

17 "John Seely Brown Interview," by Michael Schrage, *Wired,* August 2000. Also see John Seely Brown and Paul Duguid, *The Social Life of Information.* Boston: Harvard Business School Press, 2001.

18 Whyte, *The Organization Man,* p. 446.

19 See Richard Florida, "Science, Reputation and Organization." Pittsburgh: Carnegie Mellon University, unpublished working paper, January 2000. Also see Scott Stern, "Do Scientists Pay To Be Scientists?" Cambridge: National

Bureau of Economic Research, Working Paper No. 7410, October 1999. Also see Michelle Gittleman and Bruce Kogut, "Why Do Firms Do Research (By Their Own Scientists?): Science, Scientists and Innovation Among US Biotechnology Firms." Paper presented at the annual conference of the Academy of Management, Toronto, August 2000; and "Does Good Science Lead to Valuable Knowledge: Biotechnology Firms and the Evolutionary Logic of Citation Patterns." Philadelphia: Wharton School, University of Pennsylvania, Jones Center, Working Paper No. 2001–04, 2001.

20　See Paul Freiberger and Michael Swaine, *Fire in the Valley: The Making of the Personal Computer*. Berkeley: Osborne/McGraw Hill, 1984. Chapter 11, "The Big Morph," develops these themes in more detail.

21　Richard Lloyd, "Digital Bohemia: New Media Enterprises in Chicago's Wicker Park Neighborhood." Paper presented at the annual conference of the American Sociological Association, August 2001.

22　Conlin, "Job Security, No," p. 62.

23　The best expression of this may be the runaway bestseller *The Cluetrain Manifesto,* subtitled *The End of Business as Usual,* by Rick Levine, Christopher Locke, Doc Searls and David Weinberger. Cambridge: Perseus Books, 2000.

24　As quoted in Christine Canabou, "The Sun Sets on the Bohemian Workplace." *Fast Company,* August 2001, www.fastcompany.com/learning/bookshelf/ross.html, p. 3.

25　Quote from "Danger: Toxic Company." *Fast Company,* November 19, 1998, p. 152; but also see Jeffrey Pfeffer, *The Human Equation: Building Profits by Putting People First.* Boston: Harvard Business School Press, 1998.

26　Personal interviews by and communication with the author, 1999–2000.

27　Personal interviews by author, spring 2001.

Analyze

1. What does Microsoft do to manage creativity? Which of those tactics do you find most surprising? Most likely to be effective? Why?

2. More than four of ten workers described themselves as workaholics in a 1999 Gallup poll. Why does Florida think people are working that hard? Why do you think people choose to work that hard?

3. What is the no-collar workplace? How does that appeal to the creative class?

4. How does open-source software provide a model of motivation? What other examples of open-source products demonstrate similar motivations of people?

Explore

1. In the 2002 version of *The Rise of Creative Class*, Florida believed that the "creative class" was primarily composed of artists and writers. For the revised 2014 edition, which is where this selection comes from, Florida explains that the term now means job stability, and that there's a need to transform every job into a creative job. What does the term "creative class" mean to you? To your family? To your teacher? Does it presuppose the idea that everyone is inherently creative?

2. It's clear that companies have struggled to determine how best to handle creative employees. Have you worked in a situation that does it either well or quite poorly? What did your managers do? What could they have done differently? Share your experiences with classmates.

3. Imagine that you are the CEO of your own company and you have a dozen new, creative employees ready to work for you. What specifically yet reasonably can you do to create a quality work environment? Assume, too, that you have a very limited budget, so costly items/programs (like a build in daycare or gym) are out of bounds. List at least a dozen things. Compare your list with a classmate's or two. What similarities do you find? What might those similarities say about the future of managing the creative class?

Ed Catmull
"Fear and Failure"

Computer scientist **Ed Catmull** (1959–) is cofounder of Pixar Animation Studio and president of Walt Disney and Pixar Animation Studios. He has received five Academy Awards, and in 2009, the Academy of Motion Picture Arts and Sciences awarded him with the Gordon E. Sawyer Award for his lifetime of technical contributions and leadership in the field of computer graphics for the motion picture industry. "Fear and Failure" comes from his book *Creativity, Inc.: Overcoming the Unseen Forces That Stand in the Way of True Inspiration*.

The production of *Toy Story 3* could be a master class in how to make a film. At the beginning of the process, in 2007, the team that had made the original *Toy Story* gathered for a two-day off-site in a rustic cabin, 50 miles north of San Francisco, that often functions as our unofficial retreat center. The place, called the Poet's Loft, is all redwood and glass—perched on stilts over Tomales Bay, a perfect place to think. The team's goal, this day, was to rough out a movie they could imagine paying to see.

Sitting on couches with a whiteboard in the center of the room, the participants started by asking some basic questions: Why even do a third movie? What was left to say? What are we still curious about? The *Toy Story* team knew and trusted each other—over the years, they'd made stupid mistakes together and solved seemingly insurmountable problems together. The key was to focus less on the end goal and more on what still intrigued them about the characters who, by this point, felt like people we actually knew. Every so often, someone would stand up and road test what they had so far—trying to summarize a three-part story as if it were the blurb on the back of a DVD cover. Feedback would be given, and they'd go back—literally—to the drawing board.

Then somebody said the one thing that snapped everything into focus. *We've talked so much over the years, in so many different ways, about Andy growing up and growing out of his toys. So what if we just leaped right into that idea directly? How would the toys feel if Andy left for college?* While no one knew exactly how they'd answer that question, everyone present knew that we'd landed on the idea—the line of tension—that would animate *Toy Story 3*.

From that moment forward, the film seemed to fall right into place. Andrew Stanton wrote a treatment, Michael Arndt wrote a script, Lee Unkrich and Darla Anderson, the director and producer, rocked the production, and we hit our deadlines. Even the Braintrust found relatively little to argue with. I don't want to overstate this—the project had its problems—but since our founding, we'd been striving for a production as smooth as this. At one point, Steve Jobs called me to check in on our progress.

"It's really strange," I told him. "We haven't had a single big problem on this film."

Many people would have been happy with this news. Not Steve. "Watch out," he said. "That's a dangerous place to be."

"I wouldn't be too alarmed," I said. "This is our first time, in eleven movies, without a major meltdown. And besides, we have a few more meltdowns coming up."

I wasn't being glib. Over the next two years, we were about to rack up a string of costly misfires. Two of those—*Cars 2* and *Monsters University*— were solved by replacing the films' original directors. Another, a film we spent three years developing, proved so confounding that we shut it down altogether.

I'm going to talk more about our misfires, but I'm gratified to say that because we caught them midstream, before they were finished and released to the public, we were able to treat them as learning experiences. Yes, they cost us money, but the losses were not as sizable as they would have been had we not intervened. And yes, they were painful, but we emerged better and stronger because of them. I came to think of our meltdowns as a necessary part of doing our business, like investments in R&D, and I urged everyone at Pixar to see them the same way.

For most of us, failure comes with baggage—a lot of baggage—that I believe is traced directly back to our days in school. From a very early age, the message is drilled into our heads: Failure is bad; failure means you didn't study or prepare; failure means you slacked off or—worse!—aren't smart enough to begin with. Thus, failure is something to be ashamed of. This perception lives on long into adulthood, even in people who have learned to parrot the oft-repeated arguments about the upside of failure. How many articles have you read on that topic alone? And yet, even as they nod their heads in agreement, many readers of those articles still have the emotional reaction that they had as children. They just can't help it: That early experience of shame is too deep-seated to erase. All the time in my work, I see people resist and reject failure and try mightily to avoid it, because regardless of what we say, mistakes feel embarrassing. There is a visceral reaction to failure: It hurts.

We need to think about failure differently. I'm not the first to say that failure, when approached properly, can be an opportunity for growth. But the way most people interpret this assertion is that mistakes are a necessary evil. Mistakes aren't a necessary evil. They aren't evil at all. They are an inevitable consequence of doing something new (and, as such, should be seen as valuable; without them, we'd have no originality). And yet, even as I say that embracing failure is an important part of learning, I also acknowledge that acknowledging this truth is not enough. That's because failure is painful, and our feelings about this pain tend to screw up our understanding of its worth. To disentangle the good and the bad parts of failure, we have to recognize both the reality of the pain and the benefit of the resulting growth.

Left to their own devices, most people don't want to fail. But Andrew Stanton isn't most people. As I've mentioned, he's known around Pixar for repeating the phrases "fail early and fail fast" and "be wrong as fast as you can." He thinks of failure like learning to ride a bike; it isn't conceivable that you would learn to do this without making mistakes—without toppling over a few times. "Get a bike that's as low to the ground as you can find, put on elbow and knee pads so you're not afraid of falling, and go," he says. If you apply this mindset to everything new you attempt, you can begin to subvert the negative connotation associated with making mistakes. Says Andrew: "You wouldn't say to somebody who is first learning to play the guitar, 'You better think *really* hard about where you put your fingers on the guitar neck before you strum, because you only get to strum once, and that's it. And if you get that wrong, we're going to move on.' That's no way to learn, is it?"

This doesn't mean that Andrew enjoys it when he puts his work up for others to judge, and it is found wanting. But he deals with the possibility of failure by addressing it head on, searching for mechanisms that turn pain into progress. To be wrong as fast as you can is to sign up for aggressive, rapid learning. Andrew does this without hesitation.

Even though people in our offices have heard Andrew say this repeatedly, many still miss the point. They think it means accept failure with dignity and move on. The better, more subtle interpretation is that failure is a manifestation of learning and exploration. If you aren't experiencing failure, then you are making a far worse mistake: You are being driven by the desire to avoid it. And, for leaders especially, this strategy—trying to avoid failure by out-thinking it—dooms you to fail. As Andrew puts it, "Moving things forward allows the team you are leading to feel like, 'Oh, I'm on a boat that is actually going towards land.' As opposed to having a leader who says, 'I'm still not sure. I'm going to look at the map a little bit more, and we're just going to float here, and all of you stop rowing until I figure this out.' And then weeks go by, and morale plummets, and failure becomes self-fulfilling. People begin to treat the captain with doubt and trepidation. Even if their doubts aren't fully justified, you've become what they see you as because of your inability to move."

Rejecting failure and avoiding mistakes seem like high-minded goals, but they are fundamentally misguided. Take something like the Golden Fleece Awards, which were established in 1975 to call attention to government-funded projects that were particularly egregious wastes of money. (Among the winners were things like an $84,000 study on love commissioned by the National Science Foundation, and a $3,000 Department of Defense study that examined whether people in the military should carry umbrellas.) While such scrutiny may have seemed like a good idea at the time, it had a chilling effect on research. No one wanted to "win" a Golden Fleece Award because, under the guise of avoiding waste, its organizers had inadvertently made it dangerous and embarrassing for everyone to make mistakes.

The truth is, if you fund thousands of research projects every year, some will have obvious, measurable, positive impacts, and others will go nowhere. We aren't very good at predicting the future—that's a given—and yet the Golden Fleece Awards tacitly implied that researchers should know *before* they do their research whether or not the results of that research would have value. Failure was being used as a weapon, rather than as an agent of learning. And that had fallout: The fact that failing could earn you a very public flogging distorted the way researchers chose projects. The politics of failure, then, impeded our progress.

There's a quick way to determine if your company has embraced the negative definition of failure. Ask yourself what happens when an error is discovered. Do people shut down and turn inward, instead of coming together to untangle the causes of problems that might be avoided going forward? Is the question being asked: Whose fault was this? If so, your culture is one that vilifies failure. Failure is difficult enough without it being compounded by the search for a scapegoat.

In a fear-based, failure-averse culture, people will consciously or unconsciously avoid risk. They will seek instead to repeat something safe that's been good enough in the past. Their work will be derivative, not innovative. But if you can foster a positive understanding of failure, the opposite will happen.

How, then, do you make failure into something people can face without fear?

Part of the answer is simple: If we as leaders can talk about our mistakes and our part in them, then we make it safe for others. You don't run from it or pretend it doesn't exist. That is why I make a point of being open about our meltdowns inside Pixar, because I believe they teach us something important: Being open about problems is the first step toward learning from them. My goal is not to drive fear out completely, because fear is inevitable in high-stakes situations. What I want to do is loosen its grip on us. While we don't want too many failures, we must think of the cost of failure as an investment in the future.

If you create a fearless culture (or as fearless as human nature will allow), people will be much less hesitant to explore new areas, identifying uncharted pathways and then charging down them. They will also begin to see the upside of decisiveness: The time they've saved by not gnashing their teeth about whether they're on the right course comes in handy when they hit a dead end and need to reboot.

It isn't enough to pick a path—you must go down it. By doing so, you see things you couldn't possibly see when you started out; you may not like what you see, some of it may be confusing, but at least you will have, as we like to say, "explored the neighborhood." The key point here is that even if you decide you're in the wrong place, there is still time to head toward the *right* place. And all the thinking you've done that led you down that alley was not wasted. Even if most of what you've seen doesn't fit your needs, you inevitably take away ideas that will prove useful. Relatedly, if there are parts of the neighborhood you like but that don't seem helpful in the quest you're on, you will remember those parts and possibly use them later.

Let me explain what I mean by exploring the neighborhood. Years before it evolved into the funny, affecting tale of a fierce, shaggy behemoth (Sulley) and his unlikely friendship with the little girl it's his job to scare (Boo), *Monsters, Inc.* was an altogether different story. As first imagined by Pete Docter, it revolved around a thirty-year-old man who was coping with a cast of frightening characters that only he could see. As Pete describes it, the man "is an accountant or something, and he hates his job, and one day his mom gives him a book with some drawings in it that he did when he was a kid. He doesn't think anything of it, and he puts it on the shelf, and that night, monsters show up. And nobody else can see them. He thinks he's starting to go crazy. They follow him to his job, and on his dates, and it turns out these monsters are all the fears that he never dealt with as a kid. He becomes friends with them eventually, and as he conquers the fears, they slowly begin to disappear."

Anyone who's seen the movie knows that the final product bears no resemblance to that description. But what nobody knows is how many wrong turns the story took, over a period of years, before it found its true north. The pressure on Pete, all along, was enormous—*Monsters, Inc.* was the first Pixar film not directed by John Lasseter, so in some very real ways Pete and his crew were under the microscope. Every unsuccessful attempt to crack the story only heightened the pressure.

Fortunately, Pete had a basic concept that he held to throughout: "Monsters are real, and they scare kids for a living." But what was the strongest manifestation of that idea? He couldn't know until he'd tried a few options. At first, the human protagonist was a six-year-old named Mary. Then she was changed to a little boy. Then back to a six-year-old girl. Then she was seven, named Boo, and bossy—even domineering. Finally, Boo was turned into a fearless, preverbal toddler. The idea of Sulley's buddy character—the round, one-eyed Mike, voiced by Billy Crystal—wasn't added until more than a year after the first treatment was written. The process of determining the rules of the incredibly intricate world Pete created also took him down countless blind alleys—until, eventually, those blind alleys converged on a path that led the story where it needed to go.

"The process of developing a story is one of discovery," Pete says. "However, there's always a guiding principle that leads you as you go down the various roads. In *Monsters, Inc.,* all of our very different plots shared a common feeling—the bittersweet goodbye you feel once a problem"—in this case, Sulley's quest to return Boo to her own world—"has been solved. You suffer through it as you struggle to solve it, but by the end you've developed a sort of fondness for it, and you miss it when it is gone. I knew I wanted to express that, and I was eventually able to get it in the film."

While the process was difficult and time consuming, Pete and his crew never believed that a failed approach meant that *they* had failed. Instead, they saw that each idea led them a bit closer to finding the better option. And that allowed them to come to work each day engaged and excited, even while in the midst of confusion. This is key: When experimentation is seen as necessary and productive, not as a frustrating waste of time, people will enjoy their work—even when it is confounding them.

The principle I'm describing here—iterative trial and error—has long-recognized value in science. When scientists have a question, they construct hypotheses, test them, analyze them, and draw conclusions—and then they do it all over again. The reasoning behind this is simple: Experiments are fact-finding missions that, over time, inch scientists toward greater understanding. That means *any* outcome is a good outcome, because it yields new information. If your experiment proved your initial theory wrong, better to know it sooner rather than later. Armed with new facts, you can then reframe whatever question you're asking.

This is often easier to accept in the laboratory than in a business. Creating art or developing new products in a for-profit context is complicated and expensive. In our case, when we try to tell the most compelling story, how do we assess our attempts and draw conclusions? How do we determine what works best? And how do we put the need to succeed out of our minds long enough to identify a true emotional storyline that will carry a film?

There is an alternative approach to being wrong as fast as you can. It is the notion that if you carefully think everything through, if you are meticulous and plan well and consider all possible outcomes, you are more likely to create a lasting product. But I should caution that if you seek to plot out all your moves before you make them—if you put your faith in slow, deliberative planning in the hopes it will spare you failure down the line—well, you're deluding yourself. For one thing, it's easier to plan derivative work—things that copy or repeat something already out there. So if your primary goal is to have a fully worked out, set-in-stone plan, you are only upping your chances of being unoriginal. Moreover, you cannot plan your way out of problems. While planning is very important, and we do a lot of it, there is only so much you can control in a creative environment. In general, I have found that people who pour their energy into thinking about an approach and insisting that it is too early to act are wrong just as often as people who dive in and work quickly. The overplanners just take longer to be wrong (and, when things inevitably go awry, are more crushed by the feeling that they have failed). There's a corollary to this, as well: The more time you spend mapping out an approach, the more likely you are to get attached to it. The nonworking idea gets worn into your brain, like a rut in the mud. It can be difficult to get free of it and head in a different direction. Which, more often than not, is exactly what you must do.

There are arenas, of course, in which a zero failure rate is essential. Commercial flying has a phenomenal safety record because there is so much attention paid at every level to removing error, from manufacturing the engines to assembling and maintaining the planes to observing safety checks and the rules that govern air spaces. Likewise, hospitals have elaborate safeguards to make sure that they operate on the right patient, on the correct side of the body, on the right organ, and so on. Banks have protocols to prevent errors; manufacturing companies have a goal of eliminating production line errors; many industries set goals of having zero injuries.

But just because "failure free" is crucial in some industries does not mean that it should be a goal in all of them. When it comes to creative endeavors, the concept of zero failures is worse than useless. It is counterproductive.

To be sure, failure can be expensive. Making a bad product or suffering a major public setback damages your company's reputation and, often, your employees' morale. So we try to make it less expensive to fail, thereby taking some of the onus off it. For example, we've set up a system in which directors are allowed to spend years in the development phase of a movie, where the costs of iteration and exploration are relatively low. (At this point, we're paying the director's and story artists' salaries but not putting anything into production, which is where costs explode.)

It's one thing to talk about the value of people encountering a number of small failures as they grope their way to understanding, but what about a big, catastrophic failure? What about a project you sink millions of dollars into, commit to publicly, and then have to walk away from? This happened on a film we were developing a few years back, which was based on a terrific idea that originated in the mind of one of our most creative and trusted colleagues (but, notably, one who had never directed a feature film before). He wanted to tell the story of what happens when the last remaining male and female blue-footed newts on the planet are forced together by science to save the species—but they can't stand each other. When he got up and pitched the idea, we were blown away. The story was, like *Ratatouille*, a somewhat challenging concept, but if handled the right way, we could see that it would be a phenomenal movie.

Significantly, the pitch also came at a time when Jim Morris and I were thinking a lot about whether the success of Pixar was making us complacent. Among the questions we'd been asking ourselves and each other: Had we, in the interest of governing production and making it efficient, created habits and rules that were unnecessary? Were we in danger of growing lethargic and set in our ways? Were our budgets on each movie inching higher and higher for no reason? We were looking for an opportunity to change it up, to create our own little startup, within Pixar and yet separate from it, to try to tap back into the energy that permeated the place when we were young and small and striving. This project seemed to fit the bill. As we put it into production, we decided to treat it as an experiment: What if we brought in new people from the outside with fresh ideas, gave them the charter of rethinking the entire production process (and gave them experienced teammates to help carry this out), and then put them two blocks away from our main campus to minimize their contact with those who might encourage them to adopt the status quo? In addition to making a memorable movie, we were looking to challenge and improve our processes. We called the experiment the Incubator Project.

Within Pixar, some expressed doubts about this approach, but the spirit behind it—the desire not to rest on our laurels—was appealing to all. Andrew Stanton told me later that he worried from the outset about how isolated the project's crew was, even though it was by design. We were so enamored, he felt, of the possibilities of reinventing the wheel that we underestimated the impact of making so many changes at once. It was as if we'd picked four talented musicians, left them to their own devices, and hoped like hell they'd figure out how to be the Beatles.

But we didn't see that clearly then. The idea for the movie was strong, which was confirmed when we unveiled it at a presentation for the media on upcoming Pixar and Disney movies. As the website *Ain't It Cool News* reported with enthusiasm, the main character, who'd been in captivity since he was a tadpole, lived in a cage in a lab where he could see a flowchart on the wall that spelled out the mating rituals of his species. Because he was lonely, he would practice the steps day in and day out, getting ready for scientists to capture him a girlfriend. Unfortunately, he couldn't read the ninth and final mating ritual because it was obscured by the lab's coffee machine. Therein lay the mystery.

The presentation drew raves. It was classic Pixar, people gushed—offbeat, witty, while at the same time tackling meaningful, relatable ideas. But within the production, unbeknownst to us, the story was stalled. It had the beginnings of a plot—our hero gets his wish when scientists catch him a mate in the wild and bring her back to the lab—but when the unhappy couple ends up back in the natural world, the film began to fall apart. The movie was stuck, and even after a lot of thoughtful feedback, it wasn't getting better.

That fact evaded us at first because of the separateness of the enterprise. When we tried to assess how things were going, early reports seemed good. The director had a strong vision, and his crew was excited and working hard, but they didn't know what they didn't know: that the first two years of a movie's development should be a time of solidifying the story beats by relentlessly testing them—much like you temper steel. And that required decision-making, not just abstract discussion. While everyone working on it had the best intentions, it got bogged down in hypotheticals and possibilities. The bottom line was that while everyone was rowing the boat, to use Andrew's analogy, there was no forward movement.

When we finally figured this out—after a few experienced Pixar people were sent in to help and reported back about what they saw—it was too late. The Pixar way is to invest in a singular vision, and we'd done so, in a major way, on this project. We didn't consider replacing the director—the story was his, and without him as the engine, we didn't think we could push it to completion. So in May 2010, with heavy hearts, we shut it down.

There are some who will read this and conclude that putting this film into production in the first place was a mistake. An untested director, an unfinished script—it's easy to look back, after the shutdown, and say that those factors alone should have dissuaded us at the outset. But I disagree. While it cost us time and money to pursue, to my mind it was worth the investment. We learned better how to balance new ideas with old ideas, and we learned that we had made a mistake in not getting very explicit buy-in from all of Pixar's leaders about the nature of what we were trying to do. These are lessons that would serve us very well later as we adopted new software and changed some of our technical processes. While experimentation is scary to many, I would argue that we should be far more terrified of the opposite approach. Being too risk-averse causes many companies to stop innovating and to reject new ideas, which is the first step on the path to irrelevance. Probably more companies hit the skids for this reason than because they dared to push boundaries and take risks—and, yes, to fail.

To be a truly creative company, you must start things that might fail. For all of this talk about accepting failure, if a movie—or any creative endeavor—isn't improving at a reasonable rate, there is a problem. If a director devises a series of solutions that are not making a movie better, one could come to the conclusion that he or she isn't right for the job. Which is sometimes precisely the right conclusion to reach.

But where to draw that line? How many errors are too many? When does failure go from a stop on the road to excellence to a red flag that signals change is needed? We put a lot of faith in our Braintrust meetings to make sure that our directors get all the feedback and support they need, but there are problems that process can't fix. What do you do when candor is not enough?

These were the questions we faced on our various meltdowns.

We are a filmmaker-driven studio, which means that our goal is to let the creative people guide our projects. But when a movie gets stuck and it becomes clear that not only is it broken but its directors are at a loss as to how to fix it, we must replace them or shut the project down. You may ask: *If it is true that all the movies suck at first, and if Pixar's way is to give filmmakers—not the Braintrust—the ultimate authority to fix what's broken, then how do you know when to step in?*

The criteria we use is that we step in if a director loses the confidence of his or her crew. About three hundred people work on each Pixar movie, and they are used to endless adjustments and changes being made while the story is finding its feet. In general, movie crews are an understanding bunch. They recognize that there are always problems, so while they can be judgmental, they don't tend to *rush* to judgment. Their first impulse is to work harder. When a director stands up in a meeting and says, "I realize this scene isn't working, I don't yet know how to fix it, but I'm figuring it out. Keep going!"—a crew will follow him or her to the ends of the earth. But when a problem is festering and everyone seems to be looking the other way or when people are sitting around waiting to be told what to do, the crew gets antsy. It's not that they don't like the director—they usually do. It's that they lose confidence in the director's ability to bring the movie home. Which is part of why, to me, they are the most reliable barometer. If the crew is confused, then their leader is, too.

When this happens, we must act. To know when to act, we much watch carefully for signs that a movie is stuck. Here is one: A Braintrust meeting will occur, notes will be given, and three months later, the movie will come back essentially unchanged. That is not okay. You may say, "Wait a minute—I thought you just said the directors didn't *have* to obey the notes!" They don't. But directors must find ways to address problems that are raised by the group because the Braintrust represents the audience; when they are confused or otherwise dissatisfied, there's a good chance moviegoers will be too. The implication of being director-led is that the director must lead.

But any failure at a creative company is a failure of many, not one. If you're a leader of a company that has faltered, any misstep that occurs is yours as well. Moreover, if you don't use what's gone wrong to educate yourself and your colleagues, then you'll have missed an opportunity. There are two parts to any failure: There is the event itself, with all its attendant disappointment, confusion, and shame, and then there is our reaction to it. It is this second part that we control. Do we become introspective, or do we bury our heads in the sand? Do we make it safe for others to acknowledge and learn from problems, or do we shut down discussion by looking for people to blame? We must remember that failure gives us chances to grow, and we ignore those chances at our own peril.

Which raises the question: When failure occurs, how should you get the most out of it? When it came to our meltdowns, we were determined to look inward. We had picked talented, creative people to preside over these projects, so we clearly were doing something that was making it hard for them to succeed. Some worried the meltdowns were an indication that we were losing our touch. I disagreed. We never said it was going to be easy— we'd only insisted that our movies be great. Had we not stepped in and taken action, I said, *then* we'd be abandoning our values. After several misfires, though, it was important that we take a moment to reassess and to try to absorb the lessons they had to teach us.

So in March 2011, Jim Morris, Pixar's general manager, arranged an off-site with the studio's producers and directors—twenty or so people in all. On the agenda was one question: Why did we have so many meltdowns in a row? We weren't looking to point fingers. We wanted to rally the company's creative leadership to figure out the underlying problems that were leading us astray.

Jim kicked the meeting off by thanking everyone for coming and reminding us why we were there. Nothing is more critical to our continued success as a studio, he said, than the ability to develop new projects and directors, and yet we were clearly doing something wrong. We had been trying to increase the number of movies we released, but we'd hit a roadblock. Over the next two days, he said, our goal was to figure out what was missing and to chart out ways to create it and put it in place.

What became immediately apparent was that no one in the room was running from his or her role in these failures. They neither blamed the existing problems on others nor asked for someone else to solve them. The language they used to talk about the issues showed that they thought of them as their own. "Is there a way, other than Braintrust notes, that we could do a better job of teaching our directors the importance of an emotional arc?" asked one person. "I feel like I should be formally sharing my experience with other people," said another. I could not have been prouder. It was obvious that they felt they owned the problem and the responsibility for its solution. Even though we had serious problems, the culture of the place—the willingness to roll up our pant legs and wade into the muck for the good of the company—felt more alive than ever.

As a team, we analyzed our assumptions, why we'd made such flawed choices. Were there essential qualities we needed to look for in our director candidates, going forward, that we'd overlooked in the past? More significantly, how had we failed to prepare new directors adequately for the daunting job they faced? How many times had we said, "We won't let him or her fail"—only to let them fail? We discussed how we had been blinded by the fact that the directors of our first films—John, Andrew, and Pete—had each figured out how to be a director without formal training, something that we now saw was much rarer than we'd previously believed. We talked about the fact that Andrew, Pete, and Lee had spent years working side by side with John, absorbing his lessons—the need for decisiveness, for example—and his collaborative way of teasing out ideas. Andrew and Pete, the first directors at Pixar to follow in John's footsteps, had been challenged by the process but in the end had succeeded spectacularly. We assumed that others would do the same. But we had to face the fact that as we'd gotten bigger, our newer directors did not have the benefit of that experience.

Then we turned to the future. We identified individuals who we thought had the potential to become directors, listing their strengths and weaknesses and being specific about what we would do to teach them, give them experience, and support them. In the wake of our failures, we still didn't want to make only "safe" choices going forward; we understood that taking creative and leadership risks is essential to who we are and that sometimes this means handing the keys to someone who may not fit the traditional conception of a movie director. And yet, as we made those unconventional choices, everyone agreed, we needed to outline better, more explicit steps to train and prepare those we felt had the necessary skills to make movies. Instead of hoping that our director candidates would absorb our shared wisdom through osmosis, we resolved to create a formal mentoring program that would, in a sense, give to others what Pete and Andrew and Lee had experienced working so closely with John in the early days. Going forward, every established director would check in weekly with his mentees— giving them both practical and motivational advice as they developed ideas they hoped would become feature films.

Later, when I was reflecting on the off-site with Andrew, he made what I think is a profound point. He told me that he thinks he and the other proven directors have a responsibility to be teachers—that this should be a central part of their jobs, even as they continue to make their own films. "The Holy Grail is to find a way that we can teach others how to make the best movie possible with whoever they've got on their crew, because it's just logic that someday we won't be here," he said. "Walt Disney didn't do that. And without him, Disney Animation wasn't able to survive without enduring a decade and a half, if not two, of a slump. That's the real goal: Can we teach in a way that our directors will think smart when we're not around?"

Who better to teach than the most capable among us? And I'm not just talking about seminars or formal settings. Our actions and behaviors, for better or worse, teach those who admire and look up to us how to govern their own lives. Are we thoughtful about how people learn and grow? As leaders, we should think of ourselves as teachers and try to create companies in which teaching is seen as a valued way to contribute to the success of the whole. Do we think of most activities as teaching opportunities and experiences as ways of learning? One of the most crucial responsibilities of leadership is creating a culture that rewards those who lift not just our stock prices but our aspirations as well.

Discussing failure and all its ripple effects is not merely an academic exercise. We face it because by seeking better understanding, we remove barriers to full creative engagement. One of the biggest barriers is fear, and while failure comes with the territory, fear shouldn't have to. The goal, then, is to uncouple fear and failure—to create an environment in which making mistakes doesn't strike terror into your employees' hearts.

How, exactly, do you do that? By necessity, the message companies send to their managers is conflicting: Develop your people, help them grow into strong contributors and team members, and oh, by the way, make sure everything goes smoothly because there aren't enough resources, and the success of our enterprise depends on your group doing its job on time and on budget. It is easy to be critical of the micromanaging many managers resort to, yet we must acknowledge the rock and the hard place we often place them between. If they have to choose between meeting a deadline and some less well defined mandate to "nurture" their people, they will pick the deadline every time. We tell ourselves that we will devote more time to our people if we, in turn, are given more slack in the schedule or budget, but somehow the requirements of the job always eat up the slack, resulting in increased pressure with even less room for error. Given these realities, managers typically want two things: (1) for everything to be tightly controlled, and (2) to appear to be in control.

But when control is the goal, it can negatively affect other parts of your culture. I've known many managers who hate to be surprised in meetings, for example, by which I mean they make it clear that they want to be briefed about any unexpected news in advance and in private. In many workplaces, it is a sign of disrespect if someone surprises a manager with new information in front of other people. But what does this mean in practice? It means that there are pre-meetings before meetings, and the meetings begin to take on a pro forma tone. It means wasted time. It means that the employees who work with these people walk on eggshells. It means that fear runs rampant.

Getting middle managers to tolerate (and not feel threatened by) problems and surprises is one of our most important jobs; they already feel the weight of believing that if they screw up, there will be hell to pay. How do we get people to reframe the way they think about the process and the risks?

The antidote to fear is trust, and we all have a desire to find something to trust in an uncertain world. Fear and trust are powerful forces, and while they are not opposites, exactly, trust is the best tool for driving out fear. There will always be plenty to be afraid of, especially when you are doing something new. Trusting others doesn't mean that they won't make mistakes. It means that if they do (or if you do), you trust they will act to help solve it. Fear can be created quickly; trust can't. Leaders must demonstrate their trustworthiness, over time, through their actions—and the best way to do that is by responding well to failure. The Braintrust and various groups within Pixar have gone through difficult times together, solved problems together, and that is how they've built up trust in each other. Be patient. Be authentic. And be consistent. The trust will come.

When I mention authenticity, I am referring to the way that managers level with their people. In many organizations, managers tend to err on the side of secrecy, of keeping things hidden from employees. I believe this is the wrong instinct. A manager's default mode should not be secrecy. What is needed is a thoughtful consideration of the cost of secrecy weighed against the risks. When you instantly resort to secrecy, you are telling people they can't be trusted. When you are candid, you are telling people that you trust them and that there is nothing to fear. To confide in employees is to give them a sense of ownership over the information. The result— and I've seen this again and again—is that they are less likely to leak whatever it is that you've confided.

The people at Pixar have been extremely good at keeping secrets, which is crucial in a business whose profits depend on the strategic release of ideas or products when they are ready and not before. Since making movies is such a messy process, we need to be able to talk candidly, among ourselves, about the mess without having it shared outside the company. By sharing problems and sensitive issues with employees, we make them partners and part-owners in our culture, and they do not want to let each other down.

Your employees are smart; that's why you hired them. So treat them that way. They know when you deliver a message that has been heavily massaged. When managers explain what their plan is without giving the reasons for it, people wonder what the "real" agenda is. There may be no hidden agenda, but you've succeeded in implying that there is one. Discussing the thought processes behind solutions aims the focus on the solutions, not on second-guessing. When we are honest, people know it.

Pixar's head of management development, Jamie Woolf, put together a mentoring program that pairs new managers with experienced ones. A key facet of this program is that mentors and mentees work together for an extended period of time—eight months. They meet about all aspects of leadership, from career development and confidence building to managing personnel challenges and building healthy team environments. The purposes are to cultivate deep connections and to have a place to share fears and challenges, exploring the skills of managing others by wrestling together with real problems, whether they be external (a volatile supervisor) or internal (an overly active inner critic). In other words, to develop a sense of trust.

While I work with a couple of mentees, I also speak every year to the entire group. In this talk, I tell the story of how, when I was first a manager at New York Tech, I didn't feel like a manager at all. And while I liked the idea of being in charge, I went to work every day feeling like something of a fraud. Even in the early years of Pixar, when I was the president, that feeling didn't go away. I knew many presidents of other companies and had a good idea of their personality characteristics. They were aggressive and extremely confident. Knowing that I didn't share many of those traits, again I felt like a fraud. In truth, I was afraid of failure.

Not until about eight or nine years ago, I tell them, did the imposter feeling finally go away. I have several things to thank for that evolution: my experience of both weathering our failures and watching our films succeed; my decisions, post—*Toy Story*, to recommit myself to Pixar and its culture; and my enjoyment of my maturing relationship with Steve and John. Then, after fessing up, I ask the group, "How many of *you* feel like a fraud?" And without fail, every hand in the room shoots up.

As managers, we all start off with a certain amount of trepidation. When we are new to the position, we imagine what the job is in order to get our arms around it, then we compare ourselves against our made-up model. But the job is never what we think it is. The trick is to forget our models about what we "should" be. A better measure of our success is to look at the people on our team and see how they are working together. Can they rally to solve key problems? If the answer is yes, you are managing well.

This phenomenon of not perceiving correctly what our job is occurs frequently with new directors. Even if a person works side by side with an experienced director in a supporting role, a role in which they repeatedly demonstrate the abilities to take the reins on their own film, when they actually get the job it isn't quite what they thought it was. There is something scary about discovering that they have responsibilities that were not part of their mental model. In the case of first-time directors, the weight of those responsibilities is not only new, it is further amplified by the track record of our previous films. Every director at Pixar worries that his or her movie will be the one that fails, that breaks our streak of number-one hits. "That pressure is there: You can't be the first bomb," says Bob Peterson, a longtime Pixar writer and voice artist. "What you want is for that pressure to light a fire under you to make you say, 'I'm going to do better.' But there's a fear of not knowing if you can find the right answer. The directors here who are successful are able to just relax and let ideas be born out of that pressure."

Bob jokes that to relieve that pressure, Pixar should intentionally do a bad film "just to correct the market." Of course we'd never set out to make something terrible, but Bob's idea is thought-provoking: Are there ways to prove to your employees that your company doesn't stigmatize failure?

All of this attention on not only allowing but even *expecting* errors has helped make Pixar a unique culture. For proof of just how unique, consider the example of *Toy Story 3* once again. As I said at the start of this chapter, this was the only Pixar production during which we didn't have a major crisis, and after the film came out, I repeatedly said so in public, lauding its crew for racking up not a single disaster during the film's gestation.

You might imagine that the *Toy Story 3* crew would have been happy when I said this, but you'd imagine wrong. So ingrained are the beliefs I've been describing about failure at Pixar that the people who worked on *Toy Story 3* were actually offended by my remarks. They interpreted them to mean that they hadn't tried as hard as their colleagues on other films—that they hadn't pushed themselves enough. That isn't at all what I meant, but I have to admit: I was thrilled by their reaction. I saw it as proof that our culture is healthy.

As Andrew Stanton puts it, "It's gotten to the point that we get worried if a film is not a problem child right away. It makes us nervous. We've come to recognize the signs of invention—of dealing with originality. We have begun to welcome the feeling of, 'Oh, we've never had this exact problem before—and it's incredibly recalcitrant and won't do what we want it to do.' That's familiar territory for us—in a good way."

Rather than trying to prevent all errors, we should assume, as is almost always the case, that our people's intentions are good and that they want to solve problems. Give them responsibility, let the mistakes happen, and let people fix them. If there is fear, there is a reason—our job is to find the reason and to remedy it. Management's job is not to prevent risk but to build the ability to recover.

Analyze

1. In your own words, explain how Ed Catmull sees failure. How is his sense of failure—and what it means—different than that of the rest of us?
2. How does Catmull believe one can make failure into something people can face without fear?
3. Why is failure more easily accepted in a laboratory than in a business?
4. How does the Pixar Braintrust know when to step in and take over? How long will the Braintrust hold off before stepping in?

Explore

1. Think about the overplanners in your life. Is Catmull right that the longer one spends with a plan, the more attached she gets to it (even if it's a bad plan)? How does this play out with the overplanners you know? What level of planning is good? Or do you subscribe to Andy Stanton's tactic of failing as fast as you can?
2. What lessons do you see in the "last newts on earth" story that never saw the light of day? Catmull admits that they made too many changes at once, but what else do you see of value in this anecdote? What other fears or failures offer a learning opportunity here?

3. Catmull says there are two parts to any failure. "There is the event itself, with all its attendant disappointment, confusion, and shame, and then there is our reaction to it. It is this second part that we control." Think of your last failure. How did you control the second part, your reaction? Did you bury your head in the sand? Did you sulk? Did you move on as fast as you could, never looking back? Rethink how you handled the second part of that failure and come up with at least two more useful ways you could've acted. Keep those in mind the next time you encounter a failure.

4. Think about a time where you felt, as Catmull did, like a fraud. Write a short scene that presents a character in a situation like you were in, feeling as you did—like a fraud. Really explore the interiority of that character. Uncover the fears, the worries, the stress. Share your scene with a classmate while you read theirs. Take comfort in the fact that from time to time, we *all* feel like frauds. Just like Ed Catmull and the entire group at Pixar.

Tina Seelig
"The Table Kingdom"

Tina Seelig (1957–) is a Professor of the Practice in the Department of Management Science and Engineering at Stanford University as well as the Executive Director of the Stanford Technology Ventures Program. She has authored seventeen popular science books and education games. "The Table Kingdom" comes from her book *inGenius: A Crash Course on Creativity.*

Liz Gerber was running a workshop at the d.school on creative problem solving for a group of business executives, when one of the participants lamented that their team's workspace was confining, making it difficult to comfortably collaborate. The group asked if they could move to a bigger space. Liz handed them an electric screwdriver and told them to take down the plywood walls, which were easily dismantled. Their jaws dropped open when they realized that was an option, and they quickly removed the wall to create a much bigger workspace and dove into their project, filling the expanded space with artifacts and ideas.

The spaces in which we live and work are the stages on which we play out our lives. As such, they have a huge impact on our thoughts and behavior. From the moment we are born we respond to the space around us. It has been shown that children who grow up in stimulating environments have brains with a more highly developed neocortex, the outer layer of the brain. And there is evidence that such people are more capable of solving complex cognitive problems later in life. That's why new parents often try to create a rich environment for their babies and young children. They surround them with bright images and toys that activate their nervous system and spark their imagination. Kindergartens strive for an equally stimulating environment. Rooms are filled with manipulatives such as blocks and Legos®, there is an abundance of brightly colored books and games, and the furniture is designed so that kids can work independently, in groups, or as an entire class.

Unfortunately, as children get older, classrooms get less and less inspiring. Eventually, in high school and college, desks and chairs are usually lined up in rows and bolted to the floor, facing the front of the room, where the teacher lectures while students passively take notes. They have sadly graduated from an environment that is designed to stimulate their imagination to one that inadvertently crushes it. And when they head off to work, many of these graduates find themselves in offices with rows upon rows of sterile cubicles. Furthermore, in many places in the world, these offices are dimly lit and filled with cigarette smoke.

What type of messages do these environments communicate? When you enter any space, you are immersed in a narrative and become an actor in that story. You know your role and what is expected of you. For example, how do you feel and act when you walk into a lecture hall, a hotel room, an airport terminal, a doctor's office, a concert hall, or a playground? Each space compels you to respond differently. Most likely, you expect to be a passive observer in a lecture hall; you assume that others will clean up after you at a hotel; you will probably feel out of control at an airport; you know you will have to wait to see your doctor; you count on being entertained at a concert; and you expect to entertain yourself at a playground. Therefore, if you are creating an office, classroom, or family room where you want people to be inventive, you need to keep in mind that the design of the space really matters. Space is one of the key factors in all habitats, along with the rules, rewards, and constraints, which will be discussed in later chapters.

While writing this I am sitting outside at Coupa Café in Palo Alto, California, on a warm summer evening, surrounded by lots of people who are casually sipping coffee and chatting with friends. Some are in small groups, and others are sitting by themselves. This open space invites you to linger, to watch passersby, and to start a conversation with someone sitting at the next table. In fact, a young man just introduced himself to me and handed me his business card. Blazoned on the front are the words "Ryan Schwartz, entrepreneur." New to town, he wanted to meet new people and picked this spot because he understood that here it would be perfectly fine for him to introduce himself to others.

Right down the street is a restaurant with a very different ambience. I'm sure you can picture it: subdued, with small tables and quiet music, conducive to private conversations that will not be interrupted. Here it's much less likely that you would start up a conversation with someone sitting at another table. I consciously decided to sit outside at the café, because, like others, I wanted to be surrounded by the low buzz of the crowd and the potential for brief interruptions and inspiration.

This might all seem obvious. However, most of us don't take such factors into account when we design the habitats in which we live and work. When you look around your space, think of all the variables that influence how you feel and act. Consider the height of the ceiling, observe the brightness of the lights, listen to the volume of the music, and pay attention to the smells of the room. Each of these factors affects everything you do, how you feel, the way you work, how you learn, and how you play. Real estate agents know this well. That is why they turn on all the lights and often bake cookies at an open house. They know that the bright rooms and the smell of the freshly baked cookies will produce a warm feeling about the house, making you more likely to want to buy it. Even though you know what they are doing, it still works.

Architects are extremely aware of all of these variables and consider them each time they design a new building. Jeanne Gang, a renowned architect from Chicago who recently won a MacArthur "genius" award, is known for designing dramatic buildings, such as the Aqua Tower in downtown Chicago, which looks as though it is being blown by the unrelenting wind of that city, and the Starlight Theater in Rockford, Illinois, the roof of which opens like a flower. Her firm is remarkably inventive, and the team needs to work in a space that encourages the creation of innovative solutions to all the architectural challenges that come their way.

Jeanne told me that they consciously designed a work space that is slightly "out of control," filled with myriad objects that stimulate the imagination. There are found objects from all over the world, such as rocks and minerals, building materials, musical instruments, fabrics, and crafts that offer inspiration for the projects on which they are working. The building is intentionally outside the city center, in an old bank building that they gutted and made their own. It is a relaxed environment on the inside and the outside.

In addition to their open studio space, they have three unique meeting rooms, each consciously designed for different types of creative work. The rooms are different sizes and shapes, and the furniture reflects the goal for the space. The orange room is designed for all-day workshops; it has soft chairs and one big round table for group work. It opens onto both the model shop and the kitchen for easy access to prototyping materials as well as food. Another room, predominantly white, is designed for formal presentations. Outfitted with a rectangular wooden table, this room opens out to the garden. The silver room is designed for talking, not prototyping. It is an intimate space with a white round table and views of the activity in the street. Overall, Jeanne has built an environment where people aren't worried about making a mess, where everything is flexible, and where the space—both inside and outside—reflects the goals for those inside.

My favorite example of Jeanne's work is a large flowing curtain constructed of marble tiles and weighing 1,600 pounds. In this stunning piece she combines materials—stone and fabric—and unlocks previously unknown properties of marble by slicing it surprisingly thin. The interlocking pieces create a translucent marble curtain that is suspended from the ceiling. It is unlikely that ideas such as this one would have come out of a space that didn't inspire the creative connection and combination of unlikely ideas and materials.

A completely different example comes from Square, Inc., a San Francisco firm dedicated to making mobile financial transactions simple. They make a small white square device that plugs into a smartphone and allows anyone to collect creditcard payments. The firm's directors are extremely aware that the products it releases are a direct reflection of the space in which employees are working. They want their products to be simple and "breathtakingly elegant" and have explicitly designed their office space with the same aesthetic. There is one enormous room with rows of long white tables where everyone works in the open. In addition, there are elegantly designed conference rooms that are enclosed in glass for private conversations. Everything is clean, neat, and open, and all employees are required to keep their own desks clear of clutter. The message is loud and clear: this is a place where simplicity is valued and expected. In addition, the open environment is a reflection of the company's extreme transparency. According to Michael White, who works at Square, they take detailed notes at every single meeting, which are posted on the company's internal website for all to read.

I am fortunate to work in several interesting spaces at Stanford University that are designed for very different types of activities. One is the Stanford d.school, where I teach my course on creativity. It is fascinating to watch people as they walk into the d.school for the first time. Without a word from anyone, they know this is a place designed for creative endeavors. There aren't any cubicles or offices. There aren't lecture halls or chalkboards. Instead, the entire space is more like an improvisational theater, where the set changes day to day and often hour to hour to meet the needs of those using it.

One of the reasons I appreciate teaching in the d.school is that we can design the classroom differently for each session, depending upon what we are doing that day. Sometimes the students sit in small groups around tables that easily roll into place; other times the chairs face the front for presentations. Sometimes the students are arranged in pairs; and other times the room is divided into halves or quarters, with different activities happening in each section. All of the furniture, including tables, chairs, whiteboards, and foam cubes (which can be used for sitting or for carving up the space), is designed to move easily and to essentially disappear when not needed, so that the teaching space can be transformed almost instantly, sometimes several times during one class session. The room is always stocked with an endless array of prototyping materials, so anyone can quickly mock up an idea. In addition, there is a video studio where students can make movies that tell the story of their projects. And the space is filled with wonderful artifacts from past projects as inspiration.

This is not accidental. Tremendous thought went into designing a space that is optimized for creative problem solving. A "space team" at the d.school is led by Scott Doorley and Scott Witthoft, who are always evaluating the d.school environment and experimenting with new ideas. For example, recently one of the lead instructors at the d.school was sitting in the reception area. I greeted her and asked what she was doing. She told me that the space team was redesigning the experience people have when they enter the d.school. They wanted to make that experience as positive and reflective of the spirit of the school as possible. When I came by the next day, the entire reception area was changed—they were trying out a brand-new arrangement. The d.school team knows that space plays a huge role in people's experience, and they go to great lengths to find a way to build spaces that create the response they want to evoke. Scott Doorley and Scott Witthoft have captured what they've learned from their extensive experimenting with space in a new book called *Make Space: How to Set the Stage for Creative Collaboration.*[1]

Experimentation with space happens all the time at the design firm IDEO. Few things are bolted down, and people are always rearranging the space. When I met with Dennis Boyle, a partner in the firm, we sat inside an old van that is parked in the middle of the office. This started as a joke years ago. A colleague left for vacation and came back to find his office moved into the back of a transformed van, which was set right in the middle of the building. He used it for several months, after which it was turned into a meeting room that anyone can use. This type of playful experimentation with space happens all the time. When employees leave for a few weeks, they can be pretty sure that the space to which they return will be redesigned. Dennis listed dozens of examples, including turning one office into a boat while someone was on a cruise, turning another into the Eiffel Tower when a fellow designer was vacationing in France, and decking another out with a patriotic celebration in red, white, and blue when a colleague finally earned a green card.

Redecorating offices is far from frivolous. It builds on IDEO's culture of experimenting with space, and this type of experimentation has led to dramatic changes in the ways teams work together. In the early days, thirty years ago, everyone at IDEO had an office. They then moved to an open seating plan where everyone worked in cubicles. Each designer decorated the cubicle to reflect his or her interests. Now they all sit together in project teams, and there are no offices at all. These studio spaces initially evolved around long-term or secret projects. But they proved to be so successful that such "temporary empires," or dedicated studio spaces, now exist all over the company.

The first studio space at IDEO was built in 1995 when Dennis and his team were working with Palm Computing to design the Palm V handheld computer. They found that sitting together had incredible benefits. It increased the energy around the project, enhanced communication between team members, and created a place for all the project artifacts to be in plain sight. In this setup the team was always "in a meeting," making collaboration easier. Proximity is clearly an important variable when designing space. You have a very different relationship with those who work near you than with those who are far away. Studies have shown that if someone works more than fifty feet away, your collaboration and communication is comparable to that of workers who are in different buildings.

By accident, I discovered how powerfully space can contribute to creative problem solving. I was running a simulation game in my creativity class and had divided the room into two ecosystems, so that two completely different games were going on at once. Each ecosystem had four teams, each of which [was] challenged to complete a jigsaw puzzle in the shortest time. For each ecosystem I mixed together three one-hundred-piece jigsaw puzzles and then redistributed one-fourth of the total pieces to each team. Since there were fewer puzzles than there were teams, they had to figure out how to get all the pieces they needed from the other teams in their ecosystem in order to be successful.

One ecosystem was set up on one side of the room with a small table for each team, but no chairs. The other ecosystem was set up on the other side of the room with chairs for each team, but no tables. The first time I did this, the arrangement of the team spaces was not intended as a variable in the simulation, but just a way to differentiate the two ecosystems. However, this ended up being *the key variable* that affected the outcome of the game.

Remarkably, the students in the ecosystem on the side of the room with the chairs (but no tables) almost instantly started to collaborate with one another. Within minutes, the chairs were rearranged into one large circle or pushed aside altogether, as they worked on the puzzles on the floor. They figured out that by working together, they earned the maximum number of points for the game. On the other hand, the teams on the side of the room with tables (but no chairs) all anchored themselves to their respective tables. They did not collaborate at all and thus ended up limiting the number of points each team earned.

Since the tables in the room have wheels and move easily, it would have been a trivial matter to push them together to create one big team. However, in the dozens of times I have run this exercise, this *never* happens. The participants are always shocked when I point this out to them. They think that they have been making well-thought-out strategic decisions and are blown away by the realization that the space literally dictated what they would do.

Essentially, those on the side of the room with the tables see their world as framed by the tables in front of each team, and therefore they don't even consider moving them. A key takeaway from this exercise is that space dramatically affects team dynamics and creativity. The participants never imagined how important this variable would be in changing their behavior. The space told a powerful story, and each team dutifully placed itself inside that narrative. On the side of the room with the tables, the story line is "This table is our kingdom. It is up to us to build and protect it." On the side of the room with the chairs, the story line is "Our world is very flexible. With little effort we can reorganize the way we work together."

No variable should be overlooked when designing a creative space, including the color of the walls or the music played in the background. Recent studies suggest that red walls help you focus your attention, while blue walls foster creative thinking. The explanation is that blue conjures up images of the sky and thus opens up your mind. This is consistent with the finding that people have more expansive ideas when outside or in spaces with high ceilings. Architects talk about the importance of inaccessible spaces inside a building. These are spaces that you can see but cannot access. Even though you can't touch the ceiling, you are profoundly affected by its height. Consider the fact that traditional churches and concert halls usually have extremely high ceilings. They are designed to encourage lofty thoughts and feelings.

We are also influenced not just by what is in our space, but by what we see outside our windows. Whether you are looking at a wall of buildings or an expanse of trees dramatically influences how you feel. A 1984 study shows that hospital patients recover at different rates depending on the view outside their window. Researchers at a suburban Pennsylvania hospital found that twenty-three surgical patients who had rooms with windows that looked out on a natural scene had significantly shorter postoperative hospital stays and took fewer painkillers than twenty-three similar patients who were in rooms with windows that faced a building.[2]

Ambient sound also has a huge impact on how we feel. In fact, our entire life has a sound track, just like a movie. If you change the sound track, the feeling of the scene changes dramatically. Ori Brafman, the coauthor of *Click,* provided a provocative example in a lecture he gave at Stanford.[3] He showed a short video of someone skiing down a startlingly steep mountain with pounding rock music in the background. The skier's experience looks terrifying and exhilarating. Ori then played the same video clip again with melodic classical music in the background. The experience was instantly transformed. Now the skier appeared to be floating down the cliffs in a calm and meditative manner. The sound track was a primary character in the video cueing us to feel either exhilarated or serene.

I tried a similar experiment by using a classic scene from the movie *Rocky* in which Rocky Balboa is training for a big fight. The original score has bold music that foreshadows Rocky's future triumph, winning against all odds. I created a new version in which the same training scenes are accompanied by a slow, sad version of the same music. This caused the mood to shift 180 degrees. Rocky looks like a doomed failure rather than a hero with the melancholy music. His winces of pain look like fatal flaws rather than signs of strength and endurance. Of course, this tool is used in every movie or TV program we watch. The laugh tracks in comedies cue us when something is supposed to be funny, just as ominous music alerts us to impending danger in horror films.

Sound tracks don't influence only how we feel, but also our sense of taste. A study by Adrian North, in the United Kingdom, demonstrated that the way we experience wine changes significantly depending on the music in the background. In this study, participants were given both red and white wine and were asked to fill out a survey about their taste. The background music was different in each tasting. The selected music could be described as heavy, subtle and refined, light and refreshing, or mellow and soft. The survey results showed that subjects' experience of the wine matched the music in the background. In effect, the background music literally changed the taste of the wine![4]

Ewan McIntosh, who is an international expert on learning and technology, spends considerable time thinking about learning spaces. He describes seven different types of spaces that can exist in both the physical and the online world. Based upon prior work by Matt Locke, Ewan describes how different types of spaces dramatically change how we interact with one another.[5] If you are hoping to create spaces optimized for innovation, it is helpful to consider all of these types of spaces.

The first type of space is "private space." We each need to find places where we can be by ourselves for some part of the day. If we aren't given these spaces explicitly, in the form of private offices, we create them ourselves. For some people, this involves finding a quiet spot for a private phone call. For kids in school, it might mean carving out a small space on a public bench and pulling their knees up, thus creating a private space for text messaging with their friends.

Second are "group spaces," where small teams of people can work together. This might seem obvious, but so many classrooms and offices are designed to prevent this type of team interaction. We sit in rows in a lecture hall or are isolated from one another at desks that don't move or in offices that are outfitted with small cubicles. Group spaces are important, because they provide the opportunity for intense collaboration. In a home, this is often the kitchen table, where everyone gathers to share what is going on and to discuss topics of mutual interest.

Third, "publishing spaces" are designed to showcase what is going on. These occur in both the physical and the virtual world. In the virtual world publishing takes place on websites where we share our photos and videos that reflect what we have done and where we have been. In the physical world, the items displayed in the public rooms of your home, such as artwork, pictures, and souvenirs, tell visitors about you. In addition, your refrigerator and bulletin board, covered with notes and pictures, are prime examples of publishing spaces. In an office, this kind of space is often overlooked by management, leaving it to individuals to fill their cubes or offices with memorabilia. These artifacts serve both as reminders of what has happened and as stimulants for future creative endeavors.

Fourth, "performing spaces" are those where you can either share your ideas or act them out. These spaces stimulate your imagination and help bring ideas to life. They don't have to be permanent spaces, but they should be available when needed. For example, if the furniture can be moved out of the way, any room can be turned into a performance space when it is time to share ideas.

Fifth are "participation spaces." These are essentially places that allow personal engagement with what is going on. For example, Ewan suggests, if you turn a schoolyard into a public garden where students tend the plants, it is transformed from a group space into a participation space. Or if you make employees aware of their energy usage by showing real-time data about how much is being consumed, then their behavior in the space naturally changes. They become participants in the space rather than mere occupants.

The sixth type of space is for "data." This is like a library or database, where we archive information that will be needed later. It isn't necessarily in a public place, but it needs to be easily available, either physically or online. As more and more information becomes available online, we need to consider how that space affects the way we work. In the past, people would pore through reference books in the library to get the material they needed. Now a large percentage of us are plugged into the Web a good part of the day, since that is where we can most readily find the data we need.

Finally, there are "watching spaces," which allow us to passively observe what is happening around us. Sometimes we want or need to be passive observers, watching and listening to what is going on rather than being active participants. By watching we get meaningful information about the activity in our environment, which allows each of us to feel more connected to the organization.

Creative spaces lead to creative work. Pixar, the company behind mind-bendingly creative movies such as *Toy Story* and *Finding Nemo*, provides a terrific example. Large characters from Pixar movies greet you as you enter, and each designer is encouraged to create a space that reflects his or her passions. As a result, there is an office that looks like a gingerbread house, one that is designed like a tiki hut, and another that is a Lego castle. Rest assured, this is not just for fun. There is no way that the designers at Pixar would be able to come up with such innovative products without such a rich and provocative environment.

You don't need to be a hugely successful media studio to have a stimulating space. Many start-up companies adopt this philosophy. Not only does it lead to more creative work, but it also helps attract and retain employees who are eager to work in such an environment. Scribd is a great example. Run by Trip Adler, Scribd is an online publishing platform with a large open office with high ceilings. It has a zip line that runs down the length of the space; a collection of go carts, pogo sticks, NERF guns, skateboards, unicycles, and scooters; a karaoke machine; a pool table; and a pingpong table. Employees who refer a new employee to the company get a plaque next to their "toy" with their name on it. They even invented a new go-cart game called "scracing," a combination of "Scribd" and "racing." Trip says that this new game has pushed the company's creativity to new levels. They certainly don't play all day long, but the playful artifacts and games are reminders that they are encouraged to be creative in all they do.

Despite the importance of space to innovation, it is still just a shell for the people inside. As a result, it is equally important to consider *who* is in your space. Each person in your environment affects the culture and influences the topics that are discussed. This doesn't just apply to the people with whom you work directly, but also to the people you bump into when walking around the building. In fact, the random connections between people in the hallways play a big role in determining what happens in your space. This echoes Rory McDonald's research, on parallel "play" in business. He is studying how adults, just like young children, are deeply influenced by those around them even if they are not actively engaged with one another.

Space is a key factor in each of our habitats, because it clearly communicates what you should and shouldn't be doing. If you live and work in an environment that is stimulating, then your mind is open to fresh, new ideas. If, however, the environment is dull and confining, then your creativity is stifled. Just as Liz Gerber encouraged those in her workshop to do, consider rearranging the furniture, picking up a paintbrush, filling your room with art and artifacts, or even plugging in an electric screwdriver to build a space that enhances creativity.

Space is the stage on which we play out our lives. If you want to be creative, you need to build physical habitats that unlock your imagination.

NOTES

1 Scott Doorley and Scott Witthoft, *Make Space: How to Set the Stage for Creative Collaboration* (Hoboken, NJ: Wiley, 2012).

2 R.S. Ulrich, "View Through a Window May Influence Recovery from Surgery," *Science 224*, no. 4647, (1984): 420–421.

3 Ori Brafman and Rom Brafman, *Click: The Forces Behind How We Fully Engage with People, Work, and Everything We'd Do* (New York: Crown Business, 2010). You can watch a video of Ori Brafman's talk at Stanford at ecorner .stanford.edu.

4 Adrian North, "The Effect of Background Music on the Taste of Wine," *British Journal of Psychology*, September 7, 2011.

5 Ewan McIntosh, "Clicks & Bricks: When Digital, Learning, and Physical Space Meet," October 3, 2010, edu.blogs.com.

Analyze

1. What are the environmental/space differences between a kindergarten classroom and a college classroom? Why? What could/should change?

2. Compare and contrast the workspaces of Jeanne Gang's design firm in Chicago and Square, Inc.'s building in San Francisco. What is the

relationship between form and function? What buildings on your campus demonstrate such a clear relationship between form and function?

3. Why do you suspect this chapter is called "The Table Kingdom"? What point is Seelig making about space?

4. What are the seven types of learning spaces as identified by Ewan McIntosh, an international expert on learning and technology?

Explore

1. Seelig writes, "Studies have shown that if someone works more than fifty feet away, your collaboration and communication is comparable to that of workers who are in different buildings." Get out a tape measure and mark off fifty feet. Now pay attention to the actual distance between your workspace and important things, such as your teacher, the kitchen, your supply room, or the bathroom. List five things you can do to make better use of this fifty-foot rule. Consider following through and actually changing at least one thing on your list.

2. Listen to music while doing homework for an entire week. Change the type of music each day, and pay particular attention to the quality of your work with each type of music. Do you write faster with hard rock? Do you write with more passion during ballads? Do you write with fewer errors with classical music? Make a chart that details your results. Consider referring to it so you can select the best music to maximize your efforts on specific assignments in the future.

3. Write a well-researched essay on a specific work environment, taking care to analyze how space is used and how that contributes (or not) to productivity and effectiveness. Interview people, take photos, people watch, make general observations, and do whatever you need in order to make a thorough argument.

Todd Dewett
"Behold the Magic Graph" and "Long Live the Organizational Deviant"

"Tattoo addict, Harley Davidson nut, and recovering management professor" **Todd Dewett** (1971–) is an entrepreneur and author. His expertise as a leadership and life expert is viewed by millions at Lynda.com. Dewett's clients include TGI Fridays, Cox Media, Emerson, and State Farm. "Behold the Magic Graph" and "Long Live the Organizational Deviant" first appeared on the author's own website.

A t some point you may have heard me mention the Magic Graph. It is a simple but terribly powerful visual thinking aid. I use it to prod professionals into understanding the nature of creativity and innovation. It looks like this:

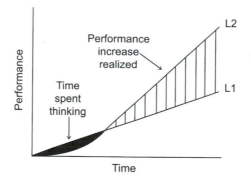

The point is simple. To the extent you wish to be creative and innovate your way to higher performance (your performance, that of your team or organization), you must invest in that little black area. The little black area represents the thinking and talking and experimenting required to move from L1 to L2. Far too often groups and organizations rave on about their love of and need for "outside the box" thinking or "discontinuous innovation." Choose the label you like, but there is no shortage of folks in industry calling for additional creativity (great ideas) and innovation (the process of getting value from ideas).

There is, however, a massive shortage of love for that little black area. Managers of all stripes hate it—and when they catch you hanging out there, they often get mad and react poorly. Too bad. For every great idea there are a few hundred, sometimes a few thousand, bad ideas. Well, not bad really: half-baked, not quite ready, under examined, etc. Fine, but they are not bad. They can't be because they are an integral part of the web of ideas which eventually, once in a while, produces a real zinger that we can all use. The half-baked ideas are in a very real sense the building blocks of innovation. Einstein used thousands of them on his way to $E=MC^2$. That's the way all great innovation happens. There are far fewer Eureka! moments than you'd believe. Innovation is more about the progressive and calculated evolution of a stew of ideas instead of a single Wow! moment. Don't get me wrong, the great moments happen, but ONLY because they are predicated on all the musings and learning moments contained in that little black area.

In fact, my love of the Magic Graph extends well beyond creativity and innovation into the examination of my career. I bet you might find it useful as well. You now sit on L1. Maybe you like it there. Maybe you're happy with the pay, challenge and status. Maybe not. To the extent you are still dreaming about L2, like I often do, you have to get serious fast. What efforts, trials and tribulations, risks, even flat out failures—all hallmarks of the little black area—do you need to seek out and endure in order to discover your own L2? This is a very productive perspective. For example, if you ever find yourself in a series of months (or maybe years . . .) defined by low job satisfaction you have a choice. You can lament your poor luck or you can chalk it up to needing more time spent in the black area—but only if you are willing and able to learn from your time there. What personal habits must you break? Create? What specific person or type of group must you reconnect with or connect with for the first time? What technical skills did you learn you do not have? Love? In general, what did you learn about your overall skills—the ones that shine and the ones that came up a bit short? Identify those things, act on those things, and you are well on your way to life at L2.

Enjoy these half-baked ideas and keep cooking.

Long Live the Organizational Deviant

Organizations don't improve unless a few people take risks. Employees and managers must risk upsetting the status quo (whether that concerns relationships, processes, technologies, or whatever) in order to move the organization forward. Ironically, most people and nearly all systems are wired to resist change. Some will acknowledge the need for change and innovation and espouse their importance. Few, however, are consistently capable of supporting the brave risk takers who actually try things. We need deviance but we hate it.

For years, I have pushed people to embrace creativity, innovation, and change. It is because I respect the personal risk involved that I must also encourage people to consider the inherent danger in supporting change. Most change agents are viewed as deviants. Not by everyone, but by enough people to make the role hazardous.

To some, this idea might seem abstract and difficult to grasp. That's why, while still employed as a professor years ago, I created a small activity designed to help graduate students understand this concept. I gave every member of the class a small bottle of bubble solution and a bubble-blowing wand. The instructions were to take these materials, leave the classroom, and roam as they please throughout the business school building sharing bubbles with others. They were told to blow many bubbles and watch people react. I told them that if they really wanted to impress me, they would enter different classrooms, not just hallways or common areas, and share their bubbles with the other classes that were in session.

What happened next was always predictable—and fun. Students would hesitate as they left my classroom. Most would walk the halls looking for unsuspecting people with whom they might share a few bubbles. A few brave souls would open the doors to other classrooms and walk in unannounced and begin blowing bubbles.

For those who ventured into classrooms, about one third of the professors in charge of the other classrooms would chuckle and tolerate my students, knowing it was I who charged them with this task. One third of the instructors would politely ask them to leave, not really amused or supportive, but not upset either. Finally, one third would explode with anger!

My favorite example of this last category involved a particularly high-strung economics instructor. When my students entered, she immediately raised her voice and asked them what they were doing.

They replied, "Blowing bubbles."

She quickly approached them. "Why are you in my classroom?"

"We wanted to share bubbles," they stated.

Her class laughed. She did not. "Did someone tell you to do this?" she demanded.

"Dr. Dewett," they responded.

Then she went nuclear. "You tell Dr. Dewett this is not funny. It is downright disrespectful and unacceptable behavior. How dare he? This is my time, not his. You don't see me bothering your class, do you? Now get out!"

A few minutes later all of my students had returned and taken their seats. During the activity debrief I asked the students to share their experiences with the class. A few weren't noteworthy. A few reported receiving very strange looks. Several reported observers with disapproving facial expressions. Others reported being stared at as if they were crazy. Three students then told us about the economics instructor. Most of my class thought that her reaction was hilarious. A minority were worried I might get in trouble.

Yes, it is a silly task, but everyone got the point. You never know how others will react to your deviance. Rock the status quo, even a tiny bit, and you face a risk. In the case of the economics instructor, I received a long e-mail late that night questioning my intellectual ability and educational methods. She informed me that I was being put on notice and that she was informing her department chair with a recommendation to speak to my department chair about my behavior. I, of course, brought the e-mail to the next class and read it to the students.

It had a strong impact. In about 10 seconds, with only a small number of bubbles, this person's world was shattered and she went ballistic. Was I wrong for creating that situation? Who knows—maybe. Were the students rude for interrupting her class? Yes, though their offense was quite small.

After I read the e-mail to the class, I said, "Imagine if I had instigated a big change. Realize that when you try to shake things up in the workplace, not just here in class, the reaction can be very strong. People don't feel the righteousness of your pursuit of creativity and innovation. They feel confusion and anger that you've moved some of the sand in their sandbox." Unfortunately, if you speak up and offer ideas for change—ones that might offer great value—that doesn't mean people will applaud. In fact, sometimes they'll kick you out of the room and send you nasty emails.

Change agents are special people. Most think it's because they have or support good ideas, or because they work hard, or maybe because they want to help. Those things are true, but the real reason they are special is because they continue to champion change in the face of an endless array of people who want to stop them. Your call, play it safe or blow some bubbles.

Analyze

1. Why are most people stuck in L1? What does one need to do in order to attain the L2 curve?
2. Dewett writes, "I must also encourage people to consider the inherent danger in supporting change. Most change agents are viewed as deviants." What dangers is Dewett talking about? Why is being a deviant hazardous?
3. What lessons can be taken from the bubble-blowing exercises and the angry economics professor?
4. "Change agents are special people," writes Dewett. Why does he think that? What do they do that others do not?

Explore

1. Seeing a visual representation of something often reveals relationships, challenge, and connections that can go unnoticed otherwise. Dewett calls his graph the Magic Graph for that reason. Create your own Magic Graph, only don't make a graph—make some other type of visual aid to help people understand the nature of creativity and innovation. Make a pie chart. Make a timeline. Make something visual and interesting and unexpected. Share your results with classmates and compare how they tackled this same Magic Graph challenge.
2. Dewett writes that "There are far fewer Eureka! moments than you'd believe. Innovation is more about the progressive and calculated evolution of a stew of ideas instead of a single Wow! moment." Discuss this idea with classmates. Do you have counterexamples from your own experiences? From this book?
3. Write a letter to your younger self, explaining how to succeed at work or school beyond what you've been able to on your own so far. Use the L1 or L2 terminology, if you want, or use your own terms and ideas. Give yourself the creative ammunition to hit the bull's-eye every time.
4. In Chapter 4 (Collaboration and Creativity), you'll find the "Collaboration in the Sandbox" piece. In what way do these selections inform each other, beyond both referring to sandboxes? Does it matter which order you read them in? Would you expect Dewett and his bubble-blowing to get along famously with Capodagli and Jackson, or would there likely be trouble? Why?

Tom Fishburne
"The 8 Types of Bad Creative Critics"

Tom Fishburne (1968–) is the founder and CEO of Marketoon Studios, a content marketing company. "I learned how to draw cartoons at Harvard Business School by doodling on the backs of business cards and publishing in the school paper and posting online in 2000. My cartoons have grown by word of mouth to reach 100,000 marketers every week and have been featured in the *Wall Street Journal, Fast Company,* and the *New York Times.*"

Analyze

1. Why are these all examples of "bad" creative critics? What would be an example of a good creative critic?
2. What's so wrong with The Blender?
3. What nontextual elements add to the effectiveness of this comic?

Explore

1. If there were a ninth type of bad creative critic, what would this person be called? What would he or she do? Draw that extra panel for this comic and create the appropriate text, too.

2. Which of these bad creative critics do you have the most experience with? Share your experiences with the class and compare them with what other classmates have to offer. As a group, decide which is the worst of the bad creative critics. And which is the "best"?

3. Consider the following by Emmy-winning actress Tyne Daly: "A critic is someone who never actually goes to the battle, yet who afterwards comes out shooting the wounded." Now write your own (amusing or not) comparison/definition of a critic.

Forging Connections

1. Which of the following quotations seems most in alignment with this chapter's readings? Why? Discuss your observations and thoughts with a classmate.

   a. "I think *Dilbert* will remain popular as long as employees are frustrated and they fear the consequences of complaining too loudly. *Dilbert* is the designated voice of discontent for the workplace. I never planned it that way. It just happened."—Scott Adams

   b. "Good intentions can often lead to unintended consequences. It is hard to image a law intended for the workforce known to Henry Ford can serve the needs of a workplace shaped by the innovations of Bill Gates."—Tim Walberg, US Congressman

   c. "On an average day, we allow ourselves the fiction that we own a piece of our workplace. That's part of what it takes to get the job done. Deeper down, we know it's all on loan."—Mary Schmich, Pulitzer Prize–winning journalist

2. Search online for "workplace" and find high-impact images that demonstrate the types of workplace environments, both good and bad, mentioned in this chapter. Endeavor to select images that have emotional depth or complexity to them versus being overly straightforward. Using ideas from the readings, create captions for these images that, taken together, create a type of multimedia experience that mirrors or responds thoughtfully to the content of this chapter.

Looking Further

1. Think broadly about what a workplace is, what it's intended to be. Now write a description of what the workplace of tomorrow will look like. Which of the readings offer clues on what this will be? Consider sketching, drawing, or making a collage to complement your written description.

2. Some companies are becoming more open to alternative ways of thinking about work and the workplace. Best Buy started a pilot program that allowed workers to show up for work when they wanted so long as they accomplished specific previously agreed-upon tasks and goals. This type of arrangement is known as ROWE (Results-Only Work Environment). Research what other companies are doing that have tried this idea and write up a case study that includes written analysis of ROWE's effectiveness. (A good place to start your research is www.gorowe.com.)

Collaboration and Creativity

4

"Few things in life are less efficient than a group of people trying to write a sentence. The advantage of this method is that you end up with something for which you will not be personally blamed."
—Scott Adams, American cartoonist

On some level, we understand that two—or more—heads are likely better than one. But when we say that, we're typically thinking about coming up with lyrics from a long-forgotten 1980s song, struggling through *The New York Times* crossword puzzle, or trying to tease out the meaning of a confusing office memo from the boss. Collaboration is far more than that, though. It's letting ideas spark off the ideas of others and being okay with things going in unexpected directions. It's choosing to gang up on a problem or

challenge, versus ganging up on each other. It's agreeing to put every resource in the best place possible. It's letting technology—Web-based
programs to file sharing to e-mail/video conferencing—bring people
together.

Phil Jackson, the winningest coach in NBA history, believes that "the
strength of the team is each individual member. The strength of each individual member is the team." Forgive him for being a little bit like the enigmatic Mr. Miyagi from the movie *The Karate Kid*—Jackson is deeply
interested in Zen and Eastern thinking. But his point is valid enough. If
everyone works together, there's an equal sense of participation. There's a
strong sense of purpose. There's access to many strengths and skills. It's
teamwork and team effort taken to a higher level. And that's good for everyone involved, whether your team is composed of classmates, coworkers,
or virtual strangers.

Perhaps the American philanthropist Andrew Carnegie said it best:
"Teamwork is the ability to work together toward a common vision. The
ability to direct individual accomplishments toward organizational objectives. It is the fuel that allows common people to attain uncommon results."
Or maybe Helen Keller nails it for you: "Alone we can do so little; together
we can do so much."

Regardless, enjoy what these experts have to say on collaboration and
creativity and their increasingly vital role in today's world.

Joshua Wolf Shenk
"The Power of Two"

Joshua Wolf Shenk (1971–) is a curator, essayist, and author whose books
include *Powers of Two: How Relationships Drive Creativity* and *Lincoln's
Melancholy*, which was named one of the best books of 2005 by *The New
York Times*, *The Washington Post*, and *The Atlanta Journal-Constitution*. He
is a founding advisor to The Moth and played a lead role in developing *The*

Moth Radio Hour, now on nearly four hundred stations worldwide. "The Power of Two" first appeared in the July/August 2014 issue of *The Atlantic.*

In the fall of 1966, during a stretch of nine weeks away from the Beatles, John Lennon wrote a song. He was in rural Spain at the time, on the set of a movie called *How I Won the War,* but the lyrics cast back to an icon of his boyhood in Liverpool: the Strawberry Field children's home, whose sprawling grounds he'd often explored with his gang and visited with his Aunt Mimi. In late November, the Beatles began work on the song at EMI Studios, on Abbey Road in London. After four weeks and scores of session hours, the band had a final cut of "Strawberry Fields Forever." That was December 22.

On December 29, Paul McCartney brought in a song that took listeners back to another icon of Liverpool: Penny Lane, a traffic roundabout and popular meeting spot near his home. This sort of call-and-response was no anomaly. He and John, Paul said later, had a habit of "answering" each other's songs. "He'd write 'Strawberry Fields,'" Paul explained. "I'd go away and write 'Penny Lane' . . . to compete with each other. But it was very friendly competition."

It's a famous anecdote. Paul, of course, was stressing the collaborative nature of his partnership with John (he went on to note that their competition made them "better and better all the time"). But in this vignette, as in so many from the Beatles years, it's easy to get distracted by the idea of John and Paul composing independently. The notion that the two need to be understood as individual creators, in fact, has become the contemporary "smart" take on them. "Although most of the songs on any given Beatles album are usually credited to the Lennon–McCartney songwriting team," Wikipedia declares, "that description is often misleading." Entries on the site about individual Beatles songs take care to assert their "true" author. Even the superb rock critic Greg Kot once succumbed to this folly. John and Paul "shared songwriting credits but little else," he wrote in 1990, "and their 'partnership' was more of a competition than a collaboration."

Kot made that observation in a review of *Beatlesongs,* by William J. Dowlding—a high-water mark of absurdity in the analysis of Lennon–McCartney. Dowlding actually tried to quantify their distinct contributions, giving 84.55 credits to John—"the winner," he declared—and 73.65 to Paul. (His tally also included 22.15 credits for George Harrison, 2.7 for

Ringo Starr, and 0.45 for Yoko Ono. For a few lines in the song "Julia," Dowlding gave 0.05 credits to the Lebanese poet Kahlil Gibran.)

For centuries, the myth of the lone genius has towered over us, its shadow obscuring the way creative work really gets done. The attempts to pick apart the Lennon–McCartney partnership reveal just how misleading that myth can be, because John and Paul were so obviously more creative as a pair than as individuals, even if at times they appeared to work in opposition to each other. The lone-genius myth prevents us from grappling with a series of paradoxes about creative pairs: that distance doesn't impede intimacy, and is often a crucial ingredient of it; that competition and collaboration are often entwined. Only when we explore this terrain can we grasp how such pairs as Steve Jobs and Steve Wozniak, William and Dorothy Wordsworth, and Martin Luther King Jr. and Ralph Abernathy all managed to do such creative work. The essence of their achievements, it turns out, was relational. If that seems far-fetched, it's because our cultural obsession with the individual has obscured the power of the creative pair.

John and Paul epitomize this power. Geoff Emerick—who served as the principal engineer for EMI on *Revolver, Sgt. Pepper's Lonely Hearts Club Band*, some of *The White Album*, and *Abbey Road*—recognized from the outset that the two formed a single creative being. "Even from the earliest days," he wrote in his memoir, *Here, There and Everywhere*, "I always felt that the artist was John Lennon and Paul McCartney, not the Beatles."

One reason it's so tempting to try to cleave John and Paul apart is that the distinctions between them were so stark. Observing the pair through the control-room glass at Abbey Road's Studio Two, Emerick was fascinated by their odd-couple quality:

> Paul was meticulous and organized: he always carried a notebook around with him, in which he methodically wrote down lyrics and chord changes in his neat handwriting. In contrast, John seemed to live in chaos: he was constantly searching for scraps of paper that he'd hurriedly scribbled ideas on. Paul was a natural communicator; John couldn't articulate his ideas well. Paul was the diplomat; John was the agitator. Paul was soft-spoken and almost unfailingly polite; John could be a right loudmouth and quite rude. Paul was willing to put in long hours to get a part right; John was impatient, always ready to move on to the next thing. Paul usually knew exactly what he wanted and would often take offense at criticism;

John was much more thick-skinned and was open to hearing what others had to say. In fact, unless he felt especially strongly about something, he was usually amenable to change.

The diplomat and the agitator. The neatnik and the whirling dervish. Spending time with Paul and John, one couldn't help but be struck by these sorts of differences. "John needed Paul's attention to detail and persistence," Cynthia Lennon, John's first wife, said. "Paul needed John's anarchic, lateral thinking."

Paul and John seemed to be almost archetypal embodiments of order and disorder. The ancient Greeks gave form to these two sides of human nature in Apollo, who stood for the rational and the self-disciplined, and Dionysus, who represented the spontaneous and the emotional. Friedrich Nietzsche proposed that the interaction of the Apollonian and the Dionysian was the foundation of creative work, and modern creativity research has confirmed this insight, revealing the key relationship between breaking and making, challenging and refining, disrupting and organizing.

John was the iconoclast. In early live shows, he would fall into the background, let Paul charm the audience, and then twist up his face, adopt a hunchback pose, and play dissonant chords. Sometimes, he deliberately kept his guitar slightly out of tune, which contributed to what the composer Richard Danielpour calls "that raw, raunchy sound." He was difficult with the press, at times even impossible. In the studio, he clamored constantly to do things differently. He wanted to be hung from the ceiling and swung around the mic. He wanted to be recorded from *behind*.

While John broke form, Paul looked to make it. He was the band's de facto musical director in the studio and, outside, its relentless champion. "Anything you promote, there's a game that you either play or you don't play," he said. "I decided very early on that I was very ambitious and I wanted to play." Among the Beatles, he said, he was the one who would "sit the press down and say, 'Hello, how are you? Do you want a drink?,' and make them comfortable."

Distinctions are a good way to introduce ourselves to a creative pair. But what matters is how the parts come together. So it's not right to focus on how John insulted reporters while Paul charmed them. John was able to insult reporters *because* Paul charmed them. Their music emerged in a similar way, with single strands twisting into a mutually strengthening double helix.

The work John initiated tended to be sour and weary, whereas Paul's tended to the bright and naive. The magic came from interaction. Consider the home demo for "Help!"—an emotionally raw, aggressively confessional song John wrote while in the throes of the sort of depression that he said made him want "to jump out the window, you know." The original had a slow, plain piano tune, and feels like the moan of the blues. When Paul heard it, he suggested a countermelody, a lighthearted harmony to be sung behind the principal lyric—and this fundamentally changed its nature. It's not incidental that in the lyrics John pleaded for "somebody . . . not just anybody." He knew he was at risk of floating away, and Paul helped put his feet back on the ground.

And John knocked Paul off his, snorting at his bromides (as with Paul's original "She was just seventeen / Never been a beauty queen") and batting against his sweet, optimistic lyrics, as in the song "Getting Better." "I was sitting there doing 'Getting better all the time,'" Paul remembered, "and John just said, in his laconic way, 'It couldn't get no worse.' And I thought, *Oh, brilliant! This is exactly why I love writing with John.*"

John lived most of his youth in his Aunt Mimi's house, a prim, stuffy place, protected—or so Mimi thought—from the wreckage of his charming but dissolute parents. Even as a boy, John was a mischief-maker, a gang leader. When he discovered music, he wanted to get his gang onstage. He insisted that his best friend, Pete Shotton, join his band, the Quarry Men, even though Pete protested that he could hardly play. John didn't mind. He could hardly play himself.

Paul, by contrast, came from a warm, close-knit family. Music occupied a central place in the McCartney home, in the form of the upright piano that dominated the tiny living room. Music for Paul was family sing-alongs and brass-band concerts with his dad. When he began to write songs, Paul wasn't thinking about rock and roll. He wanted to write for Sinatra.

John's rebellious impulse took him in dangerous directions. By the time he met Paul, his boyhood pranks had progressed to shoplifting. He said later that had he not wound up in a truly outstanding band—which is to say, had he not met Paul—he probably would have ended up like his father, a likable ne'er-do-well jostling between odd jobs and petty crime.

Paul, for his part, might have ended up teaching, or doing some other job for which he could rely on his smarts and still live inside his own mind. He was studied and careful. Even his moments of abandon (his imitations of Little Richard, say) were conducted more or less by the book. John was

20 months older—a world apart for a teenager. He was the badass older brother Paul never had. For John, Paul was a studious and charming sidekick who could do something rare: keep up with him.

Alongside their many differences, John and Paul shared uncannily similar musical tastes and drives to perform. The chemistry between them was immediate. A member of John's band who watched them on the day they met later recalled that they "circled each other like cats."

The myth is that John and Paul were enmeshed creatively in the early 1960s but that they separated after they stopped touring, in 1966. It's true that there was a new distance between them—in time spent apart, in influences, and in actual geography. Paul took up residence in London, and John moved with his wife to the tony suburbs. John plunged into LSD (he reckoned he "must have had a thousand trips"), but Paul said he "wasn't that keen on getting that weird," and dosed just a handful of times (his trip was making himself the boy king of swinging London, hobnobbing with everyone from the artist Andy Warhol to the filmmaker Michelangelo Antonioni).

But distance doesn't necessarily hinder creativity; often, it drives a pair forward. We flourish with an ongoing stream of new influences, new ideas. It's also true that we're affected by not just what people explicitly say to us, or their overt contributions to our work, but also the way they get in our heads. One sure way this happens is through competition—or what's known in business as "co-opetition," whereby two entities at once oppose and support each other. George Martin, the Beatles' longtime producer, noticed this element in John and Paul's relationship. "Imagine two people pulling on a rope, smiling at each other and pulling all the time with all their might," he said. "The tension between the two of them made for the bond."

That tension took on varying forms during the course of the Lennon–McCartney partnership. The two spun time and again through the same cycle. As the alpha, John would establish his dominance, and then Paul, like a canny prime minister under a tempestuous king, would gradually assert himself and take charge—until John, often suddenly, struck back.

This dynamic helped give birth to the two albums that represent the best of John and Paul's work together: *Sgt. Pepper's Lonely Hearts Club Band* and *The White Album*. In popular lore, *Sgt. Pepper* represents the zenith of the partnership ("It was a peak," John said), while *The White Album* represents its nadir ("the tension album," Paul called it). But the truth is that the two albums were born of the same cycle, just at different points in it.

In the *Sgt. Pepper* days, John largely let Paul run the show, during exacting and exhaustive studio sessions that stretched over many hundreds of hours, and during copious writing sessions, when John and Paul together shaped every song on the album. After seeing a drawing made by his son Julian, John initiated "Lucy in the Sky with Diamonds." He showed the picture to Paul, and the two of them saw an opportunity to flesh out the song together by playing around with *Alice in Wonderland*–style imagery. "I offered *cellophane flowers* and *newspaper taxis*," Paul said, "and John replied with *kaleidoscope eyes*... We traded words off each other, as we always did." Perhaps most famously, the two brought "A Day in the Life" into being by fusing songs they had initiated separately.

But if John was largely compliant during *Sgt. Pepper*, he soon reasserted his dominance. In the spring of 1968—after a visit to the ashram of the Maharishi Mahesh Yogi, in India, during which John and Paul whiled away many hours with their acoustic guitars and wrote dozens of songs— the Beatles were back in the studio, recording *The White Album*. Gone was the dreamy John. He was now aggressive, even hostile. He called *Sgt. Pepper* "the biggest load of shit we've ever done." Watching him in action during *The White Album*'s first session, Geoff Emerick was astonished. By the end of the session, he wrote, John was "almost psychotic."

John described the change differently. "I was again becoming as creative and dominating as I had been in the early days," he said, "after lying fallow for a couple of years."

The stock Beatles narrative attributes this change in John to the arrival in his life—and in the recording studio—of Yoko Ono. Yoko is also often blamed for breaking up the band, of course. But the crucial point is how John used Yoko to reassert his power. It was an alpha move—his way of reminding the others that he could summarily add a member to the band, just as he had decided to ask Paul to join the Quarry Men 11 years earlier. Once Yoko was on the scene, she naturally began to exert her own influence, and over time she did become a wedge between John and Paul. But at the start, despite feeling wounded by the change in John, Paul tried determinedly to make things work, by resorting to his signature style: a blend of accommodation and assertion. He saw that John was going too far, but understood that this was John's way. This had happened before; he hoped that the moment would pass, that they could get back to work.

Despite the tension—*because of* the tension—the work was magnificent. Though *The White Album* recording sessions were often tense and unpleasant (Emerick disliked them so much that he flat-out quit), they yielded an album that is among the best in music history. The album is notable for a number of role-raiding songs, with John doing the sort of ballads associated with Paul ("Julia" and "Goodnight"), and Paul drenching himself in the noise and aggression usually associated with John ("Helter Skelter," "Why Don't We Do It in the Road"). No matter how thick the tension got, it kept serving a creative purpose. At one point, maddened by endless takes of a swooning "Ob-La-Di, Ob-La-Da," John left the studio in a huff—only to return later that night, sit down at the piano, and bang out a much faster version of the song, which would become the recorded version. John and Paul also continued to answer each other's songs. On June 4, 1968, for example, John arrived at a working version of "Revolution 1," his anthem about the political struggles of the 1960s, and a week later Paul brought "Blackbird" to the studio— his statement, he said, about the civil-rights struggles in the American South. John and Paul answered each other in their romantic lives, too. Just after John brought Yoko into the studio, Paul brought in a girlfriend. And only eight days after Paul married Linda Eastman, in March 1969, John married Yoko.

Instability within a creative duo can be immensely productive, but only if sufficient support exists around it. For years John and Paul had that support, but in the late 1960s it began to fall apart. In 1967, Brian Epstein, the band's manager, died of a drug overdose, and the group failed to replace him. George Harrison, for his part, began to buck the junior role he had long been forced to play.

Still, when John and Paul devoted themselves to their music, all seemed well. At their last live performance, the iconic concert on the rooftop of the Apple Corps building, in January 1969, they assumed the positions they'd taken for 12 years: John stage left, Paul stage right, both looking out into the crowd—or, in this case, the surrounding rooftops—but able to turn in an instant to see each other. George stood to their left, facing both of them. During "Don't Let Me Down," John forgot the words to the third verse and went into a nonsense refrain, pure gibberish, but then, literally without missing a beat, he and Paul turned to each other and picked up with the correct lyrics as though nothing had happened. John beamed. Paul bobbed his head up and down in primal affirmation.

It's hard to find a better illustration of what the marriage expert John Gottman calls "repair"—a return to the strength of a partnership that tempers the effects of its weaknesses. There were other examples as the months of high tension wore on. In April 1969, John and Paul recorded the vocals for "You Know My Name (Look Up the Number)," a fantastically weird B side that Paul has said is probably his favorite Beatles track "just because it's so insane." The same month, John rushed to Paul's doorstep with a song he'd written, "The Ballad of John and Yoko." George and Ringo were unavailable, so John and Paul cut the song themselves in one long day, with John on guitar and lead vocal, and Paul on bass, drums, piano, maracas, and harmony vocals.

What ultimately brought their work together to a halt was not creative disagreements but business ones. During his power grab, John was sweet-talked by a canny, dubious manager named Allen Klein, with whom he promptly signed. George and Ringo followed—pure primate politics there. But Paul would not.

And so legend has it that the Beatles broke irrevocably apart. Except that they never really did.

It's tempting to think that a partnership ends like some scene in an opera, where two people come to dramatic conflict, sing emotionally in each other's faces, and decide to separate, weeping. But more often a split happens like it does in one of those country songs about a person leaving home and never coming back, in which no one—not the one who left, not the one who was left, not the listener—really knows why.

On April 10, 1970, a headline filled two-thirds of the front page of Britain's *Daily Mirror*. "PAUL IS QUITTING THE BEATLES" it read, with smaller type above: "Lennon–McCartney song team splits up." The story cited an interview that Paul had just distributed to the press, to accompany the release of his first solo album. The interview included the following exchanges:

Q: Are you planning a new album or single with the Beatles?

A: No.

. . .

Q: Do you foresee a time when Lennon–McCartney becomes an active songwriting partnership again?

A: No.

With those two terse answers, April 10 became fixed in the popular imagination as the day the Beatles—and John and Paul—officially split. Just a few days later, however, Paul insisted the whole business was a "misunderstanding." After he saw headlines announcing the Beatles breakup, he told a journalist, "I thought, *Christ, what have I done now?*. . . I never intended the statement to mean 'Paul McCartney quits Beatles.'"

Indeed, he had already said as much in the same interview:

Q: Is this album a rest away from the Beatles or the start of a solo career?

A: Time will tell. Being a solo album means it's "the start of a solo career..." and not being done with the Beatles means it's just a rest. So it's both.

The previous year, in September, John, too, had suggested a split: he told his bandmates he wanted a "divorce." But five months later, like Paul, he backpedaled, telling the BBC that this divorce might lead to a "rebirth." He would rough Paul up something awful in the years that followed (in his solo song "How Do You Sleep," he described Paul's songwriting as "Muzak to my ears"), but he quickly spun through his fury and returned to calling Paul his "best friend." At what turned out to be his last major public performance, on November 28, 1974, John made clear that he felt pulled in Paul's direction. That night he appeared onstage at an Elton John show at Madison Square Garden. He was so nervous beforehand that he threw up in a toilet backstage.

The crowd went wild when John appeared—so wild, according to one account, that the sprung floors of the Garden began to bounce. He and Elton played two songs together, and then John introduced "I Saw Her Standing There," the third and final song the two would play that evening. "We thought we'd do a number," he told the crowd, "of an old, estranged fiancé of mine called Paul."

As long as John and Paul were both alive, the possibility remained that they might remarry. According to Linda McCartney, during the 1970s Paul was "desperate to work with John again." John retreated from music in the second half of the decade, but in 1980 he and Yoko released *Double Fantasy.* He was murdered on December 8, 1980. Had he lived, who knows what might have happened? Jack Douglas, who produced *Double Fantasy,* said that John was actively planning to team up with Paul the following year.

Analyze

1. In what ways does this article show how misleading the myth of the lone genius is?
2. How is John Lennon described? How is Paul McCartney described?
3. What does the term "co-opetition" mean? How was it evident in the Lennon–McCartney partnership?
4. Despite everyone thinking that the Beatles "broke irrevocably apart" around April 1970, this article claims that it's not really true. Why not?

Explore

1. Listen to at least three songs from *The White Album*. Write a music review of those selections that analyzes the influences you can hear from Lennon and McCartney. Compare your reactions to those of a classmate. Are you hearing Lennon become "almost psychotic"? Where do you hear the neatnik and the whirling dervish, the diplomat and the agitator?
2. Think about your own role in a partnership or collaboration. Are you the one with the notebooks or the one wearing surfer beads? Are you Lennon, McCartney, or someone else entirely? Write a classified ad looking for a creative partner to complement you, the yin to your yang. Be specific or you might end up with Ringo Starr when you dreamed of John Lennon all along.
3. What other artistic 1-2 punches do you admire? Musician David Lee Roth and the band Van Halen? Artists Pablo Picasso and Georges Braque? Norwegian musician Bjork and designer Alexander McQueen? Social media gurus Larry Page and Sergey Brin? What is it about their relationship that makes magic? Make a short list of what each member seems to bring to the table, and what the combination of those parts adds up to. Is it ultimately like the Lennon–McCartney combo or something different? Why?
4. The article ends with this: "Jack Douglas, who produced *Double Fantasy*, said that John was actively planning to team up with Paul the following year," but he was murdered that December. Imagine that he wasn't murdered and the duo teamed up again musically in 1981. Come up with the song list for that album and annotate each one with a short description of the music. Which are mainly Lennon's songs? McCartney's? Do they still have co-opetition?

Keith Sawyer
"Small Sparks"

Dr. R. Keith Sawyer (1960–), "The Creativity Guru," has authored more than thirteen books on creativity and innovation. His research has been featured on CNN, Fox News, *TIME*, *New York Times*, National Public Radio, and other media. Dr. Sawyer is the Morgan Distinguished Professor in Educational Innovations at the University of North Carolina at Chapel Hill. "Small Sparks" is taken from his book *Group Genius*.

In May 1926, in the English department at Oxford University, C. S. Lewis first met J. R. R. Tolkien. Lewis was twenty-eight, Tolkien thirty-four. Both felt like outsiders, in part for reasons of personality—Lewis was generally unimpressed with his colleagues and Tolkien was in a political struggle with them—but also because each man had a hobby that he hid from his illustrious colleagues: writing mythical fiction and poetry. Lewis and Tolkien formed a group with other local scholars, including Lewis's brother, Warner; Hugo Dyson; and Lewis's friends R. E. Havard and Owen Barfield. Lewis came up with the name for the group: the Inklings, a pun that described them not only as writers but also as people who were searching with "vague or half-formed intimations and ideas," as Tolkien wrote. Every Tuesday, they met at the Eagle and Child pub in Oxford to discuss Nordic myths and epics, and they read aloud from their own works in progress.

Another thing made Lewis and Tolkien different from their colleagues: At a time when most Oxford scholars were avowed atheists, they were Christians. Late on the night of September 19, 1931, Lewis, Tolkien, and Dyson walked around the quadrangles until three in the morning and talked about the fine points of the New Testament myth. Tolkien argued that although Christ's death and resurrection was structured as a myth, it had nonetheless happened because God intentionally made events easier for people to understand by causing them to unfold mythically. After this conversation, Lewis became a Christian believer.

Before the Inklings formed, Lewis had written a few unremarkable poems; Tolkien had been privately writing stories about elves and wizards since he was eighteen. Gradually, as trust built within the group, both men began to share their secret writing hobby. Tolkien sent Lewis one of his early unfinished epic poems, and Lewis gave him detailed comments on the stories of Beren and his gnomish allies, the orcs and the Narog. Other members of the group began experimenting with similar mythical fiction. For Lewis, his deepening Christian beliefs led him to explore the mythical nature of Christianity.

The themes that would later appear in each writer's books first emerged during the weekly discussions of the Inklings, and all the group members focused their shared visions in different ways. When a new idea emerged in discussion, the members would return home and draft a chapter capturing the idea; then they would take turns reading their drafts aloud at the next meeting, and listen to critical suggestions from the others. Tolkien's own lens on the circle resulted in *The Hobbit* and the three-volume *The Lord of the Rings*, an epic tale of elves, wizards, dragons, and hobbits. Lewis's lens resulted in *The Chronicles of Narnia*. Without the creative circle, these works might not exist, stories that today have been read by millions—and now, seen on the big screen.

Our image of the writer is one of solitude and inner inspiration. But *The Lord of the Rings* and *The Chronicles of Narnia* were not solo works, authored by lone geniuses; they unfolded in a collaborative circle. Tolkien and Lewis aren't the only writers who tap into the power of collaboration. T. S. Eliot's most famous poem, *The Waste Land*, was heavily edited by both Ezra Pound and Eliot's wife; both of them scratched out line after line and wrote in ideas for new text. The final published version was half the length of Eliot's original.

Even such a solitary act as writing has its origins in collaboration. How did the Inklings transform C. S. Lewis from a mediocre part-time poet into a famous novelist and channel Tolkien's mythical ideas into a coherent narrative? How did Eliot and Pound work together to produce what is now considered the most important modernist English poem? To answer these questions, we need to know more about what psychologists have learned about the creative process.

The First Cash Machine

In January 1976, John Reed was resting on a beach in the Caribbean. Reed was known as the boy wonder of banking, both because he had found success at such a young age—in 1970, when he was thirty-one, he was promoted to senior vice president, the youngest in Citibank's history—and because of his innocent, boyish face. When CEO Walt Wriston first promoted Reed, the directors at Citibank did not believe that this young man could run a $100 million division of eight thousand people. On the beach in 1976, only a few industry insiders would have recognized Reed. He had worked his way up in a distinctly unglamorous part of the bank, the computerized "back room" operations that took care of bookkeeping and customers' records. And the consumer bank—the division he was now in charge of—had always been a money loser and a career dead end; the hot shots worked in investment banking and mortgage lending, or on big deals with corporations and foreign governments. Reed brazenly predicted that within ten years the consumer bank would be Citibank's biggest money-maker. Immediately after his 1970 promotion, Reed and his senior executives started to discuss the untapped potential of two new technologies: automated teller machines and a credit card authorization system that could approve a purchase while the customer waited at the counter.

Reed had a habit of taking a notebook with him everywhere he went, even onto the Caribbean beach. On this day in 1976, it wasn't long before he felt compelled to pull out his notebook and start writing down ideas. As he described it to me in an interview:

> I was on a vacation, and I started out saying, "I'm sitting on a beach thinking about the business," and it went on for thirty pages. And it turned out to be the blueprint. I didn't sit down and say, "I'm gonna write a blueprint," I said, "I'm sitting on the beach thinking," and I sort of thought through the business in a systematic way.

What happened next is still legendary at Citibank: Reed took the notepad back to New York and circulated a memo on March 9, 1976, titled, simply, "Memo from the Beach." These thirty pages turned out to be the blueprint for a new kind of bank, one based on a new technology: a network of street-level cash machines. Today, Reed is known as the person who transformed modern banking with the cash machine, with the idea to market credit cards nationally, and with many other ideas that are today a part of the everyday experience of the American consumer. When Citibank's network of cash machines came online in 1977, they were years ahead of every other New York bank. By 1981, Citibank's share of total

New York deposits had doubled, and it took the other New York banks years to catch up.

Reed's spark came when he was alone, and nowhere near the office. What does this magical moment have to do with collaboration? To see the answer, let's look at Reed's spark a little more closely. First, the cash machine had been invented years before—by Docutel, an automated baggage-handling company, and their Dallas employee Don Wetzel. Second, Citibank wasn't even the first bank to install one: Chemical Bank of New York opened the first cash machine on September 2, 1969, on Long Island, at the Rockville Centre branch at 10 North Village Avenue. Third, in the early 1970s, Citibank had already installed a network of Citicard I machines in all its branches—although these were behind the counters and could be used only by the tellers. Fourth, Reed's idea of a nationwide credit card network had been under discussion since his promotion in 1970. All these ideas occurred over time, and different people and groups contributed to each one. What made Reed's spark of insight so important was that he saw a way to bring many different ideas together—the cash machine, the credit card, the computer, the network—to create a new kind of bank.

Psychologists have discovered that creative sparks are always embedded in a collaborative process, with five basic stages:

1. *Preparation:* This involves a period of working hard, studying the problem, and talking to everyone else working on it.
2. *Time off:* The team member changes context and engages in other activities—often in conversation with others.
3. *The spark:* During the time off, a solution appears; but that solution is deeply embedded in the knowledge and social interactions of the preparation and time-off phases, and it builds on sparks that others have had.
4. *Selection:* An "Aha!" feeling doesn't always mean the idea is good. Creative people are very good at selecting the best ideas for follow-up, or they collaborate with others in selecting them.
5. *Elaboration:* Working out the idea typically requires a lot of additional ideas. Bringing them all together always requires social interaction and collaboration.

The vision captured in the memo from the beach would have meant nothing without the elaborate efforts of the entire organization; it took

$160 million for Citibank to blanket New York City with ATMs. At a time when credit cards were a high-end specialty product, it took yet more money to mass-market Visa cards. But the investments paid off: Citibank became the dominant consumer bank for the next decade, and Reed's brash 1970s prediction—that the consumer bank would be the profit leader—indeed came true. Reed wrote the memo, but hundreds of people collaborated, both before and after his 1976 vacation, to make it happen.

Bottema's Mirrors

The Hubble space telescope was carried into orbit by the shuttle *Discovery* on April 24, 1990. Hubble cost more than any other NASA spacecraft—even more than the Apollo mission that first put man on the moon. NASA decided to spend the money because every telescope on earth had a critical problem: the tiny molecules of oxygen, nitrogen, and carbon dioxide that make up our life-sustaining atmosphere also deflect light rays coming from distant stars and planets, and a telescope in the vacuum of space would provide a far clearer image. At its heart, the Hubble telescope contained a primary mirror that was less than eight feet across. The primary mirror gathered the light of distant stars and narrowed the image onto a secondary mirror that was one foot across, which then narrowed the image even further and sent it back through a tiny hole in the center of the primary mirror. Just behind the primary mirror was the brain of the telescope: a complex mechanism consisting of motors, electronics, and optics.

A few weeks after the launch, the team of twelve hundred men and women came to a horrible realization: the telescope, now orbiting Earth, had a fatal manufacturing flaw. Either the primary or the secondary mirror had been shaped to the wrong specifications; somehow, no one had noticed, in spite of years of testing. After a June 27 press conference, Senator Barbara Mikulski—who had been one of the telescope's biggest supporters—called it a "techno-turkey." The future of NASA, and of all space exploration, was on the line, because Congress wasn't going to waste billions of dollars again (at least, not on space exploration). NASA needed a creative solution—and to get it, its scientists and engineers followed the five stages of collaborative creativity.

First, the preparation stage. A team of top experts came together in July for a last-ditch effort to fix the problem. In their discussions, they quickly discovered that the flaw had occurred in the testing equipment for the lenses; it had instructed the polishing machine to shape the mirror incorrectly. The good news was that the error was systematic because it had been driven by computers.

The NASA team came up with several ideas: mechanically deforming the primary mirror, overcoating it to alter its shape, installing a corrective lens at the front of the telescope, replacing the secondary mirror. But in the selection stage, the team soon discovered that none of the suggestions would work, each for different technical reasons.

Murk Bottema, an optical expert at Ball Aerospace, then had another spark of insight: to insert a set of ten coin-sized mirrors in the light stream, just behind the tiny hole in the primary mirror. Each mirror would be deformed intentionally so that it became the exact reverse of the deformities in the main mirror. That way, the image would be corrected as the light was reflected to the five different scientific instruments at the edge of the big mirror. This time, in the selection stage, the team ran the numbers and discovered that it was technically possible to shape each tiny mirror so that its reflection would correct for the manufacturing flaw. But there was still one major problem: how could they insert the ten mirrors just behind the main mirror? That spot was a small empty space at the center of the contraption, and the original designers had never thought anyone would ever need to go in there.

Jim Crocker, one of the engineers on the team, had flown to a meeting in Germany, where the team was going to brainstorm about this new problem. Like the other experts, Crocker had been studying the problem around the clock, on his own and in frequent meetings, gathering as much information as possible. On the morning of the meeting, Crocker stepped into the shower in his hotel room. The showerhead in the European-style fixture was mounted on an arrangement of adjustable rods. A tall man, Crocker had to adjust the showerhead, and at that moment the spark came: he realized that the tiny mirrors could be mounted on similar folding arms and then unfolded into the light stream from the side. He later said, "I could see Murk Bottema's mirrors on the showerhead."

But this wasn't the end of the story—after this insight, it still took a long elaboration stage to make it happen. The corrective device had only ten mirrors, but it needed 5,300 parts to make it work. Finally, success! When Hubble's repairs were fully tested in January 1994, it performed even better than expected.

Psychologists understand preparation, selection, and elaboration; those are conscious, rational activities. And they're always deeply social because collaborative groups do the work and make the decisions. But the spark of insight seems uniquely solitary. After all, Crocker had his idea in the shower! And Reed was far from Manhattan, all alone on the beach. As it turns out, even the moment of insight, this most private of moments, depends on creative collaboration. The brain itself is suffused with collaboration, and understanding how individual creativity combines with group genius is the key to realizing creative potential.

Thinking Outside the Box

In the first half of the last century, the Gestalt psychologists studied the "Aha!" moment using what are known as *insight problems*—thought puzzles that require a sudden spark of insight to solve. One of the most famous of these is the nine-dot problem. Take a minute or two to try to solve it before turning to Appendix B for the answer. Even if you remember seeing this problem long ago, you might have trouble remembering the solution.

The Nine-Dots Problem: Connect the nine dots with four connected straight lines without lifting your pencil from the paper.

The Gestalt psychologists were known for the theory that some thoughts and perceptions can't be understood by analyzing their individual components, but have to be understood as complex wholes. These are the psychologists who created those famous illusions—the curvy goblet that suddenly turns into two faces in profile staring at each other, or the face of the haggard old woman who suddenly transforms into a young girl. No one can see both interpretations at the same time, and the transition from seeing one to the other is sudden.

Creative insight seemed to involve a similarly sudden reconfiguration. In 1926, the German Gestaltist Karl Duncker published the first study of creative insight. He began by criticizing the view of the famous American psychologist William James that sudden insights are the result of having a lot of information and being able to make connections between facts.

Instead, Duncker pointed out that some problems are solved suddenly, so fast that no chain of connections can explain the discovery. To prove his argument, Duncker created a series of twenty ingenious puzzles that he claimed couldn't be solved by incremental reasoning. One of Duncker's most famous problems is the x-ray problem:

> Suppose you are a doctor faced with a patient who has a malignant tumor in his stomach. It is impossible to operate on the patient, but unless the tumor is destroyed the patient will die. There is a kind of ray that can be used to destroy the tumor. If the rays reach the tumor all at once at a sufficiently high intensity, the tumor will be destroyed. Unfortunately, at this intensity the healthy tissue that the rays pass through on the way to the tumor will also be destroyed. At lower intensities the rays are harmless to healthy tissue, but they will not affect the tumor, either. What type of procedure might be used to destroy the tumor with the rays, and at the same time avoid destroying the healthy tissue?

If you can't solve this problem, don't feel bad about looking at Appendix B for the answer; of Duncker's forty-two subjects, only two found the solution, and even then only with hints from Duncker.

By asking his subjects to talk aloud as they tried to solve each problem, Duncker was able to identify a series of typical stages. First, you're drawn to an obvious solution, but you quickly realize that it can't work. Yet your mind is already fixated on that solution, and you're blocked from seeing the problem any other way. Prior experience is sometimes part of what leads you to fixate on the incorrect path. Then, suddenly, you overcome the fixation, you reformulate the problem and see the solution, and you experience a flash of insight.

Fixation, incubation, breakthrough. If you wanted evidence that creativity was an internal mental event, different from everyday thought, this is where you'd look. Duncker argued that prior experience doesn't help solve the problem, as it did with Reed and Crocker; it just gets in the way.

Duncker's research was suggestive, but it still couldn't tell us what was happening inside the mind, so we couldn't explore the role played by collaboration. That exploration would have to wait until the 1980s, when two research teams took very different approaches to creative insight, approaches that were not reconciled until just a few years ago.

The first approach was that of Janet Metcalfe, a Canadian psychologist who's now at Columbia University. Metcalfe is an expert in *metacognition*—how people think about their ongoing thoughts. In 1986 and 1987, she published the results of several studies that seemed to confirm the suddenness of insight solutions. First, for comparison, she collected problems that wouldn't require insight: trivia questions, simple algebra problems, and other problems that could be solved incrementally. Then she prepared another set of problems that seemed to require insight, including these two:

1. Imagine that you're a landscape gardener, and your client tells you to plant four trees. But the client wants each tree to be exactly the same distance from each of the other three. How will you do it?
2. Find ten coins. Arrange the ten coins so that you have five rows, with four coins in each row. How will you do it?

Metcalfe presented each of twenty-six volunteers with five insight problems and five non-insight problems. She pressed a mechanical clicker every fifteen seconds and asked participants to make a mark on a special sheet of paper that indicated how close they thought they were to the solution. A mark at the far left meant they were very cold, and a mark at the far right meant they were very hot. The sheet of paper had forty lines, exactly enough for the ten minutes they were allowed to work on the problem. For the algebra and trivia problems, it turned out the subjects felt warmer and warmer right up to the solution; but for the insight problems, they kept feeling cold until, suddenly, they found the solution. These studies strongly suggested that insight was different from more ordinary, incremental problem solving and the constant collaboration that accompanies it.

However, there were unexpected problems with Metcalfe's studies that the second approach would soon reveal. In 1981, Robert Weisberg and Joseph Alba, psychologists at Temple University in Philadelphia, published the first study that used the modern methods of cognitive psychology to analyze what was really going on while people solved Duncker's insight problems. Weisberg was particularly interested in the Gestaltist idea that people have trouble solving these problems because they become fixated on an incorrect solution, or on an assumption that isn't warranted. For example, in the nine-dot problem, people typically assume that the lines have to stay within the box. The nine-dot problem is hard, as the saying goes, because you can't think outside the box.

A Gestaltist would expect that once the fixation is removed, the solution will occur quickly. The Gestaltist term for this is *restructuring*—viewing the situation in a new way that doesn't depend on past experience. In contrast, Weisberg started with the belief that past experience is always the way you solve problems—even insight problems. He believed that these were difficult not because you're blocked by fixation caused by prior experience but because you don't have enough of the right kind of prior experience; that is, experience with going-outside-the-dots puzzles. Most people have a lot of experience with connect-the-dots games, and that's why they start by going from dot to dot. They soon realize that this strategy can't solve the nine-dot problem, but they don't have any experience with other strategies.

Weisberg and Alba wondered what would happen if people were given a hint—if they were told to go outside the boundaries of the square. But when people were stumped, and the researchers gave them the hint, almost everyone stayed stuck. Then they got another hint: the researchers drew the first line of the solution. A few more people were able to get it. When the researchers showed the remaining people the second line of the solution, everyone solved the problem. They concluded that thinking outside the box isn't enough to be creative; you have to know *how* to think outside the box.

What's the best way to learn how to think outside the box? Showing people simple hints didn't help that much—they had to be shown almost half the solution before they could finish the task. Weisberg and Alba decided to try another approach: they trained people to connect the dots in triangles by going outside the triangles. Sure enough, after this training, they did much better on the nine-dot problem. These results bring us back to collaboration—because you always learn *how* to think in social interactions with teachers and peers.

Weisberg and Alba's study suggested that people are more creative later if, instead of just being told the answer, they actually solved a similar problem themselves. Mary Gick decided to test this hypothesis further with two colleagues, Robert Lockhart and Mary Lamon. Here's one of the fifteen insight problems they used:

> A man who lived in a small town married twenty different women of the same town. All are still living and he never divorced a single one of them. Yet, he broke no law. Can you explain?

The solution is that the man is a clergyman. The researchers came up with two types of hints that corresponded to the two hypothesized possibilities.

In the first one, the *declarative form,* they first gave subjects the sentence "It made the clergyman happy to marry several people each week." In the second one—the *puzzle form*—they gave the sentence "The man married several people each week because it made him happy"; then, a few seconds later, they presented the word "clergyman." The puzzle form at first causes the study subjects to form an inappropriate conception—that the man is marrying each woman himself—and then they are given the clue that allows them to reconceptualize. But with the declarative form, they never have to reconceptualize because they don't form an inappropriate conception.

The people who read the declarative form ahead of time didn't do any better than people who were not given a clue; they weren't able to transfer the clue to the new problem. But the people who were given the puzzle version did far better. This study explains Weisberg and Alba's finding; what's happening is, you store information in a different way when you solve a problem than when you passively receive information. If you've eaten only at fast food restaurants all your life, you'd go into any restaurant and seat yourself. But the first time you enter an upscale restaurant, this expectation will fail. The second time you enter a restaurant that has a hostess in attendance, you can easily access your memory of the earlier failure. But if a friend simply says, "Someday you'll learn that not all restaurants are like McDonald's," that won't be stored in memory in the same way.

Experiments like these contradict several Gestaltist beliefs about creativity:

1. *We're blocked from creativity by our past experiences and our unwarranted assumptions.* To the contrary, Weisberg found that eliminating the false assumption only makes the problem slightly easier.
2. *When you break out of your fixation, the solution should come quickly and easily in a spark of insight.* That's not true, either. Instead, the "outside" hint opens up a new problem-solving domain, but that domain also requires expertise and prior experience.
3. *Insight solutions are independent of prior knowledge.* In reality, training in similar problems helps immensely.

Creativity isn't about rejecting convention and forgetting what we know. Instead, it's based on past experience and existing concepts. And the most important past experiences are in social groups filled with collaboration.

Confabulation

If insight isn't sudden—if it uses the same building blocks as other types of thought—how can we explain the many famous stories of significant artworks and ideas that seem to come out of nowhere? The English Romantic poet Samuel Taylor Coleridge said he had sparks of sudden insight all the time. He told the story of how he created his famous poem "Kubla Khan: Or, a Vision in a Dream" (referring to himself in the third person, a style common at that time):

> In the summer of 1797, the Author, then in ill health, had retired to a lonely farm-house between Porlock and Linton, on the Exmoor confines of Somerset and Devonshire. In consequence of a slight indisposition, an anodyne had been prescribed, from the effects of which he fell asleep in his chair at the moment that he was reading the following sentence, or words of the same substance, in "Purchas's Pilgrimage": "Here the Khan Kubla commanded a palace to be built . . ." On awaking he appeared to himself to have a distinct recollection of the whole [poem] and taking his pen, ink, and paper, instantly and eagerly wrote down the lines that are here preserved.

This is a classic version of a spark of insight, and books about creativity report stories like this all the time. The problem is that it's not true. Scholars who've examined Coleridge's notes have discovered that he read many different books that contributed material to the poem. Sometimes, word-for-word phrases from these books appear unmodified in his poem. And early drafts of the poem have been discovered among Coleridge's notes; further, these drafts contain versions of his insight story that describe the insight in very different ways.

Coleridge was known to be fascinated with dreams, and he was famous among his friends for making up stories about how he created his poems. A poem that he claimed to have written on "the Christmas Eve of 1794" in fact took two years to compose. Why would Coleridge lie about how he created his poems? And why does his lie so conveniently fit how we think insight works? If we can't trust what people say, the only way to understand the role of collaboration is to examine insight while it's happening.

In 1931, Norman Maier, a psychologist at the University of Michigan, revisited Duncker's insight problems. To analyze better what actually happened in the mind during the moment of insight, Maier decided to focus closely on one particular problem. In a large room filled with poles, clamps, pliers, extension cords, tables, and chairs, he hung two long ropes from the ceiling, long enough to touch the floor. With one rope next to the wall and the other in the center of the room, the ropes were far enough apart that you couldn't hold on to one and walk over to the other one. He asked each subject to come up with many different ways to tie the ropes together. The first thing they tried was to hold one rope and walk over to the other, but they quickly learned that wouldn't work.

Within ten minutes, most people came up with three solutions: (1) Stretch one rope as far toward the other as possible, tie it to one of the pieces of furniture, and then get the second rope and carry it back. (2) Take the extension cord and use it to lengthen one of the ropes. (3) Hold on to one rope and use the long pole to pull the other rope within reach. Only four in ten people also thought of a fourth solution: tie something heavy to the end of the rope in the center of the room, such as the pair of pliers; start swinging it like a pendulum; and then grab the other rope, walk toward the first, and grab it when it swings within reach.

Maier gave a subtle hint to the 60 percent who didn't think of the fourth solution within ten minutes. He got up and walked over to one of the windows. On the way, he made sure he "accidentally" brushed one of the ropes so that it would start swinging. About a minute after he did that, another 40 percent of the students experienced a sudden spark of insight and came up with the fourth solution.

When Maier asked them later how they had come up with the pendulum idea, only one of them realized it had been Maier's accidental brush. All the rest said that they'd had a sudden moment of insight: "It just dawned on me." One person gave an incredibly elaborate explanation of the idea that had occurred to him: "I thought of the situation of swinging across a river. I had imagery of monkeys swinging from trees. This imagery appeared simultaneously with the solution." When Maier asked specifically whether they had seen the cord swaying when he walked to the window, they remembered his crossing the room, but no one remembered noticing the rope swinging. This is a perfect example of the phenomenon psychologists call *confabulation:* people have no trouble coming up with explanations for their behavior after the fact. They believe they had a solitary insight, but the real story is that a social encounter was responsible for the idea.

In 1996, the psychologists Christian Schunn and Kevin Dunbar performed a similar experiment. For two days, they had biology students come into their lab, and they split the students into two groups. The students in the first group were given a virus problem on the first day. While solving the problem, they learned that viruses are dormant because they're inhibited by controlling enzymes. Students in the second group were given a different problem, one that didn't involve inhibition. On the second day, the researchers gave all the students a genetics problem in which they had to discover how a certain set of genes is controlled, the answer being that the genes are controlled through inhibition.

You won't be surprised to learn that the students who were given the virus problem on the first day were more likely to solve the genetics problem. This phenomenon, in which an earlier stimulus causes related concepts and memories to be more readily accessible to consciousness, is called *priming*. But what you might not guess is that none of the students in the first group realized that the virus problem had helped them solve the genetics problem. When they described how they solved the second problem, only two of the eighty subjects mentioned the first problem. Even when they were asked directly, "Do you see any similarities between yesterday's and today's experiments, and what are they?" the subjects didn't realize they'd been primed to solve the problem. Just like Maier's subjects back in 1931, the students didn't realize that a previous social encounter was responsible for their spark of insight.

In Metcalfe's study, even just fifteen seconds before her subjects found the answer, they all felt very cold. But people often know more than they think they know. Maier's subjects didn't remember that he'd brushed the rope; Schunn and Dunbar's subjects didn't remember the virus problem. In both studies, the subjects' insights were inspired by previous social interaction—they just didn't remember the connection.

We're all a bit like Coleridge: we can't be trusted when we describe how our insights occur. The myth that insight emerges suddenly and unpredictably persists because most people aren't consciously aware of the social and collaborative encounters that lead to their insights.

How Insights Emerge

The studies described above were groundbreaking because for the first time they demonstrated that Gestaltist ideas about creative insight are wrong. Insight isn't different from everyday thought; it moves forward, step by step, and even when we're not consciously aware of what our minds are doing, we're still using everyday brain processes. And even when we feel a solitary, sudden inspiration, the origin can often be found in collaboration—that's what happened with John Reed and Jim Crocker. The next challenge for psychologists was to delve deeper into what goes on in the mind when we have an insight. In the real world, insight is unpredictable; we needed a way to re-create reliably the "Aha!" moment in the laboratory.

One of the simplest ways to re-create insight in the laboratory is by using what's called the Remote Associates Test, with its unfortunate acronym RAT. The RAT asks you to find a fourth "target" word that's related to each of the three test words. About half of the time, people say they get an "Aha!" feeling when they finally discover the target word. Try finding the target word for each of these five rows:

```
CREAM...... SKATE........ WATER
SHOW ....... LIFE.......... ROW
CRACKER.... FLY.......... FIGHTER
DREAM...... BREAK ....... LIGHT
HOUND...... PRESSURE .... SHOT
```

The RAT was originally developed in the 1960s by the psychologist Sarnoff Mednick, and it was based on his theory that creative insights were the result of forming unusual associations between mental concepts. These triplets are designed to be difficult: Although two of the three words have a similar relation to the target word, the third word has a completely different association. For example, "fire fighter" and "fire cracker" both involve combustion, but a "fire fly" isn't a fly that's on fire. "Blood pressure" and "blood shot" both refer to vessels in the body, but a "blood hound" has nothing to do with one's body. To solve RAT problems, one must bring together words from two remote *associative clusters* by finding a link between them. Mednick's theory was that people who can do this faster than others have a more intricate network in their minds that allows them to make connections between ideas that are farther apart.

The RAT seems to support our belief in a special moment of insight: You start by getting stuck as you search through one associative cluster; then you give up and start searching your brain for another associative cluster, and you suddenly see a spark. But the way you feel while you're solving the triplets isn't the way it's really happening.

Here's an experiment, designed by the psychologist Kenneth Bowers and three of his colleagues, demonstrating that your mind is always working closer to a solution, even when you feel blocked. Bowers first chose a target word, and then created a list of fifteen words that were all remote associates of that word. For example, for the word "square" the fifteen words were these: times, inch, deal, corner, peg, head, foot, dance, person, town, math, four, block, table, box. Now, read the following list slowly and see whether you can identify the one word that is associated with all these words. As you proceed through the list, pause just after you read each word, make your best guess about what the target word is, and write it in the blank before continuing. Even if you're sure it can't be right, make sure to write something in every blank:

RED———————————

NUT ———————————

BOWL ———————————

LOOM ———————————

CUP ———————————

BASKET ———————————

JELLY ———————————

FRESH ———————————

COCKTAIL ———————————

CANDY ———————————

PIE ———————————

BAKING ———————————

SALAD ———————————

TREE ———————————

FLY ———————————

Bowers found that the average person had a first hunch after ten words and were pretty sure after twelve words. But here's the really fascinating result. Bowers had everyone write down a guess after every word, just as I instructed you to do. Then he came up with a computer program that measured how closely associated each guess was to "fruit" (the answer to the above problem). Even before people knew they were getting closer, their guesses came closer and closer to fruit, and in a strikingly linear pattern. Whether it took a person five words or fifteen words, they showed the same incremental, linear pattern of getting closer and closer up to the end. But these same people often said the answer had come to them in a sudden flash of insight—even though the researchers had just gathered data showing it didn't happen that way.

If creativity is based in everyday thought—if there's no magical moment of insight, no mysterious subconscious incubation working on these problems—why did Jim Crocker and John Reed have to take time off from the problems they were working on? And if creativity is always collaborative, why did they have their sparks of insight when they were far away from the office? Stories such as theirs are what make us believe that we need distance from a problem to gain a significant insight, and that we need to get away from the group to be creative. If creativity is so collaborative, why does taking time off help the sparks fly?

The answer lies in understanding exactly what's happening in the mind when you're being creative.

Analyze

1. What have psychologists discovered are the five basic stages of an effective collaborative process?
2. What are insight problems? Which of the insight problems that Sawyer offers challenged you most? Did you have to look up the answer or did you come up with it on your own? What insight does this experience give you into the idea of insight? (The answers to all of his insight problems are in Appendix B.)
3. Sawyer uses the term "metacognition." What is it? And why is that a useful term to appear in this chapter?
4. What is "confabulation"? What examples of it have you encountered in your own life?

Explore

1. Sawyer mentions how "English Romantic poet Samuel Taylor Coleridge said he had sparks of insight all the time." One example is his poem

"Kubla Khan: Or, a Vision in a Dream." How many other writers, artists, or other creative people do you know who claim their work comes from sparks of insight? What do you make of this idea when Coleridge scholars "discovered that he read many different books that contributed material to the poem" and "these [early] drafts [of the poem] contain versions of his insight story that describe the insight in very different ways"?

2. Sawyer's examples drive home the point that "we can't be trusted when we describe how our insights occur." Do you agree? Thinking back to your most recent sparks of creativity, what do you remember? How clearly can you explain what happened to a classmate? How certain are you of what you're explaining?

3. Create your own insight or noninsight problem. Use Sawyer's examples as models or look up more examples online. Share your problem with a classmate and see how effective it is. Discuss the results and modify your problem accordingly, as needed.

4. Write an essay that examines "Gestaltism" or "Gestalt psychology," terms that Sawyer used a number of times in this reading. Explore it from a bird's-eye view or select one specific aspect of it, such as the Law of Closure, and go deeply into that aspect. Bring in outside sources, make connections, and create examples as needed.

Bill Capodagli and Lynn Jackson
"Collaboration in the Sandbox"

Bill Capogdagli (1948–) has coauthored *The Disney Way: Harnessing the Management Secrets of Disney in Your Company, The Disney Way Fieldbook, The Pixarians,* and *Innovate the Pixar Way: Business Lessons from the World's Most Creative Corporate Playground,* among others. With Lynn Jackson, he runs Capodagli Jackson Consulting.

    Lynn Jackson (1955–) has been leading corporate playground activities for over twenty years. She is the coauthor of *The Disney Way: Harnessing the Management Secrets of Disney in Your Company, The Disney Way Fieldbook,* and *Innovate the Pixar Way: Business Lessons from the World's Most*

Creative Corporate Playground, among others. With Bill Capodagli, she runs Capodagli Jackson Consulting. "Collaboration in the Sandbox" first appeared in their coauthored book, *Innovate the Pixar Way*.

Have you ever watched the interplay of children in a sandbox? The younger ones watch with curiosity how the older children build their sandcastles. From time to time, the older children will mentor the younger ones, suggesting ideas and providing instruction for using the essential construction tools—shovels and buckets. Kids don't need to take "Sandcastle Building 101" to learn how to build a sandcastle. They learn from intense observation and by trial and error in a collaborative environment.

In 1887, after only two semesters, the legendary architect Frank Lloyd Wright left the University of Wisconsin–Madison. It wasn't long before he went to Chicago to meet with Louis Sullivan, father of the modern-day skyscraper, and told him that he wanted to become an architect. Sullivan was impressed with the young man and hired him. On his first day of work, Wright asked him, "What should I do?" Sullivan told him to sit down and watch. In later years, Wright opened his own college where students learned through watching other architects and assisting on real projects, just the way Sullivan instructed Wright and just like in the sandbox.

Walt Disney once said, "Every child is born blessed with a vivid imagination. But just as a muscle grows flabby with disuse, so the bright imagination of a child pales in later years if he ceases to exercise it." Truly creative people exhibit a level of enthusiasm for imagination and discovery that harkens back to the days of childhood. Indeed, innovation begins with a beginner's mind and is often stimulated by a catalyst.

Merriam-Webster's defines *catalyst* as "an agent that provokes or speeds significant change or action." For Frank Lloyd Wright, that agent was Louis Sullivan. For Ed Catmull, it was his two childhood idols—Walt Disney and Albert Einstein. For John Lasseter, it was Bob Thomas's book, *The Art of Animation*, about the history of the Disney Studios. For Randy Nelson, it was Ed Catmull and a memo written by Walt Disney that inspired the creation of Pixar University. And for the kids in the Tucson Unified School District (TUSD), it is the now nationally recognized Opening Minds through the Arts (OMA) program.

Pixar University and the Tucson Unified School District's OMA program are both catalysts that encourage educational change in their respective worlds of corporate America and the U.S. public school system. Seemingly worlds apart, they share a long-term commitment to a learning process that encourages collaborative creativity. They both have "champions" of their respective learning models and, in their own unique ways, make art a team sport.

At the completion of *Toy Story*, Pixar's Ed Catmull and John Lasseter began discussions on the importance of continuing education in building a top-notch studio—one in which not only new employees could learn the skills they need, but also veteran staff could expand their learning horizons beyond their fields of expertise, and a place where everyone would learn collaboratively. Like Walt Disney before them, Ed and John planned a studio-based school, and they sought out a leader who was not an artist in the traditional sense of the word. Pixar University (John said, "We picked the name just for its initials, P.U.") was soon to be under the direction of Randy Nelson, a former technical trainer at NeXT (founded in 1985 by Steve Jobs) and one of the founding members of the world-famous juggling troupe the Flying Karamazov Brothers. It stands to reason, if you are going to offer a highly diverse array of courses, why not hire a guy with a highly diverse background as the leader? As Ed said, "He had an unusual combination of skills, which I felt was an asset. I figured I'd rather have a world-class juggler running the program than a mediocre artist. People who have experience doing great work understand something that can be applied to other things."

Walt Disney's studio-based school of the 1930s was the inspiration for Pixar University nearly a half century later. Walt once said, "I think we shouldn't give up until we have found out all we can about how to teach these young [people].... There are a number of things that could be brought up in these discussions to stir [their] imagination, so that when they get into actual animation, they're not just technicians, but they're actually creative people." This was a key message in the eight-page memo Walt Disney wrote to Don Graham (legendary art instructor at Chouinard Art Institute in downtown Los Angeles and author of *Composing Pictures,* an out-of-print classic coveted by both art students and animators) just before Christmas in 1935. At that time, Walt was planning the production of *Snow White and the Seven Dwarfs* and needed to hire and train new animators in short order. In his memo, he outlined "a very systematic training course for young animators, and also outlined a plan of approach for [our] older animators." With Walt's detailed plan for developing the finest artists in the industry, Don Graham carried forth the creation of a curriculum that included courses on drawing, comedy, music, dialogue, and motion, and intertwined them in a holistic fashion, as Walt described, "to stir up the men's minds more."

The now famous Walt Disney memo would remain at Disney for decades, eventually falling into the hands of Ed Catmull, John Lasseter, and Randy Nelson. Walt's missive inspired and motivated them. Since being crowned dean of Pixar University in 1997 (Randy says he's a "fake" dean and "at the same level as the guy at McDonald's Hamburger University"), Randy Nelson has gone from juggling knives on Broadway to juggling an extensive lineup of courses (and is still juggling foot-long knives in gesture-drawing class at P.U.!) that rivals some of the finest public institutions offering art degrees. With more than 110 courses on everything from improv to the Israeli self-defense system Krav Maga, "Big Art"—the boxy brick building that is home to P.U.—is always buzzing. And don't let Randy's charismatic persona fool you. He's fun, to be sure, but he is dead serious about integrating learning opportunities into the work lives of Pixar's approximately 1,000 employees. "We're all filmmakers here," says Randy. "We all have access to the same curriculum. In class, people from every level sit right next to our directors and the president of the company." So passionate about building a strong base of "interested" people, Pixar challenges employees to dedicate up to four hours of every single week to their education. Pixar University has been a vital catalyst for employees who are encouraged to take a great deal of responsibility for their own learning and for collaborating with one another. Randy maintains that "the skills we develop are skills we need everywhere in the organization. Why teach drawing to accountants? Because drawing class doesn't just teach people to draw. It teaches them to be more observant. There's no company on earth that wouldn't benefit from having people become more observant."

Walt Disney felt each person in his company should "plus" another's ideas to make them bigger, even better. Pixar has certainly "plus-ed" Walt Disney's idea for a "little" art school. Since its inception in 1995, Pixar University has truly lived up to its reputation as a "secret weapon"—one that challenges, in Steve Jobs words, "the densest group of really brilliant people that I've ever seen in my life" to continue to push the boundaries of their art.

If you set out to develop a plan for creating a learning environment for children to prepare them for working in an environment such as Pixar, you'd surely be benchmarking the OMA project in Tucson, Arizona. In less than a decade, what began as one man's dream of integrating the arts into the entire learning experience within a single school district is now the cutting edge of a new paradigm in public education.

OMA was created around children's neurological development and brain-based learning theories. The program employs teaching artists—professionals from Tucson's cultural institutions—who use music, dance, and visual arts to teach concepts and skills applied in academic subjects like reading, writing, math, and science. Carroll Reinhart, OMA cofounder, said, "What I get excited about with the OMA project is that I see artists helping classroom teachers helping principals to understand the very essence of what art is." The curriculum is designed to engage specific skills targeted to each grade level, and the results have been amazing. Since 2001, OMA has been working with WestEd, a nationally recognized educational research firm, to conduct a study comparing three "research" schools that were fully implementing the OMA model and three "control" schools that were utilizing standard teaching methodology. WestEd's research focused on answering two primary questions: does OMA have a positive effect on test results in reading, writing, and math; and does OMA improve teacher effectiveness? The answer to both was a resounding "yes."

When Bill observed the OMA program, he was particularly impressed by the first-grade opera experience. For the first half of the year, students learn opera by watching members of the Tucson Opera perform a short opera, and then performing the same parts themselves. During the second half of the year, the students write their own opera and perform it as their final class project. These are *first* graders! One of the first-grade OMA lesson plans reads like a Pixar University course description: "Use Beethoven's song 'The Mighty Monarch' to teach students sequencing through two different means—first, by explaining the writing process (poet, composer, performer), and then by using the characters and the sequence of the story." What a way to begin an educational journey!

Not only are OMA students being exposed to the art form of opera, but these children also learn vocabulary, story construction, collaboration, and "failure recovery" while having fun. It's a lot like the sandbox or the Frank Lloyd Wright example—observe, try, learn, and try again within a supportive team. According to Rick Warner, OMA program coordinator, "OMA creates an environment in the school where the children feel safe to risk making mistakes and recover from those mistakes in the process of inquiry and exploration. They come to understand that that's not crippling, but somehow we build mastery through that." The children of OMA courageously explore and share new ideas with one another, with the belief that other students' ideas are assets in the exploration process. In short, they learn that more knowledge, creativity, and ideas can be found in two minds than in one, and that even more can be found in five or ten. Rick explained, "What I think is so valuable at OMA has to do with core values. . . . It's completely opposed to the typical assessment and evaluation of children being evaluated on how I answer these questions in a multiple-choice fashion on this piece of paper."

Steve Seidel, director of Harvard University's Project Zero (whose stated mission is "to understand and enhance learning, thinking, and creativity in the arts, as well as humanistic and scientific disciplines, at the individual and institutional levels"), recently said, "OMA had better be ready to grow, because in a few years, this will be the standard by which all other programs will be judged, and it will be the model for the entire country." He spoke these words to J. Eugene "Gene" Jones, the founding "dreamer" and major champion of OMA who is now a retired entrepreneur after earning a fortune turning around troubled companies. The 93-year-old Gene focuses his enormous energy into two of his lifelong passions: music and education. As incoming president of the Tucson Symphony in 2000, Gene attended an annual symphony leadership meeting in North Carolina and happened to stumble upon a class where the music director was using music as a classroom educational tool. After walking through that door and watching the creativity and energy pouring forth from the children, he said to himself, "If that is what music will do, that's what we are damn well going to do and do it better." His passion for creating an innovative arts-education program in his own community was so great that he donated more than $1 million of his own money to launch OMA, which currently operates in more than half of Tucson's elementary schools and a quarter of its middle schools.

Joan Ashcraft, director of fine and performing arts at TUSD and co-founder of OMA, said, "I was so grateful to have Gene Jones say to me, 'Just do it. . . . Find people that support your dreams.'" Roger Pfeuffer, former superintendent of TUSD, said that it was imperative that the "dream" team challenge the local naysayers who feared "bringing a Cadillac model to a Chevrolet town." Roger—who clearly understood the immense value of an arts integration curriculum in developing fully functioning individuals— explained, "The OMA model isn't an add-on; it's got to be part of the core.

You've also got to have a long-term view, what is needed in higher education and beyond." And as OMA cofounder Jan Vesely added, "We integrated art and music into the learning because I believe that higher-order thinking comes when you integrate."

Today, the cofounders and champions of OMA—Gene Jones, Joan Ashcraft, Carroll Rinehart, Jan Vesely, and John Snavely—remain fully engaged in building a world-class educational arena where an "art is a team sport" culture facilitates student achievement and social growth. "Our district is taking on the amazing challenge of moving OMA to the next level . . . designing the learning that will meet the future needs of our 'digital native' students," says superintendent Elizabeth Fagen. And who knows? They may also be preparing the future generation of Pixarians!

"Art is a team sport" is the very essence of learning and working in a collaborative fashion at Pixar. Pixar encourages employees to share their ideas and art-in-process, and to accept feedback from others without worrying about being labeled a failure. Fittingly, the Pixar University crest bears the inscription "Alienus Non Diutius," Latin for "alone no longer." "It's the heart of our model," Randy Nelson says, "giving people opportunities to fail together and to recover from mistakes together." Remember—this is an environment of mutual respect and trust, two vital ingredients required for innovation in teams. As Ed Catmull, whose leadership sets the tone for Pixar's culture of safe risk taking, said, "Everyone at the company will tell you there are no bad ideas at Pixar, even if they don't end up in a movie." And when it comes to developing new stories and technologies, Ed humbly admits, "We're constantly figuring it out. We don't have all the answers." But, with a workforce of truly interested people who band together and constantly explore new ways to fulfill their dreams, it is clearly apparent why Pixar continues to succeed.

Pixar goes to great lengths to hire people who are interested in working together as a "network . . . in solving problems, building and supporting each other," as Ed describes it. Four common proficiencies—depth, breadth, communication, and collaboration—are vital to making "art a team sport." Here are definitions of these proficiencies according to Randy Nelson:

- **Depth**—demonstrating mastery in a subject or a principal skill such as drawing or programming; having the discipline to chase dreams all the way to the finish line.

- **Breadth**—possessing a vast array of experiences and interests; having empathy for others; having the ability to explore insights from many different perspectives; and being able to effectively generate new ideas by collaborating with an entire team. Randy described people who have breadth: "They amplify *you*. They want to know what *you* want to know." In problem solving, they are the ones who lean in, rather than pulling back.

- **Communication**—focusing on the receiver; receiving feedback to ascertain whether the message sent was truly understood. According to Randy, "Communication is not something the emitter can measure." Only the listener can say, "I understand."

- **Collaboration**—bringing together the skills (including depth, breadth, and communication), ideas, and personality styles of an entire team to achieve a shared vision. "Yes, and . . ." (rather than "No, this is better") is part of Pixar's common lexicon that fosters collective creativity and keeps the vibe and energy in the room upbeat and alive.

Collaboration is critical to the process of generating ideas and solving problems in any organization. At Pixar, there are literally thousands of ideas that are considered during the making of a film. As Catmull explained, "Everyone is trying to solve these problems, and a lot of ideas are thrown out there that don't work. . . . You get in a group of people, they look at it, you get ideas . . . and you come back and you make the performance better. . . . If you think about it, this is creative problem solving."

Those who gain mastery in anything have become comfortable with the process of failure recovery. From the technicians to the artists, these gifted and talented team members have needs and concerns that emerge from "errors" in their independent work—ones that motivate them to seek solutions. Sharing breadth, however, leads them to collaborate with others to do so. In truly living the Pixar University mantra of "alone no longer," employees do not struggle in isolation. When team members come together to find a solution to a problem, they are energized and strive to discover creative options for accomplishing their goals. They don't get trapped into thinking that an answer is the *only* answer.

Pixarians working in a team environment (standard operating procedure at Pixar) are open to alternative answers helping foster an outward focus. They understand that an outward focus is a requirement for seeking and accepting new inputs and ideas in a playground where "art is a team sport." As John Lasseter stated, "Pixar is actively expanding its talent base. We have younger filmmakers experiment with ideas and technology. The next thing you know, we have assigned them to come up with feature ideas." When asked about the process of making *Up*, codirector Pete Docter said, "This is a very personal film, yet it's intensely collaborative. No one person could do this. . . . So as a director . . . [I don't] tell them too specifically what I want. 'On frame seven, I want him to grab the bottle.' It's more the feeling, 'Remember, he's just run seven miles. He's exhausted, he's angry.' Just tell [the animators] those sorts of details and think of them more like an actor. Let them bring their ideas to the thing."

Pixar employees care enough about one another and are emotionally secure enough, as Randy Nelson explained, to make their "partner(s) look good." Team members continually "plus" one another's work—all in the spirit of sorting through and refining a multitude of ideas that gel together to produce, in the words of Ed Catmull, a "wonderful magical whole."

Pixar's really magical stories come to life through the able hands of *interested* people—a quality Randy says is much more valuable than simply being *interesting*. How, you may ask, do we cultivate the gift of being truly *interested*—opening the mind to new ideas and possibilities, persistently seeking answers to questions, and digging deep to find the best solutions to problems? Pixar University's model of education enables employees to do just that.

We wonder what it will take to change the culture of formal education that all too often stifles the imaginations of children and adults alike. We must leave behind the culture of answering questions *correctly* and adopt a culture of safe inquiry, exploration, and discovery. OMA's Rick Warner is in sync with Pixar president Ed Catmull in building a culture where try, learn, and try again—failure recovery—is integral to making "art a team sport." Rick explained, "The process of artistic inquiry is exploration and discovery, and it's making mistakes a million thousand times, and it's throwing away a million thousand things that you come to . . . and saving and valuing specific things out of this pool of things you discover. That's what you hold on to as an artist and [what] is ultimately woven into the content of any kind of product you create."

As is true of Pixar, the advantage in this world will always go to *interested* people who can outcollaborate and outinnovate their competitors— and the fully engaged OMA children will someday be ready to do just that! Choose your sandbox. Will it set the stage for opening minds through experiential collaborative learning opportunities or merely opening minds and pouring in the facts?

> I happen to be an inquisitive guy and when I see things I don't like, I start thinking why do they have to be like this and how can I improve them.
>
> —Walt Disney

Analyze

1. Why do articles on creativity so often talk about a sandbox? Why does that example communicate so effectively?
2. What are some of the lessons/skills/courses being taught at Pixar University? Would you prefer attending a university such as that? Why?
3. What is the OMA model? Do you have OMA models in schools or businesses in your area? How successful do they seem?
4. Ed Catmull wants to make "art a team sport," and he believes what four proficiencies are vital to making that happen?

Explore

1. Ed Catmull has his own piece in this book—"Fear and Failure" in Chapter 3: The Creative Workplace. What points of comparison and contrast do you find between this piece—where Catmull features heavily—and the one he himself wrote? What type of leader does Catmull appear to be?
2. Create your own collaboration via social media. On Facebook, put up a post that has a fill-in-the-blank portion—such as "Writing a term paper is like _____ because _____" or "The best thing about a snowstorm is _____"—and allow responses to come in over a couple of days. Which responses surprised you? Which ones were far better than anything you imagined (which is to say, the collaboration was a success)? Share the best three with classmates and compare with the results they got on their own social media collaborations. What other social media outlets might this work on? Twitter? Instagram? Something new?
3. The Pixar University mantra is "alone no longer." What is/should be the mantra of your school? Your family? Your workplace? Rewrite

those mantras in the spirit of creativity and collaboration. Do what you can to make those new mantras a reality.

4. The next time you are watching a movie you really enjoy, let it roll all the way through the credits. Pay attention to the sheer volume of people who collaborated to create something artistic that you enjoyed. Appreciate it. That's all. Just appreciate the power of effective collaboration.

Hugh Hart
"Yes, and . . . 5 More Lessons in Improv-ing Collaboration and Creativity from Second City"

Los Angeles freelance writer **Hugh Hart** (1950–) writes about music, television, art, design, and New Media for the *Los Angeles Times, New York Times*, and Fast Company. "Yes, and . . . 5 More Lessons in Improv-ing Collaboration and Creativity from Second City" first appeared on www.fastcocreate.com.

Second City execs Tom Yorton and Kelly Leonard do not claim their new book *Yes, And* will teach you how to become a world-class comedian. However, they *do* argue that the same improv techniques absorbed at The Second City in Chicago by Tina Fey, Steve Carrell, Stephen Colbert, Amy Poehler, and dozens of other funny alumni can be used to jumpstart creativity in the workplace.

Yorton, who oversees improv workshops for corporate clients as CEO of Second City Works, says, "When we teach comedy in the business world, it's not in the service of pure entertainment. We're doing it to help change behavior and get people to try things they otherwise wouldn't do within the typical stiff, boring patterns of communication."

Yorton and Leonard, a longtime Second City producer, held forth from their snowbound Chicago headquarters to talk about how gibberish, "Following the Follower," and other brainstorming games foster outrageous ideas and tight-knit ensembles.

Just Say Yes

Y ou may have heard a lot—too much—about the "Yes, And" approach, but there's a reason it's jumped from the improv world into more mainstream usage. "Yes, And" improvisers always agree with the partner's statement, then build on that premise with something new. Shooting down the initial idea squashes creativity, Kelly says. "What you learn about improvisation when you apply 'Yes, And' is that there's a bounty of ideas, way more than will ever get used. Everyone in the ensemble produces hundreds of ideas, so even though most of (the ideas) will die and never be seen again, people don't hold on out of fear that they'll have nothing to offer at the end."

In the business environment, he adds, "Fear does creep into the process; it's the job of the boss to remind everybody that it's okay to fail because when you say 'Yes, And,' you're dealing with an abundance of possibilities. This creates an environment where ultimately you get the richest material."

Second City's "Yes, And" exercise "Word at a Time" trains people to create a tall tale by taking turns building sentences one word at a time.

Give Shy People a Voice

M ost Second City improv exercises, developed by Chicago social worker Viola Spolin and later adapted by her son Paul Sills when he co-founded the troupe in 1959, train participants in the simple art of listening. "When you're a very smart domineering alpha personality, a lot of people shut up around you because they see you're smart and maybe think 'I'm never going to have more stuff to offer,' says Yorton."

In a corporate environment, Leonard notes, "Some people feel like they need to control the conversation out of fear that they're not going to be top dog or God forbid, someone else will get a little bit of credit. But the truth is, you're only so smart for so long. You're only original for so long, so at Second City we like to say, 'All of us is better than one of us.'"

For "String of Pearls," the group forms a line. The person at one end is given the first sentence of a story. The person at the end of the line is given the last sentence. Each person in between takes a turn improvising a line of dialogue aimed at making the story progress logically to its pre-set end point.

In "Last Word Response," two people converse. Each person must begin the first word of his or her sentence with the last word of the partner's sentence. Both exercises hammer home a simple message: pay attention.

Forget "Team," Build an "Ensemble"

Second City performances draw their power from ensemble thinking that pulls equally from each player. Yorton points out, "In the business world, people who've had too many lousy team-building experiences become jaded to the point where 'team' becomes a loaded word. 'Ensemble' gives that idea a fresh look because when you put together an ensemble, you're looking for different points of view. To use a baseball analogy, you don't want to stack your lineup with nine sluggers; you don't want the ensemble full of alphas."

You also don't want an ensemble full of "straight white men," observes Kelly. For decades, Second City troupes rarely included more than one or two woman and people of color. That all changed in 1995. "Tina Fey was in the first gender-equal cast, and then, after the 9/11 attacks, we had Keegan Michael Key performing on stage, relating to that event in a completely different way than his cast mates," recalls Kelly. "As a creativity laboratory, we've seen the shows have become better and stronger and deeper since we started using more diverse casts."

The strength-in-diversity concept applies to corporate structures, Leonard says. "It's just a fact. Ensembles become more powerful when they express the differences that exist inside an organization."

Follow the Follower

Successful improv performance depends on a willingness to share the spotlight. In the workplace, Leonard observes, "Yes, And" concepts go a long way toward dismantling unproductive control freak behavior. "Top down hierarchical management style doesn't work anymore," he says. "In a global, web-enabled environment, teams disband and form all the time; when you've got software developers working on a product around the clock, you don't know who's going to lead, who's going to follow. This idea of a pyramid with one person at the top supported by legions of underlings has fallen away as the world itself becomes more improvisational."

The second City exercise "Follow the Follower" compels shy people to assert themselves while "Giver Taker" forces everyone in the group to take turns being the center of attention. Yorton says, "A smart company embraces the 'Follow the Follower' style knowing that there are times when you need to cede control to another person."

Dare to Offend . . . Honestly

Each time The Second City creates a new satiric revue, its "Dare to Offend" slogan is never far from mind, says Leonard. "We challenge convention. What that means when we go into the business world is we don't avoid the thing that everybody in the audience would be talking about later at the bar when they've had a couple of drinks in them. If a merger hasn't worked out and the two cultures hate each other, comedy is a good way to pop the tension bubble around a thorny issue because what creates cynicism is when everybody pretends the problem's not there."

Leonard says, "'Daring to Offend' does not mean we're going to drop F bombs, but we do help companies be honest. At Second City, if somebody screws up on stage, acknowledge it. When a sketch starts out and somebody's name is Tom, then later an actor calls him Ted, the first actor might say, 'So when did you learn my true identity?' If you bring the audience in, they'll love you for it and it's the same thing with companies. Comedy is a safe way to hold a mirror up to reality and when you do that as management, you gain enormous credibility."

Analyze

1. In your own words, explain what the "Yes, And" technique is. How might it be useful in the world of creativity?
2. How important is listening to the Second City performer? How do you know? (If you've ever watched an episode of *Inside the Actor's Studio*, you'll probably here it there too. The #1 answer to the question "What's the most important skill an actor can have?" Listening.)
3. What's the difference between an ensemble and a team? What makes a good ensemble?
4. What is "Dare to Offend"? In what situations might it be useful? (Do you already have a class clown or a wise-cracking uncle who does this?)

Explore

1. Who are some of the comedians who came through the Second City program? Which of these do you find particularly creative? Which of the techniques from this article do you see them practicing to good effect?

2. With a number of classmates, try the "String of Pearls" assignment. How easy is it to improve your line and still make the story follow logically toward the predetermined end point? What's the biggest challenge in this assignment? Where does creativity play into things?

3. One thing comedians might do when working with a group of businessmen is to give them ten minutes to create a story that's built around the things at work that annoy them. Once it's time to get volunteers to perform the story, there's never a shortage. People are laughing, sharing, and learning more about others than they ever expected. This type of exercise is always a hit because the little silos they've lived and worked in have begun to come down, and that means collaboration is now possible. Where might you use this same technique to generate connection, positivity, and fun? In your classroom? At work? With an intramural sports team? Try it, and report back to the class with your results.

Forging Connections

1. Good managers have their own techniques for bringing people together. Some have five- to ten-minute get-togethers—"meetings" is too formal, so "huddles" or "confabs" might be the term—that are launched with a good, provocative quotation. If you were a good manager and you were calling one of these short huddles, what would be a quotation from this chapter that you might use to launch a fruitful pep talk? What does that quotation mean to you? How would it serve to motivate others?

2. You're the teacher of your class and you've only got enough time to assign two of the four readings in this chapter before having to move on to other things. Which two readings would you assign and why? What ways do they speak to each other? What are the takeaways from the combined readings? What are you missing by skipping the others? How hard is to be a teacher (or an editor of a book like this!) who has to make these tough choices?

Looking Further

1. Ken Blanchard, management expert and author of the hugely successful book *The One-Minute Manager*, says, "None of us is as smart as all of us." Is that universally true? Is there ever a situation where collaboration gets in the way of getting things done? For the Beatles, two was enough. Think about the factors that play into an effective collaboration. What are they? What makes a collaboration an ineffective one? When you're asked to partner/group up in class (or at work or on a sports field), are you being set up for a successful collaboration or not? Blanchard says that one of the biggest problems in companies is that they don't know what success looks like, so they never know how well they did/didn't perform. Keep that in mind for the day you're running Pixar, 3M, or your own company.

2. Consider the various ideas discussed in this chapter—including improv, partnerships, earning environments, and deviance—and then use the Internet to find relevant articles, interviews, Top 10 lists, and blogs. Compare and contrast what those sources say and what you found in the chapter. Create a presentation that delivers the most useful material on collaboration and creativity. Which sources were the most helpful in making the presentation? Why?

Creativity and the Arts

5

"Go and make interesting mistakes, make amazing mistakes, make glorious and fantastic mistakes. Break rules. Leave the world more interesting for your being here. Make. Good. Art."
—Neil Gaiman, English author

This chapter investigates the deep relationship between creativity and the arts, with a special emphasis on writing—the subtitle of every book in this Oxford University Press series is "A Reader for Writers" after all! But let's allow writers, artists, and a few other creative people to help "write" the introduction to this chapter. A little wisdom before the wisdom included in the chapter, as it were. Savor the artistic good-ness! Delight in such pithy knowledge!

"Don't think. Thinking is the enemy of creativity. It's self-conscious, and anything self-conscious is lousy. You can't try to do things. You simply must do things."—Ray Bradbury, American author

"The thing about creativity is, people are going to laugh at it. Get over it."—Twyla Tharp, American dancer, choreographer, and author

"I invent nothing, I rediscover."—Auguste Rodin, French sculptor

"From 30,000 feet, creating looks like art. From ground level, it's a to-do list."—Ben Arment, American author and Founder of Story: An Uncom-mon Creativity Conference

"If I create from the heart, nearly everything works; if from the head, almost nothing."—Marc Chagall, Russian-French artist

"The whole culture is telling you to hurry, while the art tells you to take your time. Always listen to the art."—Junot Diaz, Dominican American writer

"The reason that art (writing, engaging, and all of it) is valuable is pre-cisely why I can't tell you how to do it. If there were a map, there'd be no art, because art is the act of navigating without a map."—Seth Godin, American author, entrepreneur, and marketer

"No great artist ever sees things as they really are. If he did, he would cease to be an artist."—Oscar Wilde, Irish author, playwright, and poet

Howard Gardner
"Creativity across the Domains"

A MacArthur "Genius" Prize Fellow in 1981, **Howard Gardner** (1943–) is the John H. and Elisabeth A. Hobbs Professor of Cognition and Education at the Harvard Graduate School of Education. He has twice been selected by *Foreign Policy* and *Prospect* magazines as one of the one hundred most influential public intellectuals in the world. He has authored thirty books and several hun-dred articles and is perhaps best known for his theory of multiple intelligences. "Creativity across the Domains" first appeared in his book *Creating Minds*.

In the preceding chapters, I have related the stories of seven remarkable human beings, each of whom made an indelible mark in one or more domains while also contributing uniquely to the shape of the modern era. Their stories are, I trust, of interest in their own right. Yet, given my focus on the conceptualization of creativity, I need to step back and discuss which lessons hold for the study of creativity in general.

Revisiting the Organizing Framework

In my book *Creating Minds*, I introduced a framework for treating the complex issues of creativity. Explicitly developmental, that framework features a concern with the creators' childhoods, as related to their adult creativity; an interest in phases of development across the life span; and a focus on the finer-grained steps that characterize moments of break-through. I posited a dynamic that appears to characterize all creative activity: an ongoing dialectic among talented *individuals*, *domains* of expertise, and *fields* charged with judging the quality of creations. According to my formulation, this dynamic is often characterized by various kinds of tensions and asynchronies: provided that the asynchronies are not overwhelming, they should prove conducive to the fostering of creative individuals, processes, and products. Finally, I suggested a set of guiding themes, most of which provided background for the study, but two of which emerged, unexpectedly, from the study itself.

That framework has now been put to work, implicitly in the case studies and more explicitly in the three interludes. In this concluding chapter, I examine explicitly a number, but certainly not all, of the issues raised thus far. I touch on the major questions that motivated the study, providing, when possible, a rough quantitative survey of "data" relevant to the issue in question.

Earlier I indicated that the current work on creativity ought to be framed by two stances: the detailed views of individual creators, of the sort undertaken by Howard Gruber and his associates; and the large-scale quantitative studies undertaken by Dean Keith Simonton and his colleagues. In my work I have sought to integrate these stances, which have traditionally been termed *idiographic* and *nomothetic,* respectively; I have approached this integration by looking at seven individuals deliberately chosen from diverse domains and yet searching for generalizations applicable to all or at least most of their cases.

One person's generalization is another person's exception. Depending on how one defines a term or carves out a category, one can either collapse individuals together or cleave them apart. In what follows I offer my current impressions about which findings are likely to qualify ultimately as reliable generalizations, and which are better described as either domain-specific or unique to particular individuals. Those who have detailed knowledge about specific individuals, who have available arrays of data and powerful statistical techniques, or who are wedded to different conceptual frameworks may well carve the pattern somewhat differently. I hope to have at least set up a structure that merits debate.

A Portrait of the Exemplary Creator

I need not focus here on the many important ways these seven creators differ. Even to place Gandhi and Stravinsky, or Graham and Einstein, in the same comparative study involves a suspension of customary categorical schemes. Moreover, my own theoretical bias has predisposed me to look for differences across domains of accomplishment; I believe that this study confirms the distinctive character of the activities typical of each of the creators.

That said, I have been struck by the extent to which common themes nonetheless emerge in the lives of these creators. While no theme emerges with equal force for all the creators, and an exception can be found to each of the emerging generalizations, I feel comfortable in putting forth a portrait of the Exemplary Creator, whom I shall nickname E.C. and speak of as female.

E.C. comes from a locale somewhat removed from the actual centers of power and influence of her society, but not so far away that she and her family are entirely ignorant of what is going on elsewhere. The family is neither wealthy nor in dire financial straits, and life for the young creator is reasonably comfortable, in a material sense. The atmosphere at home is more correct than it is warm, and the young creator often feels a bit estranged from her biological family; even though E.C. has close ties to one of her parents, she feels ambivalence, too. Intimate ties are more likely to exist between E.C. and a nanny, a nursemaid, or a more distant member of her family.

E.C.'s family is not highly educated, but they value learning and achievement, about which they hold high expectations. In a word, they are prototypically bourgeois, holding dear the ambitions, respectability, and valuing of hard work that have come to be associated with that class, particularly in the late nineteenth century. E.C.'s areas of strength emerged at a relatively young age, and her family encouraged these interests, though they are ambivalent about a career that falls outside of the established professions. There is a moral, if not a religious, atmosphere around the home, and E.C. develops a strict conscience, which can be turned against herself but also against others who do not adhere to behavioral patterns she expects. The creator often passes through a period of religiosity that is rejected and that may, but need not, be revisited in later life.

There comes a time when the growing child, now an adolescent, seems to have outgrown her home environment. E.C. has already invested a decade of work in the mastery of a domain and is near the forefront; she has little in addition to learn from her family and from local experts, and she feels a quickened impulse to test herself against the other leading young people in the domain. And so, as an adolescent or young adult, E.C. ventures toward the city that is seen as a center of vital activities for her domain. With surprising speed, E.C. discovers in the metropolis a set of peers who share the same interests; together, they explore the terrain of the domain, often organizing institutions, issuing manifestos, and stimulating one another to new heights. Sometimes E.C. proceeds directly to work in a chosen domain although she might just as well have flirted with a number of different career lines until a crystallizing moment occurred.

Experiences within domains differ from one another, and there is no point in trying to gloss over these here. Still, with greater or lesser speed, E.C. discovers a problem area or realm of special interest, one that promises to take the domain into uncharted waters. This is a highly charged moment. At this point E.C. becomes isolated from her peers and must work mostly on her own. She senses that she is on the verge of a breakthrough that is as yet little understood, even by her. Surprisingly, at this crucial moment, E.C. craves both cognitive and affective support, so that she can retain her bearings. Without such support, she might well experience some kind of breakdown.

Of course, in the happy circumstances that we have examined, E.C. succeeds in effecting at least one major breakthrough. And, the field rather rapidly acknowledges the power of the breakthrough. So special does E.C. feel that she appears willing to enter into special arrangements—a Faustian bargain—to maintain the flow that comes from effective, innovative work. For E.C., this bargain involves masochism and unbecoming behavior toward others, and, on occasion, the feeling of a direct pact with God. E.C. works nearly all the time, making tremendous demands on herself and on others, constantly raising the ante. In William Butler Yeats formation, she chooses perfection of the work over perfection of the life. She is self-confident, able to deal with false starts, proud and stubborn, and reluctant to admit mistakes.

Given E.C.'s enormous energy and commitment, she has an opportunity for a second breakthrough, which occurs about a decade after the first one. The succeeding breakthrough is less radical, but it is more comprehensive and more intimately integrated with E.C.'s previous work in the domain. The nature of E.C.'s domain determines whether an opportunity for further breakthroughs arises. (Remaining highly creative is easier in the arts than in the sciences.) E.C. attempts to retain her creativity; she will seek marginal status or heighten the ante of asynchrony to maintain freshness and to secure the flow that accompanies great challenges and exciting discoveries. When E.C. produces an outpouring of works, a few of them stand out as *defining*, both for E.C. herself and for members of the surrounding field.

Inevitably with aging, limits on E.C.'s creative powers emerge. She sometimes exploits young persons as a means of rejuvenation. Finding it increasingly difficult to achieve original new works, E.C. becomes a valued critic or commentator. Some creators die young, of course, but in the case of our E.C., she lives on until old age, gains many followers, and continues to make significant contribution until her death.

I am well aware of the limitations of this hypothetical portrait. Behind each sentence are arrayed not only the seven individuals in the study but also many others, at least some of whom appear directly to contradict this composite portrait. If most creators come from an intact and reasonably supportive family, certainly the Brontë sisters did not; if many live to an old age, Keats and Mozart certainly did not; if a majority come from somewhat marginal backgrounds, most members of the Bloomsbury set certainly did not. Thus, when it comes to offering generalizations about creativity, one must assess how essential each generalization is. In all probability, no single one of the factors just highlighted is critical for a creative life; but it may be that one needs at least a certain proportion of them, if the chances for a creative breakthrough are to be heightened. To evaluate the importance of different factors, I move now to a more explicit consideration of the central issues that guided my research. It should be stressed that the patterns proposed here are illustrative rather than definitive; one would need larger samples, and more precise measures, to establish the validity of any proposed pattern.

Major Issues: A Reprise

Individual Level

Cognitive. My slant in this study has been determinedly cognitive. A major assumption has been that creators differ from one another in the kinds of intelligences that they exhibit; and indeed, each of the creators was selected because he or she was thought to exemplify one of the seven intelligences that I detailed in *Frames of Mind.*

I conclude that creators differ from one another not only in terms of their dominant intelligence but also in terms of breadth and the combination of intelligences. Freud and Eliot had strong scholastic abilities (which reflect linguistic and logical intelligences), and they presumably could have made contributions in many academic areas. Picasso, on the other hand, was weak in the scholastic area, while exhibiting quite strongly targeted strengths in spatial, bodily, and personal spheres. Stravinsky and Gandhi were indifferent students, but one senses that their lackluster performances arose more out of lack of interest in school than out of any fundamental intellectual flaw. Graham had broad intellectual strengths but was never fully engaged until she encountered the world of dance. A rough summary of their intellectual profiles follows:

	Strength	*Weakness*
Freud	linguistic, personal	spatial, musical
Einstein	logical-spatial	personal
Picasso	spatial, personal, bodily	scholastic
Stravinsky	musical, other artistic	
Eliot	linguistic, scholastic	musical, bodily
Graham	bodily, linguistic	logical-mathematical
Gandhi	personal, linguistic	artistic

Just as the creators exhibited distinctive intellectual strengths, so, too, their relation to prodigiousness was also quite different. Freud was precocious in scholastic matters but did not discover his true vocation until in his late thirties; Graham did not begin to dance until she was over twenty; Gandhi ambled from one role to another until he discovered his political-religious calling; Stravinsky did not compose seriously until he was well into his twenties. Einstein and Eliot can be seen as having done important work when still quite young, but neither was seen as a prodigy in his chosen area. Indeed, of the seven creators, only Picasso comes close to the classic view of the prodigy—an individual performing at a master level while still a child. The other creators were distinguished chiefly by rapid growth, once they had committed themselves to a domain.

Personality and Motivation.   In many respects, the picture of creators that emerged from the study closely parallels that reported in the classic empirical studies emanating from the Institute of Personality Assessment at the University of California at Berkeley and from other research centers. Individuals of the E.C. type are indeed self-confident, alert, unconventional, hardworking, and committed obsessively to their work. Social life or hobbies are almost immaterial, representing at most a fringe on the creators' worktime.

I have reluctantly concluded that these characterizations may traditionally have been taken in too positive a way. That is, the self-confidence merges with egotism, egocentrism, and narcissism: each of the creators seems highly self-absorbed, not only wholly involved in his or her own projects, but likely to pursue them at the cost of other individuals. The British psychologist Hans Eysenck has suggested that there may even be a genetic basis to this amalgam of creativity and hard-headedness.

Nuances of differences exist. While as self-absorbed as any other creator, Einstein seems to have directed little overtly negative behavior toward others; he wanted chiefly to be left alone. Picasso represents the opposite extreme: he seems to have obtained sadistic pleasure, if not creative inspiration, from inducing discomfort in others. The remaining five creators can be placed somewhere in between these two extremes, perhaps somewhat like this:

Disregarding others		*Difficult toward others*	*Frankly sadistic*
Einstein	Eliot	Gandhi	Picasso
		Stravinsky	
		Graham	
		Freud	

A related dimension concerns the degree of effort attached to self-promotion. One can be quite distanced from, or even sadistic toward, others and still devote considerable energy to self-promotion. All seven creators recognized the importance of bringing their work to the attention of others; and in the absence of a parent, spouse, or aide who could accomplish this task on their behalf, they were expected to do so themselves. Much of the self-promotion was dedicated to the work; as far as I can determine, Gandhi was much more interested in bringing attention to his program than to his own person, but his efforts at self-promotion were still striking. I would array our creators in this approximate order:

Ordinary self-promotion			*Extraordinary self-promotion*		
Einstein	Picasso	Eliot	Stravinsky	Gandhi	Freud
		Graham			

A notable characteristic of creativity, I have argued, is its special amalgam of the childlike and the adultlike. This amalgam can occur both in the sphere of personality and in the sphere of ideas. It can be more positively tinged (when the childlike feature is innocence or freshness) or more negatively tinged (when the childlike feature is selfishness or retaliation). A brief comment is in order on the relation between the child and adult "faces" in these seven creators:

• In the realm of personality, the adult Freud showed few childlike features; if anything, he sought to present himself as mature and judicious. However, his interests in the unconscious, in the stream of consciousness, and in childhood wishes, fantasies, dreams, and sexual preoccupations underscore the extent to which the consciousness of the child remained crucial to his thinking.

• Einstein prided himself on the preservation of certain childlike features, such as curiosity and a defiance of convention. Like other creators, he placed the mind and spirit of the young child on a pedestal. While his concepts were technical contributions, they represented attempts to answer the same kinds of questions that preoccupy young children—Piaget-style questions about the basic nature of the universe and of experience.

• Like Einstein, Picasso cultivated certain childlike personality features. Besides his clowning for the media, his enormous quest for possessions (human as well as material) and his desire to control all aspects of his life (and others' lives) can be fairly described as infantile. In his artwork, he cultivated the fragmentation of forms, searched for the simplest underlying shapes, and strove to capture all aspects of a visual experience simultaneously on paper—all characteristics of the art of young children.

• Stravinsky was interested in the world of children, but certainly did not dote on his own childhood and took no special pleasure in appearing to act like a child. He probably was most reminiscent of a child in his extraordinarily litigious nature—his desire to pick, and then to win, every fight and, if possible, humiliate "the enemy" in the process. Like other modern artists, he anchored his work in the most basic elements of the medium— primitive rhythms and harmonies of the sort that had so impressed him when he was a young child.

• In Freudian terms, Eliot was the most rigid and repressed of the seven personalities, in his life, if not in his work. He had seemed old when young, and he enjoyed the role of the elder statesman. Yet even he retained a certain childlike nature, loving puzzles, producing bawdy doggerel, as well as verses designed for children; and he did not let his conservative political views undermine his appreciation of the novel and the offbeat. In the fragmented nature of his verse and its concern with unconscious and symbolic themes, he inhabits the same childlike universe of the artist Stravinsky and the scientist Freud.

• Martha Graham sought to remain forever young in her person and her work; any sign of aging terrified her. Her self-centeredness, furious temper, and single-minded passion speak to the preservation of certain behavioral patterns of the young. Both the art form that she selected (use of the body for expression) and the kind of elemental expressions that she favored draw on the reservoir of the child's imagination.

• We think of Gandhi as elderly and wise, yet in many ways he was very childish and even cultivated the look of the young child—naked to the world, proud of his body, excessively interested in its functions. Moreover, his major conceptual breakthrough—*satyagraha*—can be seen as childlike in the best sense of that term: individuals confronting one another in terms of actual equality and ensuring that they each feel renewed by a mutually satisfactory arrangement. Of course, it takes a most mature individual to bring this vision to fruition.

Having touched on the childlike component of each creator, I shall conclude this discussion of personality features by considering two remaining elements. The extent to which each of the creators engaged in public display of emotions, particularly the powerful ones of passion and rage, raises a complex issue. While each creator no doubt experienced very powerful feelings, some expressed them directly, while others preferred to "speak" through their works. There are few works of the period more powerful than *The Waste Land*, yet Eliot struck many observers as lifeless, without affect, frighteningly shy and reserved. Picasso and Graham, on the other hand, were as dramatic in their bedrooms and their working spaces as they were expressive in their works of art. The same contrast can be observed among our more scholarly creators. Einstein kept his feelings under wraps but wrote compellingly of the aesthetic elements of doing science; Freud took a clinical approach to emotion in his writings, but he was not afraid to confront his emotions, to express his feelings directly, and to mastermind and lead an intellectual revolution.

Particularly at the time of greatest creative tension, these creators felt under siege. So far as I can tell, all of them experienced periods of despondency when work was not going well, and virtually all had some kind of documented breakdown. The only possible exception here is Gandhi, who appears to have experienced two significant periods of depression. These preceded his decisions to return to a far simpler life: in his South African period (1906 to 1910) and in his return to India in the 1930s following the disastrous London conference.

Social-Psychological Aspects.   Though each of these creators seems to have come from a reasonably supportive household, unconditional intimacy and warmth may have been in short supply, except perhaps in the care of a nanny. When there was a close tie to the mother (Freud, Einstein, Eliot) or the father (Gandhi, Graham, Picasso), it seems to have been conditioned on achievement. Perhaps these contexts of early life stimulated the creators to regard work as the area where they would feel most whole. The French writer Gustave Flaubert once declared, "I love my work with a love that is frantic and perverted, as an ascetic loves the hairshirt that scratches his belly."

Strictness also marked most of the households. A disciplined "Protestant ethic"–style regimen led to children who were able to stick to tasks and to advance quickly in their studies or in their area of expertise. Ultimately, each of the creators rebelled against control: Freud, by calling explicit attention to the various motivational forces that had been covert in Vienna; Einstein by reveling in the permissiveness of the Aarau school and by confronting his teachers; Picasso, by rejecting his family, and particularly his father; Stravinsky, by spurning a legal career and finding a new father figure (Rimsky-Korsakov); Eliot, in similar fashion, by choosing a non-professorial career and leaving his native land for good; Gandhi, by rejecting aspects of his Hindu heritage and leaving home for over twenty years; and Graham, by choosing a dance profession, pursuing a unique life-style, and offering explicitly erotic performances.

I do not think that such a rebellion would have been possible without two factors: (1) sufficient skill and talent to allow one the option of a life different from one's forbears, and (2) positive models in childhood of a creative life. The homes of these seven creators may have been strict and conservative, but hints were given, either inside or around the home, that it was permissible to strike out on one's own, so long as one gave a good account of oneself. Freud's parents ultimately approved of his pursuing whichever career he liked; Einstein's uncle Jakob and his older friend Max Talmey promoted curiosity and scholarly pursuit; Picasso's uncle funded his study trips abroad; Stravinsky's family home served as a congregating place for artists of the time; Eliot's mother was herself a poet; Graham's father had an artistic side, nicely revealed in his decision to escort young Martha to a performance by Ruth St. Denis; and Gandhi's family was judicious in personal matters and permissive in religious matters.

Despite the support that the young creators received from their families, the theme of marginality pervades this work. Some of the creators were distinctly marginal by accident of their birth: Einstein and Freud as Jews in German-speaking countries, Graham as a woman in a male-oriented world. Others were marginal by virtue of where they came to live, by choice or by necessity: the Indian Gandhi abroad in the British empire; the Russian Stravinsky in Western Europe and the United States; the American Eliot in London; the Spaniard Picasso in Paris.

In addition to their demographic marginality, each of our creators used his or her marginality as a leverage in work. Not only did they exploit their marginality in what they worked on and how they worked on it; more important, whenever they risked becoming members of "the establishment," they would again shift course to attain at least intellectual marginality. Freud became suspicious whenever his work was too readily accepted; Einstein labored for thirty years on the unpopular side of the quantum-mechanical enterprise; Picasso and Stravinsky renounced first the mainstream artistic heritage and, in later decades, their own unrelenting departures from it; Eliot embraced unfashionable political and social ideas and then attempted in midlife to become a playwright; Graham took on new and challenging genres throughout her life, finally making the shift to choreography successfully (if reluctantly) in her eighties; and Gandhi constantly embraced unpopular causes and controversial groups.

While each creator was determinedly marginal and was willing to give up much to retain this marginality, it is too simple to say that each was simply aloof from the world of other people. At least two further patterns were at work. First, these creators often moved from a period of life in which they were comfortable with many persons to a period of maximum isolation, at the moment of their major discovery, only to return to a larger, and perhaps more accepting, world in the later years of life. Second, at the time of their greatest isolation, these creators needed, and benefited from, a special relation to one or more supportive individuals.

I return to this special relation at the conclusion of this chapter, but let me comment now on the general shift in the texture of interpersonal relations across the life span. Freud is the prototypical figure here—popular and engaged as a youth, increasingly isolated as he seeks his own domain, and then a firm leader of an ever-expanding crusade in the last decades of his life. Einstein's life pattern is somewhat similar, but in his case, the ultimate relationship to the wider world took a more distanced form, as he concerned himself with weighty issues of war, peace, philosophy, and religion. Gandhi's trajectory reflects aspects of both of these models: the need to organize a small group of loyal lieutenants, in the spirit of Freud's psychoanalytic circle, coupled with the capacity to relate to larger segments of humanity in a more distanced way, through writings, through the media of mass communication, and through his inspiring personal example.

With respect to the four artists, I discern a somewhat different pattern. Whatever their configuration of childhood relations, all experienced a period of isolation when they were working on their pioneering compositions. Once their work began to be accepted, they found themselves necessarily enmeshed in a political network. Stravinsky seems to have been most energized by this political world; Eliot accepted it as part of the territory and negotiated it surprisingly well; Picasso and Graham, in their different ways, left as much as possible to other individuals, and yet rose effectively to the occasion when their own presence was wanted.

If I can risk another generalization, none of these individuals had a particular need for friends who could be treated as equals. Rather, they used others to advance their professional work, being charming, seductive, and at least superficially loyal, while dropping these peers quietly or dramatically when the usefulness was judged to be at an end. The carnage around a great creator is not a pretty sight, and this destructiveness occurs whether the individual is engaged in a solitary pursuit or ostensibly working for the betterment of humankind.

Life Patterns: The Shape of Productivity.   Without wishing to invest more magic in a numeral than is warranted, I have been struck throughout this study by the operation of the ten-year rule. These seven creators can be well described in terms of careers in which important events and breakthroughs occurred at approximately ten-year intervals, with the number of such ten-year periods allotted to the creators differing across domains. As has already been well documented in studies of cognitive psychology, it takes about ten years for an individual to gain initial mastery of a domain. Should one begin at age four, like Picasso, one can be a master by the teenage years; composers like Stravinsky and dancers like Graham, who did not begin their creative endeavors until later adolescence, did not hit their stride until their late twenties.

The decade of an apprenticeship heightens the likelihood of a major breakthrough. Such a breakthrough generally follows a series of tentative steps, but when it occurs, it represents a decisive break from the past. In this vein I have described Freud's "Project," Einstein's special theory of relativity, Picasso's *Les demoiselles d'Avignon*, Stravinsky's *Le sacre du printemps*, Eliot's *The Waste Land*, Graham's *Frontier*, and Gandhi's strike at Ahmedabad as breakthrough events.

In the years that follow, the creator comes to terms with his or her breakthrough. The appeal of innovation rarely atrophies, but generally speaking, the subsequent breakthrough is of a broader and more integrative sort, with the creator proceeding in a more nuanced way, tying innovations more directly to what has gone on in the past of the domain and to what others have been executing in the domain. Freud's *Interpretation of Dreams* (or perhaps *Totem and Taboo*), Einstein's general theory of relativity, Picasso's *Guernica*, Stravinsky's *Les noces*, Eliot's *Four Quartets*, Graham's *Appalachian Spring*, and Gandhi's salt march are candidates for a second, culminating breakthrough.

What happens after the second breakthrough is more a reflection of the nature of the domain than of the skills and aspirations of the creator. If the domain is wide open, freshly charted, and graced with relatively little competition, the creator retains the opportunity to continue to be innovative for as long as he or she remains active. This is what happened to Graham, Freud, Stravinsky, Gandhi, and Picasso. (Freud, in fact, thought that he had a breakthrough every seven years.) If, however, the domain is already well delineated, there are many other younger individuals working in the domain, or the creator's energies are sapped, then the possibility of further innovation is reduced. Neither Eliot nor Einstein was able to continue his innovations beyond the second decade of efforts, though Eliot wrote plays and Einstein worked on theoretical and philosophical issues until his death. The varying permeability of the domains cuts across the arts and the sciences: lyric poetry ends up as closer to physics than to painting.

After the second decade, a different kind of opportunity arises. The individual may begin to look back on the relevant domain in a historical or reflective way. Picasso, Stravinsky, and Graham each pursued an impressive neoclassical period; Eliot tried to do so, but with less pronounced success. One can also become a metacommentator on one's field, as did Einstein and Eliot. When there exists a respected role within the domain, as there has been in literary criticism, one can continue in this reflective vein indefinitely. In the sciences, however, people who become philosophers of science are considered to have left their domain; thus, in the final decades of his life, Einstein was not considered central to the discussions pursued by the most innovative scientists.

In table 5.1 I summarize the trajectories of creativity across the decades. The radical breakthrough is indicated by a single asterisk, and the comprehensive work by two asterisks. Note that no two creators exhibit exactly the same trajectory, but that the "ten-year rule" still proves suggestive. The issue of productivity may appear to be a confounding factor. In some domains one can produce works at an enormous rate. Picasso produced on the average of one work a day throughout his adult life; Freud produced dozens of books and hundreds of papers. On the other hand, Eliot wrote less than fifty poems, some of them very brief, and Einstein's published scientific works were far fewer than Freud's. Yet there are first-class poets (like W. H. Auden) and major scientists (like the chemist Carl Djerassi) who prove that creativity in literature and in science is also compatible with fecundity.

Table 5.1   **The Ten-Year Rule at Work**

	Origin	10 Years	20 Years	30 Years and Beyond
Freud	Charcot	"Project"* *The Interpretation of Dreams***	*Three Contributions to the Theory of Sex*	Social works
Einstein	Light-beam thought experiment	Special theory of relativity*	General theory of relativity**	Philosophical works
Picasso	Barcelona circle	*Les demoiselles d'Avignon** Cubism	Neoclassical style	*Guernica***
Stravinsky	Rimsky-Korsakov influenced works	*Le sacre du printemps**	*Les noces***	Later styles
Eliot	"Prufrock" Juvenilia	*The Waste Land**	*Four Quartets***	Playwright/ critic
Graham	St. Denis troupe	First recital	*Frontier**	*Appalachian Spring*** Neoclassical style
Gandhi	Natal	So. Africa Satyagraha	Ahmedabad*	Salt march**

Radical breakthrough
**Comprehensive work*

While even creative individuals can differ enormously in terms of energy, I think it is important not to dwell on the actual number of products listed in an encyclopedia. What strikes me about our subjects is that they were each productive every day. Eliot may not have written poetry, but he wrote hundreds of reviews, edited major publications, and issued books on a wide range of subjects. Gandhi's literary output fills ninety volumes. Einstein worked on questions of physics until the last years of his life, even though his publication output lagged. It would be more opportune to monitor the number of new ideas or separate projects than to count the number of "final products" by a painter, poet, or physicist. Picasso may have made a thousand paintings over a five-year period, but in his own mind one or two of them were far more important (in my terms, "defining works") than the others. Freud may have written a dozen papers a year, but he could be repetitive in these essays, and he stressed his own need to search actively for new ideas. The ten-year period is revealing in this respect because it suggests that, independent of the number of discrete works issued by an individual, there may be a limit to the number of genuinely innovative works or ideas that an individual can produce in a finite period of time.

Domain Level

If the level of the individual reveals as many similarities as differences, the domain level constitutes the crucial location for the most telling differences across the creators. Youths interested in some aspect of their world evolve into young adults who choose (or are chosen) to work in a recognized domain or discipline within the culture. Each will be working in a domain for decades, and so the nature of that domain becomes crucial.

When I embarked on this study, I believed one could describe the steps of creativity across domains in a relatively comprehensive way. Building on Graham Wallas well-known fourfold scheme—from preparation and incubation, to illumination and revision—I described elsewhere the nature of local disturbances, the initial surgery undertaken to fix them, the unsatisfactory nature of this stop-gap measure, and the gradual emergence of the need to create some kind of a new language or symbol system adequate to the problem at hand. And I posited an "afterlife" to this emerging scheme, where other knowledgeable individuals attempted to understand the new symbolic scheme and to promulgate it, and where the new invention, as understood by others, gradually became accepted by the field and even contributed to the reformulation of the domain.

I still stand by this scheme, in a general sense, but I now believe that it leaves out two very important, related dimensions. First, the kinds of symbol systems with which individuals work in different domains vary strikingly; one cannot simply lump them together under the broad rubric of symbol systems. Freud worked with words as shorthand for scientific concepts about human dreams and behaviors, and with simple diagrammatic schemes. Einstein thought in terms of complex spatial schemes, bodily imagery, and mathematical equations, with words entering as afterthoughts at the end of the process. Picasso dealt with colors, textures, lines, and forms as they relate to objects in the world and, increasingly, in terms of their own intrinsic features. Stravinsky treated analogous elements in the world of sound (timbre, rhythm, pitch, color); though these bear some relation to the world of experience, they gain significance chiefly in terms of intramusical associations. The verbal elements, allusions, and sounds used by Eliot lead in a wholly different direction from the words used by a Freud or an Einstein. Graham worked chiefly with the materials of the human body, attempting to capture plot, emotion, and formal relations in explicit gestures, and integrating them with the accompanying music and decor. And, finally, Gandhi's texts and talks represented an effort to paint a convincing picture of the experiences of a group of people: he built a model of current beliefs and behaviors within a group, as well as a model of how to change them, through the mounting of certain pivotal performances ranging from ritualistic to high-stake.

Not only do these symbols and symbol systems differ dramatically from one another, but the kinds of mental skills needed to work with them, and to communicate discoveries to others, are distinctly different—so much so, that grouping them all together as symbol systems obscures as much as it clarifies. Indeed, as described in the Interludes, these creative individuals were involved, respectively, in at least five distinct kinds of activities:

1. *Solving a particular problem* (usually a scientific one). Einstein's early papers, for example, on Brownian motion, reflect such a practice. Particular assignments tackled in the course of artistic training, such as Stravinsky's reorchestration of classical pieces, constitute examples from a different domain.

2. *Putting forth a general conceptual scheme.* Whatever their original missions, Einstein and Freud are most remembered for the broad schemes they developed—relativity theory, by Einstein, and the psychoanalytic theory of unconscious processes, by Freud.

3. *Creating a product.* Artists create small-scale products, such as preliminary sketches or brief poems, or larger-scale ones, such as murals, operas, or novels. These works embody ideas, emotions, and concepts, but they are not well described, overall, as efforts to solve problems or to create conceptual schemes. Rather, they are often highly original instances of works within a genre, or attempts to initiate a new genre. Picasso, Stravinsky, and Eliot fall into this scheme, as does Graham in her guise as a choreographer.

4. A *stylized kind of performance.* In forms like dance or drama, an individual creator may embody the art form; in this case the "autographic" work does not exist apart from a particular realization by one person at a

specific historical moment. The performance may be prescribed in various ways, but opportunities always exist for innovation, improvisation, and interpretation. The condition of the body and the exigencies of the historical moment circumscribe such performances.

4. A *performance for high stakes*. When one enters the political or spiritual realm, an individual's own public words and actions become the terrain in which the creativity unfolds. Gandhi may have had brilliant or scatterbrained ideas; but in the end it was his capacity to appear credible to his followers, and to the rest of the world, by virtue of his example at specific historical moments, that constituted the central aspects of his creation. Unlike the ritualistic dancer or dramatic artist, the high-stakes performer is risking security, health, and even life in the service of a mission. In Clifford Geertz's famous phrase, it is a form of very "deep play."

In light of the new distinctions introduced—a consideration of the nature of specific symbol systems and a position of five different kinds of activities that merit the term *creative*—it is necessary to conceptualize a more complicated scheme, which entails three components:

1. The particular symbol system(s) employed
2. The nature of the creative activity
3. Particular moments in the course of a creative breakthrough or performance

Rather than simply speaking generically of incubation, one needs to configure such dimensions in light of whether one is dealing (1) with words, gestures, or mathematical concepts, for example; (2) with the solving of a problem, the creating of a work, or the influencing of behavior among individuals living in one's community; and (3) with the period of conceptualization, the execution of the work, or the actual time when a performance is unfolding.

So far I have focused on the kinds of symbol systems and activities that characterize each domain. But domains differ as well in terms of their *structures* at a given historical moment. One key structural aspect is the extent to which a domain may be considered paradigmatic. In the way in which this word is usually employed, only physics can lay claim to the status of a *scientific paradigm*—a domain in which established practices and norms are accepted by all members. Psychology in Freud's time and even psychology today are preparadigmatic: the principal issues differ between rival schools, not between rival interpretations of mutually agreed upon phenomena and findings. But the physics paradigms associated with Newton, with Maxwell and Faraday, or with Mach and Helmholtz were not adequate either; the uneasiness with current concepts expressed by Lorentz and Poincare around 1900 pointed to the possibility that a new paradigm might soon be needed.

The term *paradigm* can be stretched, or analogized, outside of science. When one performs such stretching, it becomes clear that there are times in other domains where there is also a dominant paradigm. In the late eighteenth century, Western classical music embraced a paradigm of composition; by the same token, in British law courts today, there are accepted paradigms for handling disputes.

At the beginning of the century, it seems fair to say, there were no equivalently entrenched paradigms in the major art forms. The romantic approach in music and literature and the academic and impressionist movements in the visual arts were in their waning phases; dance was not taken seriously as an art form. Thus, these domains can be considered "paradigmless" and, hence, open for new and competing approaches. If one can use the term *paradigm* for relationships between geographical entities within the British empire, it can perhaps be said that the British still believed that they knew what was best for their colonies and colonists, while the indigenous residents themselves were becoming increasingly restive.

The hegemony of a single paradigm is probably the best prognosticator of the rapidity with which a new approach can be broadly accepted. Despite some initial skepticism, the merit of Einstein's breakthrough could be readily and rapidly appreciated within the physics community. On the other hand, the very centripetal nature of a paradigmatic domain also means that younger individuals can soon make contributions that build on the new paradigm, and they thereupon become competitive with the originator of the new paradigm. What happened to Einstein has happened to other paradigm makers at work in established domains; he was soon overtaken by the younger scientists, who readily mastered his contributions and were able to build on it.

None of the other six creators had to confront this situation; in a sense, all of them had enough work to last a lifetime. And, indeed, the creators did continue to work and make innovations throughout the rest of their lengthy lives. The chief exception is Eliot. Of the various possibilities, the explanation that I have favored here pertains to the nature of the domain of lyric poetry, as I mentioned earlier. While other kinds of writing seem relatively resistant to the processes of aging, lyric poetry is a domain where talent is discovered early, burns brightly, and then peters out at an early age. There are few exceptions to this meteoric pattern. Eliot attempted to lengthen his creative life by becoming a playwright and critic: his accomplishments, particularly in the critical sphere, are notable, but they do represent a lifeline different from that pursued by other creators; the closest analogy would be Graham after she had been forced to stop dancing.

Field Level

Once the creators have begun to advance within a chosen domain, they inevitably encounter other individuals with whom they must interact. Typically, each creator will have one or more mentors; if reasonably successful, she will also spawn colleagues, rivals, and followers, and she will become involved in political battles, to at least a limited degree. How do each of the creators fare on these field dimensions?

It would be virtually inconceivable to envision any mature expert devoid of at least some competent mentoring. Still, our creators differ noticeably in the kind and degree of mentoring to which they were exposed. Freud had perhaps the most traditional mentoring picture: a number of strong father figures, ranging from Bruecke to Charcot to Breuer, who introduced him to important disciplines, problems, and methods. Einstein was unusual for a scientist in the relative lack of personal mentors. His mentoring seems to have occurred at a greater distance, by virtue of the reading that he did, first in popular accounts, and then in the writings of Mach, Poincaré, Maxwell, and other major professional figures. In this way he is reminiscent of certain artistic titans of the past, like Shakespeare or Beethoven, who are not considered to have had major personal mentoring figures.

Each of the four artists benefited from mentors. Stravinsky had the most traditional experience, with Rimsky-Korsakov serving as a primary musical mentor and Diaghilev introducing him to other aspects of the theatrical world. Eliot was influenced by several of his teachers at Harvard, by the slightly older and more daring Pound, and by the writings of Laforgue and Symons. Picasso benefited most directly from his father; thereafter, he was exposed to a multiplicity of figures from the recent and distant past, no one of whom seems to have dominated his artistic formation. Graham had relatively demarcated mentoring from the team of Ruth St. Denis and Ted Shawn; thereafter, as we have seen, her close confidant Louis Horst doubled as her best teacher.

Again, Gandhi seems anomalous here. One can point to some individuals whom he knew well, like Gokhale and Rajchandra, and to those whose writings he admired, such as Tolstoy and Ruskin. He also had a circle of confidants, such as Polak and Schleslin. Yet to a greater extent than with most other creative figures, Gandhi seems to have invented himself. Perhaps this explains why he wrote so much about his own experiments on himself and why, in certain senses, he felt on an equal footing with the religious innovators of the past and with his own God.

Earlier I touched on the generally dismal relationships between the creators and other human beings. What can be said more specifically about the creators' relationships with others in their chosen field? The paper trail can be a confounding factor here, for those who liked to write, like Freud, Stravinsky, and Eliot, have provided much more evidence about their relations to others in the field than have those who did not conventionally resort to correspondence, memos, and diaries.

With respect to the seven creators, I would locate Freud and Stravinsky at one end of the continuum, with most other practitioners close by, and Einstein at the other end. Freud and Stravinsky were both intensely competitive individuals who saw—and labeled—many others as rivals. They doggedly protected their territory, divided the world into supporters and enemies, proved quick to reward loyalty and to punish apparent disloyalty. They perceived the sociopolitical scene in zero-sum terms: if you were not for them, you were against them. Each had an ensemble of followers who did their bidding, and neither welcomed close colleagues, perhaps because they felt that few of their domain peers were their equals. It is no accident that their closest, least charged friendships occurred with individuals outside of their own domain.

Picasso was at least as competitive as Freud and Stravinsky, and probably far more ruthless toward men and women than either of the others. But perhaps because, from a fairly early age, he could afford to have others negotiate for him, and because he did not have as ready a recourse to writing, he does not qualify as quite so politically embroiled as Freud and Stravinsky. Eliot became involved in political relations as well and proved quite skilled at them; but I perceive little relish on his part about this sphere of life, and he seems to have been happy to metamorphose into the role of an elder statesman. Additionally, in comparison with other figures, Eliot seems to have devoted less effort to discovering enemies, labeling them as such, and seeking to destroy them. Graham's relationships with colleagues were charged, and she gave at least as well as she received; but her focus on her work and on the performance was primary; and she was pleased to leave financial and logistic arrangements to other people.

Gandhi and Einstein constitute the exceptions here. Einstein was simply less interested in the personal and political sphere surrounding his work, rarely taking a chance to defend himself or to attack others, unless controversy hinged on a nonscientific issue. More so than the other creators, Einstein was content to allow the work to speak for itself, though he occasionally encouraged his supporters. As for Gandhi, he often affirmed the essential political nature of what he was doing and was endlessly enterprising in promoting his own work. Yet, as the central portion of his message had to do with maintaining peace with his adversaries, he could not afford to be openly jealous or competitive with them. Still, his sorry record with his own family indicates that Gandhi could be very difficult interpersonally, especially when he could not prevail over those who were closest to him. The master at large-scale politics proved a disaster in more intimate relations.

A final dimension of the field points to the complementary concept of the domain. I refer here to the extent to which a field is organized hierarchically and the extent to which one's position in the hierarchy influences one's behavior. Here the differences across fields are again striking. Early on, Einstein was placed at the summit of the hierarchy of physics, and his position remained secure even after his death; but he himself took little interest in this position, except perhaps insofar as it permitted him to focus on his scientific work and to bring attention to his nonscientific interests. Freud was never highly ranked in any internationally acknowledged field, so he created his own. Thenceforth, controlling the hierarchical structure of psychoanalysis became a chief preoccupation.

Picasso's position as the outstanding painter of the century was also widely acknowledged from the start of his middle age. Picasso was far more interested in his own work and his own success than he was in influencing the behavior of other painters; and while he retained relationships with some artists, only Matisse seems to have occupied a significant part of his consciousness. For Stravinsky, the hierarchy was more complex, inasmuch as the rival schools of music continued throughout his life. For many years he saw himself as locked in competition with Schönberg, the leader of the rival school; only after Schönberg's death did Stravinsky himself feel free to grapple with twelve-tone music. Graham found herself similarly embattled with other leaders of modern dance; and though Graham had trained most of the best of the next generation, she desired ardently to remain the figure emblematic of dance, even after her long-delayed retirement.

A major part of Eliot's assignment as an editor and critic was precisely to attend to the cultivation of the domain of literature, spanning fiction and poetry. Seldom has an honored practitioner also served as its chief evaluator (Freud might be considered another exemplar of this dual role within psychoanalysis). Eliot performed this task with more generosity of spirit than one might have predicted; he believed in a hierarchy of literary quality, susceptible to judgment apart from political and social attitudes. At the same time, particularly with respect to predecessors, he enjoyed playing an iconoclastic role; and in his rewriting of literary history, he was, whether or not consciously, attempting to boost his own stock.

The model of a field, with a set of judges operating consensually, is perhaps least germane in a consideration of Gandhi. In one way, his domain, politics, was the oldest and broadest; but in another way, *satyagraha*, like psychoanalysis, was a domain of his devising, and as the founder, he was by definition in the best position in the field to render judgments about its practitioners and practices. But Gandhi was not in the business of making evaluations; he was in the business of bringing about change. Here he was playing for very high stakes; and his competitors were the major political figures of his time, like Lenin and Churchill, and the major religious thinkers of other times, like Christ and Buddha. Gandhi was surely aware of these considerations, though he seems to have been genuinely humbled by such lofty comparisons. In the end, Gandhi's creativity is closely linked to the success of his reform efforts: he was amazingly successful in the middle years of his life, but far less successful thereafter.

With this discussion of individual, domain, and field considerations, I conclude a review of the "data" relevant to the theoretical and empirical issues that guided my study. Definitive answers about these issues remain elusive. At the same time, however, one may speak of strong trends with regard to certain issues—for example, the prevalence of marginality or the unimportance of prodigiousness; and of striking domain differences with respect to other issues, such as the possibility of lifelong creativity or the inevitability of political strife. As others add data points from these and other domains, and from this and other eras, we should be able to facilitate the transition from an idiographic, Gruber-like effort to a nomothetic, Simonton-style research enterprise.

Asynchronies Assessed

In *Creating Minds,* I introduced an organizing framework, designed in response to the question "Where is creativity?" The essential burden of the "triangle of creativity" has been to investigate the dialectics among the *individual* person, or talent; the *domain* in which the individual is working; and the *field* of knowledgeable experts who evaluate works in the domain. No matter how talented the individual is, in some abstract sense, unless he or she can connect with a domain and produce works that are valued by the relevant field, it is not possible to ascertain whether that person in fact merits the epithet "creative." In some cases, of course, there may not be a fit initially between the nodes of the triangle; but unless some kind of rapprochement can be arranged among individual, domain, and field, an ultimate decision about an individual's creativity cannot be made.

Occasionally, an almost perfect fit among individual, domain, and field will exist: this is the textbook example of a prodigy. Indeed, in some societies, such alignment is all that is ever wanted. In our modern world, however, few if any prodigies make a ready transition to the world of the creative adult. That is because we seek from adults a kind of innovation, a departure from the norm, that not even the most talented youth can fathom. The closest that one comes to the adult prodigy is an individual like Mozart or Picasso, who was blessed with a stunning talent and who eventually became an acknowledged master; but as is well known, both men experienced anything but a smooth transition from youthful to adult practice. More commonly, as I have shown, the individuals who made the most remarkable breakthroughs could not have been considered prodigies by any strict definition of that term.

What seems defining in the creative individual is the capacity to exploit, or profit from, an apparent *misfit* or *lack of smooth connections* within the triangle of creativity. From an analytic point of view, there are six possible areas of asynchrony: within the individual, within the domain, within the field; between individual and domain; between individual and field; and between domain and field. Individuals who avoid any kind of asynchrony may well be prodigies or experts, but they are unlikely to become creative people; those who experience asynchrony at all points may be overwhelmed. I have hypothesized that an individual will be judged creative to the extent that he or she exhibits several asynchronies and yet can withstand the concomitant strain.

In the previous pages I have provided evidence of each of these kinds of asynchronies. It would be possible to look for each kind of asynchrony in each case study, but such a quest for forty-two or more asynchronies would be forced and, therefore, not revealing. Instead, I want to recall some of the more striking asynchronies that have emerged.

At the level of the individual, I noted the asynchrony between Picasso's excellent spatial and bodily capacities, on the one hand, and his meager scholastic capacities, on the other. Within the domain of physics, the strains at work in the years before Einstein's cutting of the Gordian knot were apparent. Within the field of clinical psychiatry, there were the deep divisions between those who valued Freud's work and those who felt that it was errant nonsense; and, of course, the tension between mass (low) and elite (high) fields characterizes the several art forms.

One can with equal readiness amass instances of asynchronies across nodes. Freud exhibited a set of intelligences that were unusual for a natural scientist but that finely tuned the newly formed domain of psychodynamic practice. Graham's early dances were remote from the tastes of regular concertgoers, but they excited pivotal newspaper reviewers, who helped create a new field for modern dance. Finally, with Gandhi, the domain of legalistic or militaristic conflict resolution functioned adequately within a British setting but made less sense to the field of twentieth-century Indians seeking to build their own society.

A problem with the hypothesis of fruitful asynchrony is that one can all too readily find instances of asynchronies. Do creative individuals really experience or exhibit more asynchronies, or are they simply better at exploiting them? Here the example of marginality is useful. By definition, most individuals are not marginal within their community; hence, to the extent that there is a larger proportion of marginal individuals within the ranks of the creative, one has evidence that asynchronies may actually be associated with creative output in a statistically verifiable way. But it seems equally true that creative individuals, once they have felt the pain and pleasure of asynchrony, often continue to seek asynchrony, even as many other individuals "escape from freedom" and rush to the comfort of majority status.

I maintain that each of our individuals stands out in the extent to which he or she *sought* conditions of asynchrony, receiving a kind of thrill or flow experience from being "at the edge" and eventually finding it difficult to understand why anyone would *not* wish to experience the fruits of asynchrony. Such a pattern clearly characterizes each of the creators, independent of the degree of asynchrony or marginality with which each began. Though highly gifted in many areas, Freud was riven with asynchronies within himself and with respect to other individuals and to the several domains in which he worked. And whenever it looked like he might be moving somewhat closer to the establishment, Freud made the move typical of creators of traveling closer to the edge, confronting yet more complex issues, making even stronger demands on those around him.

Though by any definition as creative and successful as Freud, Einstein may not have had the same drive to be asynchronous in his life or his work. At an early age he had already identified the issues on which he wished to work, and like the bear of which his secretary spoke, he would have continued to work on them for the next millennium. Einstein's personality and gifts had suited him well for his revolutionary discoveries between 1905 and 1920. In that sense, the world of physics interacted perfectly with his particular strengths and style. Thereafter, his asynchrony with physics became too great. He distinguished himself as a commentator on the world scene and on the enterprise of science.

Each of the four artists was characterized by considerable asynchrony, but this lack of fit affected them in different ways. From an established family and with strong academic and professional credentials, Eliot had to stretch the most to induce asynchrony. But the combination of his strange personality, difficult marriage, and decision to live abroad on his own finances, yielded an almost desperately asynchronous individual by the end of the First World War. Thereafter, the asynchronies lessened somewhat, perhaps mirroring a muting of his creative talent. Graham can be seen as an opposite to Eliot, since she had neither the family connections nor the social advantage, as then defined, of being male. By personality, she was strengthened by challenges (as Eliot was probably not), and so she was able to thrive under asynchronies of her own devising, as well as those inherent in her situation.

Stravinsky and Picasso can be seen as similar on some dimensions, opposite on others. Stravinsky came from a family that was centrally involved in the musical arts, while Picasso's father, though an artist, possessed distinctly limited talent. Whereas Stravinsky wished to escape from bourgeois complacency, Picasso wanted to escape from provinciality. Both men could have remained with their early successes—the music of *Firebird* and *Petrouchka*, the art of the blue and the pink periods—but both were impelled to strike out in more radical directions. And despite the eventual success that greeted their frankly iconoclastic works, they were stimulated for the rest of their lives to search for asynchronies in both their professional efforts and in their relations to other individuals.

Once again, Gandhi presents a complex picture. On demographic grounds, both within his country and as a citizen of the world, Gandhi was most asynchronous with his surroundings. In addition, his decidedly odd personality and philosophy helped ensure that he would always stand out from those around him. At the same time, however, his work was predicated on the assumption that he could illustrate, indeed exemplify, deep connections to the rest of his society: that he could appear as a typical representative of the larger Indian community. Thus, he had to cultivate, to embody, a being who was at once synchronous with the rest of society and humanity and distinctly marginal, someone positioned to bring about radical social change. Perhaps this dual assignment can itself be seen as a form of asynchrony; that is, it may be even more anomalous for the creator to retain one foot in the camp of the ordinary than to be completely dissociated from one's society.

Those in search of asynchronies can feel rewarded by these case studies, which document considerable initial asynchrony as well as a decided taste for creating more. In this way, the creative individual certainly differs from the individual who does not seek to stand out in any way. But is the creator also different from members of a reasonable control group—a group composed of individuals in a related domain who are equally ambitious but perhaps less successful, such as Wilhelm Fliess in the domain of medicine or Pierre Janet in the domain of psychiatry? My own hunch is that our seven model creators *are* different, and that the degree and type of asynchrony they represent is somehow more fruitful—more fruitful, say, than Wilhelm Fliess's scheme, which was too bizarre, or Pierre Janet's scheme, which was less sharply delineated and less expertly disseminated. But in the absence of convincing methods for evaluating both asynchrony and fruitfulness, this must remain a speculation.

The Two Emerging Themes

Any researcher embarking on a large-scale study must be guided by certain assumptions. In the absence of such a rough roadmap, his or her journey is almost impossible to envision. Yet, at the same time, most researchers remain open to the possibility of surprises or of new discoveries: after all, if one knew exactly what one expected to find, then the journey would hardly be worth undertaking. Here, as elsewhere, the favorable degree of asynchrony is delectable.

Two themes I had not anticipated emerged during my work on these case studies. Consistent with the developmental perspective, one theme represents a relatively brief period of time, during which the creator made a major breakthrough; the second theme covers a significant portion of the creator's adult life.

The Matrix of Support at the Time of Breakthrough

Because of my familiarity with Freud's life, I had known that, during the time of his greatest loneliness, he had gained sustenance from his relationship with Fliess. While few scholars have felt that Freud obtained indispensable ideas from Fliess, Freud clearly needed the latter's support and listening ear. And since Freud destroyed Fliess's correspondence, we cannot determine the extent to which he gave Freud either valuable ideas or acute criticisms.

When I began to learn about other creators, I gradually became struck by the fact that, far from being an isolated case, the Freud–Fliess confidant relationship represented the norm. As we have seen in the preceding chapters, Braque played much this role for Picasso; Horst, for Graham; Pound (along with Vivien Eliot), for Eliot; and the Diaghilev circle (along with special figures like Roerich and Ramuz), for Stravinsky.

It is possible to stretch the facts to cover the remaining two creators as well. For Einstein, the first rank of support came from the members of the Olympiad, with whom he had such regular and intimate contact during the years before his epochal discoveries. More proximal support for his relativity theory came from his close friend Besso and, with reasonable likelihood, from his wife Mileva as well.

I feel less secure in invoking the name of one or a few individuals who served as confidants for Gandhi. But the defining moment at Ahmedabad might not have been possible if Gandhi had not been aligned with one family member (Anasyra Sarabhai) and against another (Ambalal Sarabhai), to both of whom he felt powerfully connected. Perhaps, in this sense, I can legitimately include the Gandhi example within the pattern of confidants as well.

There is more to be said about this confidant relationship. First, under ideal circumstances, it ought to have two dimensions: an affective dimension, in which the creator is buoyed with unconditional support; and a cognitive dimension, where the supporter seeks to understand, and to provide useful feedback on, the nature of the breakthrough. The prototypical supporters—Fliess, Horst, and Braque—apparently assumed both roles. Certainly, between them, Pound and Vivien Eliot cover the waterfront, too. With Einstein, the need for affective support may have been less pronounced; with Stravinsky, the various kinds of support may well have been distributed among diverse figures, including Fokine, Nijinsky, Benois, Monteux, Roerich, and Diaghilev himself. Again, I have the least to say about Gandhi, though it might be relevant to remark that the support of large multitudes of strikers, workers, religious individuals, and his own loyal team of intimates must have meant a great deal to the Indian leader.

As I have perceived it, these relationships harken back to important associations early in life. One model entails the exchanges that take place between the mother and the infant, as the mother attempts to teach the child the language and rules of the culture in which they will both live. Thanks to the mother's constant efforts at interpretation, the infant passes here from a state of ignorance to a state of knowledge. Another model entails the exchanges that take place between close friends—siblings or peers—as they explore the unfamiliar world together and relate to one another what they have discovered.

Such processes must be replayed at the time of the breakthrough. The difference is that the language being forged is new not just for a single child but for the rest of humankind. The creator is in the throes of discovering this language, as a means of solving certain issues—often personal as well as discipline-based—and, perhaps, of illuminating others as well. The creator must be able to devise and understand the language well enough to use it and then gain sufficient mastery to communicate it to others (lest it be autistic). In so doing, the creator draws on earlier models of teaching a new language to an ignorant but willing pupil.

It would be bizarre and unnecessary to maintain that this form of communication represents any kind of a conscious replay of the mother–child dialogue, or of the kind of intimate conversations that take place in early life, for instance, between siblings, twins, or close friends. Yet, I find these analogies helpful in conveying the phenomenal flavor of this exchange. I would submit, further, that a creator who has not gone through an earlier effective communication process, such as the mother–child or nurse–infant dialogue or the conversation between close friends, would have difficulties in effecting this most radical kind of adult communication. It is notable that this support in adult life is related specifically to the creation of new work—a replaying of an earlier situation in which elders rewarded a gifted young child's achievements.

My claim, then, is that the time of creative breakthrough is highly charged, both affectively and cognitively. Support is needed at this time, more so than at any other time in life since early infancy. The kind of communication that takes place is unique and uniquely important, bearing closer resemblance to the introduction of a new language early in life, than to the routine kinds of conversations between individuals who already share the same language. The often inarticulate and still struggling conversation also represents a way for the creator to test that he or she is still sane, still understandable by a sympathetic member of the species.

The Faustian Bargain and a Creative Life

I have alluded to a Faustian bargain struck by each creator. The Faust legend is but the best-known exemplar of a widely held belief that creative individuals are special by virtue of their gift, and that they must pay some kind of a price or adhere to some kind of an agreement to sustain that gift. In a trivial sense, of course, this proposition has to be true: one cannot remain an expert writer or performer unless one practices one's craft regularly. In its more dramatic sense, however, this claim has the air of fancy: after all, why should we think that a creator need be in communication, or in cahoots, with a personal god or a private devil?

I was quite surprised to find that the creators, in order to maintain their gifts, went through behaviors or practices of a fundamentally superstitious, irrational, or compulsive nature. Usually, as a means of being able to continue work, the creator sacrificed normal relationships in the personal sphere. The kind of bargain may vary, but the tenacity with which it is maintained seems consistent. These arrangements are typically not described as pacts with anyone, but at least to me, they resemble that kind of semimagical, semimystical arrangement in the West we have come to associate with Dr. Faustus and Mephistopheles. Equally, they have a religious flavor, as if each creator had, so to speak, struck a deal with a personal god.

The only allusion I found to a deliberate experience of this sort was in the biography of Picasso, the most overtly superstitious of the seven creators, regarding his sworn oath to stop painting if one of his sisters recovered from a critical illness (indeed, a singular bargain). Picasso elected to devote his life to painting when she died, and I argue that Picasso took this commitment as a license to sacrifice not only himself but others in the service of his painting; the bargain that had not been honored gave rise to a "counterbargain" that sanctioned his otherwise outrageous behavior toward so many other people over the course of his life.

The extreme asceticism associated with the lives of Freud, Gandhi, and Eliot represents another variant of the bargain. Freud and Gandhi both renounced sexual relations at a very young age and subjected themselves to many kinds of seemingly unnecessary (and perhaps unwise) deprivations. In addition to being virtually celibate, Eliot endured a miserable marriage for many years, seemingly as part of the bargain that he had forged to lead the poetic life. Revealingly, following his divorce, and especially following his second marriage, he became much happier, but also much less productive.

And what of the other figures? Graham did not renounce the pleasures of the flesh, but she was wary of maintaining an intimate love relationship for many years, denying herself not only a spouse but also children. She seems to have been celibate once her marriage broke down. Stravinsky seems not to have been notably ascetic or abstemious, but, like Picasso, he retained a singularly cruel attitude toward other people—possibly, in his mind, a necessary part of his creative personality. The fact that he wrote legal documents on the very day that he completed *Le sacre du printemps* underscores to me the close relationship that he discerned between the committed innovator and the embattled litigant (cf. Picasso's reported equation of Rape and Work). Of these seven figures, Einstein seems the least likely to have made any kind of conscious or unconscious pact with respect to his own creativity; yet he commented so often on his distance from other individuals, and his inability to relate to them, as to suggest that he viewed this disjunction from the human sphere as part of the price he had to pay for being able to think originally about the physical world.

As with the many empirical issues just discussed, it would be an exaggeration to maintain that either of my emerging themes constitutes a prerequisite for a creative breakthrough. I have tried to introduce various nuances while considering each creative figure. But I believe that the two emerging themes do open a unique window into the experience of being highly creative. If one feels in possession of (or possessed by) an enormous talent, one may well feel that the talent comes with a price; and one may seek to make that covenant as explicit and unmistakeable as possible. By the same token, when one is working at the edge of one's creative powers, invading territories never touched before, the need for help and support is unprecedently great: at least in some ways, the best model for this is the time, shortly after birth, when the caretaker helps the infant make initial sense of a new world.

Remaining Questions

Even if this study is convincing in its major lines, it raises a host of questions. I will comment on five raised frequently by those who have become familiar with my point of view.

• *Did I select the right people?* My original intention in this study was to choose individuals representing each of the several intelligences. I then decided to add the condition that the individuals must have lived in the shadow of the twentieth century. By dealing with individuals who lived at roughly the same time and were exposed to the same general international currents, I could gain some control over at least one source of variation. At the same time, I would have to restrict the emerging portrait of creativity to its practice during a specific historical era.

Of course, within any domain, or set of domains, many individuals could have been chosen. In addition to the significance of the figures I was considering, my major criteria were individuals on whom considerable information existed, and individuals to whose work I was personally attracted. While I sympathize with those who might have preferred a cohort with fewer white males or more non-Europeans, I hope that the study will be judged on its power for explaining the work of these seven individuals, rather than on the costs of not including subjects who represent other populations.

• *Did I select the proper domains?* Again, the decision to deal with a manageable number of domains meant that many areas had to go unsampled. Dealing with a poet meant that I could not deal with a novelist; dealing with a physicist left no room for a biologist, mathematician, chemist, or astronomer; a focus on high art involved a neglect of popular art; and neither inventors nor business people nor athletes have infiltrated my sample. Again, I hope that readers can focus on the insights gained from the present analysis and, if so motivated, extend this study to other individuals, other domains, or other populations. Only additional studies will reveal whether the generalizations offered in this chapter can withstand extension to domains, eras, or individuals that I failed to sample.

• *Has my focus been too cognitive?* Without question, a study of equal length could have been carried out with an entirely different focus: a focus on personality, on conscious or unconscious motivation, on social supports. Similarly, instead of focusing on individuals, I could have focused on the field, as a sociologist might have done, or on the domain, as a historian, a philosopher of science, or a philosopher of art might have done. I focus on the cognitive area both because it is the one that I know the best and because I think it is the one that can currently provide the most illumination. At the same time, I am well aware that the cognitive story is not the whole story; I hope that I have at least construed the cognitive domain in a relatively broad way, ultimately reaching to affect, religion, and spirituality. Even so, determined cognitivists will note that I do not probe as deeply as I might have into the specific mental processes used by the creators, nor do I propose any model of information processing by the creative person.

• *Have I really focused on creativity?* While most readers will accept my list of individuals as creative, some will balk at my criteria. For example, acceptance by the field indicates to some that I am looking at popularity or worldly success rather than sheer creativity. And many will point to individuals whom they consider to be at least as creative as the members of the cohort I selected.

I do not insist on the notion of acceptance by the field because I believe that creativity is a popularity contest, but rather because I know of no other criterion that is reliable in the long run. The phrase "in the long run" is critical here; probably at any historical moment during the first half of this century, the individuals listed here would not have been considered the best by the relevant fields. Certainly, the number of negative, and even outraged, reviews of the works of Freud, Graham, or Stravinsky would give anyone pause. But I believe that, with the passage of time, individuals of merit do come to stand out; and I underscore my belief that there *is* such a thing as merit within a domain. Of course, this by no means denies the existence of many other meritorious individuals who happen to have been missed by the field. It is just that we have not even heard of these people, or, if we have, we do not (at least yet) quite know what to make of them.

- *To what extent are the results of this study limited to the modern era?* Having deliberately selected individuals who are roughly contemporaneous, I am not in a position to say whether my findings about creativity would apply to another time. My own guess is that certain findings are time-bound, while others would have recurred whether I was looking at ancient Athens, Renaissance Italy, France in the Enlightenment, or China in the T'ang dynasty. However, it is clear to me that other factors, such as the nearly instant availability of information about one's own domain and about events in the world, color the picture I have presented. Moreover, I think that the variety of creativity on which I have focused, with its radical, revolutionary, breakthroughs, is characteristic of our own era in the West, rather than a generic property of all creativities in all societies.

Analyze

1. What is the framework Gardner has for treating the complex issues of creativity? How might that framework help someone understand it more fully?
2. What is E.C.? And what's the story of E.C.?
3. "Particularly at the time of greatest creative tension, these creators felt under siege," writes Gardner. "So far as I can tell, all of them experienced periods of despondency when work was not going well, and virtually all had some kind of documented breakdown." Why do you think this is so? Where does he offer reasons for this common despair?
4. Gardner makes a generalization about friendships for these individuals. What is that generalization? What type of friendships do these creative people have?

Explore

1. Using the strength/weakness chart (as well as the other charts) Gardner provides, decide to explore the life and work of one of the seven people he lists. Any will do. List as many observations as you can about this person's relationship to the arts throughout his or her lifetime. Does it ever alter? If so, hypothesize why. Once you're done with your list, consider reading Gardner's profile of your person in his book *Creating Minds*, which is where this reading comes from. How much do your impressions sync up with those of Gardner?

2. Gardner writes, "A notable characteristic of creativity, I have argued, is its special amalgam of the childlike and the adultlike." He goes on to give examples in the lives of numerous geniuses. How does this idea link up with Mihaly Csikszentmihalyi's "The Creative Personality" in Chapter 1: The Creative Process? Create a compare/contrast essay on this point between the two authors or choose any other aspect of their work that seems particularly fruitful to explore.

3. What is the ten-year rule? Select a creative person not on Gardner's list and research his or her life to see how this rule holds up. Make a chart like Gardner does. Does the trajectory of this person's creativity across the decades match up nicely? Why or why not?

4. While this text could easily have appeared in Chapter 6: The Creative Genius, it belongs here as well. Offer some specific reasons why. Share your thoughts with a classmate and together debate the best location for this reading in the book. Does it matter that it's listed as first in this chapter, too? Would it be better to come after Shahn? After Langer? Somewhere else?

Ben Shahn
"On Nonconformity"

A Lithuanian-born American artist, **Ben Shahn** (1898–1969) was deeply involved in the social realism movement during the Depression and after. Whether he was creating art, writing, or lecturing, Shahn always strove to combat injustice and raise social awareness. His most popular lectures were collected in his book *The Shape of Content,* which is where "On Nonconformity" first appeared.

The artist is likely to be looked upon with some uneasiness by the more conservative members of society. He seems a little unpredictable. Who knows but that he may arrive for dinner in a red shirt . . . appear unexpectedly bearded . . . offer, freely, unsolicited advice . . . or even ship off one of his ears to some unwilling recipient? However glorious the history of art, the history of artists is quite another matter. And in any well-ordered household the very thought that one of the young may turn out to be an artist can be a cause for general alarm. It may be a point of great pride to have a Van Gogh on the living room wall, but the prospect of having Van Gogh himself in the living room would put a good many devoted art lovers to rout.

A great deal of the uneasiness about artists is based upon fiction; a great deal of it also is founded upon a real nonconformity which artists do follow, and which they sometimes deliberately exaggerate, but which seems nevertheless to be innate in art. I do not mean to imply at all that every artist is a nonconformist or even that most artists are nonconformists. I daresay that if we could somehow secure the total record it would show that an enormous majority of painters, sculptors, and even etchers have been impeccably correct in every detail of their behavior. Unfortunately, however, most of these artists have been forgotten. There seems to have been nothing about them, or even about their work actually, that was able to capture the world's attention or affection. Who knows? Perhaps they were too right, or too correct, but in any case we hardly remember them or know who they were.

There was a great commotion aroused in Paris around 1925 when it was proposed by officials that one of the pavilions of the coming Exposition des Arts Décoratifs be housed in that space traditionally reserved for the Salon of the Independents. It was suggested that, in view of the new enlightenment, there was actually no further need of an Independents' show in Paris. An indignant critic promptly offered to give twenty-five reasons why the Independents' show ought to be continued.

The twenty-five reasons proved to be twenty-five names—those of the winners of the Prix de Rome over as many years, the Prix de Rome being the most exalted award that can be extended to talented artists by the French

Government. But all these names, excepting that of Rouault, were totally unknown to art. The critic then called off twenty-five other names, those of artists who had first exhibited with the Independents, who had not won a Prix de Rome, and who could not by any stretch of the imagination have won such an award. They were Cézanne, Monet, Manet, Degas, Derain, Daumier, Matisse, Utrillo, Picasso, Van Gogh, Toulouse-Lautrec, Braque, Gauguin, Léger, and so on and on.

This incident has great bearing upon the matter of conformity. For it was through the questionable virtue of conformity that the Prix de Rome winners had prevailed. That is to say, they had no quarrel with art as it stood. The accepted concepts of beauty, of appropriate subject matter, of design, the small conceits of style, and the whole conventional system of art and art teaching were perfectly agreeable to them. By fulfilling current standards drawn out of past art, the applicants had won the approval of officials whose standards also were based upon past art, and who could hardly be expected to have visions of the future. But it is always in the future that the course of art lies, and so all the guesses of the officials were wrong guesses.

What is it about us, the public, and what is it about conformity itself that causes us all to require it of our neighbors and of our artists and then, with consummate fickleness, to forget those who fall into line and eternally celebrate those who do not?

Might not one surmise that there is some degree of nonconformity in us all, perhaps conquered or suppressed in the interest of our general well-being, but able to be touched or rekindled or inspired by just the quality of unorthodoxy which is so deeply embedded in art?

I doubt that good psychological or sociological opinion would allow such a view. On the contrary, I think that the most advanced opinion in these fields holds that we are by our natures doomed to conformity. We seem to be hemmed in by peer groups, hedged by tradition, struck dumb by archetypes; to be other-directed, inner-directed, outer-directed, over-directed. We are the organization man. It is not allowed that we may think for ourselves or be different or create something better than that which was before.

Since I do not myself aspire to being a sociologist, I do not feel particularly committed to correct sociological behavior. I don't care a rap about my peer group. And as for my tradition, brave though it may be and nostalgic, still I feel that I am on the whole well out of it. I cannot believe in Statistical Man or Reisman Man (Reis-Man?) and I can even dream of a day when perhaps both shall be ranged alongside Piltdown Man in some wonderful museum of scientific follies.

Nonconformity is not only a desirable thing, it is a factual thing. One need only remark that all art is based upon nonconformity—a point that I shall undertake to establish—and that every great historical change has been based upon nonconformity, has been bought either with the blood or with the reputation of nonconformists. Without nonconformity we would have had no Bill of Rights or Magna Carta, no public education system, no nation upon this continent, no continent, no science at all, no philosophy, and considerably fewer religions. All that is pretty obvious.

But it seems to be less obvious somehow that to create anything at all in any field, and especially anything of outstanding worth, requires nonconformity, or a want of satisfaction with things as they are. The creative person—the nonconformist—may be in profound disagreement with the present way of things, or he may simply wish to add his views, to render a personal account of matters.

Let me indicate the mildest kind of nonconformity that I can think of. A painter, let us say, may be perfectly pleased and satisfied with art just as it stands. He may like the modern and lean toward the abstract. Within the abstract mode, however, he may envision possibilities and powers not yet exploited. Perhaps he is interested in light. He may feel confident that with the enormous freedom of manipulation afforded by abstract techniques he himself can produce something new. He may believe that by relating colors and forms in a certain way—by forcing them perhaps—he can produce unheard-of luminosities. Even though many of his friends may feel that he is engaged upon a ridiculous project, he will pursue his vision, and he will probably ultimately realize it. Such a man may be perfectly circumspect in his behavior, and may have no quarrel even with art. The point of his nonconformity will be just at the point of his new vision, of his confidence that it can be realized. There he takes lessons from no one, and is his own authority.

If there is nothing in the code, if there is no doctrine which holds that light is a wrong and undesirable thing, then the artist's nonconformity is taken for granted as part of the art process. But if there happens to exist some such stricture, some rule or academic principle, or some official body or tribunal to obstruct his work or take issue with his purpose, then nonconformity becomes rebellion, intransigence.

One thinks of Turner, for this great innovator did manipulate colors and suppress forms to create light. He anticipated Impressionism by so many years, and he violated every accepted canon of academic art. Radical though he was, Turner created no outright explosion, simply because his work encountered little opposition beyond being called "tinted steam" by Constable and "soapsuds and whitewash" by someone else.

How different was the case with the Impressionists who, with objectives almost the same as those of Turner, were made the outlaws and the outcasts of art, their paintings ostracized by academic edict. The French Academy, which held official status and some material power, had been able to set up a certain absolutism of standards. It had pronounced upon the proper aims and objectives of painting, and the creation of pure and unalloyed light was not among them—particularly light gained at the expense of the entrenched method of underpainting in black, a heritage from the now-sacred Renaissance. The Academy did seek to obstruct and curtail Impressionist nonconformity, and thus produced the greatest art upheaval in history.

Nonconformity, even on a vast scale, does not necessarily imply any sort of violent or total overthrow. The transition from Medieval art into that of the Renaissance was accomplished by the modest personal ventures of such gentle painters as Giotto, Cimabue, Duccio, and Ambrogio Lorenzetti, each of whom created his humane and freshly observed images within the framework of the Medieval manner.

The Renaissance was of course a time of extraordinary artistic latitude, a time tolerant of nonconformity, able to expand to accommodate all sorts of styles and viewpoints, to endure the mediocre as well as to applaud the great, to be at once religious and pagan and classic. The world has enjoyed few such respites from rigidity of mind—perhaps a space of a few hundred years in Greece, a period in France from the Enlightenment almost to the present, Victorian England—but whenever they have occurred a flowering has taken place—in the arts, in science, in literature, and most significantly, in life.

Every successive change in the look of art, that is, every great movement, has been at issue with whatever mode was the then prevailing one. Protestantism in art seems almost to have preceded Protestantism in religion. The high style of the Italians, even though it constituted the very model and ideal of Dutch and Flemish and German painters, still appears somehow too florid for the lean and frugal Northern temperament. Holbein, Dürer, Grünewald, and Bosch were earth-oriented and did not or could not aspire to such sky-ey matters as the wonderful cloud-surrounded Transfigurations and Apotheoses at which the Italians excelled.

Protestant art itself was conscientiously, defiantly, earth-oriented, and in opposition to it there was created the art of the Catholic Counter-Reformation with the almost studied return to splendor. To Rubens, its greatest artistic spokesman, no excess of elaboration, ornamentation, or glorification of Church and nobility seemed unacceptable. As such lavishness descended to Rococo, there arose almost as if in revulsion the severe Neo-Classicism of David and Ingres, a fast after too-prolonged feasting. The Romanticism of Gericault and Delacroix may well have been a recoil from just that neo-classic sterility. The Realism of Courbet took issue with romantic effulgence; Impressionism and all the Isms that followed it were a fragmentation of Realism, and then a denial and then an outright opposition to Realism. All of which is not to elaborate upon the history of art movements, but only to point out the essential fact of nonconformity.

The artist occupies a unique position vis-à-vis the society in which he lives. However dependent upon it he may be for his livelihood, he is still somewhat removed from its immediate struggles for social status or for economic supremacy. He has no really vested interest in the status quo.

The only vested interest—or one might say, professional concern—which he does have in the present way of things rests in his ability to observe them, to assimilate the multifarious details of reality, to form some intelligent opinion about the society or at least an opinion consistent with his temperament.

That being the case, he must maintain an attitude at once detached and deeply involved. Detached, in that he must view all things with an outer and abstracting eye. Shapes rest against shapes; colors augment colors, and modify and relate and mingle mutually. Contrasts in life move constantly across the field of vision—tensions between the grotesque and the sad, between the contemptible and the much-loved; tensions of such special character as to be almost imperceptible; dramatic, emotional situations within the most banal settings. Only the detached eye is able to perceive these properties and qualities of things.

Within such contrasts and juxtapositions lies the very essence of what life is today, or any day. Whoever would know his day or would capture its essential character must maintain such a degree of detachment.

But besides perceiving these things, the artist must also feel them. Therein he differs from the scientist, who may observe dispassionately, collate, draw conclusions, and still remain uninvolved. The artist may not use lines or colors or forms unless he is able to feel their rightness. If a face or a figure or a stretch of grass or a formal passage fails in that sense, then there is no further authority for it and no other standard of measurement. So, he must never fail to be involved in the pleasures and the desperations of mankind, for in them lies the very source of feeling upon which the work of art is registered. Feeling, being always specific and never generalized, must have its own vocabulary of things experienced and felt.

It is because of these parallel habits of detachment and of emotional involvement that artists so often become critics of society, and so often become partisans in its burning causes. And also it is why they are so likely to be nonconformists in their personal lives. Michelangelo, Leonardo, and Rembrandt were all noted nonconformists, each one of them expanding freely the set limits of mind and art and behavior. Dürer was a passionate admirer of the heretical Martin Luther, David a prime figure in the French Revolution; Courbet helped push over the Vendôme Column during the period of the Paris Commune, calling it a symbol of war and imperialism. Even the American Revolution had an artist participant in Charles Willson Peale (not to mention Paul Revere). The instances are numerous: I remember the Paris of the twenties when the cafés teemed with talk of the still-to-be-created New World, and when every smallest aesthetic deviation had its own political manifesto; then the thirties in New York and the depression, when almost no artist was without some sort of identification with political or social theory, a solution for his time.

But considerably more revealing than active engagement or the personal behavior of artists has been the passionate testament of their sympathies as it is written across the canvases and walls of the world and carved into its buildings and filed away within its archives in engravings, woodcuts, lithographs, and drawings. Here the intransigent sentiments are stamped indelibly and are inseparable from the art itself.

One of the earliest of such testaments was painted by Ambrogio Lorenzetti in the early 1300's and spreads over three vast walls of the Council Chamber in the Palazzo Púbblico in Siena. A dissertation upon the sins of bad government and the virtues of good, it remains a monument to the medieval *Free City*, a beautiful and majestic dream of justice. One of the latest of such testaments is Picasso's "Guernica."

Compassion with human woes threads through all art from Masaccio's anguished "Adam and Eve" to the bitter sufferers of Käthe Kollwitz' "Weavers' Strike" and on down to the present, although for the moment it may have thinned. Partisanship on the side of the humble has been an ever recurring passion in art—Brueghel, Rembrandt, Daumier. And with these three and so many others, there is always the other side of the coin, the thrusts and satires upon social and political malpractice. *Nonconformity.*

While artists try to make their nonconformity as clear and unmistakable as possible, one of the challenging tasks of criticism seems to be to smooth over such nonconformity, and to make it appear that this or that artist was a very model of propriety. We read this sort of thing, "The coarseness of Goya is hardly noticeable unless we set out to look for it." Or again, "There is no evidence to prove that Goya actively assisted in any scheme of protest against the established order of society." But of course Goya did actively assist; indeed he protested with the most crying, the most effective, the most unforgettable indictment of the horrors of religious and patriotic fanaticism that has ever been created in any medium at all. Beauty? Yes it is beautiful, but its beauty is inseparable from its power and its content. Who is to say when a weeping face becomes a trenchant line? And who may presume to know that the line might have been trenchant apart from the face? Who can say that this passage of color, that formal arrangement, this kind of brush-stroking could have come into being were it not for the intensity of belief which demanded it?

And so one reads of the color, the form, the shape, the structure—all of this apart from the meaning which they hold, and apart from the context of life in which they took place. The fierce and dreadful fantasies of Brueghel become "cryptic iconography" with little reference to the reality of tortures, violence, and burnings at the stake, those common practices of the Spanish occupation and its own peculiar tribunal—the Blood Council.

Of course these artists were nonconformists. Indeed each of them stands out as an island of civilized feeling in an ocean of corruption. Civilization has freely vindicated them in everything but their nonconformity.

It is an amusing contradiction of our time that we do applaud a sort of copy-book nonconformity. Everyone laments the increase in conformity; everyone knows that too much conformity is bad for art and literature and politics, and that it may deal the deathblow to National Greatness. The deadening effects of over-conformity are well understood. Yet, when it comes to the matter of just what kind of nonconformity shall be encouraged, liberality of view recedes. There seems to be no exact place where nonconformity can be fitted in. It must not be admitted into the university curriculum—that would produce chaos. In politics it is certainly inadvisable—at least for the time being. It cannot be practiced in journalism—witness the recent stoppage of Eric Severeid's broadcast upon a free press. In science—least of all, alas! As to nonconformity on the part of people in public office, the trials of Mr. Secretary Wilson ought to be enough to warn anyone against excessive outspokenness.

Without the person of outspoken opinion, however, without the critic, without the visionary, without the nonconformist, any society of whatever degree of perfection must fall into decay. Its habits (let us say its virtues) will inevitably become entrenched and tyrannical; its controls will become inaccessible to the ordinary citizen.

But I do not wish to underrate the importance of the conformist himself—or perhaps an apter term would be the conservative. In art, the conservative is the vigorous custodian of the artistic treasures of a civilization, of its established values and its tastes—those of the past and even those present ones which have become accepted. Without the conservative we would know little of the circumstances of past art; we would have lost much of its meaning; in fact, we would probably have lost most of the art itself. However greatly the creative artist may chafe at entrenched conservatism, it is still quite true that his own work is both sustained and enriched by it.

It is natural and desirable that there should occur some conflict between these two kinds of people so necessary to each other and yet so opposite in their perspectives. I have always held a notion of a healthy society as one in which the two opposing elements, the conservative and the creative (or radical, or visionary, or whatever term is best applied to the dissident), exist in a mutual balance. The conservative, with its vested interest in things as they are, holds onto the present, gives stability, and preserves established values (and keeps the banks open). The visionary, always able to see the configuration of the future in present things, presses for change, experiment, the venture into new ways. A truly creative artist is inevitably of this part of the society.

There takes place from time to time an imbalance between the stabilizing and the visionary elements in society. Conformity is then pressed upon everyone, and growth and change and art come to a standstill.

In the year 1573, the painter Veronese was summoned before the Inquisition to answer a charge of blasphemy. In a painting of the Last Supper he had created an outer scene of worldliness in contrast to the inner scene of solemnity. Among the figures of the outer scene was a dog, and it was the dog that constituted the blasphemy. Ten years earlier the Council of Trent had decided upon the proper iconography for this and other religious scenes; their decision was held to be final, and a dog was not among the items listed.

The painter sought to explain the formal considerations which had led to his arrangement. His explanation was disregarded and he was ordered to substitute a Magdalene for the dog or be subject to whatever penalty the Holy Tribunal should decide to impose. Veronese did not yield; he retained the dog and changed the title of the painting. But let us note that art itself did yield to the increased pressure for conformity. It was in an atmosphere of enforced acts of faith, of fear of heresy, of trial and ordeal, and of the increasing harshness of the Inquisition that three hundred years of Renaissance greatness came to a close in Italy.

In our own generation, there is a record of a Russian trial not dissimilar to that of Veronese. A Soviet painter named Nikritin was accused of decadent Western formalism in a painting which he had made of a sports event, the specific complaint being that he had employed symbolic devices at the expense of Soviet Realism. Defending himself before a tribunal made up of fellow-artists and a member of a cultural bureau, Nikritin explained the artistic reasons which had prompted his choice and arrangement of figures. His defense was unsuccessful. It was decided that such symbolic treatment as that which he had employed was not understandable to workers and was indeed an affront to them. One of his fellow-artists described him as "one of those fellows who want to talk at all cost about themselves . . . an undesirable type of artist." The verdict: "What we see here is calumny; it is a class attack inimical to Soviet power. The picture must be removed and the appropriate steps taken."

Perhaps equally significant is a story related by my brother after he had returned from a trip to the Soviet Union. He was curious about the status of art there and arranged to meet a number of artists. After he had visited several studios he was struck by the fact that all the artists seemed to be working in groups rather than singly and to be producing more or less the same subject matter. After a great deal of inquiring he learned of one man who painted alone, and he made his way to this man's studio. There he found the solitary painter, the individualist, who in spite of hardships was carrying on. When my brother looked at his work he was astonished to find that this man was painting exactly the same subject matter—the idealized workers, anti-capitalist themes, and portraits of heroes which the collective artists were doing. Conformity is a mood and an atmosphere, a failure of hope or belief or rebellion.

I do not know of any trials which actually took place during the Hitler regime in Germany. But it is well known that the function of art was determined by edict during that time, that art was charged with carrying out the policies of the State. It was to be Nordic; it was to reject the so-called degenerate forms current in the Democracies; it was to be purged of Semitic influences. German Expressionism, one of the most brilliant art movements of modern times, came to an abrupt end. Its artists scattered across Europe and America—those that were fortunate enough to escape in time. And there arose in its place a cloying art of *kirche, küche,* and *kinder,* stillborn and unremembered.

Nonconformity is the basic pre condition of art, as it is the precondition of good thinking and therefore of growth and greatness in a people. The degree of nonconformity present—and tolerated—in a society might be looked upon as a symptom of its state of health.

The greater number of artists at any time whatever are no doubt complete conformists—not the outstanding ones, but the numerical majority. That is simply because mediocrity is commoner than that accumulation of talents which is called genius. There is always an impressive number of artists who are overwhelmed by the nearest outstanding figure. They adopt his point of view and mannerisms and become a school; that is one kind of art conformity.

Another kind of conformity is derived from the wholly venal business of catering to a popular market. Still another results from trends and the yearning of artists—an almost irresistible yearning—to be in the forefront of things. I am sure that every professional writer on art feels the need to produce at least one wave of the future per season, and once he has hit upon it, there is a considerable rush among artists to be seen at the crest. I will have a little more to say about this sort of conformity at a later time.

All these kinds of conformity are inevitable and to be expected. But there has grown around us a vastly increased conformity. One could say "conformism" here; for this is conformity by doctrine and by tribunal.

We are all prone to attribute the new conformity to television and mass communications, and indeed they do play their part. But television is not so much guilty as it is itself the victim of conformism. For it has been tried on the basis of possible disloyalty; it has been purged, but not exonerated. It remains in a state of suspended verdict, liable to re-examination at any time.

So with radio; so with films; so with the press; so with education; so with all those professions which involve the exercise of judgment, intellect, and creativity.

Art has not yet come in for its official purgation although it is understood to be on the docket. Nevertheless it has had its own ordeal of conformity. And it has its own Congressional scourge in the person of a Midwestern Congressman who provides the *Congressional Record* with periodic messages under the heading: "Extension of Remarks by Congressman Dondero." In the shelter of his privilege he has recorded a list of artists whom he has designated as "international art thugs," "art vermin," "subversives of art," and so on. To museums and museum directors, that is, those interested in contemporary art, he has attributed reprehensible motives and practices. He regards modern art forms as a disguised plot to undermine our morals and our "glorious American art." Such are the bludgeons of conformity.

So alerted, some sections of the public have felt that the call was for them, and have rallied to the cause of watchfulness. Civic groups or veterans' groups—all sorts of organizations and their committees and their auxiliaries have assumed the solemn duties of the judging and screening of art. Crusades have developed in a number of places with some work of art as their subject. A mural in the process of execution in a federal building just barely survived a campaign to have it removed because it contained a portrait of Roosevelt. Another just barely survived because someone thought it failed to express American ideals. On a sail in a painting of a regatta a city councilman professed to have discovered a Communist symbol, and he sought to close the exhibition of which the painting was a part. (The symbol turned out to be that of a Los Angeles yachting club.) Another large painting was vetoed because it contained nudes.

The most recent of the civic crusades—to my knowledge—was directed against a very large exhibition of sports themes, paintings, drawings, and prints which had been laboriously assembled by *Sports Illustrated* with the assistance of the American Federation of Arts, and was to have been displayed in Australia at the time of last summer's Olympic meet. The exhibition was circulated in a number of American cities before it was to be shipped abroad. It came to grief in Dallas, Texas. There a local patriotic group discovered among the exhibitors some names which had appeared under "The Extension of Remarks by Congressman Dondero." So great was the Texas commotion (and probably so delicate the political balance there), that the exhibition was not sent on to Australia.

In such a climate all art becomes suspect. And while the paint-alone métier has itself come under considerable attack, it is on the whole a safer category to be in than is the more communicative kind of art. In paint alone there are at least no daring commitments to the future, no indiscretions, no irreverence toward relatively sacred individuals, or toward their manners, emblems, or favored slogans. The aesthetic of line, color, and form, like any other way of painting, may always grow in the hands of a gifted painter; but today it has become the norm and the model of conformity. Young artists complain that their galleries freely press them into working in such a manner. Art departments in schools and colleges are literally minting art of the content-less kind. One department head claims that he sees no further necessity for forcing upon his students the hard archaic disciplines of academic study since they will abandon them anyway.

The daily reviews in the newspapers are a concatenation of like descriptions of this artist's circles, or that artist's squares, or a third artist's spirals. A few days ago a reviewer, casting about for fresh adjectives with which to describe an unbroken yellow canvas, suddenly broke off with the inspired words, "Since there's nothing to look at, there's nothing to say!"

Today's conformity is, more than anything else, the retreat from controversiality.

Tomorrow's art, if it is to be at all stirring, will no doubt be performed upon today's forbidden territory.

I remember a story that my father used to tell of a traveler in thirteenth-century France who met three men wheeling wheelbarrows. He asked in what work they were engaged and he received from them the following three answers: the first said, "I toil from sunup to sundown and all I receive for my pains is a few francs a day." The second said, "I am glad enough to wheel this wheelbarrow for I have been out of work for many months and I have a family to support." The third said, "I am building Chartres Cathedral."

I always feel that the committees and the tribunals and the civic groups and their auxiliaries harbor no misgivings about the men who wheel their wheelbarrows for however many francs a day; the object of their suspicions seems, inevitably, to be the man who is building Chartres Cathedral.

Analyze

1. Why does Shahn recount the "great commotion aroused in Paris around 1925" where it was proposed that in view of the new enlightenment,

there was no longer a need for an Independents' Show in Paris? What does this say, too, about the Prix de Rome, at least in that era?

2. Without conformity, what does Shahn say "is pretty obvious" that we would not have?

3. Why was the English Romanticist landscape painter J. M. W. Turner largely left alone but the Impressionists—who shared many of Turner's objectives—were "outlaws and the outcasts of art"? What was the difference in how they were received? (Feel free to research Turner to learn more about why this might have happened.)

4. What does Shahn mean when he says that the artist "has no really vested interest in the status quo"?

Explore

1. Answer Shahn's own question: "What is it about us, the public, and what is it about conformity itself that causes us all to require it of our neighbors and of our artists and then, with consummate fickleness, to forget those who fall into line and eternally celebrate those who do not?" What seems to be Shahn's answer? What is your answer? Why?

2. Refresh your memory on the Bill of Rights and the Magna Carta, two things Shahn says we would not have without nonconformity. Is he right? What about these things stems directly from a desire to not conform? What else could you add to the list of important things that come about because of nonconformity?

3. Shahn mentions the peaceful transition from medieval art into that of the Renaissance, citing such "gentle painters" as Giotto, Cimabue, Duccio, and Ambrogio Lorenzetti. Select any one of these gentle painters and locate some of their work. Then compare it to painters of the Renaissance. What differences do you note? What similarities? Are you surprised to find that the transition from one style to another went so smoothly? To what do you attribute that smooth transition?

4. Shahn writes that "art departments in schools and colleges are literally minting art of the content-less kind." This text was written by Shahn in the 1950s. Is his assessment of what art departments do still valid today? Speak to contemporary artists to find out their opinion, or do research on your own. In what other areas of art might there be instances of people minting the content-less kind? What do you make of that?

Ellen Langer
"The More We Know the More Blind We Become"

The first woman to ever be tenured in psychology at Harvard University, **Ellen Langer** (1947–) is a social psychologist who has authored eleven books and more than two hundred research articles on mindful aging, decision making, and health. She is often described as the "mother of mindfulness." "The More We Know the More Blind We Become" first appeared in her book *On Becoming an Artist*.

"The most beautiful thing we can experience is the mysterious."

—Albert Einstein

"Only when he no longer knows what he is doing does the painter do good things."

—Edgar Degas

Most people think it is in their best interest to learn things so well that they become second nature to us. But is that true? We have all learned that stop signs are red and octagonal, and we slow our cars automatically when we see one, without really reading what a particular sign might actually say. Would it take significantly longer to make sure we read it? What are the costs when we don't?

The psychologist Elizabeth Loftus has conducted a number of important studies that demonstrate how susceptible we are as a result of our everyday blindness. In one of them, participants were shown a videotape of an automobile accident that took place at a typical stop sign. Experimenters then asked them a series of leading questions about the accident that referred to the events having taken place at "the yield sign." When they were later asked to recount the accident, participants placed the accident at a yield sign.

The ramifications of this finding for eyewitnesses in court cases are important. There is now a good deal of research that shows how poor eyewitness accuracy is. In fact, the confidence people feel when they look and can identify what they see is the very thing that prevents witnesses from seeing what is otherwise in plain view. An interesting finding in this work is that confidence and accuracy are not correlated. That is, people may be absolutely sure of what they have seen, and they may be wrong.

The Greek philosopher Empedocles offered a theory of vision which maintained that sight arises from an active relationship between the seer and the seen. Perhaps the Greeks saw more than we typically do. Why didn't we learn from them? The Indian shamans of Peru, Buddhists, Sufis, and others may also have a better phenomenological understanding of what sight means than most of us do. Things started to run amok for us as we moved toward a rationalist view, in which we see the objective world existing independent of ourselves. Seeing is typically a passive process for us. The movement toward objectivity began with Plato's dichotomy between pure thought and material reality. In the 1400s, the Black Plague left people frightened of uncertainty. Science was to rescue us and remove that uncertainty, but in doing so it may have blinded us to sensuous knowledge. I am a scientist, so of course, I am not decrying science or suggesting science has done more harm than good. Instead, I am suggesting that there is a way to treat the "people-created objective" so that we don't lose sight.

With the rise of science, possibilities gave way to probabilities. As we search for the "right" answer, the potential opportunities that result from many alternatives and the vagaries of our intuition are problems to be ignored or held constant. We learn early on to break up experience into units—activities have beginnings and ends, days have minutes and hours, and so on. In her book *Sight and Sensibility: The Ecopsychology of Perception*, Laura Sewall maintains that these "broken experiences are unnatural and fundamentally discontinuous." They help create the illusion of separation between us and nature.

Yet, with a little thought, we could realize that what we see is dependent on relationships and not on discrete units. Figure–ground relationships or the context in which the target appears allows us to see it. It is the relationship between the signals from more than one receptor—one thing in relation to another—that leads us to see. According to Sewall, the edges *between* things—between the mountains and the sky, the sea and the shore—are of paramount importance. The edge marks both the figure and the ground. It is these edges that we become aware of when we decide to paint or take a photograph.

One way to start seeing, according to Sewall, is to attend to the spaces *in between,* in other words, the negative space. If we do so, Sewall says our attention will naturally widen and we will see more deeply into things. The primary function of our imagination is to bridge this negative space and close the gap between dualities. This is what makes things seem seamlessly real. Seeing, by contrast, could, and perhaps should, be an active process. In my view, we've become so adept at mindlessly naming things, forgetting that the "name" and the "named" are not the same, that perceiving the external world seems effortless. But in this adeptness, we rob ourselves of what could be seen if we only looked more mindfully.

Sewall tells of an exercise she uses in teaching vision improvement. She spills onto a table some kitchen utensils, scissors, matches, a can opener, batteries, and tape, and asks students to close their eyes and visualize a pair of scissors. Once the image is clearly formed in their minds, she tells them to open their eyes and try to find the can opener. It takes them much longer to do so than it does for those asked to search for the scissors. Imagining something makes it easier to see, and seeing that object repeatedly makes it easier to imagine. The neural networks subserving a particular image are strengthened each time we see or imagine it, and each time the world we see becomes more integrated and seemingly less a function of how we perceive it. The easier it becomes to see the world we expect to see, the harder it becomes to see the unexpected.

Imagining something, however, may make it easier to see only if there is a strong physical relationship between the imagined and the seen. Consider, for example, the not infrequent occurrence of looking for something we expect to find that is right where we are looking, but still we fail to see it. I was looking for a large painting I did on Masonite board that I couldn't seem to find anywhere. As I searched, I tried hard to imagine the painting, thinking that doing so would help. It turned out this may have been the very thing that prevented me from seeing it. The painting was facing the wall. Later, when a friend had found it for me, I was surprised at how wrong I had been all along about the size of the painting. I was looking for a much larger painting, and so I didn't see it. Let's imagine that I'm looking for my wallet. If my memory of the wallet is not exactly as the wallet looks now (that is, if it's sitting at a different orientation, the light is different, et cetera), sharpening my old image of what I thought it looked like should make it harder to find.

If we learn something mindfully, we essentially enshroud it in some uncertainty, and this uncertainty is what allows us to see. Psychologists have found that some of us are better at "finding the hidden object" than others. Typically males are more field independent than females are, and females are typically field dependent. *Field independence* is an ability to separate figure from ground; field dependence is an inability to separate figure from ground. I see this concept very differently. Years ago, Benzion Chanowitz and I were preparing stimulus materials for a study we were designing. We counted the hidden objects in a picture from a children's magazine. There was a fish on a child's pants leg. Benzion saw it as a hidden figure. But I saw it as a design on the pants. That difference gave rise to the idea that perhaps females like me were field sensitive, able to integrate figure and ground. That would make males like Benzion field insensitive, unable to integrate figure and ground. Thus, while field dependence seems bad, field integration seems good. The more mindful one is, the better one should be at integrating when integrating is desired and being field independent when that is desired. That is, mindfulness provides us with choices.

Right now most of us see what we expect to see without realizing that there is a choice. In an experiment designed by psychologist Dan Simons, participants were shown a videotape of a basketball game and asked to count the number of passes made by one of the teams. In the middle of the game, a person dressed in a gorilla suit quite clearly walks onto the court, stops, and beats his chest. No one could have missed that, you would think. Well, approximately half of the participants did not see him. When asked if they had noticed anything unusual during the game, they reported that they had not. When told of the gorilla, they were surprised and had to be shown the tape again.

While discussing the experiment in our lab, we noticed that many of us saw the gorilla when we first viewed the tape. Was it because we were more mindful than others? Kevin Williams and I recently showed the videotape to my class to see whether mindful observers were more likely to notice the gorilla. Before we showed the tape, we randomly handed out two sets of written instructions. Half of the participants received instructions that were the same as those Dan gave his research participants, to "count the number of passes that are made." The other half were given instructions on being mindful. We explained that each basketball game is similar to all others in some ways, which is why we call them by the same name, but also that each is different in some ways from any other game they may have seen. We asked the participants to notice the ways this game of basketball was both similar to and different from the last basketball game they saw. Most of those who were instructed to be mindful noticed the gorilla, while those who counted passes did not.

Finding Perspective and Gaining Control

> "In the end, she will manage to look just like it."
> Pablo Picasso, upon being told that his portrait of Gertrude
> Stein looked nothing like her

I magine we are sitting across a table from each other. If I ask you to envision the scene from my perspective, you are likely to look directly at me in an attempt to do so. Of course, you aren't really gaining my perspective at all; what I see from my perspective is you. For many beginning artists (and even writers, in a sense) the most frustrating aspect of early efforts is getting the perspective right. But whose perspective do we mean?

I once invited my friend the artist Barbara Cohen over to see a painting I had just finished. It was an early painting on a canvas measuring about three feet by four feet. I had depicted a woman sitting at a table, working on her computer, with another woman standing supportively behind her, looking over her shoulder. There are canvases strewn about and dogs resting in several places. There was also a couch in the room. A sweet smile came over Barbara's face as she studied the couch. I asked what she found amusing. She said she'd tell me if I promised not to change anything in the painting. I wouldn't agree, but I convinced her to tell me anyway. She pointed out that the couch was on its back with the legs pointed into the room. I was aghast. How could I have been so blind, I thought. As soon as she had left, I quickly "moved" the furniture in the painting, which turned out to be a good deal harder than if the couch had actually been on its back in my living room.

I had looked at the original painting many times but saw no problem with it. Why hadn't I noticed this obvious thing? Late that night, it struck me. I might have been new to painting, but I had been looking at things all my life. Why did I paint the room that way? I looked again at the painting and realized that I had painted the couch from the perspective of the people in the painting. It was they, after all, who would use the couch. Why hadn't I first seen it from Barbara's perspective? Just as interesting, one might counter, why didn't she see it from mine? If either I or Barbara had been aware of the perspective from which I was painting, it would have made sense. In fact, as I looked at the painting again, I saw that the odd perspective had been one of its more interesting aspects. It still troubles me that I so easily become blinded to my own perspective and adopt someone else's ideas.

To know that our work can be more engaging precisely because we don't have it quite right is liberating. Barbara still claims that I have furniture dyslexia, and that would seem to be true in at least one sense. I often paint furniture from my mind's inner perspective, and it can be quite cockeyed when I look at the finished painting from a new perspective. In fact, I've learned often to vary the perspective as I paint, which can make things very interesting indeed. And so, I have rejected her use of the word *dyslexia* and choose to see what I paint as simply my vision of furniture. Indeed, it may be this very "problem" that makes some of the work more interesting. Soon, I might even stop using the rather mindless word *cockeyed* to describe these paintings.

Armed with the awareness of how different things look depending on perspective, we open up many more choices for ourselves. Change the perspective and we have a new painting.

Openness to different points of view is an important aspect of being mindfully creative. As already noted, social psychologists have long written about the differences between the perspective of an actor and that of an observer. Research has shown that we are likely to blame circumstances for our negative behavior: "The elevator always makes me late." If the very same behavior is engaged in by someone else, however, we tend to blame that individual: "He is chronically behind schedule."

Once we become mindfully aware of views other than our own, we start to realize that there are as many views as there are observers. Such awareness is potentially liberating. Imagine that someone has just told you that you are rude, but you thought you were being frank. If only one perspective can be correct, you can't both be right. But with an awareness that there are many legitimate perspectives, you could accept that you are both right and instead focus on whether your words had the effect you wanted to produce. When we cling to our own point of view, we may blind ourselves to our impact on others; if we are too vulnerable to other people's definitions of our behavior, we can feel undermined, for observers are typically less flattering of us than we are of ourselves. It is easy to see that any interaction between people can have *at least* two interpretations: spontaneous versus weak, intense versus emotional, and so on.

This is not meant to give the impression that for every act there are two set, polarized interpretations. As we said, there are potentially as many interpretations as there are observers. Every idea, person, or object is simultaneously many things depending on the perspective from which it is viewed.

A steer may be steak to a rancher, a sacred object to a Hindu, and a collection of genes and proteins to a molecular biologist. Instead, we need to remain aware that the number of possible perspectives will never be exhausted.

The consequences of trying out different perspectives are important. First, we gain more choice in how to respond. A single-minded label produces an automatic reaction, which reduces our options. Also, to understand that other people may not be so different allows us empathy and enlarges our range of responses. We are less likely to feel locked into a polarized struggle.

Second, when we apply this open-minded attitude to our own behavior, change becomes more possible. When I used to do clinical work, it seemed odd to me that not only did many people in therapy have strong motivation to change (hence their visits to me) but the desired behavior was already in their repertoires. What was stopping them? In looking back, I realize that they were probably trying to change behavior (for example, "being impulsive") they actively enjoyed but from another point of view ("being spontaneous"). With this realization, changing one's behavior might be seen not as changing something negative but as making a choice between two positive alternatives (for example, "being reflective" versus "being spontaneous").

If seeing depends in large part on believing, then how can we learn to see more? We have already seen and learned much about the world. How can we learn to see it all again? By recognizing that evaluation is not stable and independent of context, for example, or by putting people back in the equation, we should increase our uncertainty. It is in this uncertainty that we have the possibility of creating new options for ourselves.

Any new activity we undertake has the potential to reveal to us that which we don't know. The uncertainty before us will serve us well as long as we make a universal, rather than a personal, attribution for it. That is, uncertainty is the rule for all of us, not just for the individual. If I don't know but think "it" is knowable, i.e., certain, then I feel insecure and am afraid to go forward. When I realize that I don't know but neither does anyone else, I am less afraid. Stability is a mindset, and those with unbridled confidence that they are right confuse the stability of their mind-sets with the stability of the underlying phenomena. Confidence and certainty are not the same.

Painting, writing, learning to play an instrument, or any other new activity provokes mindfulness and reveals much of what was hidden for us. In the past I would have described trees as green. Now I see a multitude of colors when I look at trees, even when I just think about them. I now know that I don't know what any particular tree will look like without first seeing it, and even then it is likely to be more than I see.

Do artists paint what they see, what they know, or what they imagine? If we view any painting from a single perspective, we think if the artist doesn't paint what we see she must have worked from imagination. Wouldn't it be interesting to consider that what we are looking at is what the artist actually saw? For example, to consider pre-Columbian art to be realistic rather than symbolic. What's more, if I pretend I am the thing I want to draw or paint, I may see it better. If I reduce its size or make it much larger, that which stays constant can reveal to me what I take to be important.

If I paint a portrait, I'm painting what feels to me like the essence of the person. If I take the time to give the nose and other facial features depth, the emotion often fades for me. I didn't realize this until I was able to paint a nose so that it did indeed look the way a nose is "supposed" to look. I'm not interested in painting noses very often, however. I usually want to paint a portrait wherein the individual parts are less than the whole. When we look at the work of self-taught artists or untrained artists, we should be careful not to think that the choices they made were made by default, because of limited possibility of expression.

Can you draw a reasonably straight line? A curved line? A thick, bold line or curve? A thin line or curve? Can you recognize different colors? If so, all that is left to be able to draw or paint is to learn how to see. To play an instrument, all you need to learn is to hear. It is that simple.

Analyze

1. In your own words, explain what everyday blindness is. Where is everyday blindness particularly a problem, according to Langer?
2. What does field independence mean? Who tends to be better at field independence? Why does that matter?
3. What does it mean to be mindful? How does the man in the gorilla suit anecdote support the value of mindfulness?
4. What are the benefits of trying out different perspectives?

Explore

1. Why do you think Langer was troubled by her misuse of perspective in her painting and her subsequent "fixing" it? She writes, "It still troubles

me that I so easily become blinded to my own perspective and adopt someone else's ideas" after all. When have you immediately changed something artistic because of someone else's opinion or perspective? Why did you do that? Did you experience the same kind of remorse Langer did? Why or why not?

2. Langer asks, "Do artists paint what they see, what they know, or what they imagine?" Which do you think is most true? And how does the idea of perspective and mindfulness play into it?

3. This reading uses two quotations as epigraphs. The first is by Edgar Degas: "Only when he no longer knows what he is doing does the painter do good things." The second is by Albert Einstein: "The most beautiful thing we can experience is the mysterious." Which one resonates more with you? With this text? Why? What is the purpose of an epigraph? Which one does a better job of meeting that purpose? Discuss your thoughts with a classmate.

4. Write a poem about the intersection and or interconnectedness of creativity and the arts. Strive to make your poem emotionally strong, linguistically powerful, and appropriate in length (which is, of course, whatever you decide). Beyond that, all the artistic choices are yours to make!

Henriette Klauser
"Going to the Movies: Creative Visualization and Writing"

Henriette Klauser is the president of Writing Resources, a seminar and consulting organization. Her work has appeared in *Redbook*, *Glamour Magazine*, *Good Housekeeping*, *O! The Oprah Magazine*, and others. She is also the author of *Writing on Both Sides of the Brain: Breakthrough Techniques for People Who Write*, *Put Your Heart on Paper: Staying Connected in a Loose-Ends World*, and two other books. "Going to the Movies: Creative Visualization and Writing" first appeared in her book *Writing on Both Sides of the Brain*.

"I learned . . . that inspiration does not come like a bolt, nor is it kinetic, energetic striving, but it comes to us slowly and quietly and all the time, though we must regularly and every day give it a little chance to start flowing, prime it with a little solitude and idleness."

—Brenda Ueland, *If You Want to Write*

The Five R's of whole-brained writing will make your task more relaxed and more profitable. The tips and techniques of editing will make your finished piece more polished. But didn't I promise I would also make writing fun, a glorious adventure, a mind-expanding experience? That is what this chapter is all about.

Creative Visualization

Creative visualization is the technique of using your imagination to create images and feelings inside your head; it is a powerful way to tap into the message center of the right brain. Creative visualization is like going to the movies inside your own head. In today's world of high-priced entertainment, it is a handy talent to cultivate. Visualization is no longer an esoteric practice, reserved for Buddhist monks and California psychics. Now it is in the mainstream to see pictures in your head. It's even in *Time* magazine.

When the Americans who were held captive in Iran were released, they told of overcoming the stress of 444 days in captivity through various strategies. One hostage mentally remodeled a whole house, nail by nail, board by board; another went, in his mind's eye, on the Orient Express and recorded mentally every detail down to the menu. According to *Time*, the State Department doctors at Wiesbaden, Germany, called these survival tactics "Going to the Movies" and considered them good devices for "warding off the helplessness that comes with captivity."

Not only captives in Iran need to ward off feelings of helplessness, and, fortunately, you don't have to be behind bars to get a free pass to this theater. In fact, you are carrying around in your own head a very rich source of entertainment and inspiration, a huge 3-D screen to play out life's mysteries and messages.

This chapter is a whetstone to make you keen and eager to incorporate the skill of visualization into your life and to show you how to apply it directly to your writing. Using visualization, you can bring the perfect writing environ-ment to wherever you are, picture your success scenario, get inside the head of the person driving the car in front of you on the freeway. You can become your favorite author or ask an authority for personal advice with editing.

From Sports to Schools to Sneakers

It is no secret that today's Olympic contenders not only have athletic coaches, they have mind coaches. A popular book like *The Miracle of Sports Psychology*, by James Pravitz and James Bennett, attests to the power of the mind in achieving sports goals. Visualization is an accepted part of today's sports world. San Francisco outfielder Jim Wohlford, speaking of baseball, put it eloquently: "Ninety percent of this game," he said, "is half mental."

Schools are also discovering, to the delight of student and teacher alike, how the use of relaxation techniques and guided imagery improves compre-hension and raises grades and self-esteem. Studies done by Dr. Beverly-Colleene Galyean (see her book *Mind Sight*) show that students taught their other subjects with visualization improve academically and are less unruly, less truant, more motivated, more secure. Not only the students but also the teachers find the classroom a more pleasant place to be: learning is easier, teaching is easier, and both are more fun when visualization or guided imagery is incorporated into the curriculum.

And it is happening all over the world. *Paris Match,* for example, quotes Micheline Frank, a Parisian teacher, who emphasizes that relaxation and visualization are not "the corollary of passivity." On the contrary, she as-serts, these techniques make possible greater concentration of attention, alertness, and receptivity to learning.

Visualization is even good for your heart. Dr. George Sheehan, the famous running guru, after spending 195 pages of his book, *Dr. Sheehan on Running,* extolling the virtues of jogging for the physically fit, then tells of this interesting experiment done in Canada with heart patients. The study divided cardiac patients into two groups for postoperative care. The one group trained strenuously, running and exercising every day. Those in the second group, under the guidance of a psychiatrist, were put into a hypnotic trance, in which they pictured themselves running through a field, with the wind in their faces and oxygen filling their lungs going straight to their hearts. After one year the results in both groups were identical. Weight down, blood pressure down, less body fat, grip strength increased to an identical degree. EKG readings showed the same improvement.

So visualization is here to stay and can even cut down on the cost of your sneakers! To visualize, you don't need training of any kind. You needn't be an expert. Even if you are skeptical, it will still happen if you let it. Because it is there already inside of you.

Part of You Knows the Answer

Did you ever walk over, say, to a cupboard or a drawer and forget what you went there for as you stood in front of it? The interior monologue at such times usually goes something like this:

"Dumb me! What did I come over here for? I must be losing my mind. How dumb!"

When that happens to me now, I say instead, "Wow. What smart feet I have. They knew to come this way even though I can no longer articulate why I am here."

Then I take a deep breath, close my eyes in a satisfied way, and let the image of what I came to get cross back over my corpus callosum into words.

When we sit down to write, we are often at the stage of "knowing but not knowing," as Perl and Egendorf name it in their study of the process of creative discovery.

"Knowing but not knowing" is that sense that you know what to say but do not know how to say it. Your feet were smart enough to get you to the desk. You knew enough to pull out the paper and pick up the pen. Now you must somehow, as the computer people say, "access" the nonverbal information that will tell you what to write and how to write it.

Listen to what I am saying here! It is very important. Attending to your nonverbal side, quieting down the static and listening to your inner self, will help you get in touch with your feelings about a particular writing project and what may be blocking you. What I am suggesting here is even more radical, more powerful. I am suggesting that the thought itself (in nonverbal form), the shape and direction, the whole piece that you know but do not know, the content as well as the context, can be discovered by this same pathway. And that is what this chapter is about.

The right brain sends messages in terms of pictures and feelings. *Attend* to those images and you will be rewarded with knowledge.

Let Your Brain Waves Do the Walking

In the past, when I mislaid some object, I would frantically search every logical place for the missing item. I have been known to waste an hour or more in thankless rummage. Now, I take a deep breath, sit still, and say calmly, "The right side of my brain knows where it is." Often the place pops right into mind. If not, I mentally go through each room of the house, each nook and cranny at the office. When I inwardly arrive at the right corner, I actually see the item there or feel a sensation inside me. Sometimes there is a heat radiating from that spot (remember the game "Hot or Cold" we played as children?). Sometimes the space seems to glow, or shout, or vibrate. Whatever the signal, the sense of it is strong and definite.

Then I open my eyes, get up, and go for it. And there it is.

In preparing to write this chapter, I located a magazine article that had been missing for four years, using the same approach. I found the article in a crawl space under the stairs, in an abandoned desk rack, in with old recipes, report cards, a summer aerobics schedule, an old tape of Beethoven's *Eroica*, an opera program, an immunization form, and a personality profile test, filled out and never sent in for scoring. In other words, in with things that had no connection at all with the article I was searching for, in a place it had no right being. Yet the movies of my mind led me directly to it.

When you incorporate the movies of your mind into your writing, it not only gives you a healthy and playful attitude towards words and ideas; it also often supplies the missing links. Below are several exercises that tap into this reserve. Use your own imagination to come up with others.

Set Up the Screen, Turn on the Projector

You don't need any fancy equipment for creative visualization. In fact, you already own the projector and some pretty sophisticated camera equipment. You even have some footage in there already that is waiting to be unrolled. All you need to do is quiet down inside and let it happen. The *let* is integral to the process. Do not force the image or come ready with expected responses. Be mindful not to reject whatever comes, even if its usefulness is not immediately apparent to you. *Let* it happen. *Let* the sense unfold, the "opening up" come forward; *let* the meaning "pop" from the image.

You might want to read some of the exercises below slowly into a tape recorder in a monotone voice, then play the tape back with your eyes closed and the lights low. Or have a friend read a section to you in a soothing voice, or just close your eyes, relax, and trust yourself to remember whatever part is important to you. I encourage you to prepare your own scripts based on these suggestions.

Exercise 16: Character Formation

If you are writing fiction or doing character sketches of any kind, learning to see the world from behind another's eyes is invaluable. But even for those of you who are writing nonfiction business letters, reports, or proposals, this exercise is a fun way to keep your movie apparatus in gear, to keep all that million-dollar equipment in good working order. As we will see below, it will also sharpen your wits in preparation for using a powerful editing tool: getting inside the head of the person who will read your stuff.

You could be sitting on a park bench or driving in the car. Pick a person in front of you and imagine what it might be like to experience the world from his or her perspective. Where did he just come from? Where is she going next? Tune into her mind: turn up the volume a bit so you can hear the concerns and worries, the mutterings. Sit down in the movie theater of his mind for a moment and watch the pictures on his screen. Do not force anything, just let the images and sounds come.

Here's an example of how it works. While driving through morning traffic down a busy commercial street in town, I saw two things almost simultaneously. One was a sign in front of a gas station. In large letters it read, "RED EYE IS BACK!" At the same moment, my eye caught a man standing at a bus stop, with his shoulders bent and his head down. He was wearing a bowler (true!) and carrying an umbrella, even though it was only overcast, not raining. He looked defeated and discouraged, as though he were facing yet another dreary day. Before I knew what was happening, the two images coalesced. I kept on driving, but inside my head was a new voice, not my own. It was husky and depressed.

"I wish I were Red Eye. Sure, he's got a foul mouth and drinks too much, but everybody loves him. He can get away with murder. Roughhewn, but damn good. They love him. They put up a big sign when he comes back."

"Ha! Nobody cares whether I'm at work or not. Can you picture them putting up a sign for me?"

"And Mildred! If I have one more fight with Mildred going out the door, I'm not..."

Mildred! That's when I hit the brakes. Who let Mildred in?

You get the idea. You see how easy it is.

By the way, I do not necessarily recommend that you make any attempt to verify your cinematic snooping. Several months after the experience described above, I was in that very gas station buying gas.

Said I, "I'd like to meet your mechanic, the one you call Red Eye."
The attendant looked at me queerly.
I continued. "A few months back, you put up a big sign when he re-
turned. 'Red Eye Is Back' it said." I gave my shoulders a little self-effacing
shrug. "I'd just like to meet the guy."
"Lady. There ain't no guy named Red Eye. Red Eye is the name of an oil.
We've been out of it for awhile, and so we put up a sign when we got it back
in stock. Sorry to disappoint you."
Ah well. But for all I know, the little man in the bowler *was* feeling
down and *did* just have a morning spat with a wife named Mildred.

Exercise 17: The Success Scenario

Maybe you have heard about, or even experienced, how visualizing
something you want can help make it happen. This exercise is part of
that fine tradition, with a twist. Here, you use the theater of your mind to
enjoy the pleasure of a well-written piece, and—even more dramatically—
to help create the piece that brings such joy. I call this the success scenario.

Quieten yourself in whatever way works best for you. In your mind's eye,
picture whatever, for you, would be the success scenario of the piece you are
currently working on. If you are a lawyer preparing a brief, it might be hearing the opinion of the court and knowing that you won. A playwright
might picture the party at Sardi's with champagne and streamers and ex-
clamatory reviews pouring in. A manager who has been having trouble
with her staff might picture her ideas being implemented and everyone
friendly and smiling. For myself, it is the autograph party with the lines
going out the door, all ages patiently waiting to have a moment to talk with
me, maybe the Phil Donahue show, a write-up in *Time* magazine. Success
for you might be a big hoopla or a quiet thing. It might include crowds of
people, lots of noise, or it may be simply one person you care about patting
you on the back.

Larry, an attorney, wanted to write an article for the *New York Times*.
He had a colleague at the firm who was always lording it over him, and
Larry knew that an article in the *Times* would be a neat way to match wits.
Larry's scene of success and its accompanying good feeling was very simple.
First he got quiet, inside and out, slowed his breathing, relaxed his muscle
tension, and then he imagined this same fellow coming over to his desk.

"Larry, I saw your piece in this morning's *Times*." "It was nothing," Larry answers with a shrug.

So a success scenario does not require fanfare. The idea is to immerse yourself thoroughly in that scene. Be playful. Have some fun. Let the smile cross your face. Let the happy and satisfied feeling suffuse your whole body. Let the glow of success start from your toes and move right up to your head. Get giddy from the rush of it. Pay particular attention to what people are saying, all the wonderful comments about your job well done. Let your ears burn. Nod and smile and soak it up. You've worked hard for this moment, and you deserve to bask in it. Reach out and touch whatever is tangible— the desk, the chair, the hand to shake. Become part of that scene, and enjoy it for as long as you want.

Here comes the twist. After playing with your success scene for awhile, let the noise die down, the crowd dissipate, the colleague walk away, the TV talk-show interview end—not abruptly but in a pleasant, relaxed kind of way. The people are gone, but the residual good feelings of success are still with you. You are alone now but feeling fine. Shake your head in a gesture of pleased wonderment. And now—this is the fun part—turn your attention to the writing that has been getting such praise and accolades. Pick up the brief off the courtroom table, open the cover of your new book, look at the memo on your desk that had exactly the results that you wanted, and now, as you read it for the first time, copy it down.

Here's an example of how it worked for me. When I first designed the brochure advertising my writing workshop, I wanted it to double as a poster as well as a flier. That way I would be able not only to send it through the mail but also to post it around town and ask various companies and organizations to tack it up on their bulletin boards.

I sat in a quiet library, away from distractions, and tried again and again to write the opening copy. It wouldn't click. It got worse. I started to feel uptight, and I heard my Critic say, "This is a fine kettle of fish, Ollie. You plan to save others, and yourself you cannot save." My adrenaline was rising, my foot tapping, my fingers tightening around the pencil. I knew it was time for a relaxation break. Staying at my chair, I put down my pencil, closed my eyes, and took a deep breath. I became conscious of my breathing and thought that my breath was like a pump, breathing out any tension, breathing in peace and relaxation. I said that very phrase several times to myself: "Out with tension; in with peace and relaxation. Out with tension; in with peace and relaxation." Soon the words matched the reality.

In my mind's inner eye I found myself going up and down the avenue in the university section of town, posting my brochure in bookstores, cafés, and on kiosks. I was interacting with various people, and all of them were very complimentary about my brochure and my workshop.

"May I post this in your window?"

"Certainly. Sounds like an interesting workshop. I'd like to go myself. When is it?"

Soon, people were following me down the street—I was like the Pied Piper—stopping to read what I had posted, and asking me excited questions about my workshop and where they could sign up. I felt like a little kid at the zoo with a red balloon, skipping and happy. As I held the stapler in my hand, I could feel the rough texture of the kiosk and hear the satisfying clunk as the staple penetrated the wood where many millions of staples before had sunk their metal teeth. Other posters vied for visual attention, but my poster stood out, almost glowed. It beckoned and enticed. The crowds were jostling with each other in a friendly way, all wanting to read about this wonderful workshop.

"Where can I sign up?"

"May I have another copy of that brochure for a friend?"

"This is dynamite. Count me in."

"Just what I've been waiting for."

"Tell you the truth, it was your opening paragraph that caught my eye."

That last comment made me curious: How did the winning paragraph read? I resisted the temptation to look at it; I wanted to bask some more in the stunning results. I was having fun. Anyone looking over to me in my carrel in the library would have seen a totally relaxed person with a blissful smile.

I waited until the crowds dispersed a bit and then quietly tacked my last brochure over the "Post No Notices" stencil on a poster-covered fence.

Now I stood back from it a moment, and this time I read it. I read the words that were creating such a positive response, read the opening hook that captured such attention. *As I read it, I wrote it down.*

Professional writers call it writer's block, but panic before a blank page is not exclusive to writers who are professional. Writing anxiety can immobilize anyone: business executives behind in correspondence, students struggling over term papers, lawyers laboring over legal briefs, nurses or social workers dreading report deadlines. People with writing apprehension have been known to let it determine the paths of their lives, choosing majors in college, and later jobs, that have few writing demands. Some let it limit their earning and advancement potential. Or those who have been writing successfully for years suddenly find their creative juices run dry. Others have stories inside them that they want to tell, but they just can't get the words out. This workshop is for all of you.

Perhaps you've even taken some courses, or read some books that have given you hints and tips on breaking out of this syndrome. This workshop does more than give tips and strategies to fight the immediate problem—it arms you with tools to be your own best strategist from now on. Discover why you can't write on those days when the writing drags, and why you can write on those days when everything flows. Armed with that information, your writing will be productive for the rest of your life.

If you ever hesitate in writing, this workshop is for you.

It was almost cheating. The words were printed there so clearly before me. I could actually see them, not handwritten on a yellow pad but printed on a page with my twisted-pencil logo blown up on the side. I simply surreptitiously copied them down.

This approach is a wonderful catalyst, but do not think that just because you've seen it in print it does not need improvement. I needed to emend my brochure copy: a dangling participle, the enemy of the people, had crept into the last line of the second paragraph, and that line needed to be ruthlessly rearranged. I changed it to "Armed with that information, you can be a productive writer for the rest of your life." Then I took out the mixed metaphor of "arms you with tools;" in doing that, corrected as well the redundancy of "arms" and "armed."

So your mental manuscript starts out with a burst of energy and playfulness, but like everything else you write, it undergoes the same scrutiny of the Five R's of whole-brained writing. Visualization is actually just another way of doing Step 1.

There are many other dramatic examples of this creative construction. Chuck Loch, in an article called "How to Feed Your Brain and Develop Your Creativity," tells of a songwriter who "used to see the titles of his unwritten songs listed on a mental jukebox. In his mind, he would drop in a quarter and sit back and listen to his song, copying it down as he heard it played."

Or take the example of the senior executive of a large shipping company who told me that he was having a dreadful problem with phone etiquette in his firm. He had sent out many memos, most of them curt and authoritarian in tone, but they did not get the kind of response he wanted. In fact, they made things even worse. Most of his memos began with phrases like "It has come to my attention. . ." and "Unfortunately, it is once again necessary to inform you that. . . ."

Not only did the phone problem persist, but he had created a tension among his employees that ran counter to his usual management style and disturbed the atmosphere he liked to maintain in his company.

While taking my workshop, he played around with the success scenario of the perfect memo. He felt himself back in his office, even noticed what he was wearing and saw the items and papers on his desk. Mostly, though, he was conscious of a feeling of well-being, a sense of contentment around the office that he had missed. People were courteous without being stiff; there was a genuine feeling of camaraderie and goodwill. It was a nice place to be. There was almost a perceptible hum in the office of people working together. In his mind's eye he stayed with that feeling of satisfaction and went about his own work eagerly, knowing that all the people around him were working hard and happily. He told me later that it resembled the unexpressed sense of harmony you feel when the whole family is working on projects in different corners of the house. He still didn't know how it had happened, and in some ways it didn't matter. He was just enjoying the aftermath.

Then his eye strayed to a copy of the morning memo on his desk. He read:

> We are all part of a family here, and as any growing family knows, there are times when we need to pitch in together to make changes necessary for the betterment of the whole.

As he read it, it pleased him. He wrote it down.

He could hardly wait to get back to his office and make that memo a reality. He made a few minor changes in what he had copied from his mind's memo and sent it out to the people in his company the next day. Guess what? The results were almost exactly as he had envisioned them. Once again, his company was a pleasant place to work, and an almost tangible team spirit prevailed.

Exercise 18: Carry Your Perfect Writing Environment Wherever You Go

How many times have you said, "I could write *if only. . .?*" If only I were someplace else, free from distractions. If only I could be in a room without clutter, without fingerprints. Or are you like the boss who tells me that she always brings her writing home, even though it irritates her husband, because she does her best writing outside the office? Save your marriage—and your sanity!

I remember a time in Newport when I wrote so fluently, so much, that I couldn't stop writing—it was a supportive atmosphere, free from distractions, free from pressure and responsibility. I wrote and wrote and wrote. I wrote so much that I even took the pad into the bathroom with me. I got up in the middle of the night and started writing. I was all charged up with a "Here-we-go! Don't-stop-now!" kind of energy and excitement. Ah! Where did that energy come from? It came from inside *me!* So I can re-create it anywhere, bring that space and that energy to my computer room, to my office, to my dining room table.

In *Sadhana* Anthony de Mello speaks of the mystic's ability to bring the past into the present by going in and out of the experience, each time noting what changes occur. Let's say that you did your best writing on the beach in Atlantic City or that time you were visiting the people with no children in Denver and the walls were white and had no handprints. That energy, that ability to write came from inside YOU! And it is yours for the asking to recapture it. Here's how.

First, relax. Get into a comfortable position. Close your eyes. Take a deep breath. Start with the top of your head and gently relax every muscle, working your way down to the very soles of your feet. Once your body is relaxed, go in your mind's eye to your perfect writing environment. In that quiet center, see yourself writing and writing, the energy and heat coming off the very page, burning a hole in the paper. It is wonderful to write like that. It is energizing and exciting. And the writing is good—clear and lucid, and so human. Keep on writing. What does it feel like to be writing like that? How does it feel inside of you, in your gut, in the center of your being? How does your hand feel, what is your head like? Can you locate the feeling in a part of your body? Can you taste it, smell it, touch it?

Now, return to the room you are in, but not abruptly or fully. How does it feel to come back to this room? Are you cold? Do you have less energy? Is it demoralizing, draining, sapping your vitality? Do you notice even a slight carryover from your perfect writing state? Stay with that feeling for a moment. Then return to the fullness of your perfect environment. Play with it, move back and forth, until you sense a strong transference of the vibes of the past scene into the present.

Exercise 19: Become the Audience

François Rochaix, a stage director, says that the last thing he does before the final production of an opera is become like the audience to test his design:

> I do all I can to prepare for a production ahead of time, with reading and thinking and working with designers. But once the rehearsals begin I have to turn into someone else too. Without forgetting what it is I set out to do, I must become like a member of the audience, see it all as they will see it, so that I can help the singers know what is the effect that we make. What they bring to it now is what matters most, because it is only that which makes it all come together and come to life.

Even though editing is basically a left-brained task, the right can contribute in its strength to make the task easier, more pleasant, more fun—and more effective. Remember the goal in writing on both sides of the brain is to get that corpus callosum crackling, and this exercise is one sure way to make that happen.

Creative visualization builds audience awareness in a profound way. I suggest that you have a little fun with this. Using the approach outlined in Exercise 16, get inside the mind of your intended reader. You might know specifically who that person will be (such as a difficult person to whom you have drafted a tactful letter), or it might just be a generic type.

So quiet down inside. Take a deep breath. ("Your breathing is your greatest friend," says de Mello, quoting a Tibetan sage. "Return to it in all your troubles, and you will find comfort and guidance.") Close your eyes, relax, and bring to mind the person who will be reading your piece.

Think of where he might be when he receives this letter, what she might be doing right before this memo crosses her desk. Is the judge reading your brief in his chambers; has your boss gone through a stack of infuriating papers and finally worked her way down to your proposal; is the editor up to here with queries and now opening up yours?

Notice the body posture and the expression on the face. What insights do these clues give you into how that person feels? What concerns occupy her thoughts? Is the phone ringing off the hook, has she just had another cup of coffee or an upsetting encounter with another employee? What kind of effect are you going for? Get as much into the mind and the environment of that person (your reader) as possible. Put the reading of your piece in context—in the same context it will be received in. Does the reader seem hostile to your subject? If so, it is even more important to play with this projection for awhile. Become the audience. What is it like to be him? What is it like to be her? Stay with that image, using all of your senses: see, hear, taste, smell, and touch the world with your reader's eyes, ears, nose, mouth, and fingers. Now, inside his head, not your own, pick up your writing with his hands, read it through with her eyes, feel their visceral response to it.

Is it "Oh, here's _____. I always like to read her byline"? Or is it "I'm mad already just seeing the return address" or perhaps "Wouldn't you know, another letter from the boss finding fault with me again—brace yourself"?

Now read your piece. What happens? Are you impressed? Are you entertained? Are you insulted, or pleased? Or confused? Does the writing keep you moving along in a pleasant pace, or are you bored and tempted to put it aside and come back to it later? Are you confused, angry, upset? Does a word strike you as harsh? Mark in the margin all the places where it pings.

Exercise 20: Confer with Expert

Once you learn, using any of the forms above, to tap into your creative center, ask for a guide to meet you there. This guide might arrive in the form of a friend or an animal or someone famous in your field. I like to invite John Fowles, Geoffrey Chaucer, or Jane Austen to help me edit. Jane Austen, in particular, was a great friend to me during the editing stages of this book. At one point, when I was feeling overwhelmed by the sheer amount of work ahead of me, I took a breather. I moved to a comfortable chair (my Ruminating Chair, in fact). What would Jane Austen do? I wondered. I know she reworked her novels meticulously right up to her death. I slowed my breathing, letting relaxation flow over me. In my imagination, I was walking along a forest path, an actual spot that is a favorite comforting place. There are majestic evergreens all around, but it is not a closed or confined place, nor is it dark and forbidding. The trees line a path that beckons forward to an expansive vista. The sun was streaming along that path in an invitational way, and it was from this clearing that Jane Austen came forward to greet me. She hailed me warmly. She was dressed in an Empire gown of antique ivory hue, with an umber sash beneath the bodice. She was business-like but kind.

She took me by the elbow and, demonstrating for me even as she led me to follow, she said, "Henriette. Like this. Look at your feet. One step. Good. Now the next step. Good. Now another. Step by step. You can do it. One step at a time. Come on—"(still urging me on by my elbow)"—I'm with you now. Step by step."

I went back to my work renewed, and instead of keeping the giant mass of raw unworked pages of the complete manuscript on my desk, I put the bulk of it aside and took one chapter at a time, one page at a time. Whenever I faltered, I said, "Look at your feet, not ahead. One foot after the other. Come on, one foot—that's it—after the other." It was good advice. I am grateful to Jane Austen for passing it on.

Another time, I invited John Fowles to meet me in the library of my mind, and when he showed up, he had brought a friend, Tony Buzan. Tony was exactly the fellow I needed to talk to then, so I was flabbergasted and delighted that John had brought him along.

Maureen Murdoch, in her book *Spinning Inward*, tells of using a technique with children that she calls "Skill Rehearsal with a Master Teacher." The results are astonishing. "Children report invoking Pele to improve soccer kicks, Haydn to tutor piano, and Mark Twain to put some humor into their writing," she relates.

Invite me, if you don't mind your work being a bit cavalier in spots. I'll be glad to help you in any way I can.

Chuck Loch, in an article mentioned earlier, suggests an intriguing variation of this exercise. His idea is to "imagine yourself going back in time, back to another lifetime when you were a famous writer of the past." The more vivid you can make the scene, the better. "Feel yourself in that writer's study, sitting at that writer's desk, taking pen in hand, writing a 'lost' manuscript." Then all you need to do is write the words along with the celebrated author and produce your own masterpiece. Loch gives several examples of students who had successfully employed this playful technique, and he once told me that he uses it in his own writing.

These ideas, and others like them, work, according to Loch, because they "generate strong synchronized brain waves," which emulate the pattern, confirmed by research, of the electric wave activity in the brain during peak moments of creative inspiration. Such exercises "reestablish the balance between both sides of the brain. They recreate the brain wave pattern for creative inspiration in which all parts work together."

In other words, you are writing on both sides of your brain.

A Parting Word

We have a parting expression in our family that I would like to share with you. When our children have studied hard for a test, or worked long hours on a dramatic recital, or prepared carefully for a presentation of any sort, we do not send them off with the usual "Good luck!" They have worked hard for whatever triumph awaits them, and their work needs to be acknowledged and validated. They have used part of their brain that was theirs to claim. Luck has nothing to do with it.

Working through the exercises in this book took dedication and commitment on your part, and whatever was revealed was talent you had in you all along. The world of fluent, productive, on-time writing is at your command. It's already yours. It's already there.

The human mind has all kinds of software we are not using, simply because no one ever showed us how. Reclaim your birthright! And when you do, give yourself tremendous credit. Give yourself a big pat on the back. Send yourself off with a big smile on your face and a spring in your step. You are wonderful. Quite brilliant. Genius class. And it was there all along. What a marvel you are!

Send yourself off with these words of praise and acknowledgment ringing in your ears. Before you began reading this book, you had enormous talent that you brought to the work. Now you know how to get at it. It is only the beginning. A time capsule of internal combustion is planted inside you. Go for it, 100 percent!

Good skill!

Analyze

1. What does Klauser mean by "going to the movies"? How is this a useful creative effort?

2. How does Perl and Egendorf's explanation of "knowing but not knowing" prove for writers? When was the last time that you encountered this state?

3. This piece is a chapter from Klauser's book *Writing on Both Sides of the Brain*. What type of promise is that title making? Which of these exercises seems to accomplish that promise most effectively?

4. How can someone carry her perfect creative environment with her wherever she goes?

Explore

1. Reread Klauser's Exercise 16 and give it a whirl. Through creative visualization and the power of the written word, put yourself in someone else's shoes. As she suggests, "Do not force anything, just let the images and sounds come" from the movie theater of this other person's mind. And then write. How does this compare to your normal writing process in terms of how easily the words come out? How might you use this type of tactic for a school essay? An admissions essay for graduate school? A Facebook post?

2. Reread Klauser's Exercise 17 and try that on your own. Imagine your success moment—it could be an interview with Oprah, a ticker tape parade, or something else. But once you lock into that feeling of success, flip the situation like Klauser did and copy the writing that gave you such success right out of your own creative visualization. Think about that songwriter who "saw" the titles to his unwritten songs in a jukebox, and he'd drop in quarter after quarter, then write down the songs as he heard them played. Where might this technique help you with your own writing? Would it work as well in other artistic endeavors such as painting, web design, or fashion? Give this technique a try on your next assignment from this book or elsewhere.

3. Because this text has so many exercises in it, it almost ended up in Chapter 7: Creative Strategies and Hacks. What other chapters might this text fit? Why? Is it more about creativity, writing, art, or something else? Discuss your thoughts with a classmate.

4. In the final exercise of this chapter, Klauser talks about how you can summon up a living, long-dead, or imaginary mentor to give you advice and/or work on a creative project. Summon up the most creative person

you can think of and allow this person to coach you on creativity. Align your brain waves with this person's. Let your voice become hers. What does she say? What advice is offered? What breakthroughs occur?

Forging Connections

1. What is it about a work of art that allows viewers to identify it as art, as distinct from an ordinary object or event? What would Shahn say? What would Csikszentmihalyi say? How necessary is it that we understand the aesthetic perspective of other cultures? In what ways might creativity—artistic or otherwise—be understood differently in other cultures?

2. Add another chapter to this book entitled "Creativity and _____." What word or phrase would you add to create your chapter title? Why is this a useful chapter to include? What relationships do you see between your word or phrase and the idea of creativity? Which of the authors of this chapter's texts would you imagine to write the most useful piece for your chapter? Why? What would the author say?

Looking Further

1. What current artists, musicians, or writers do you think will stand the test of time? Are these the ones you feel are most creative? Why or why not? What does it take for a work of art to stand the test of time?

2. Visit Poetry Daily (www.poems.com) and using the archives feature, select three poems to read. Which poem strikes you as being most creative? Why? Are poets generally more creative with language than prose writers? Why or why not? Write your own poem about any topic you choose, using any style you wish. The only caveat? Use language in creative, innovative ways. Refer to Chapter 7: Creativity Strategies and Hacks for advice or tips, as needed.

The Creative Genius

6

The list of geniuses is easy to populate because geniuses typically become fairly well known. Their creativity is undoubtable and quite public. Beethoven. Kurt Vonnegut. Shakespeare. Bobby Fischer. Oscar Niemeyer. Ben Franklin. Michelangelo. Andrew Carnegie. The list of geniuses throughout the course of human history goes on and on.

But what is genius? At first blush, it seems obvious. Geniuses are people who have managed to realize their extraordinary potential. But that doesn't quite seem to cover it. Is it perhaps then that genius is the state of being connected to—or informed by—forces bigger than ourselves? After all, Plato linked artistic creation to the inspiration from the gods, saying that poets did their best work while in "the grip of something divine." Socrates, too, believed he was advised by a *daimon*, an intellectual being that spoke to him so clearly that it was like hearing an angel whispering into his ear.

The more we try to clarify what genius is, however, the more elusive it seems to be, and the more questions seem to emerge. To what extent is genius innate? Is it something that can be cultivated? What is its relationship to IQ? Can we create conditions in which genius might flourish?

One thing seems clear: most geniuses are productive. Bach wrote a cantata every week. While Einstein is best remembered for his paper on relativity, he also published 248 other papers. Mozart produced 600+ pages of music. Thomas Edison had 1,000+ patents. As creativity researcher Dean Keith Simonton explains, geniuses produce great works and they produce mundane or even bad work, but they produce and produce and produce, period.

This chapter looks to shed a bit more light on how creativity works in the minds of the truly exceptional.

Mihaly Csikszentmihalyi
"Where Is Creativity?"

Born in Italy in 1934, **Mihaly Csikszentmihalyi** (pronounced me-HIGH chick-sent-me-HIGH-ee) immigrated to the United States at age twenty-two to study psychology. The author of numerous books on creativity and psychology, he serves as the Distinguished Professor of Psychology and Management at Claremont Graduate University. He is also the founding codirector of the Quality of Life Research Center, a nonprofit research institute that studies positive psychology, such as optimism, creativity, intrinsic motivation, and responsibility. "Where Is Creativity?" first appeared in his book *Creativity*.

The answer is obvious: Creativity is some sort of mental activity, an insight that occurs inside the heads of some special people. But this short assumption is misleading. If by creativity we mean an idea or action that is new and valuable, then we cannot simply accept a person's own account as the criterion for its existence. There is no way to know whether a thought is new except with reference to some standards, and there is no way to tell whether it is valuable until it passes social evaluation. Therefore, creativity does not happen inside people's heads, but in the interaction between a person's thoughts and a sociocultural context. It is a systemic rather than an individual phenomenon. Some examples will illustrate what I mean.

When I was a graduate student I worked part-time for a few years as an editor for a Chicago publishing house. At least once a week we would get in the mail a manuscript from an unknown author who claimed to have made a great discovery of one sort or another. Perhaps it was an eight-hundred-page tome that described in minute detail how a textual analysis of the *Odyssey* showed that, contrary to received opinion, Ulysses did not sail around the Mediterranean. Instead, according to the author's calculations, if one paid attention to the landmarks, the distances traveled, and the pattern of the stars mentioned by Homer, it was obvious that Ulysses actually traveled around the coast of Florida.

Or it might be a textbook for building flying saucers, with extremely precise blueprints—which on closer inspection turned out to be copied from a service manual for a household appliance. What made reading these manuscripts depressing was the fact that their authors actually believed they had found something new and important and that their creative efforts went unrecognized only because of a conspiracy on the part of philistines like myself and the editors of all the other publishing houses.

Some years ago the scientific world was abuzz with the news that two chemists had achieved cold fusion in the laboratory. If true, this meant that something very similar to the perpetual motion machine—one of the oldest dreams of mankind—was about to be realized. After a few frenetic months during which laboratories around the world attempted to replicate the initial claims—some with apparent success, but most without—it became increasingly clear that the experiments on which the claims were based had been flawed. So the researchers who at first were hailed as the greatest creative scientists of the century became somewhat of an embarrassment to the scholarly establishment. Yet, as far as we know, they firmly believed that they were right and that their reputations had been ruined by jealous colleagues.

Jacob Rabinow, himself an inventor but also an evaluator of inventions for the National Bureau of Standards in Washington, has many similar stories to tell about people who think they have invented perpetual motion machines:

> I've met many of these inventors who invent something that cannot work, that is theoretically impossible. But they spent three years developing it, running a motor without electricity, with magnets. You explain to them it won't work. It violates the second law of thermodynamics. And they say, "Don't give me your goddamn Washington laws."

Who is right: the individual who believes in his or her own creativity, or the social milieu that denies it? If we take sides with the individual, then creativity becomes a subjective phenomenon. All it takes to be creative, then, is an inner assurance that what I think or do is new and valuable. There is nothing wrong with defining creativity this way, as long as we realize that this is not at all what the term originally was supposed to mean—namely, to bring into existence something genuinely new that is valued enough to be added to the culture. On the other hand, if we decide that social confirmation is necessary for something to be called creative, the definition must encompass more than the individual. What counts then is whether the inner certitude is validated by the appropriate experts—such as the editors of the publishing house in the case of far-out manuscripts, or other scientists in the case of cold fusion. And it isn't possible to take a middle ground and say that sometimes the inner conviction is enough, while in other cases we need external confirmation. Such a compromise leaves a huge loophole, and trying to agree on whether something is creative or not becomes impossible.

The problem is that the term "creativity" as commonly used covers too much ground. It refers to very different entities, thus causing a great deal of confusion. To clarify the issues, I distinguish at least three different phenomena that can legitimately be called by that name.

The first usage, widespread in ordinary conversation, refers to persons who express unusual thoughts, who are interesting and stimulating—in short, to people who appear to be unusually bright. A brilliant conversationalist, a person with varied interests and a quick mind, may be called creative in this sense. Unless they also contribute something of permanent significance, I refer to people of this sort as *brilliant* rather than creative—and by and large I don't say much about them in this book.

The second way the term can be used is to refer to people who experience the world in novel and original ways. These are individuals whose perceptions are fresh, whose judgments are insightful, who may make important discoveries that only they know about. I refer to such people as *personally creative,* and try to deal with them as much as possible. But given the subjective nature of this form of creativity, it is difficult to deal with it no matter how important it is for those who experience it.

The final use of the term designates individuals who, like Leonardo, Edison, Picasso, or Einstein, have changed our culture in some important respect. They are the *creative* ones without qualifications. Because their achievements are by definition public, it is easier to write about them, and the persons included in my study belong to this group.

The difference among these three meanings is not just a matter of degree. The last kind of creativity is not simply a more developed form of the first two. These are actually different ways of being creative, each to a large measure unrelated to the others. It happens very often, for example, that some persons brimming with brilliance, whom everyone thinks of as being exceptionally creative, never leave any accomplishment, any trace of their existence—except, perhaps, in the memories of those who have known them. Whereas some of the people who have had the greatest impact on history did not show any originality or brilliance in their behavior, except for the accomplishments they left behind.

For example, Leonardo da Vinci, certainly one of the most creative persons in the third sense of the term, was apparently reclusive, and almost compulsive in his behavior. If you had met him at a cocktail party, you would have thought that he was a tiresome bore and would have left him standing in a corner as soon as possible. Neither Isaac Newton nor Thomas Edison would have been considered assets at a party either, and outside of their scientific concerns they appeared colorless and driven. The biographers of outstanding creators struggle valiantly to make their subjects interesting and brilliant, yet more often than not their efforts are in vain. The accomplishments of a Michelangelo, a Beethoven, a Picasso, or an Einstein are awesome in their respective fields—but their private lives, their everyday ideas and actions, would seldom warrant another thought were it not that their specialized accomplishments made everything they said or did of interest.

By the definition I am using here, one of the most creative persons in this study is John Bardeen. He is the first person to have been awarded the

Nobel Prize in Physics twice. The first time it was for developing the transistor; the second for his work on superconductivity. Few persons have ranged as widely and deeply in the realm of solid state physics, or come out with such important insights. But talking with Bardeen on any issue besides his work was not easy; his mind followed abstract paths while he spoke slowly, haltingly, and without much depth or interest about "real life" topics.

It is perfectly possible to make a creative contribution without being brilliant or personally creative, just as it is possible—even likely—that someone personally creative will never contribute a thing to the culture. All three kinds of creativity enrich life by making it more interesting and fulfilling. But in this context I focus primarily on the third use of the term, and explore what is involved in the kind of creativity that leaves a trace in the cultural matrix.

To make things more complicated, consider two more terms that are sometimes used interchangeably with creativity. The first is *talent*. Talent differs from creativity in that it focuses on an innate ability to do something very well. We might say that Michael Jordan is a talented athlete, or that Mozart was a talented pianist, without implying that either was creative for that reason. In our sample, some individuals were talented in mathematics or in music, but the majority achieved creative results without any exceptional talent being evident. Of course, talent is a relative term, so it might be argued that in comparison to "average" individuals the creative ones are talented.

The other term that is often used as a synonym for "creative" is *genius*. Again, there is an overlap. Perhaps we should think of a genius as a person who is both brilliant and creative at the same time. But certainly a person can change the culture in significant ways without being a genius. Although several of the people in our sample have been called a genius by the media, they—and the majority of creative individuals we interviewed—reject this designation.

The Systems Model

We have seen that creativity with a capital *C*, the kind that changes some aspect of the culture, is never only in the mind of a person. That would by definition *not* be a case of cultural creativity. To have any effect, the idea must be couched in terms that are understandable to others, it must pass muster with the experts in the field, and finally it must be included in the cultural domain to which it belongs. So the first question I ask of creativity is not *what* is it but *where* is it?

The answer that makes most sense is that creativity can be observed only in the interrelations of a system made up of three main parts. The first of these is the *domain*, which consists of a set of symbolic rules and procedures. Mathematics is a domain, or at a finer resolution algebra and number theory can be seen as domains. Domains are in turn nested in what we usually call culture, or the symbolic knowledge shared by a particular society, or by humanity as a whole.

The second component of creativity is the *field*, which includes all the individuals who act as gatekeepers to the domain. It is their job to decide whether a new idea or product should be included in the domain. In the visual arts the field consists of art teachers, curators of museums, collectors of art, critics, and administrators of foundations and government agencies that deal with culture. It is this field that selects what new works of art deserve to be recognized, preserved, and remembered.

Finally, the third component of the creative system is the individual *person*. Creativity occurs when a person, using the symbols of a given domain such as music, engineering, business, or mathematics, has a new idea or sees a new pattern, and when this novelty is selected by the appropriate field for inclusion into the relevant domain. The next generation will encounter that novelty as part of the domain they are exposed to, and if they are creative, they in turn will change it further. Occasionally creativity involves the establishment of a new domain: It could be argued that Galileo started experimental physics and that Freud carved psychoanalysis out of the existing domain of neuropathology. But if Galileo and Freud had not been able to enlist followers who came together in distinct fields to further their respective domains, their ideas would have had much less of an impact, or none at all.

So the definition that follows from this perspective is: Creativity is any act, idea, or product that changes an existing domain, or that transforms an existing domain into a new one. And the definition of a creative person is: someone whose thoughts or actions change a domain, or establish a new domain. It is important to remember, however, that a domain cannot be changed without the explicit or implicit consent of a field responsible for it.

Several consequences follow from this way of looking at things. For instance, we don't need to assume that the creative person is necessarily different from anyone else. In other words, a personal trait of "creativity" is not what determines whether a person will be creative. What counts is whether the novelty he or she produces is accepted for inclusion in the domain. This may be the result of chance, perseverance, or being at the right place at the right time. Because creativity is jointly constituted by the interaction among domain, field, and person, the trait of personal creativity may help generate the novelty that will change a domain, but it is neither a sufficient nor a necessary condition for it.

A person cannot be creative in a domain to which he or she is not exposed. No matter how enormous mathematical gifts a child may have, he or she will not be able to contribute to mathematics without learning its rules. But even if the rules are learned, creativity cannot be manifested in the absence of a field that recognizes and legitimizes the novel contributions. A child might possibly learn mathematics on his or her own by finding the right books and the right mentors, but cannot make a difference in the domain unless recognized by teachers and journal editors who will witness to the appropriateness of the contribution.

It also follows that creativity can be manifested only in existing domains and fields. For instance, it is very difficult to say "This woman is very creative at nurturing" or "This woman is very creative in her wisdom," because nurturance and wisdom, although extremely important for human survival, are loosely organized domains with few generally accepted rules and priorities, and they lack a field of experts who can determine the legitimacy of claims. So we are in the paradoxical situation that novelty is more obvious in domains that are often relatively trivial but easy to measure; whereas in domains that are more essential novelty is very difficult to determine. There can be agreement on whether a new computer game, rock song, or economic formula is actually novel, and therefore creative, less easy to agree on the novelty of an act of compassion or of an insight into human nature.

The model also allows for the often mysterious fluctuations in the attribution of creativity over time. For example, the reputation of Raphael as a painter has waxed and waned several times since his heyday at the court of Pope Julius II. Gregor Mendel did not become famous as the creator of experimental genetics until half a century after his death. Johann Sebastian Bach's music was dismissed as old-fashioned for several generations.

The conventional explanation is that Raphael, Mendel, and Bach were always creative, only their reputation changed with the vagaries of social recognition. But the systems model recognizes the fact that creativity cannot be separated from its recognition. Mendel was not creative during his years of relative obscurity because his experimental findings were not that important until a group of British geneticists, at the end of the nineteenth century, recognized their implications for evolution.

The creativity of Raphael fluctuates as art historical knowledge, art critical theories, and the aesthetic sensitivity of the age change. According to the systems model, it makes perfect sense to say that Raphael was creative in the sixteenth and in the nineteenth centuries but not in between or afterward. Raphael is creative when the community is moved by his work, and discovers new possibilities in his paintings. But when his paintings seem mannered and routine to those who know art, Raphael can only be called a great draftsman, a subtle colorist—perhaps even a personally creative individual—but not creative with a capital *C*. If creativity is more than personal insight and is cocreated by domains, fields, and persons, then creativity can be constructed, deconstructed, and reconstructed several times over the course of history. Here is one of our respondents, the poet Anthony Hecht, commenting on this issue:

> Literary reputations are constantly shifting. Sometimes in trifling, frivolous ways. There was a former colleague of mine who, at a recent meeting of the English Department, said that she thought it was now no longer important to teach Shakespeare because among other things he had a very feeble grasp of women. Now that seems to me as trifling an observation as can be made, but it does mean that, if you take this seriously, nobody's place in the whole canon is very secure, that it's constantly changing. And this is both good and bad. John Donne's position was in the nineteenth century of no consequence at all. The *Oxford Book of English Verse* had only one poem of his. And now, of course, he was resurrected by Herbert Grierson and T. S. Eliot and he's one of the great figures of seventeenth-century poetry. But he wasn't always. This is true of music, too. Bach was eclipsed for two hundred years and rediscovered by Mendelssohn. This means that we are constantly reassessing the past. And that's a good, valuable, and indeed necessary thing to do.

This way of looking at things might seem insane to some. The usual way to think about this issue is that someone like van Gogh was a great creative genius, but his contemporaries did not recognize this. Fortunately, now we have discovered what a great painter he was after all, so his creativity has been vindicated. Few flinch at the presumption implicit in such a view. What we are saying is that we know what great art is so much better than van Gogh's contemporaries did—those bourgeois philistines. What—besides unconscious conceit—warrants this belief? A more objective description of van Gogh's contribution is that his creativity came into being when a sufficient number of art experts felt that his paintings had something important to contribute to the domain of art. Without such a response, van Gogh would have remained what he was, a disturbed man who painted strange canvases.

Perhaps the most important implication of the systems model is that the level of creativity in a given place at a given time does not depend only on the amount of individual creativity. It depends just as much on how well suited the respective domains and fields are to the recognition and diffusion of novel ideas. This can make a great deal of practical difference to efforts for enhancing creativity. Today many American corporations spend a great deal of money and time trying to increase the originality of their employees, hoping thereby to get a competitive edge in the marketplace. But such programs make no difference unless management also learns to recognize the valuable ideas among the many novel ones, and then finds ways of implementing them.

For instance, Robert Galvin at Motorola is justly concerned about the fact that in order to survive among the hungry Pacific Rim electronic manufacturers, his company must make creativity an intentional part of its productive process. He is also right in perceiving that to do so he first has to encourage the thousands of engineers working for the company to generate as many novel ideas as possible. So various forms of brainstorming are instituted, where employees free-associate without fear of being ridiculously impractical. But the next steps are less clear. How does the field (in this case, management) choose among the multitude of new ideas the ones worth pursuing? And how can the chosen ideas be included in the domain (in this case, the production schedule of Motorola)? Because we are used to thinking that creativity begins and ends with the person, it is easy to miss the fact that the greatest spur to it may come from changes outside the individual.

Creativity in the Renaissance

A good example is the sudden spurt in artistic creativity that took place in Florence between 1400 and 1425. These were the golden years of the Renaissance, and it is generally agreed that some of the most influential new works of art in Europe were created during that quarter century. Any list of the masterpieces would include the dome of the cathedral built by Brunelleschi, the "Gates of Paradise" crafted for the baptistery by Ghiberti, Donatello's sculptures for the chapel of Orsanmichele, the fresco cycle by Masaccio in the Brancacci Chapel, and Gentile da Fabriano's painting of the Adoration of the Magi in the Church of the Trinity.

How can this flowering of great art be explained? If creativity is something entirely within a person, we would have to argue that for some reason an unusually large number of creative artists were born in Florence in the last decades of the fourteenth century. Perhaps some freak genetic mutation occurred, or a drastic change in the education of Florentine children suddenly caused them to become more creative. But an explanation involving the domain and the field is much more sensible.

As far as the domain is concerned, the Renaissance was made possible in part by the rediscovery of ancient Roman methods of building and sculpting that had been lost for centuries during the so-called Dark Ages. In Rome and elsewhere, by the end of the thirteen hundreds, eager scholars were excavating classical ruins, copying down and analyzing the styles and techniques of the ancients. This slow preparatory work bore fruit at the turn of the fifteenth century, opening up long-forgotten knowledge to the artisans and craftsmen of the time.

The cathedral of Florence, Santa Maria Novella, had been left open to the skies for eighty years because no one could find a way to build a dome over its huge apse. There was no known method for preventing the walls from collapsing inward once the curvature of the dome had advanced beyond a certain height. Every year eager young artists and established builders submitted plans to the Opera del Duomo, the board that supervised the building of the cathedral, but their plans were found unpersuasive. The Opera was made up of the political and business leaders of the city, and their personal reputations were at stake in this choice. For eighty years they did not feel that any proposed solution for the completion of the dome was worthy of the city, and of themselves.

But eventually humanist scholars became interested in the Pantheon of Rome, measured its enormous dome, and analyzed how it had been constructed. The Pantheon had been rebuilt by the emperor Hadrian in the second century. The diameter of its 71-foot-high dome was 142 feet. Nothing on that scale had been built for well over a thousand years, and the methods that allowed the Romans to build such a structure that would stand up and not collapse had been long forgotten in the dark centuries of barbarian invasions. But now that peace and commerce were reviving the Italian cities, the knowledge was slowly being pieced back together.

Brunelleschi, who in 1401 appears to have visited Rome to study its antiquities, understood the importance of the studies of the Pantheon. His idea for how to complete the dome in Florence was based on the framework of internal stone arches that would help contain the thrust, and the herringbone brickwork between them. But his design was not just a restatement of the Roman model—it was influenced also by all the architecture of the intervening centuries, especially the Gothic models. When he presented his plan to the Opera, they recognized it as a feasible and beautiful solution. And after the dome was built, it became a liberating new form that inspired hundreds of builders who came after him, including Michelangelo, who based on it his design for the cupola of St. Peter's in Rome.

But no matter how influential the rediscovery of classical art forms, the Florentine Renaissance cannot be explained only in terms of the sudden availability of information. Otherwise, the same flowering of new artistic forms would have taken place in all the other cities exposed to the ancient models. And though this actually did happen to a certain extent, no other place matched Florence in the intensity and depth of artistic achievement. Why was this so?

The explanation is that the field of art became particularly favorable to the creation of new works at just about the same time as the rediscovery of the ancient domains of art. Florence had become one of the richest cities in Europe first through trading, then through the manufacture of wool and other textiles, and finally through the financial expertise of its rich merchants. By the end of the fourteenth century there were a dozen major bankers in the city—the Medici being only one of the minor ones—who were getting substantial interest every year from the various foreign kings and potentates to whom they had lent money.

But while the coffers of the bankers were getting fuller, the city itself was troubled. Men without property were ruthlessly exploited, and political tensions fueled by economic inequality threatened at any moment to explode into open conflict. The struggle between pope and emperor, which divided the entire continent, was reproduced inside the city in the struggle between the Guelf and Ghibelline factions. To make matters worse, Florence was surrounded by Siena, Pisa, and Arezzo, cities jealous of its wealth and ambitions and always ready to snatch away whatever they could of Florentine trade and territory.

It was in this atmosphere of wealth and uncertainty that the urban leaders decided to invest in making Florence the most beautiful city in Christendom—in their words, "a new Athens." By building awesome churches, impressive bridges, and splendid palaces, and by commissioning great frescoes and majestic statues, they must have felt that they were weaving a protective spell around their homes and businesses. And in a way, they were not wrong: when more than five hundred years later Hitler ordered the retreating German troops to blow up the bridges on the Arno and level the city around them, the field commander refused to obey on the grounds that too much beauty would be erased from the world—and the city was saved.

The important thing to realize is that when the Florentine bankers, churchmen, and heads of great guilds decided to make their city intimidatingly beautiful, they did not just throw money at artists and wait to see what happened. They became intensely involved in the process of encouraging, evaluating, and selecting the works they wanted to see completed. It was because the leading citizens, as well as the common people, were so seriously concerned with the outcome of their work that the artists were pushed to perform beyond their previous limits. Without the constant encouragement and scrutiny of the members of the Opera, the dome over the cathedral would probably not have been as beautiful as it eventually turned out to be.

Another illustration of how the field of art operated in Florence at this time concerns the building of the north and especially the east door of the baptistery, one of the uncontested masterpieces of the period, which Michelangelo declared was worthy of being the "Gate of Paradise" when he saw its heart-wrenching beauty. In this case also a special commission had been formed to supervise the building of the doors for this public edifice. The board was composed of eminent individuals, mostly the leaders of the guild of wool weavers that was financing the project. The board decided that each door should be of bronze and have ten panels illustrating Old Testament themes. Then they wrote to some of the most eminent philosophers, writers, and churchmen in Europe to request their opinion of which scenes from the Bible should be included in the panels, and how they should be represented. After the answers came in, they drew up a list of specifications for the doors and in 1401 announced a competition for their design.

From the dozens of drawings submitted the board chose five finalists—Brunelleschi and Ghiberti among them. The finalists on the short list were given a year to finish a bronze mock-up of one of the door panels. The subject was to be "The Sacrifice of Isaac" and had to include at least one angel and one sheep in addition to Abraham and his son. During that year all five finalists were paid handsomely by the board for time and materials. In 1402 the jury reconvened to consider the new entries and selected Ghiberti's panel, which showed technical excellence as well as a wonderfully natural yet classical composition.

Lorenzo Ghiberti was twenty-one years old at the time. He spent the next twenty years finishing the north door and then another twenty-seven finishing the famed east door. He was involved with perfecting the baptistery doors from 1402 to 1452, a span of a half century. Of course, in the meantime he finished many more commissions and sculpted statues for the Medicis, the Pazzis, the guild of merchant bankers, and other notables, but his reputation rests on the Gates of Paradise, which changed the Western world's conception of decorative art.

If Brunelleschi had been influenced by Roman architecture, Ghiberti studied and tried to emulate Roman sculpture. He had to relearn the technique for casting large bronze shapes, and he studied the classic profiles carved on Roman tombs on which he modeled the expressions of the characters he made emerge from the door panels. And again, he combined the rediscovered classics with the more recent Gothic sculpture produced in Siena. However, one could claim without too much risk of exaggeration that what made the Gates of Paradise so beautiful was the care, concern, and support of the entire community, represented by the field of judges who supervised their construction. If Ghiberti and his fellows were driven to surpass themselves, it was by the intense competition and focused attention their work attracted. Thus the sociologist of art Arnold Hauser rightly assesses this period: "In the art of the early Renaissance ... the starting point of production is to be found mostly not in the creative urge, the subjective self-expression and spontaneous inspiration of the artist, but in the task set by the customer."

Of course, the great works of Florentine art would never have been made just because the domain of classical art had been rediscovered, or because the rulers of the city had decided to make it beautiful. Without individual artists the Renaissance could not have taken place. After all, it was Brunelleschi who built the dome over Santa Maria Novella, and it was Ghiberti who spent his life casting the Gates of Paradise. At the same time, it must be recognized that without previous models and the support of the city, Brunelleschi and Ghiberti could not have done what they did. And that with the favorable conjunction of field and domain, if these two artists had not been born, some others would have stepped in their place and built the dome and the doors. It is because of this inseparable connection that creativity must, in the last analysis, be seen not as something happening within a person but in the relationships within a system.

Domains of Knowledge and Action

It seems that every species of living organism, except for us humans, understands the world in terms of more or less built-in responses to certain types of sensations. Plants turn toward the sun. There are amoebas sensitive to magnetic attraction that orient their bodies toward the North Pole. Baby indigo buntings learn the patterns of the stars as they look out of their nests and then are able to fly great distances at night without losing their way. Bats respond to sounds, sharks to smell, and birds of prey have incredibly developed vision. Each species experiences and understands its environment in terms of the information its sensory equipment is programmed to process.

The same is true for humans. But in addition to the narrow windows on the world our genes have provided, we have managed to open up new perspectives on reality based on information mediated by symbols. Perfect parallel lines do not exist in nature, but by postulating their existence Euclid and his followers could build a system for representing spatial relations that is much more precise than what the unaided eye and brain can achieve. Different as they are from each other, lyric poetry and magnetic resonance spectroscopy are both ways to make accessible information that otherwise we would never have an inkling about.

Knowledge mediated by symbols is extrasomatic; it is not transmitted through the chemical codes inscribed in our chromosomes but must be intentionally passed on and learned. It is this extrasomatic information that makes up what we call a culture. And the knowledge conveyed by symbols is bundled up in discrete domains—geometry, music, religion, legal systems, and so on. Each domain is made up of its own symbolic elements, its own rules, and generally has its own system of notation. In many ways, each domain describes an isolated little world in which a person can think and act with clarity and concentration.

The existence of domains is perhaps the best evidence of human creativity. The fact that calculus and Gregorian chants exist means that we can experience patterns of order that were not programmed into our genes by biological evolution. By learning the rules of a domain, we immediately step beyond the boundaries of biology and enter the realm of cultural evolution. Each domain expands the limitations of individuality and enlarges our sensitivity and ability to relate to the world. Each person is surrounded by an almost infinite number of domains that are potentially able to open up new worlds and give new powers to those who learn their rules. Therefore, it is astounding how few of us bother to invest enough mental energy to learn the rules of even one of these domains, and live instead exclusively within the constraints of biological existence.

For most people, domains are primarily ways to make a living. We choose nursing or plumbing, medicine or business administration because of our ability and the chances of getting a well-paying job. But then there are individuals—and the creative ones are usually in this group—who choose certain domains because of a powerful calling to do so. For them the match is so perfect that acting within the rules of the domain is rewarding in itself; they would keep doing what they do even if they were not paid for it, just for the sake of doing the activity.

Despite the multiplicity of domains, there are some common reasons for pursuing them for their own sake. Nuclear physics, microbiology, poetry, and musical composition share few symbols and rules, yet the calling for these different domains is often astonishingly similar. To bring order to experience, to make something that will endure after one's death, to do something that allows humankind to go beyond its present powers are very common themes.

When asked why he decided to become a poet at the age of seven, György Faludy answered, "Because I was afraid to die." He explained that creating patterns with words, patterns that because of their truth and beauty had a chance to survive longer than the body of the poet, was an act of defiance and hope that gave meaning and direction to his life for the next seventy-three years. This urge is not so very different from physicist John Bardeen's description of his work on superconductivity that might lead to a world without friction, the physicist Heinz Maier-Leibnitz's hope that nuclear energy will provide unlimited power, or the biochemical physicist Manfred Eigen's attempt to understand how life evolved. Domains are wonderfully different, but the human quest they represent converges on a few themes. In many ways, Max Planck's obsession with understanding the Absolute underlies most human attempts to transcend the limitations of a body doomed to die after a short span of years.

There are several ways that domains can help or hinder creativity. Three major dimensions are particularly relevant: the clarity of structure, the centrality within the culture, and accessibility. Say that pharmaceutical companies A and B are competing in the same market. The amount of money they devote to research and development, as well as the creative potential of their researchers, is equal. Now we want to predict whether company A or B will come up with the most effective new drugs, basing our prediction solely on domain characteristics. The questions we would ask are the following: Which company has the more detailed data about pharmaceuticals? Where is the data better organized? Which company puts more emphasis in its culture on research, relative to other areas such as production and marketing? Where does pharmaceutical knowledge earn more respect? Which company disseminates knowledge better among its staff? Where is it easier to test a hypothesis? The company where knowledge is better structured, more central, and more accessible is likely to be the one where—other things still being equal—creative innovations are going to happen.

It has been often remarked that superior ability in some domains—such as mathematics or music—shows itself earlier in life than in other domains—such as painting or philosophy. Similarly, it has been suggested that the most creative performances in some domains are the work of young people, while in other domains older persons have the edge. The most creative lyric verse is believed to be that written by the young, while epics tend to be written by more mature poets. Mathematical genius peaks in the twenties, physics in the thirties, but great philosophical works are usually achieved later in life.

The most likely explanation for these differences lies in the different ways these domains are structured. The symbolic system of mathematics is organized relatively tightly; the internal logic is strict; the system maximizes clarity and lack of redundancy. Therefore, it is easy for a young person to assimilate the rules quickly and jump to the cutting edge of the domain in a few years. For the same structural reasons, when a novelty is proposed—like the long-awaited proof of Fermat's last theorem presented by a relatively young mathematician in 1993—it is immediately recognized and, if viable, accepted. By contrast, it takes decades for social scientists or philosophers to master their domains, and if they produce a new idea, it takes the field many years to assess whether it is an improvement worth adding to the knowledge base.

Heinz Maier-Leibnitz tells the story of a small physics seminar he taught in Munich, which was interrupted one day by a graduate student who suggested a new way to represent on the blackboard the behavior of a subatomic particle. The professor agreed that the new formulation was an improvement and praised the student for having thought of it. By the end of the week, Maier-Leibnitz says, he started getting calls from physicists at other German universities, asking in effect, "Is it true that one of your students came up with such and such an idea?" The next week, calls began to come in from American universities on the East Coast. In two weeks, colleagues from Cal Tech, Berkeley, and Stanford were asking the same question.

This story could never have been told about my branch of psychology. If a student stood up in a psychology seminar at any school in the world and uttered the most profound ideas, he or she would not create a ripple beyond the walls of the classroom. Not because psychology students are less intelligent or original than the ones in physics. Nor because my colleagues and I are less alert to our students' new ideas. But because with the exception of a few highly structured subdomains, psychology is so diffuse a system of thought that it takes years of intense writing for any person to say something that others recognize as new and important. The young student in Maier-Leibnitz's class was eventually awarded the Nobel Prize in Physics, something that could never happen to a psychologist.

Does this mean that a domain that is better structured—where creativity is easier to determine—is in some sense "better" than one that is more diffuse? That it is more important, more advanced, more serious? Not at all. If that were true, then chess, microeconomics, or computer programming, which are very clearly structured domains, would have to be considered more advanced than morality or wisdom.

But it is certainly true that nowadays a quantifiable domain with sharp boundaries and well-defined rules is taken more seriously. In a typical university it is much easier to get funding for such a department. It is also easier to justify promotion for a teacher in a narrowly defined domain: ten colleagues will willingly write letters of recommendation stating that professor X should be promoted because she is the world's authority on the mating habits of the kangaroo rat or on the use of the subjunctive in Dravidic languages. It is much less likely that ten scholars would agree on who is a world authority on personality development. From this it is easy to make the regrettable mistake of inferring that personality development is a scientifically less respectable domain than the one that studies the mating practices of the kangaroo rat.

In the current historical climate, a domain where quantifiable measurement is possible takes precedence over one where it does not. We believe that things that can be measured are real, and we ignore those that we don't know how to measure. So people take intelligence very seriously, because the mental ability we call by that name can be measured by tests; whereas few bother about how sensitive, altruistic, or helpful someone is, because as yet there is no good way to measure such qualities. Sometimes this bias has profound consequences—for instance, in how we define social progress and achievement. One of futurist Hazel Henderson's life goals is to convince world governments to start computing less easily measured trends in their Gross Natural Product. As long as the costs of pollution, depredation of natural resources, decline in the quality of life, and various other human costs are left out of the reckoning of the GNP, she claims, entirely distorted pictures of reality result. A country may pride itself on all its new highways while the resulting auto emissions are causing widespread emphysema.

Fields of Accomplishment

If a symbolic domain is necessary for a person to innovate in, a field is necessary to determine whether the innovation is worth making a fuss about. Only a very small percentage of the great number of novelties produced will eventually become part of the culture. For instance, about one hundred thousand new books are published every year in the United States.

How many of these will be remembered ten years from now? Similarly, about five hundred thousand people in this country state on their census forms that they are artists. If each of them painted only one picture a year, it would amount to about fifteen *million* new paintings per generation. How many of these will end up in museums or in textbooks on art? One in a million, ten in a million, one in ten thousand? One?

George Stigler, the Nobel laureate in economics, made the same point about new ideas produced in his domain, and what he says can be applied to any other field of science:

> The profession is too busy to read much. I keep telling my colleagues at the *Journal of Political Economy* that anytime we get an article that fifteen of our profession, of the seven thousand subscribers, read carefully, that must be truly a major article of the year.

These numbers suggest that the competition between memes, or units of cultural information, is as fierce as the competition between the units of chemical information we call genes. In order to survive, cultures must eliminate most of the new ideas their members produce. Cultures are conservative, and for good reason. No culture could assimilate all the novelty people produce without dissolving into chaos. Suppose you had to pay equal attention to the fifteen million paintings—how much time would you have left free to eat, sleep, work, or listen to music? In other words, no person can afford to pay attention to more than a very small fraction of new things produced. Yet a culture could not survive long unless all of its members paid attention to at least a few of the same things. In fact it could be said that a culture exists when the majority of people agree that painting X deserves more attention than painting Y, or idea X deserves more thought than idea Y.

Because of the scarcity of attention, we must be selective: we remember and recognize only a few of the works of art produced, we read only a few of the new books written, we buy only a few of the new appliances busily being invented. Usually it is the various fields that act as filters to help us select among the flood of new information those memes worth paying attention to. A field is made up of experts in a given domain whose job involves passing judgment on performance in that domain. Members of the field choose from among the novelties those that deserve to be included in the canon.

This competition also means that a creative person must convince the field that he or she has made a valuable innovation. This is never an easy task. Stigler emphasizes the necessity of this difficult struggle or recognition:

> I think you have to accept the judgment of others. Because if one were allowed to judge his own case, every one of us should have been president of the United States and received all the medals and so forth. And so I guess I am most proud of the things in which I succeeded in impressing other people with what I have done. And those would be things like the two areas of work in which I received the Nobel Prize, and things like that. So those and certain other works that my profession has liked would be, as far as my professional life goes, the things of which I'm most proud.
>
> I have always looked upon the task of a scientist as bearing the responsibility for persuading his contemporaries of the cogency and validity of his thinking. He isn't entitled to a warm reception. He has to earn it, whether by the skill of his exposition, the novelty of his ideas, or what. I've written on subjects which I thought had promise which haven't amounted to much. That's all right. That may well mean that my judgment wasn't good, because I don't think any one person's judgment is as good as that of a collection of his better colleagues.

Fields vary greatly in terms of how specialized versus how inclusive they are. For some domains, the field is as broad as society itself. It took the entire population of the United States to decide whether the recipe for New Coke was an innovation worth keeping. On the other hand, it has been said that only four or five people in the world initially understood Einstein's theory of relativity, but their opinion had enough weight to make his name a household word. But even in Einstein's case, the broader society had a voice in deciding that his work deserved a central place in our culture. To what extent, for instance, did his fame depend on the fact that he looked like a scientist from Hollywood central casting? That he was persecuted by our enemies, the Nazis? That many interpreted his discoveries as supportive of the relativity of values, and thus offering a refreshing alternative to binding social norms and beliefs? That while yearning to overthrow old beliefs, we also thirst for new certainties, and Einstein was said to have come up with an important new truth? Although none of these considerations bears in the least on the theory of relativity, they were all very much part of how the media portrayed Einstein—and it is these traits rather than the profundity of his theory that presumably convinced most people that he was worth including in the cultural pantheon.

Fields can affect the rate of creativity in at least three ways. The first way is by being either reactive or proactive. A reactive field does not solicit or stimulate novelty, while a proactive field does. One of the major reasons the Renaissance was so bountiful in Florence is that the patrons actively demanded novelty from artists. In the United States, we make some effort to be proactive in terms of stimulating scientific creativity in the young: science fairs and prestigious prizes like the Westinghouse, which goes to the one hundred best high school science projects each year, are some examples. But of course much more could be done to stimulate novel thinking in science early on. Similarly, some companies like Motorola take seriously the idea that one way to increase creativity is for the field to be proactive.

The second way for the field to influence the rate of novelty is by choosing either a narrow or a broad filter in the selection of novelty. Some fields are conservative and allow only a few new items to enter the domain at any given time. They reject most novelty and select only what they consider best. Others are more liberal in allowing new ideas into their domains, and as a result these change more rapidly. At the extremes, both strategies can be dangerous: it is possible to wreck a domain either by starving it of novelty or by admitting too much unassimilated novelty into it.

Finally, fields can encourage novelty if they are well connected to the rest of the social system and are able to channel support into their own domain. For instance, after World War II it was easy for nuclear physicists to get all sorts of money to build new laboratories, research centers, experimental reactors, and to train new physicists, because politicians and voters were still enormously impressed by the atomic bomb and the future possibilities it represented. During a few years in the 1950s, the number of students in theoretical physics at the University of Rome went from seven to two hundred; the proportions were not so far off elsewhere around the world.

There are several ways that domains and fields can affect each other. Sometimes domains determine to a large extent what the field can or cannot do; this is probably more usual in the sciences, where the knowledge base severely restricts what the scientific establishment can or cannot claim. No matter how much a group of scientists would like their pet theory accepted, it won't be if it runs against the previously accumulated consensus. In the arts, on the other hand, it is often the field that takes precedence: The artistic establishment decides, without firm guidelines anchored in the past, which new works of art are worthy of inclusion in the domain.

Sometimes fields that are not competent in the domain take control over it. The church interfered in Galileo's astronomical findings; the Communist party for a while directed not only Soviet genetics but art and music as well; and fundamentalists in the United States are trying to have a voice in teaching evolutionary history. In more subtle ways, economic and political forces always influence, whether intentionally or not, the development of domains. Our knowledge of foreign languages would be even less if the U.S. government stopped subsidizing Title IV programs. Opera and ballet would virtually disappear without massive outside support. The Japanese government is heavily invested in stimulating new ideas and applications in microcircuitry, while the Dutch government, understandably enough, encourages pioneering work in the building of dams and hydraulic devices. The Romanian government was actively involved in the destruction of the art forms of its ethnic minorities in order to maintain the purity of Dacian culture; the Nazis tried to destroy what they considered "degenerate" Jewish art.

At times fields become unable to represent well a particular domain. A leading philosopher in our study maintains that if a young person wants to learn philosophy these days, he or she would be better advised to become immersed in the domain directly and avoid the field altogether: "I'd tell him to read the great books of philosophy. And I would tell him not to do graduate study at any university. I think all philosophy departments are no good. They are all terrible." By and large, however, jurisdiction over a given domain is officially left in the hands of a field of experts. These may range from grade school teachers to university professors and include anyone who has a right to decide whether a new idea or product is "good" or "bad." It is impossible to understand creativity without understanding how fields operate, how they decide whether something new should or should not be added to the domain.

The Contributions of the Person

Finally we get to the individual responsible for generating novelty. Most investigations focus on the creative person, believing that by understanding how his or her mind works, the key to creativity will be found. But this is not necessarily the case. For though it is true that behind every new idea or product there is a person, it does not follow that such persons have a single characteristic responsible for the novelty.

Perhaps being creative is more like being involved in an automobile accident. There are some traits that make one more likely to be in an accident—being young and male, for instance—but usually we cannot explain car accidents on the basis of the driver's characteristics alone. There are too many other variables involved: the condition of the road, the other driver, the type of traffic, the weather, and so on. Accidents, like creativity, are properties of systems rather than of individuals.

Nor can we say that it is the person who starts the creative process. In the case of the Florentine Renaissance one could just as well say that is was started by the rediscovery of Roman art, or by the stimulation provided by the city's bankers. Brunelleschi and his friends found themselves in a stream of thought and action that started before they were born, and then they stepped into the middle of it. At first it appears that they initiated the great works that made the epoch famous, but in reality they were only catalysts for a much more complex process with many participants and many inputs.

When we asked creative persons what explains their success, one of the most frequent answers—perhaps the most frequent one—was that they were lucky. Being in the right place at the right time is an almost universal explanation. Several scientists who were in graduate school in the late 1920s or 1930s remember being among the first cohorts to be exposed to quantum theory. Inspired by the work of Max Planck and Niels Bohr, they applied quantum mechanics to chemistry, to biology, to astrophysics, to electrodynamics. Some of them, like Linus Pauling, John Bardeen, Manfred Eigen, Subrahmanyan Chandrasekhar, were awarded Nobel Prizes for extending the theory to new domains. Many women scientists who entered graduate school in the 1940s mention that they wouldn't have been accepted by the schools, and certainly they wouldn't have been given fellowships and special attention from supervisors, except for the fact that there were so few male students left to compete against, most of them having gone to war.

Luck is without doubt an important ingredient in creative discoveries. A very successful artist, whose work sells well and hangs in the best museums and who can afford a large estate with horses and a swimming pool, once admitted ruefully that there could be at least a thousand artists as good as he is—yet they are unknown and their work is unappreciated. The one difference between him and the rest, he said, was that years back he met at a party a man with whom he had a few drinks. They hit it off and became friends. The man eventually became a successful art dealer who did his best to push his friend's work. One thing led to another: a rich collector began to buy the artist's work, critics started paying attention, a large museum added one of his works to its permanent collection. And once the artist became successful, the field discovered his creativity.

It is important to point out the tenuousness of the individual contribution to creativity, because it is usually so often overrated. Yet one can also fall in the opposite error and deny the individual any credit. Certain sociologists and social psychologists claim that creativity is all a matter of attribution. The creative person is like a blank screen on which social consensus projects exceptional qualities. Because we need to believe that creative people exist, we endow some individuals with this illusory quality. This, too, is an oversimplification. For while the individual is not as important as it is commonly supposed, neither is it true that novelty could come about without the contribution of individuals, and that all individuals have the same likelihood of producing novelty.

Luck, although a favorite explanation of creative individuals, is also easy to overstate. Many young scientists in Linus Pauling's generation were exposed to the arrival of quantum theory from Europe. Why didn't they see what this theory implied for chemistry, the way he saw it? Many women would have liked to become scientists in the 1940s. Why did so few take the opportunity when the doors to graduate training were opened to them? Being in the right place at the right time is clearly important. But many people never realize that they are standing in a propitious space/time convergence, and even fewer know what to do when the realization hits them.

Internalizing the System

A person who wants to make a creative contribution not only must work within a creative system but must also reproduce that system within his or her mind. In other words, the person must learn the rules and the content of the domain, as well as the criteria of selection, the preferences of the field. In science, it is practically impossible to make a creative contribution without internalizing the fundamental knowledge of the domain. All scientists would agree with the words of Frank Offner, a scientist and inventor: "The important thing is that you must have a good, a very solid grounding in the physical sciences, before you can make any progress in understanding." The same conclusions are voiced in every other discipline. Artists agree that a painter cannot make a creative contribution without looking, and looking, and looking at previous art, and without knowing what other artists and critics consider good and bad art. Writers say that you have to read, read, and read some more, and know what the critics' criteria for good writing are, before you can write creatively yourself.

An extremely lucid example of how the internalization of the system works is given by the inventor Jacob Rabinow. At first, he talks about the importance of what I have called the *domain*:

> So you need three things to be an original thinker. First, you have to have a tremendous amount of information—a big database if you like to be fancy. If you're a musician, you should know a lot about music, that is, you've heard music, you remember music, you could repeat a song if you have to. In other words, if you were born on a desert island and never heard music, you're not likely to be a Beethoven. You might, but it's not likely. You may imitate birds but you're not going to write the Fifth Symphony. So you're brought up in an atmosphere where you store a lot of information.
>
> So you have to have the kind of memory that you need for the kind of things you want to do. And you do those things which are easy and you don't do those things which are hard, so you get better and better by doing the things you do well, and eventually you become either a great tennis player or a good inventor or whatever, because you tend to do those things which you do well and the more you do, the easier it gets, and the easier it gets, the better you do it, and eventually you become very one-sided but you're very good at it and you're lousy at everything else because you don't do it well. This is what engineers call positive feedback. So the small differences at the beginning of life become enormous differences by the time you've done it for forty, fifty, eighty years as I've done it. So anyway, first you have to have the big database.

Next Rabinow brings up what the *person* must contribute, which mainly a question of motivation, or the enjoyment one feels when playing (or working?) with the contents of the domain:

Then you have to be willing to pull the ideas, because you're interested. Now, some people could do it, but they don't bother. They're interested in doing something else. So if you ask them, they'll, as a favor to you, say: "Yeah, I can think of something." But there are people like myself who *like* to do it. It's fun to come up with an idea, and if nobody wants it, I don't give a damn. It's just fun to come up with something strange and different.

Finally he focuses on how important it is to reproduce in one's mind the criteria of judgment that the *field* uses:

And then you must have the ability to get rid of the trash which you think of. You cannot think only of good ideas, or write only beautiful music. You must think of a lot of music, a lot of ideas, a lot of poetry, a lot of whatever. And if you're good, you must be able to throw out the junk immediately without even saying it. In other words, you get many ideas appearing and you discard them because you're well trained and you say, "That's junk." And when you see the good one, you say, "Oops, this sounds interesting. Let me pursue that a little further." And you start developing it. Now, people don't like this explanation. They say, "What? You think of junk?" I say, "Yup. You must." You cannot a priori think only of good ideas. You cannot think only of great symphonies. Some people do it very rapidly. And this is a matter of training. And by the way, if you're not well trained, but you've got ideas, and you don't know if they're good or bad, then you send them to the Bureau of Standards, National Institute of Standards, where I work, and *we* evaluate them. And *we* throw them out.

He was asked what constitutes "junk." Is it something that doesn't work, or—

It doesn't work, or it's old, or you know that it will not gel. You suddenly realize it's not good. It's too complicated. It's not what mathematicians call "elegant." You know, it's not good poetry. And this is a matter of training. If you're well trained in technology, you see an idea and say, "Oh, God, this is terrible." First of all, it's too complicated. Secondly, it's been tried before. Thirdly, he could have done it in three different easier ways. In other words, you can evaluate the thing. That doesn't mean that he wasn't original. But he simply didn't do enough. If he were well trained, if he had the experience I had, and had good bosses and worked with great people, he could say this is not really a good idea. It's an idea, but it's not a *good* idea. And you have arguments with people. And you say, "Look, this is not a good way. Look at the number of parts you're gluing together. Look at the amount of energy it'll take. This is really not good." And the guy says, "But to me it's new." I say, "Yup. To you it's new. It may be new to the world. But it's still not good."

To say what is beautiful you have to take a sophisticated group of people, people who know that particular art and have seen a lot of it, and say this is good art, or this is good music, or this is a good invention. And that doesn't mean everybody can vote on it; they don't know enough. But if a group of engineers who work on new stuff look at it and say, "That's pretty nice," that's because they know. They know because they've been trained in it.

And a good creative person is well trained. So he has first of all an enormous amount of knowledge in that field. Secondly, he tries to combine ideas, because he enjoys writing music or enjoys inventing. And finally, he has the judgment to say, "This is good, I'll pursue this further."

It would be very difficult to improve on this description of how the systems model works after it is internalized. Drawing on over eighty years of varied experience, Rabinow has distilled with great insight what is involved in being a creative inventor. And as his words suggest, the same process holds for other domains, whether poetry, music, or physics.

Analyze

1. Who is right? The individuals who believe in their own creativity? Or the social milieu that denies them? What does this text have to say about this? What do you have to say?

2. What are the three phenomena that can legitimately be called creativity?

3. Who is John Bardeen, and why does he merit special attention?

4. Csikszentmihalyi claims that it makes the most sense to observe creativity in the interrelations of a system comprised of three parts. What are those three parts? And how do they help us get a better handle on what is creative or not?

5. Why was the Florentine Renaissance—between 1400 and 1425—so special and noteworthy? Why weren't similar cities in the area which were exposed to the same cultural and other forces similarly blessed with such creativity and talent?

Explore

1. Csikszentmihalyi cites how one's creative stock—yes, kind of like the stock market, which has wild fluctuations due to market forces, which in this case have to do with changing audiences, culture, and sensibilities—goes up and down throughout the years. Who are some on-and-off-again geniuses whose literary or artistic or intellectual stock has moved a lot in your lifetime? Why did that happen? Does it truly mean they weren't special the entire time? Was John Donne really a forgettable poet before being resurrected by T. S. Eliot and Herbert Grierson?

2. What point is Csikszentmihalyi trying to make about American businesses striving to enhance creativity but doing so poorly? How does his example of Robert Galvin at Motorola illustrate this point? What companies, schools, or even families have similar problems? Why?

3. Csikszentmihalyi suggests that certain domains will primarily be for older people, and certain ones will find young people making great contributions. He writes: "Mathematical genius peaks in the twenties, physics in the thirties, but great philosophical works are usually achieved later in life." What other domains are typically reserved for certain age groups? What about composing symphonies? Painting murals? Dancing ballet? What counterexamples to this idea of age groups and certain domains come to mind?

4. What is the domain(s) in which you work (or aspire to work)? What are the fields? How do these fields inspire and stimulate creativity? How do they inhibit it? What would you need to do to be creative in your work?

Nancy C. Andreasen
"Secrets of the Creative Brain"

Nancy C. Andreasen (1938–) is the Andrew H. Woods Chair of Psychiatry at the University of Iowa College of Medicine. She has authored eight books and more than five hundred articles on a range of topics, though her Ph.D. is in English literature with a Renaissance literature specialization. Her research interests include creativity, spirituality, neuroimaging, genomics, and schizophrenia. "Secrets of the Creative Brain" first appeared in the July/August 2014 issue of *The Atlantic*.

As a psychiatrist and neuroscientist who studies creativity, I've had the pleasure of working with many gifted and high-profile subjects over the years, but Kurt Vonnegut—dear, funny, eccentric, lovable, tormented Kurt Vonnegut—will always be one of my favorites. Kurt was a faculty member at the Iowa Writers' Workshop in the 1960s, and participated in the first big study I did as a member of the university's psychiatry department. I was examining the anecdotal link between creativity and mental illness, and Kurt was an excellent case study.

He was intermittently depressed, but that was only the beginning. His mother had suffered from depression and committed suicide on Mother's Day, when Kurt was 21 and home on military leave during World War II. His son, Mark, was originally diagnosed with schizophrenia but may actually have bipolar disorder. (Mark, who is a practicing physician, recounts his experiences in two books, *The Eden Express* and *Just Like Someone Without Mental Illness Only More So,* in which he reveals that many family members struggled with psychiatric problems. "My mother, my cousins, and my sisters weren't doing so great," he writes. "We had eating disorders, codependency, outstanding warrants, drug and alcohol problems, dating and employment problems, and other 'issues.'")

While mental illness clearly runs in the Vonnegut family, so, I found, does creativity. Kurt's father was a gifted architect, and his older brother Bernard was a talented physical chemist and inventor who possessed 28 patents. Mark is a writer, and both of Kurt's daughters are visual artists. Kurt's work, of course, needs no introduction.

For many of my subjects from that first study—all writers associated with the Iowa Writers' Workshop—mental illness and creativity went hand in hand. This link is not surprising. The archetype of the mad genius dates back to at least classical times, when Aristotle noted, "Those who have been eminent in philosophy, politics, poetry, and the arts have all had tendencies toward melancholia." This pattern is a recurring theme in Shakespeare's plays, such as when Theseus, in *A Midsummer Night's Dream,* observes, "The lunatic, the lover, and the poet/Are of imagination all compact." John Dryden made a similar point in a heroic couplet: "Great wits are sure to madness near allied,/And thin partitions do their bounds divide."

Compared with many of history's creative luminaries, Vonnegut, who died of natural causes, got off relatively easy. Among those who ended up losing their battles with mental illness through suicide are Virginia Woolf, Ernest Hemingway, Vincent van Gogh, John Berryman, Hart Crane, Mark Rothko, Diane Arbus, Anne Sexton, and Arshile Gorky.

My interest in this pattern is rooted in my dual identities as a scientist and a literary scholar. In an early parallel with Sylvia Plath, a writer I admired, I studied literature at Radcliffe and then went to Oxford on a Fulbright scholarship; she studied literature at Smith and attended Cambridge on a Fulbright. Then our paths diverged, and she joined the tragic list above. My curiosity about our different outcomes has shaped my career. I earned a doctorate in literature in 1963 and joined the faculty of the University of Iowa to teach Renaissance literature. At the time, I was the first woman the university's English department had ever hired into a tenure-track position, and so I was careful to publish under the gender-neutral name of N. J. C. Andreasen.

Not long after this, a book I'd written about the poet John Donne was accepted for publication by Princeton University Press. Instead of feeling elated, I felt almost ashamed and self-indulgent. Who would this book help? What if I channeled the effort and energy I'd invested in it into a career that might save people's lives? Within a month, I made the decision to become a research scientist, perhaps a medical doctor. I entered the University of Iowa's medical school, in a class that included only five other women, and began working with patients suffering from schizophrenia and mood disorders. I was drawn to psychiatry because at its core is the most interesting and complex organ in the human body: the brain.

I have spent much of my career focusing on the neuroscience of mental illness, but in recent decades I've also focused on what we might call the science of genius, trying to discern what combination of elements tends to produce particularly creative brains. What, in short, is the essence of creativity? Over the course of my life, I've kept coming back to two more-specific questions: What differences in nature and nurture can explain why some people suffer from mental illness and some do not? And why are so many of the world's most creative minds among the most afflicted? My latest study, for which I've been scanning the brains of some of today's most illustrious scientists, mathematicians, artists, and writers, has come closer to answering this second question than any other research to date.

The first attempted examinations of the connection between genius and insanity were largely anecdotal. In his 1891 book, *The Man of Genius,* Cesare Lombroso, an Italian physician, provided a gossipy and expansive account of traits associated with genius—left-handedness, celibacy, stammering, precocity, and, of course, neurosis and psychosis—and he linked them to many creative individuals, including Jean-Jacques Rousseau, Sir Isaac Newton, Arthur Schopenhauer, Jonathan Swift, Charles Darwin, Lord Byron, Charles Baudelaire, and Robert Schumann. Lombroso speculated on various causes of lunacy and genius, ranging from heredity to urbanization to climate to the phases of the moon. He proposed a close association between genius and degeneracy and argued that both are hereditary.

Francis Galton, a cousin of Charles Darwin, took a much more rigorous approach to the topic. In his 1869 book, *Hereditary Genius,* Galton used careful documentation—including detailed family trees showing the more than 20 eminent musicians among the Bachs, the three eminent writers among the Brontës, and so on—to demonstrate that genius appears to have a strong genetic component. He was also the first to explore in depth the relative contributions of nature and nurture to the development of genius.

As research methodology improved over time, the idea that genius might be hereditary gained support. For his 1904 *Study of British Genius,* the English physician Havelock Ellis twice reviewed the 66 volumes of *The Dictionary of National Biography.* In his first review, he identified individuals whose entries were three pages or longer. In his second review, he eliminated those who "displayed no high intellectual ability" and added those who had shorter entries but showed evidence of "intellectual ability of high order." His final list consisted of 1,030 individuals, only 55 of whom were women. Much like Lombroso, he examined how heredity, general health, social class, and other factors may have contributed to his subjects' intellectual distinction. Although Ellis's approach was resourceful, his sample was limited, in that the subjects were relatively famous but not necessarily highly creative. He found that 8.2 percent of his overall sample of 1,030 suffered from melancholy and 4.2 percent from insanity. Because he was relying on historical data provided by the authors of *The Dictionary of National Biography* rather than direct contact, his numbers likely underestimated the prevalence of mental illness in his sample.

A more empirical approach can be found in the early-20th-century work of Lewis M. Terman, a Stanford psychologist whose multivolume *Genetic Studies of Genius* is one of the most legendary studies in American psychology. He used a longitudinal design—meaning he studied his subjects repeatedly over time—which was novel then, and the project eventually became the longest-running longitudinal study in the world. Terman himself had been a gifted child, and his interest in the study of genius derived from personal experience. (Within six months of starting school, at age 5, Terman was advanced to third grade—which was not seen at the time as a good thing; the prevailing belief was that precocity was abnormal and would produce problems in adulthood.) Terman also hoped to improve the measurement of "genius" and test Lombroso's suggestion that it was associated with degeneracy.

In 1916, as a member of the psychology department at Stanford, Terman developed America's first IQ test, drawing from a version developed by the French psychologist Alfred Binet. This test, known as the Stanford–Binet Intelligence Scales, contributed to the development of the Army Alpha, an exam the American military used during World War I to screen recruits and evaluate them for work assignments and determine whether they were worthy of officer status.

Terman eventually used the Stanford–Binet test to select high-IQ students for his longitudinal study, which began in 1921. His long-term goal was to recruit at least 1,000 students from grades three through eight who represented the smartest 1 percent of the urban California population in that age group. The subjects had to have an IQ greater than 135, as measured by the Stanford–Binet test. The recruitment process was intensive: students were first nominated by teachers, then given group tests, and finally subjected to individual Stanford–Binet tests. After various enrichments—adding some of the subjects' siblings, for example—the final sample consisted of 856 boys and 672 girls. One finding that emerged quickly was that being the youngest student in a grade was an excellent predictor of having a high IQ. (This is worth bearing in mind today, when parents sometimes choose to hold back their children precisely so they will not be the youngest in their grades.)

These children were initially evaluated in all sorts of ways. Researchers took their early developmental histories, documented their play interests, administered medical examinations—including 37 different anthropometric measurements—and recorded how many books they'd read during the past two months, as well as the number of books available in their homes (the latter number ranged from zero to 6,000, with a mean of 328). These gifted children were then reevaluated at regular intervals throughout their lives.

"The Termites," as Terman's subjects have come to be known, have debunked some stereotypes and introduced new paradoxes. For example, they were generally physically superior to a comparison group—taller, healthier, more athletic. Myopia (no surprise) was the only physical deficit. They were also more socially mature and generally better adjusted. And these positive patterns persisted as the children grew into adulthood. They tended to have happy marriages and high salaries. So much for the concept of "early ripe and early rotten," a common assumption when Terman was growing up.

But despite the implications of the title *Genetic Studies of Genius,* the Termites' high IQs did not predict high levels of creative achievement later in life. Only a few made significant creative contributions to society; none appear to have demonstrated extremely high creativity levels of the sort recognized by major awards, such as the Nobel Prize. (Interestingly, William Shockley, who was a 12-year-old Palo Alto resident in 1922, somehow failed to make the cut for the study, even though he would go on to share a Nobel Prize in Physics for the invention of the transistor.) Thirty percent of the men and 33 percent of the women did not even graduate from college. A surprising number of subjects pursued humble occupations, such as semiskilled trades or clerical positions. As the study evolved over the years, the term *gifted* was substituted for *genius.* Although many people continue to equate intelligence with genius, a crucial conclusion from Terman's study is that having a high IQ is not equivalent to being highly creative.

Subsequent studies by other researchers have reinforced Terman's conclusions, leading to what's known as the threshold theory, which holds that above a certain level, intelligence doesn't have much effect on creativity: most creative people are pretty smart, but they don't have to be *that* smart, at least as measured by conventional intelligence tests. An IQ of 120, indicating that someone is very smart but not exceptionally so, is generally considered sufficient for creative genius.

But if high IQ does not indicate creative genius, then what does? And how can one identify creative people for a study?

One approach, which is sometimes referred to as the study of "little *c*," is to develop quantitative assessments of creativity—a necessarily controversial task, given that it requires settling on what creativity actually is. The basic concept that has been used in the development of these tests is skill in "divergent thinking," or the ability to come up with many responses to carefully selected questions or probes, as contrasted with "convergent thinking," or the ability to come up with the correct answer to problems that have only one answer. For example, subjects might be asked, "How many uses can you think of for a brick?" A person skilled in divergent thinking might come up with many varied responses, such as building a wall; edging a garden; and serving as a bludgeoning weapon, a makeshift shot put, a bookend. Like IQ tests, these exams can be administered to large groups of people. Assuming that creativity is a trait everyone has in varying amounts, those with the highest scores can be classified as exceptionally creative and selected for further study.

While this approach is quantitative and relatively objective, its weakness is that certain assumptions must be accepted: that divergent thinking is the essence of creativity, that creativity can be measured using tests, and that high-scoring individuals are highly creative people. One might argue that some of humanity's most creative achievements have been the result of convergent thinking—a process that led to Newton's recognition of the physical formulae underlying gravity, and Einstein's recognition that $E = mc^2$.

A second approach to defining creativity is the "duck test": if it walks like a duck and quacks like a duck, it must be a duck. This approach usually involves selecting a group of people—writers, visual artists, musicians, inventors, business innovators, scientists—who have been recognized for some kind of creative achievement, usually through the awarding of major prizes (the Nobel, the Pulitzer, and so forth). Because this approach focuses on people whose widely recognized creativity sets them apart from the general population, it is sometimes referred to as the study of "big *C*." The problem with this approach is its inherent subjectivity. What does it mean, for example, to have "created" something? Can creativity in the arts be equated with creativity in the sciences or in business, or should such groups be studied separately? For that matter, should science or business innovation be considered creative at all?

Although I recognize and respect the value of studying "little *c*," I am an unashamed advocate of studying "big *C*." I first used this approach in the mid-1970s and 1980s, when I conducted one of the first empirical studies of creativity and mental illness. Not long after I joined the psychiatry faculty of the Iowa College of Medicine, I ran into the chair of the department, a biologically oriented psychiatrist known for his salty language and male chauvinism. "Andreasen," he told me, "you may be an M.D./Ph.D., but that Ph.D. of yours isn't worth sh—, and it won't count favorably toward your promotion." I was proud of my literary background and believed that it made me a better clinician and a better scientist, so I decided to prove him wrong by using my background as an entry point to a scientific study of genius and insanity.

The University of Iowa is home to the Writers' Workshop, the oldest and most famous creative writing program in the United States (UNESCO has designated Iowa City as one of its seven "Cities of Literature," along with the likes of Dublin and Edinburgh). Thanks to my time in the university's English department, I was able to recruit study subjects from the workshop's ranks of distinguished permanent and visiting faculty. Over the course of 15 years, I studied not only Kurt Vonnegut but Richard Yates, John Cheever, and 27 other well-known writers.

Going into the study, I keyed my hypotheses off the litany of famous people who I knew had personal or family histories of mental illness. James Joyce, for example, had a daughter who suffered from schizophrenia, and he himself had traits that placed him on the schizophrenia spectrum. (He was socially aloof and even cruel to those close to him, and his writing became progressively more detached from his audience and from reality, culminating in the near-psychotic neologisms and loose associations of *Finnegans Wake*.) Bertrand Russell, a philosopher whose work I admired, had multiple family members who suffered from schizophrenia. Einstein had a son with schizophrenia, and he himself displayed some of the social and interpersonal ineptitudes that can characterize the illness. Based on these clues, I hypothesized that my subjects would have an increased rate of schizophrenia in family members but that they themselves would be relatively well. I also hypothesized that creativity might run in families, based on prevailing views that the tendencies toward psychosis and toward having creative and original ideas were closely linked.

I began by designing a standard interview for my subjects, covering topics such as developmental, social, family, and psychiatric history, and work habits and approach to writing. Drawing on creativity studies done by the psychiatric epidemiologist Thomas McNeil, I evaluated creativity in family members by assigning those who had had very successful creative careers an A++ rating and those who had pursued creative interests or hobbies an A+.

My final challenge was selecting a control group. After entertaining the possibility of choosing a homogeneous group whose work is not usually considered creative, such as lawyers, I decided that it would be best to examine a more varied group of people from a mixture of professions, such as administrators, accountants, and social workers. I matched this control group with the writers according to age and educational level. By matching based on education, I hoped to match for IQ, which worked out well; both the test and the control groups had an average IQ, of about 120. These results confirmed Terman's findings that creative genius is not the same as high IQ. If having a very high IQ was not what made these writers creative, then what was?

As I began interviewing my subjects, I soon realized that I would not be confirming my schizophrenia hypothesis. If I had paid more attention to Sylvia Plath and Robert Lowell, who both suffered from what we today call mood disorder, and less to James Joyce and Bertrand Russell, I might have foreseen this. One after another, my writer subjects came to my office and spent three or four hours pouring out the stories of their struggles with mood disorder—mostly depression, but occasionally bipolar disorder. A full 80 percent of them had had some kind of mood disturbance at some time in their lives, compared with just 30 percent of the control group—only slightly less than an age-matched group in the general population. (At first I had been surprised that nearly all the writers I approached would so eagerly agree to participate in a study with a young and unknown assistant professor—but I quickly came to understand why they were so interested in talking to a psychiatrist.) The Vonneguts turned out to be representative of the writers' families, in which both mood disorder and creativity were overrepresented—as with the Vonneguts, some of the creative relatives were writers, but others were dancers, visual artists, chemists, architects, or mathematicians. This is consistent with what some other studies have found. When the psychologist Kay Redfield Jamison looked at 47 famous writers and artists in Great Britain, she found that more than 38 percent had been treated for a mood disorder; the highest rates occurred among playwrights, and the second-highest among poets. When Joseph Schildkraut, a psychiatrist at Harvard Medical School, studied a group of 15 abstract-expressionist painters in the mid-20th century, he found that half of them had some form of mental illness, mostly depression or bipolar disorder; nearly half of these artists failed to live past age 60.

While my workshop study answered some questions, it raised others. Why does creativity run in families? What is it that gets transmitted? How much is due to nature and how much to nurture? Are writers especially prone to mood disorders because writing is an inherently lonely and intro-spective activity? What would I find if I studied a group of scientists instead?

These questions percolated in my mind in the weeks, months, and even-tually years after the study. As I focused my research on the neurobiology of severe mental illnesses, including schizophrenia and mood disorders, studying the nature of creativity—important as the topic was and is—seemed less pressing than searching for ways to alleviate the suffering of patients stricken with these dreadful and potentially lethal brain disorders. During the 1980s, new neuroimaging techniques gave researchers the abil-ity to study patients' brains directly, an approach I began using to answer questions about how and why the structure and functional activity of the brain is disrupted in some people with serious mental illnesses.

As I spent more time with neuroimaging technology, I couldn't help but wonder what we would find if we used it to look inside the heads of highly creative people. Would we see a little genie that doesn't exist inside other people's heads?

Today's neuroimaging tools show brain structure with a precision ap-proximating that of the examination of post-mortem tissue; this allows researchers to study all sorts of connections between brain measurements and personal characteristics. For example, we know that London taxi drivers, who must memorize maps of the city to earn a hackney's license, have an enlarged hippocampus—a key memory region—as demonstrated in a magnetic-resonance-imaging, or MRI, study. (They know it, too: on a recent trip to London, I was proudly regaled with this information by several different taxi drivers.) Imaging studies of symphony-orchestra musicians have found them to possess an unusually large Broca's area—a part of the brain in the left hemisphere that is associated with language—along with other discrepancies. Using another technique, functional magnetic resonance imaging (fMRI), we can watch how the brain behaves when engaged in thought.

Designing neuroimaging studies, however, is exceedingly tricky. Capturing human mental processes can be like capturing quicksilver. The brain has as many neurons as there are stars in the Milky Way, each connected to other neurons by billions of spines, which contain synapses that change continuously depending on what the neurons have recently learned. Capturing brain activity using imaging technology inevitably leads to oversimplifications, as sometimes evidenced by news reports that an investigator has found the location of something—love, guilt, decision making—in a single region of the brain.

And what are we even looking for when we search for evidence of "creativity" in the brain? Although we have a definition of creativity that many people accept—the ability to produce something that is novel or original and useful or adaptive—achieving that "something" is part of a complex process, one often depicted as an "aha" or "eureka" experience. This narrative is appealing—for example, "Newton developed the concept of gravity around 1666, when an apple fell on his head while he was meditating under an apple tree." The truth is that by 1666, Newton had already spent many years teaching himself the mathematics of his time (Euclidean geometry, algebra, Cartesian coordinates) and inventing calculus so that he could measure planetary orbits and the area under a curve. He continued to work on his theory of gravity over the subsequent years, completing the effort only in 1687, when he published *Philosophiæ Naturalis Principia Mathematica*. In other words, Newton's formulation of the concept of gravity took more than 20 years and included multiple components: preparation, incubation, inspiration—a version of the eureka experience—and production. Many forms of creativity, from writing a novel to discovering the structure of DNA, require this kind of ongoing, iterative process.

With functional magnetic resonance imaging, the best we can do is capture brain activity during brief moments in time while subjects are performing some task. For instance, observing brain activity while test subjects look at photographs of their relatives can help answer the question of which parts of the brain people use when they recognize familiar faces. Creativity, of course, cannot be distilled into a single mental process, and it cannot be captured in a snapshot—nor can people produce a creative insight or thought on demand. I spent many years thinking about how to design an imaging study that could identify the unique features of the creative brain. Most of the human brain's high-level functions arise from the six layers of nerve cells and their dendrites embedded in its enormous surface area, called the cerebral cortex, which is compressed to a size small enough to be carried around on our shoulders through a process known as gyrification— essentially, producing lots of folds. Some regions of the brain are highly specialized, receiving sensory information from our eyes, ears, skin, mouth, or nose, or controlling our movements. We call these regions the primary visual, auditory, sensory, and motor cortices. They collect information from the world around us and execute our actions. But we would be helpless, and effectively nonhuman, if our brains consisted only of these regions.

In fact, the most extensively developed regions in the human brain are known as association cortices. These regions help us interpret and make use of the specialized information collected by the primary visual, auditory, sensory, and motor regions. For example, as you read these words on a page or a screen, they register as black lines on a white background in your primary visual cortex. If the process stopped at that point, you wouldn't be reading at all. To read, your brain, through miraculously complex processes that scientists are still figuring out, needs to forward those black letters on to association-cortex regions such as the angular gyrus, so that meaning is attached to them; and then on to language-association regions in the temporal lobes, so that the words are connected not only to one another but also to their associated memories and given richer meanings. These associated memories and meanings constitute a "verbal lexicon," which can be accessed for reading, speaking, listening, and writing. Each person's lexicon is a bit different, even if the words themselves are the same, because each person has different associated memories and meanings. One difference between a great writer like Shakespeare and, say, the typical stockbroker is the size and richness of the verbal lexicon in his or her temporal association cortices, as well as the complexity of the cortices' connections with other association regions in the frontal and parietal lobes.

A neuroimaging study I conducted in 1995 using positron-emission tomography, or PET, scanning turned out to be unexpectedly useful in advancing my own understanding of association cortices and their role in the creative process.

This PET study was designed to examine the brain's different memory systems, which the great Canadian psychologist Endel Tulving identified. One system, episodic memory, is autobiographical—it consists of information linked to an individual's personal experiences. It is called "episodic" because it consists of time-linked sequential information, such as the events that occurred on a person's wedding day. My team and I compared this with another system, that of semantic memory, which is a repository of general information and is not personal or time-linked. In this study, we divided episodic memory into two subtypes. We examined *focused* episodic memory by asking subjects to recall a specific event that had occurred in the past and to describe it with their eyes closed. And we examined a condition that we called *random* episodic silent thought, or REST: we asked subjects to lie quietly with their eyes closed, to relax, and to think about whatever came to mind. In essence, they would be engaged in "free association," letting their minds wander. The acronym REST was intentionally ironic; we suspected that the association regions of the brain would actually be wildly active during this state.

This suspicion was based on what we had learned about free association from the psychoanalytic approach to understanding the mind. In the hands of Freud and other psychoanalysts, free association—spontaneously saying whatever comes to mind without censorship—became a window into understanding unconscious processes. Based on my interviews with the creative subjects in my workshop study, and from additional conversations with artists, I knew that such unconscious processes are an important component of creativity. For example, Neil Simon told me: "I don't write consciously—it is as if the muse sits on my shoulder" and "I slip into a state that is apart from reality." (Examples from history suggest the same thing. Samuel Taylor Coleridge once described how he composed an entire 300-line poem about Kubla Khan while in an opiate-induced, dreamlike state, and began writing it down when he awoke; he said he then lost most of it when he got interrupted and called away on an errand—thus the finished poem he published was but a fragment of what originally came to him in his dreamlike state.)

Based on all this, I surmised that observing which parts of the brain are most active during free association would give us clues about the neural basis of creativity. And what did we find? Sure enough, the association cortices were wildly active during REST.

I realized that I obviously couldn't capture the entire creative process—instead, I could home in on the parts of the brain that make creativity possible. Once I arrived at this idea, the design for the imaging studies was obvious: I needed to compare the brains of highly creative people with those of control subjects as they engaged in tasks that activated their association cortices.

For years, I had been asking myself what might be special or unique about the brains of the workshop writers I had studied. In my own version of a eureka moment, the answer finally came to me: creative people are better at recognizing relationships, making associations and connections, and seeing things in an original way—seeing things that others cannot see. To test this capacity, I needed to study the regions of the brain that go crazy when you let your thoughts wander. I needed to target the association cortices. In addition to REST, I could observe people performing simple tasks that are easy to do in an MRI scanner, such as word association, which would permit me to compare highly creative people—who have that "genie in the brain"—with the members of a control group matched by age and education and gender, people who have "ordinary creativity" and who have not achieved the levels of recognition that characterize highly creative people. I was ready to design Creativity Study II.

This time around, I wanted to examine a more diverse sample of creativity, from the sciences as well as the arts. My motivations were partly selfish—I wanted the chance to discuss the creative process with people who might think and work differently, and I thought I could probably learn a lot by listening to just a few people from specific scientific fields. After all, each would be an individual jewel—a fascinating study on his or her own. Now that I'm about halfway through the study, I can say that this is exactly what has happened. My individual jewels so far include, among others, the filmmaker George Lucas, the mathematician and Fields Medalist William Thurston, the Pulitzer Prize–winning novelist Jane Smiley, and six Nobel laureates from the fields of chemistry, physics, and physiology or medicine. Because winners of major awards are typically older, and because I wanted to include some younger people, I've also recruited winners of the National Institutes of Health Pioneer Award and other prizes in the arts.

Apart from stating their names, I do not have permission to reveal individual information about my subjects. And because the study is ongoing (each subject can take as long as a year to recruit, making for slow progress), we do not yet have any definitive results—though we do have a good sense of the direction that things are taking. By studying the structural and functional characteristics of subjects' brains in addition to their personal and family histories, we are learning an enormous amount about how creativity occurs in the brain, as well as whether these scientists and artists display the same personal or familial connections to mental illness that the subjects in my Iowa Writers' Workshop study did.

To participate in the study, each subject spends three days in Iowa City, since it is important to conduct the research using the same MRI scanner. The subjects and I typically get to know each other over dinner at my home (and a bottle of Bordeaux from my cellar), and by prowling my 40-acre nature retreat in an all-terrain vehicle, observing whatever wildlife happens to be wandering around. Relaxing together and getting a sense of each other's human side is helpful going into the day and a half of brain scans and challenging conversations that will follow.

We begin the actual study with an MRI scan, during which subjects perform three different tasks, in addition to REST: word association, picture association, and pattern recognition. Each experimental task alternates with a control task; during word association, for example, subjects are shown words on a screen and asked to either think of the first word that comes to mind (the experimental task) or silently repeat the word they see (the control task). Speaking disrupts the scanning process, so subjects silently indicate when they have completed a task by pressing a button on a keypad.

Playing word games inside a thumping, screeching hollow tube seems like a far cry from the kind of meandering, spontaneous discovery process that we tend to associate with creativity. It is, however, as close as one can come to a proxy for that experience, apart from REST. You cannot force creativity to happen—every creative person can attest to that. But the essence of creativity is making connections and solving puzzles. The design of these MRI tasks permits us to visualize what is happening in the creative brain when it's doing those things.

As I hypothesized, the creative people have shown stronger activations in their association cortices during all four tasks than the controls have. This pattern has held true for both the artists and the scientists, suggesting that similar brain processes may underlie a broad spectrum of creative expression. Common stereotypes about "right brained" versus "left brained" people notwithstanding, this parallel makes sense. Many creative people are polymaths, people with broad interests in many fields—a common trait among my study subjects.

After the brain scans, I settle in with subjects for an in-depth interview. Preparing for these interviews can be fun (rewatching all of George Lucas's films, for example, or reading Jane Smiley's collected works) as well as challenging (toughing through mathematics papers by William Thurston). I begin by asking subjects about their life history—where they grew up, where they went to school, what activities they enjoyed. I ask about their parents—their education, occupation, and parenting style—and about how the family got along. I learn about brothers, sisters, and children, and get a sense for who else in a subject's family is or has been creative and how creativity may have been nurtured at home. We talk about how the subjects managed the challenges of growing up, any early interests and hobbies (particularly those related to the creative activities they pursue as adults), dating patterns, life in college and graduate school, marriages, and child-rearing. I ask them to describe a typical day at work and to think through how they have achieved such a high level of creativity. (One thing I've learned from this line of questioning is that creative people work much harder than the average person—and usually that's because they love their work.)

One of the most personal and sometimes painful parts of the interview is when I ask about mental illness in subjects' families as well as in their own lives. They've told me about such childhood experiences as having a mother commit suicide or watching ugly outbreaks of violence between two alcoholic parents, and the pain and scars that these experiences have inflicted. (Two of the 13 creative subjects in my current study have lost a parent to suicide—a rate many times that of the general U.S. population.) Talking with those subjects who have suffered from a mental illness themselves, I hear about how it has affected their work and how they have learned to cope.

So far, this study—which has examined 13 creative geniuses and 13 controls—has borne out a link between mental illness and creativity similar to the one I found in my Writers' Workshop study. The creative subjects and their relatives have a higher rate of mental illness than the controls and their relatives do (though not as high a rate as I found in the first study), with the frequency being fairly even across the artists and the scientists. The most-common diagnoses include bipolar disorder, depression, anxiety or panic disorder, and alcoholism. I've also found some evidence supporting my early hypothesis that exceptionally creative people are more likely than control subjects to have one or more first-degree relatives with schizophrenia. Interestingly, when the physician and researcher Jon L. Karlsson examined the relatives of everyone listed in Iceland's version of

Who's Who in the 1940s and '60s, he found that they had higher-than-average rates of schizophrenia. Leonard Heston, a former psychiatric colleague of mine at Iowa, conducted an influential study of the children of schizophrenic mothers raised from infancy by foster or adoptive parents, and found that more than 10 percent of these children developed schizophrenia, as compared with zero percent of a control group. This suggests a powerful genetic component to schizophrenia. Heston and I discussed whether some particularly creative people owe their gifts to a subclinical variant of schizophrenia that loosens their associative links sufficiently to enhance their creativity but not enough to make them mentally ill.

As in the first study, I've also found that creativity tends to run in families, and to take diverse forms. In this arena, nurture clearly plays a strong role. Half the subjects come from very high-achieving backgrounds, with at least one parent who has a doctoral degree. The majority grew up in an environment where learning and education were highly valued. This is how one person described his childhood:

> Our family evenings—just everybody sitting around working. We'd all be in the same room, and [my mother] would be working on her papers, preparing her lesson plans, and my father had huge stacks of papers and journals . . . This was before laptops, and so it was all paper-based. And I'd be sitting there with my homework, and my sisters are reading. And we'd just spend a few hours every night for 10 to 15 years—that's how it was. Just working together. No TV.

So why do these highly gifted people experience mental illness at a higher-than-average rate? Given that (as a group) their family members have higher rates than those that occur in the general population or in the matched comparison group, we must suspect that nature plays a role—that Francis Galton and others were right about the role of hereditary factors in people's predisposition to both creativity and mental illness. We can only speculate about what those factors might be, but there are some clues in how these people describe themselves and their lifestyles.

One possible contributory factor is a personality style shared by many of my creative subjects. These subjects are adventuresome and exploratory. They take risks. Particularly in science, the best work tends to occur in new frontiers. (As a popular saying among scientists goes: "When you work at the cutting edge, you are likely to bleed.") They have to confront doubt and rejection. And yet they have to persist in spite of that, because they believe strongly in the value of what they do. This can lead to psychic pain, which may manifest itself as depression or anxiety, or lead people to attempt to reduce their discomfort by turning to pain relievers such as alcohol.

I've been struck by how many of these people refer to their most creative ideas as "obvious." Since these ideas are almost always the opposite of obvious to other people, creative luminaries can face doubt and resistance when advocating for them. As one artist told me, "The funny thing about [one's own] talent is that you are blind to it. You just can't see what it is when you have it. . . . When you have talent and see things in a particular way, you are amazed that other people can't see it." Persisting in the face of doubt or rejection, for artists or for scientists, can be a lonely path—one that may also partially explain why some of these people experience mental illness.

One interesting paradox that has emerged during conversations with subjects about their creative processes is that, though many of them suffer from mood and anxiety disorders, they associate their gifts with strong feelings of joy and excitement. "Doing good science is simply the most pleasurable thing anyone can do," one scientist told me. "It is like having good sex. It excites you all over and makes you feel as if you are all-powerful and complete." This is reminiscent of what creative geniuses throughout history have said. For instance, here's Tchaikovsky, the composer, writing in the mid-19th century:

> It would be vain to try to put into words that immeasurable sense of bliss which comes over me directly [when] a new idea awakens in me and begins to assume a different form. I forget everything and behave like a madman. Everything within me starts pulsing and quivering; hardly have I begun the sketch ere one thought follows another.

Another of my subjects, a neuroscientist and an inventor, told me, "There is no greater joy that I have in my life than having an idea that's a good idea. At that moment it pops into my head, it is so deeply satisfying and rewarding. . . . My nucleus accumbens is probably going nuts when it happens." (The nucleus accumbens, at the core of the brain's reward system, is activated by pleasure, whether it comes from eating good food or receiving money or taking euphoria-inducing drugs.)

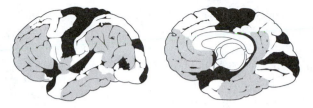

Figure 6.1   The images on the left show the brain of a creative subject (top) and a matched control subject during a word-association task. The images on the right show brain activation as the subjects alternate between an experimental task (word association) and a control task (reading a word). The line representing the creative subject's brain activation moves smoothly up and down as the task changes, reflecting effective use of the association cortices in making connections. The control subject's activation line looks ragged by comparison.

As for how these ideas emerge, almost all of my subjects confirmed that when eureka moments occur, they tend to be precipitated by long periods of preparation and incubation, and to strike when the mind is relaxed—during that state we called REST. "A lot of it happens when you are doing one thing and you're not thinking about what your mind is doing," one of the artists in my study told me. "I'm either watching television, I'm reading a book, and I make a connection. . . . It may have nothing to do with what I am doing, but somehow or other you see something or hear something or do something, and it pops that connection together."

Many subjects mentioned lighting on ideas while showering, driving, or exercising. One described a more unusual regimen involving an afternoon nap: "It's during this nap that I get a lot of my work done. I find that when the ideas come to me, they come as I'm falling asleep, they come as I'm waking up, they come if I'm sitting in the tub. I don't normally take baths . . . but sometimes I'll just go in there and have a think."

Some of the other most common findings my studies have suggested include:

Many creative people are autodidacts. They like to teach themselves, rather than be spoon-fed information or knowledge in standard educational settings. Famously, three Silicon Valley creative geniuses have been college dropouts: Bill Gates, Steve Jobs, and Mark Zuckerberg. Steve Jobs—for many, the archetype of the creative person—popularized the motto "Think different." Because their thinking is different, my subjects often express the idea that standard ways of learning and teaching are not always helpful and may even be distracting, and that they prefer to learn on their own. Many of my subjects taught themselves to read before even starting school, and many have read widely throughout their lives. For example, in his article "On Proof and Progress in Mathematics," Bill Thurston wrote:

> My mathematical education was rather independent and idiosyncratic, where for a number of years I learned things on my own, developing personal mental models for how to think about mathematics. This has often been a big advantage for me in thinking about mathematics, because it's easy to pick up later the standard mental models shared by groups of mathematicians.

This observation has important implications for the education of creatively gifted children. They need to be allowed and even encouraged to "think different." (Several subjects described to me how they would get in trouble in school for pointing out when their teachers said things that they knew to be wrong, such as when a second-grade teacher explained to one of my subjects that light and sound are both waves and travel at the same speed. The teacher did not appreciate being corrected.)

Many creative people are polymaths, as historic geniuses including Michelangelo and Leonardo da Vinci were. George Lucas was awarded not only the National Medal of Arts in 2012 but also the National Medal of Technology in 2004. Lucas's interests include anthropology, history, sociology, neuroscience, digital technology, architecture, and interior design. Another polymath, one of the scientists, described his love of literature:

> I love words, and I love the rhythms and sounds of words . . . [As a young child] I very rapidly built up a huge storehouse of . . . Shakespearean sonnets, soliloquies, poems across the whole spectrum . . . When I got to college, I was open to many possible careers. I actually took a creative-writing course early. I strongly considered being a novelist or a writer or a poet, because I love words that much . . . [But for] the academics, it's not so much about the beauty of the words. So I found that dissatisfying, and I took some biology courses, some quantum courses. I really clicked with biology. It seemed like a complex system that was tractable, beautiful, important. And so I chose biochemistry.

The arts and the sciences are seen as separate tracks, and students are encouraged to specialize in one or the other. If we wish to nurture creative students, this may be a serious error.

Creative people tend to be very persistent, even when confronted with skepticism or rejection. Asked what it takes to be a successful scientist, one replied:

> Perseverance . . . In order to have that freedom to find things out, you have to have perseverance . . . The grant doesn't get funded, and the next day you get up, and you put the next foot in front, and you keep putting your foot in front . . . I still take things personally. I don't get a grant, and . . . I'm upset for days. And then I sit down and I write the grant again.

Do creative people simply have *more* ideas, and therefore differ from average people only in a quantitative way, or are they also qualitatively different? One subject, a neuroscientist and an inventor, addressed this question in an interesting way, conceptualizing the matter in terms of kites and strings:

> In the R&D business, we kind of lump people into two categories: inventors and engineers. The inventor is the kite kind of person. They have a zillion ideas and they come up with great first prototypes. But generally an inventor . . . is not a tidy person. He sees the big picture and . . . [is] constantly lashing something together that doesn't really work. And then the engineers are the strings, the craftsmen [who pick out a good idea] and make it really practical. So, one is about a good idea, the other is about . . . making it practical.

Of course, having too many ideas can be dangerous. One subject, a scientist who happens to be both a kite and a string, described to me "a willingness to take an enormous risk with your whole heart and soul and mind on something where you know the impact—if it worked—would be utterly transformative." The *if* here is significant. Part of what comes with seeing connections no one else sees is that not all of these connections actually exist. "Everybody has crazy things they want to try," that same subject told me. "Part of creativity is picking the little bubbles that come up to your conscious mind, and picking which one to let grow and which one to give access to more of your mind, and then have that translate into action."

In *A Beautiful Mind,* her biography of the mathematician John Nash, Sylvia Nasar describes a visit Nash received from a fellow mathematician while institutionalized at McLean Hospital. "How could you, a mathematician, a man devoted to reason and logical truth," the colleague asked, "believe that extraterrestrials are sending you messages? How could you believe that you are being recruited by aliens from outer space to save the world?" To which Nash replied: "Because the ideas I had about supernatural beings came to me the same way that my mathematical ideas did. So I took them seriously."

Some people see things others cannot, and they are right, and we call them creative geniuses. Some people see things others cannot, and they are wrong, and we call them mentally ill. And some people, like John Nash, are both.

Analyze

1. In your own words, explain why author Kurt Vonnegut was "an excellent case study" in creativity. Have you read any of this writing? If so, did you sense the genius within his work? Within the man?

2. How many of "history's creative luminaries" does Andreasen point out lost their battles with mental illness through suicide? Are you surprised by these names? What other creative luminaries who died by suicide come to mind?

3. What connections does Andreasen have with Sylvia Plath, another creative person who committed suicide?

4. What is one simple way researchers found that they could likely identify students with a high IQ? What does Andreasen say about the validity of that method today?

5. How did "The Termites"—the subjects of Terman's study—debunk some stereotypes about creativity and high IQ? What new paradoxes did they introduce?

Explore

1. Because Andreasen talks about the archetype of the mad genius, this piece could also fit in Chapter 2: Creativity Myths. She cites examples of the madness and creativity via a heroic couplet by John Dryden,

thematic issues in the work of Shakespeare, and lines by Aristotle. What have other writers in this book said about the archetype of the mad genius? What have writers not represented in this book said about it? What do you say/think/feel about it? Would you want to be a genius if it 100% came with a form of madness?

2. Andreasen herself asks two questions that her research seeks to answer. "What differences in nature and nurture can explain why some people suffer from mental illness and some do not? And why are so many of the world's most creative minds among the most afflicted?" What answers—full or partial—to these do you get from her piece here? From the entire book?

3. What is the "duck test"? How does it relate to creativity (or the Big C)? Who do you know passed the duck test? How valid do you think the duck test is?

4. Andreasen writes that "When eureka moments occur, they tend to be precipitated by long periods of preparation and incubation, and to strike when the mind is relaxed." She explains, too, the story of Newton figuring out gravity in 1666 when an apple fell from a tree and struck him on the head, but that prior to this, he'd taught himself Euclidean geometry, algebra, and Cartesian coordinates, and he invented calculus to better measure planetary orbits and area under a curve. What "Aha!" or "Eureka!" moments have you experienced? What type of preparation had you done prior to that sudden moment? Prior to now, had you realized that—in Andreasen's terms—you were undergoing an "ongoing, iterative process"?

Phillippe Petit
"Chaos & Order"

Often called the "poet laureate of the high wire," French-born **Phillippe Petit** (1949–) taught himself to walk the high wire at age sixteen despite being expelled from five schools. He went on to teach himself Spanish, German, Russian, and English as he performed throughout the world. His illegal walk between the towers of the World Trade Center in 1974 became the subject of the award-wining film *Man on Wire*. In addition to his high-wire work, Petit writes, draws, performs close-up magic and street juggling, practices lock picking and eighteenth-century timber framing, plays chess, and studies French wines. "Chaos & Order" first appeared in his book *Creativity*.

Passion is explosive.

It knows no bounds.

It can't be measured.

I let it boil over—to the point that sometimes I think and talk in all directions.

Do you speak to yourself? I often do (silently).

In keeping with our outlaw enterprise, why don't you eavesdrop on me as I interview myself?

The Gallop of Chaos

So, how does the outlaw artist go about embarking on the "perfect crime"? What's the first step? What's the recipe?

There is no recipe.

Okay. What is the first step?

My first step?

Chaos.

That's how I set my artistic crimes in motion.

I toy with an idea until it becomes a fixation. The French have a name for it: *idée fixe*. It is an idea that you lodge in your brain with the understanding that it will refuse to leave.

The word *chaos* is Greek and means "that which gapes wide open." It's a beautiful word. I see a wide-open mouth hungry to swallow the world's knowledge. I do not fear chaos; I welcome it. Chaos for me cannot be still: I make it move! I gallop as fast as I can along its path, to keep the pace of my excitement high. I must not lose the passion that drives me.

In chaos, all is possible. Every incoming idea is welcomed, with no regard for reality. Forget time, money or reason; embrace a brimming universe! Because if you start with rules, your creation will be stillborn.

But ideas should not be left floating around aimlessly; I tie them to one another—in no particular order—with the rope of intuition. They are my prisoners; I know where to find them at all times. This gives me power and freedom: I can break rules, I can be daring.

Where do those ideas come from?

I have amassed considerable archival material throughout my life: clippings, journals, specialized books, objects, iconographies on specific topics, posters, programs, random notes . . .

I keep this material in innumerable files. Some topics sleep in a single folder, others fill an entire trunk. When I am in search of ideas, I go through the files that I suspect hide gems or mysterious ingredients that may become part of my personal *parkour* and—like Jean-Baptiste Grenouille, the master perfumer in Patrick Süskind's novel *Perfume*—I extract their essence.

Can you give examples of such files?

No. In this particular case, examples would be misleading. So let's have it all!

MAGIC, STREET-JUGGLING, HIGH-WIRE WALKING, ROCK CLIMBING, BULLFIGHTING, TEXTS, LANGUAGES, EIGHTEENTH-CENTURY BARN BUILDING, HAND TOOLS, PICKPOCKET, LOCK-PICKING, CRIME, CORDAGE, KNOTS, RIGGING, RUE LAPLACE, SAINT JOHN THE DIVINE, DRAWINGS, SACRED GEOMETRY, GYPSY, CHILDREN'S BOOKS, GRAPHICS, IMAGES, COSTUMES, MUSIC . . .

Hold on, some of this is obscure. What is "Rue Lapl—"

Wait!

. . . PHOTOGRAPHS, CHESS, THEATER, TRAVELS, GREAT RESTAURANTS, COOKING, WINES, ENGINEERING, ALTERNATIVE LIVING SYSTEMS, SURVIVAL, BRIDGES, BLACKSMITHING, FILMS, PEOPLE, LECTURES, WORKSHOPS, SCALE MODELS, QUIZZES & PUZZLES, ESCAPES, PROJECTS

AND NOS. (This last one is a chest filled with projects I developed that, for whatever reason, were turned down.)

I will also go to the special shelf where I keep the books that are most dear to me. I'll check for notes left in the margins and for press clippings I am in the habit of slipping under the covers.

And simultaneously...

I understand, but how does all of this—

Hold on!

... and simultaneously with this frantic hunt, I welcome the avalanche of thoughts coming my way. However tiny, however absurd, anything that passes through my mind gets caught in my net. Organization? At this stage I have no use for it!

Why an avalanche? Why not a neat, manageable stack?

Because from the start I place myself in a state of extreme focus and urgency about the subject at hand. I am frenzied, you could say.

Excess rules! Leaving something important behind would be a giant mistake. So I amass... until later, when the intellectual law of selection confiscates what's not essential.

Pick two topics at random from your excessive list, and use them to illustrate this process of "intellectual industry" that inhabits you.

Sure.

LOCK-PICKING and CHILDREN'S BOOKS.

These days, unless you're a certified locksmith, if you're caught with "burglar tools" in your pocket, you go directly to jail—three years. Thus, a criminal lock-picker learns to make his own tools, wherever he goes.

Lock-picking (which I learned from poorly designed clandestine manuals, CIA pamphlets and the book of trial and error) is based on a simple fact: a system involving parts designed to function in harmony with one another can do so only if the system is imperfect—that is, if there is a minuscule space between the parts. Craftsmen call this "mechanical tolerance."

Without such tolerance, a door would not open; a key would not turn in a lock; the world as we know it would not function.

The art of lock-picking consists of exploiting mechanical tolerance by introducing tiny metal tools inside a locked mechanism and rearranging its moving parts until it opens.

Why did the "hot" topic of lock-picking jump to mind? Joy! I take pleasure in finding imperfections in a system; I use them as tiny portals through which I sneak in, to explore, to understand, to create.

To turn to my other topic, children's books, it's joy again: I delight in children's books.

But mostly the ones I make.

It started when I wanted to remind my daughter, Gypsy, that her traveling father was thinking lovingly about her from far away—

I would tear striking images from magazines and mix them up with text and rough drawings I'd quickly make with thick markers. Minutes later, with the help of scissors and adhesive tape, a simple story was born and a one-of-a-kind album was assembled and put in the mail.

As I kept making them, the stories became more interesting, the drawings more sophisticated and the finished products more "professional-looking."

Soon, I was giving children's books to friends for their kids' birthdays. That's why to this day I always keep my IMAGES portfolio full.

And why do homemade children's books illustrate so well my creative process? Perhaps because it surprises me how an imposed starting point (sometimes I ask the kids to provide a character, an animal, a color, a time, for their story)—or an existing series of images (the ones I tear from magazines) opens my imagination in an instant, leading to an utterly personal, original result.

Okay. So these are elements in the avalanche, the frenzy and the excess. Now what do you do with the whole chaotic pile?

I allow it to slumber.

I let its powder sprinkle my mind, which reminds me of Simon Verity, the master stone carver who for years could be seen with stone dust in his hair, hitting his chisel with his mallet—*toc-toc, toc-toc-toc*—against the blocks of the Portal of Paradise at the Cathedral of St. John the Divine. By the end of the day his dark hair had turned handsomely gray, sprinkled with minuscule particles of limestone. The next morning, he came to work with the powder still clinging to his head, wearing it all day like a crown, smiling like a prince.

Then I take a break.

For example, thinking about this book, I'll play awhile with the concept of its cover.

Although I'm aware it is the graphic designer, not the author, who designs the cover, this fooling around is far from pointless: it adds lines to the switchboard of my ongoing creative network; it provides new mental connections that will surface—somewhere, someday, book or no book—when I wake them up. I'm fond of triggers.

After all, I'm the person who ordered a magnificent door handle from a blacksmith and upon receiving it declared: "Now that I have a way to open the door, all I need to do is build a barn around it!"

Oh! And to deal with what you call the *chaotic pile*, I now start a fresh filing container, dedicated to the project, which will stand open on my desk until completion of the work.

With separate indexed folders?

Now you're getting it!

Yes, with separate indexed folders (color coded, of course) that cover all aspects of the endeavor I am building—from excavation to opening celebration.

I'll keep old drafts in the back of the container, and in the front I'll have a large open envelope labeled À classer (to file) where I'll throw things that I will sort out when I feel like it.

How long do you stay with chaos?

Until *order* emerges. Which it does, at its own pace.

And the space between chaos and order also gets my full attention. For me, it is the oft-neglected void between particles—particles of artistic nature—that changes beauty into perfection. Why are we mesmerized when we look at the stars? Because of the space between them! Can music be defined in part by the void between its notes, as the supreme wire-walk proves dependent on the ever-so-brief suspension between each of the *funambule's* steps? Yes.

Believe it or not, chaos always brings order.

I help in a deceptively simple manner.

I fish topics from the pile.

Then I file them in the open container, adding here and there a little link, a little thought.

Do you use any tools at this stage of the process?

Tools?

My fingers, my eyes, my brain.

For writing, a fountain pen with sepia ink. Adhesive tape and glue if I have the urge to cover the walls with key words, which I call *master words*.

We're miles from the laptop.

For me, the tactile experience provides a tangible link between what I formulate and the solid creation I must achieve.

Try using a pencil in the early stages of your own undertakings. Notice how your fingers absentmindedly play with the pencil while you're thinking. (Mine performs somersaults around my fingers.)

The pencil moves because it is impatient to receive orders to write. Some people chew their pencils as they think—as if to extract the creative juices from their tongues to give to the writing instrument.

Consider it a blessing when your pencil needs sharpening. During that interruption your mind must hold on to a thought not yet "at hand." Look! It bounces back and forth like a child impatient to go play.

Welcome all those side motions, all these delays; they keep your imagination on the dance floor!

So you follow something of a recipe!

Hmm.

Actually, no. I think of all my steps as unpremeditated. They just happen when I set my horse loose at full gallop. Another theory of mine: turning in circles and getting lost is important! You find yourself when you get lost. And there can be no distractions. I must work nonstop.

But you have to sleep.

We spend almost a third of our lives asleep and a third of that time dreaming. The brain areas that restrict our thinking to the familiar and the logical are much less active during REM sleep; I take advantage of that.

I write and solve problems in my sleep.

How do you do that?

When I'm about to fall asleep, I place one unsolved problem, one only, under my pillow—metaphorically speaking, of course.

Once the opacity of sleep has sheltered my mind from the outside world, my subconscious decides on the right direction and travels at sonic speed. It retrieves the solution I need, which sails from outer space to paint my whirling inner space. When the motion stops, I wake up.

I must immediately jot down the solution my unconscious holds at its fingertips, or else the whole thing evaporates in the moonlight.

Yesterday I fell asleep with one precise question inside my head: *Are genius discoveries the music of chance?* I wished for an answer in a single sentence, however long.

During my sleep, fifty-five words came dancing. When the music abruptly stopped, each hurried to find a chair. Believe it or not, the chairs were in the order of a full answer to my question. I woke up and wrote it down:

Sometimes, yes: after hearing too many times Michael Corleone's long scream of despair at the end of The Godfather: Part III, *the editor working on the film temporarily muted the first half of the scream and came up with an accidental yet magisterial cinematographic effect that was kept in the final version of the movie.*

I also write effortlessly when I fly. At thirty thousand feet, the words that I could not capture during sleep float around in the rarefied, cold air and are sucked in by the vacuum the aircraft creates in its wake . . . which collects them like a magnet and brings them right to my seat.

Why do you think I always place a pad and pen under my seat belt?

You're crazy!

A compliment I appreciate.

The Scent of Order

The con man, the bank robber, the illegal wire-walker all begin a coup in the same way: they collect information about their target. The CIA agent preparing for an op does the same, but calls it *gathering intelligence.*

The process may involve steaming open a sealed envelope, zooming in on satellite images, or—in the case of my adventure at the World Trade Center—quick-changing into an architect's disguise in order to "borrow" a blueprint from the construction site.

Whatever it takes, in preparation for a coup I always "do my homework," an expression I despise because for me—be it under strict deadline or with the world against me—the action it describes always spells adventure, never work.

Still writing by hand, I make a complete list of what my research has produced.

But the list is always too long and some entries are not relevant to the project I'm pursuing. Impatiently, I start editing: No time! Let's go! Gloves off! Give no quarter!—as medieval axe-wielding warriors used to scream across the battlefield. The result—raw, as I like it—is not alphabetized or sorted in any other way.

This semi-organized chaos forces me to go through the entire list each time I want to find something. And the repetitive scanning unconsciously drives me to dismiss the redundant and the unworthy while validating the most important elements.

Today, working on this book, my first list is a two-page eclectic enumeration that includes some intriguing notions—TERRITORY, USELESSNESS, NEGATIVE SPACE, VULNERABILITY and IMPROVISED WEAPONS—each with thoughts and stories reverberating inside my head. For instance, if I see ARTS COLLUSION, I think about going to Thailand for a performance. I do not bring trunks filled with preconceived elements—costume, music and ideas. It would be as if the country were of no importance. Instead I bring the minimum (props I've trained, tools I work with) and have my costume inspired by Thai style, my music influenced by Thai compositions, my ideas nourished by Thai culture, history and spirit.

If my eyes land on SIMPLICITY & ELEGANCE, I see the continually creating designer Ken Carbone. He always surprises me (he says I always surprise him).

When Ken agreed to design my barn book, the first thing he did was change its title: *A Square Peg in a Round Hole* became *A Square Peg*. With the same nod to simplicity, he transformed a thick manuscript crowded with drawings into an exquisite, almost Japanese-like album, full of white!

Clarity. Simplicity. Balance. Perfection.

Like a secret agent, I continue *processing my intelligence*. I add words where needed. I use stars or question marks to give ratings.

That's list number two.

The indubitable SPATIAL ALCHEMY, AUTODIDACT, PRIDE and PERFECTION get one star; the indecisive ARROGANCE, CHEATING and USELESS INVENTIONS merit at the moment only a question mark.

Then, to marry certain notions, I create links (*créer des liens* in French, the definition Antoine de Saint-Exupéry in *The Little Prince* gives to the verb

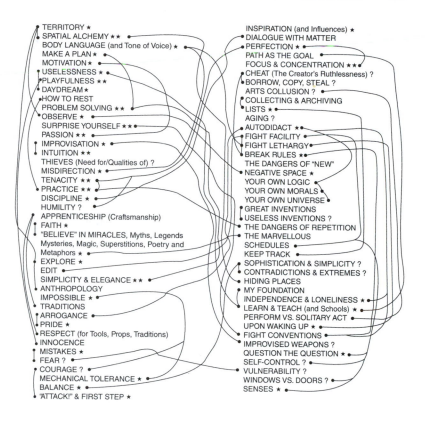

TERRITORY ★
SPATIAL ALCHEMY ★★
BODY LANGUAGE (and Tone of Voice) ★
MAKE A PLAN ★
MOTIVATION ★
USELESSNESS ★
PLAYFULNESS ★★
DAYDREAM ★
HOW TO REST
PROBLEM SOLVING ★★
OBSERVE ★
SURPRISE YOURSELF ★★
PASSION ★★
IMPROVISATION ★
INTUITION ★★
THIEVES (Need for/Qualities of) ?
MISDIRECTION ★
TENACITY ★★
PRACTICE ★★
DISCIPLINE ★
HUMILITY ?
APPRENTICESHIP (Craftsmanship)
FAITH ★
"BELIEVE" IN MIRACLES, Myths, Legends
Mysteries, Magic, Superstitions, Poetry and
Metaphors ★
EXPLORE ★
EDIT
SIMPLICITY & ELEGANCE ★★
ANTHROPOLOGY
IMPOSSIBLE ★
TRADITIONS
ARROGANCE
PRIDE ★
RESPECT (for Tools, Props, Traditions)
INNOCENCE
MISTAKES ★
FEAR ?
COURAGE ?
MECHANICAL TOLERANCE ★
BALANCE ★
"ATTACK!" & FIRST STEP ★

INSPIRATION (and Influences) ★
DIALOGUE WITH MATTER
PERFECTION ★
PATH AS THE GOAL
FOCUS & CONCENTRATION ★★
CHEAT (The Creator's Ruthlessness) ?
BORROW, COPY, STEAL ?
ARTS COLLUSION ?
COLLECTING & ARCHIVING
LISTS ★
AGING ?
AUTODIDACT ★★
FIGHT FACILITY
FIGHT LETHARGY
BREAK RULES ★★
THE DANGERS OF "NEW"
NEGATIVE SPACE ★
YOUR OWN LOGIC
YOUR OWN MORALS
YOUR OWN UNIVERSE
GREAT INVENTIONS
USELESS INVENTIONS ?
THE DANGERS OF REPETITION
THE MARVELLOUS
SCHEDULES
KEEP TRACK
SOPHISTICATION & SIMPLICITY ?
CONTRADICTIONS & EXTREMES ?
HIDING PLACES
MY FOUNDATION
INDEPENDENCE & LONELINESS ★
LEARN & TEACH (and Schools) ★
PERFORM VS. SOLITARY ACT ★
UPON WAKING UP ★
FIGHT CONVENTIONS
IMPROVISED WEAPONS ?
QUESTION THE QUESTION ★
SELF-CONTROL ?
VULNERABILITY ?
WINDOWS VS. DOORS ?
SENSES ★

apprivoiser—a term generally rendered as "to tame," but essentially untranslatable into English).

This process generates list number three, which I share with you here, more for you to glance at than to read thoroughly.

Notice how FIGHT FACILITY pairs with BODY LANGUAGE, for example, and connects to SCHEDULES, SELF-CONTROL and QUESTION THE QUESTION . . .

Finally, I rearrange the list in accordance with the links I have established and I get rid of the connecting lines.

That's list number four, not yet final, but you may read it.

OBSERVE ★
EXPLORE ★
ANTHROPOLOGY
TERRITORY ★
SPATIAL ALCHEMY ★★
NEGATIVE SPACE ★
HIDING PLACES

BODY LANGUAGE (and Tone of Voice) ★
MISDIRECTION ★
FIGHT LETHARGY
UPON WAKING UP ★

MAKE A PLAN ★
PROBLEM SOLVING ★★
SIMPLICITY & ELEGANCE ★★
GREAT INVENTIONS
USELESS INVENTIONS ?

MOTIVATION ★
PASSION ★★

PRACTICE ★★
TENACITY ★★
THE DANGERS OF REPETITION
DISCIPLINE ★
HOW TO REST
FOCUS & CONCENTRATION ★★
HUMILITY ?
DIALOGUE WITH MATTER
PERFECTION ★

INTUITION ★★
IMPROVISATION ★
IMPROVISED WEAPONS ?

THIEVES (Need for/Qualities of) ?

APPRENTICESHIP (Craftsmanship)
RESPECT (for Tools, Props, Traditions)
TRADITIONS

FAITH ★
"BELIEVE" IN MIRACLES (and in Myths,
Legends, Mysteries, Magic, Superstitions, Poetry,
Metaphors and the Marvellous) ★

IMPOSSIBLE ★
COURAGE ?
"ATTACK!" & FIRST STEP ★
MECHANICAL TOLERANCE ★

BALANCE ★
SOPHISTICATION & SIMPLICITY ?
CONTRADICTIONS & EXTREMES ?

MISTAKES ★
FEAR ?
VULNERABILITY ?

INSPIRATIONS (and Influences) ★

BREAK THE RULES ★
FIGHT CONVENTIONS
SURPRISE YOURSELF! ★★
CHEAT (The Creator's Ruthlessness) ?
BORROW, COPY, STEAL ?
ARROGANCE
PRIDE ★
AUTODIDACT ★
YOUR OWN LOGIC
YOUR OWN MORAL
YOUR OWN UNIVERSE
INDEPENDENCE & LONELINESS ★

ARTS COLLUSION ?
PERFORM VS. SOLITARY ACT

COLLECTING & ARCHIVING
LISTS ★
KEEP TRACK

AGING ?

FIGHT FACILITY
EDIT
SELF-CONTROL ?
QUESTION THE QUESTION ★
SCHEDULES

THE DANGERS OF "NEW"

MY FOUNDATION
LEARN & TEACH (Schools) ★
SENSES ★
USELESSNESS ★
PLAYFULNESS ★★
INNOCENCE
DAYDREAM ★
WINDOWS VS. DOORS ?
PATH AS THE GOAL

Making lists is my way of raking ideas into a critical mass before I work them out. While my pen scribbles and *order* settles in, my imagination runs ahead, anticipating creation.

I invite you to be curious about where your passion leads, to transport its explosive demeanor into the kind of chaos that finds order. What are the wonders with which you wish your creative cornucopia to be filled when you wake up in the middle of the night? List them!

PARKOUR

Spelling the French word with a *k* does not change the essence of the thing: parkour has been around for a long time.

It started in France. People in the countryside found a way to let their creative physicality explode, for joy and good health, by running a special course made up of individual segments that mixed gymnastic achievements with playfulness—an activity that became known as *"faire un parcour."*

I remember as a little kid being brought with my sister to La Forêt de Meudon (a vast wood on the outskirts of Paris) for early-Sunday-morning parcours directed by our father. We had to walk on tree trunks across streams, crawl under bushes and climb rocks. What I liked very much were the little competitions that here and there interrupted our jogging: throwing a pebble from afar to demolish a pyramid of stones; creating the most skips across a pond; collecting in a minute the most items whose names started with a given letter of the alphabet. These little challenges seemed to happen by chance; it did not occur to me, young as I was, that they had been planted in our path. The parcours we were enjoying in 1954 came from "La Méthode Hébert," created by the influential physical educator Georges Hébert, which was growing in popularity at the time. It was a great test of agility, balance, precision and imagination.

When I was a teenager on vacation in the Jura Mountains, my favorite activity aside from bouldering was to go to the middle of a roaring brook and run toward its source by jumping from rock to rock. Stopping meant being thrown into the water by my own momentum, so I acquired a special technique that had me bouncing nonstop from one rock to another. In midair I had to make the split-second decision where to land next. I became so good at it that I was able upon each brief landing to scream the name of a letter from the Russian alphabet (a language I was teaching myself).

And then the parcour took over the city of Paris. Monuments and façades of buildings replaced rocks and trees. Of course a certain amount of illegality was involved, as you're not ordinarily permitted to climb a lamppost, balance on a train track or leap from roof to roof singing!

It became a sport, then a sport of sorts, then a novel activity that reached America and spread elsewhere throughout the world. Today, parkour, with thousands of practitioners, has turned into a way of living, almost a philosophy—with its own ethics, followers and gods.

I delight in watching a champion negotiate a short parkour with complexity, fluidity, speed, playfulness and elegance.

Surely parkour has a place in any manifesto on creativity.

Analyze

1. In your own words, explain what the French term "idée fixe" means? What was your own last experience with this phenomenon?
2. Where do Petit's ideas come from?
3. What is Petit's relationship to a pencil? What does his pencil do that yours does not? What does yours do that his does not?
4. What does Petit say, "Surely parkour has a place in any manifesto on creativity"?

Explore

1. What is "mechanical tolerance"? Where in your own life have you experienced mechanical tolerance? What is its relationship to creativity?
2. As Petit did, make your own children's book. "Tear striking images from magazines and mix them up with text and rough drawings" you quickly make with thick markers. Don't feel bound by rules or guidelines. Petit certainly doesn't! Open your imagination and you'll be left with "an utterly personal, original result."
3. For your next writing assignment, follow the advice of the prolific Petit. "I think of all of my steps as unpremeditated. They just happen when I set my horse loose at full gallop. Another theory of mine: turning in circles and getting lost is important! You find yourself when you get lost. And there can be distractions. I must work nonstop." Channel his energy and complete that writing assignment as Petit would. How did it work for you? Where/when did you most feel the creative energy brimming to life? How might you incorporate some of these tactics/ techniques into your regular writing routine?
4. Do as Petit did and interview yourself on creativity. Ask yourself at least eight good, leading questions. Answer them accordingly. Be honest. The interviewer will know if you're not! Share your interview with a classmate.

Forging Connections

1. Who is someone that most consider a genius that you would not? Why? What is your working definition of *genius*? What is the main difference between talent and genius? Between intellect and genius? Do you think someone can become a genius if he or she works hard, eats the right foods, or trains properly? Why or why not?

2. Which of the three quotations below by Albert Einstein—a true historical genius—resonates most deeply with you? Why? What quotation would you pull from the text by Petit—a contemporary genius—to pin on your wall or put on a bumper sticker? What does that quotation mean to you?

   a. "I have no special talent. I am only passionately curious."

   b. "The difference between genius and stupidity is that genius has its limits."

   c. "Everybody is a genius. But if you judge a fish by its ability to climb a tree, it will live its whole life believing that it is stupid."

Looking Further

1. The TV network Lifetime has a competition series entitled "Child Genius," where twenty of America's smartest kids test their skills in an eight-week competition. In no more than twenty seconds, these whiz kids are asked questions in mathematics (without using paper or calculators), world geography, human body, spelling, zoology, and inventions. A few examples (answers in Appendix B):

   - Calculate $14 \times 8 - 11 \times 2$.
   - What is the official currency of Kenya?
   - Which is the scientific name of the shinbone?
   - Spell "triskaidekaphobia."
   - What is the order of bats called?
   - What device did Trevor Baylis invent in 1991?

   What do you think the authors included in this chapter would say about this TV show? What do you think about this TV show? Are these kids geniuses or something else?

2. One of the five most popular TED talks is "Your Elusive Creative Genius" by *Eat, Pray, Love* author Elizabeth Gilbert. View it online, then ask yourself how her view of genius connects with that of the

authors in this chapter. Who does she most align with? What do you think she'd make of Ray Bradbury, who wrote in his book *Zen in the Art of Writing* that taking credit for his own writing is nearly an act of plagiarism since it was really written by "the other me"? What do you find most useful/illuminating about Gilbert's talk?

Creativity Strategies and Hacks

7

"Conditions for creativity are to be puzzled; to concentrate; to accept conflict and tension; to be born every day; to feel a sense of self."

—Erich Fromm, German sociologist, philosopher, and psychoanalyst

"You can't just give someone a creativity injection. You have to create an environment for curiosity and a way to encourage people and get the best out of them."

—Sir Ken Robinson, English creativity expert

Talk to any productive writer, artist, or musician, and odds are they have specific strategies for getting into a creative mode. *Dilbert* creator Scott Adams blogged about this in August 2014, citing these four tactics: work near crowd noise (such as a coffee shop), take a walk, drive a car, and take a shower. He explains, "My armchair guess about what is going on with the brain distractions is that we evolved to keep some important part of the brain on high alert for danger, food, and mating opportunities. If you distract that part of the brain with driving, walking, showering, and background noise, it loosens its hold on the creative processing part of your brain." Singer Sinead O'Connor says, "My creative process is quite slow. I hear melodies in my head while washing the dishes and I allow my subconscious to do the work." Writer Henriette Klauser recommends that writers write when they're tired and sleepy, because in that state, the conscious and subconscious begin to blur, and that can lead to surprising insight that's fueled by having access to the part of the brain where dreams come from.

But the important question is this: no matter what tactics or strategies for creativity we have in place already, can we take a more active approach to having more of it? Can we find our own personal muse and bring her—any time, day or night—into action? Is there a checklist, a tip, or a process that can jumpstart our own creativity and get us roaring along?

This chapter offers a host of conceptual as well as nuts-and-bolts options to improving your own creativity.

A. J. Jacobs
"How to Be More Creative"

The author of four *New York Times* bestsellers, **A. J. Jacobs** (1968–) is a journalist, lecturer, and self-proclaimed "guinea pig." Jacobs is editor at large at *Esquire*, a commentator on National Public Radio, and a columnist for *Mental Floss*. He has appeared on *Oprah, The Today Show, Good Morning*

America, CNN, The Dr. Oz Show, and *The Colbert Report.* "How to Be More Creative" first appeared on RealSimple.com.

I am not typing this article at my desk. I am sprawled on my floor, because an artist told me a change of perspective would boost my creative thinking.

I've spent the last hour warming up my imagination muscles: I devised 50 new uses for a spoon (drumstick, mini catapult, ineffective shield). I surrounded myself with blue, since a University of British Columbia study showed it's a creativity-enhancing color. I played the violin as Einstein did. (Actually, I don't own a violin, so I played my son's ukulele.) In short, I am using as many creativity-boosting strategies as possible. (Well, I'm not taking LSD, which may have helped Steve Jobs achieve those world-changing insights.)

I'm in the middle of a monthlong project to see if I can reignite my creative spark. I'm a writer, so creativity is part of my job description. But in the last few years I've started to worry that my middle-aged brain is ossifying. And as I've discovered, continued creativity may be crucial not just for my livelihood but for my longevity, too. A 2006 George Washington University study of 300 senior citizens found that creative activities, such as art and writing, slow the aging process, resulting in fewer doctor visits and better mental health.

Every day, even those of us who aren't Left Bank watercolor painters engage in creative thinking. "Creativity is critical to solving problems in all parts of our lives," says Richard Restak, a neurologist in Washington, D.C., and the author of *Think Smart.* That includes work, parenting, and arranging our medicine cabinets.

And here's the good news: "Just as you can learn techniques to improve your memory," says Restak, "you can learn techniques to be more creative." We'll see.

Welcoming Bad Ideas

My first call is to Rex Jung, an assistant professor of neurosurgery at the University of New Mexico, in Albuquerque, who specializes in the brain and creativity. He tells me that we tend to think of creative people as churning out one work of genius after another, but brilliance is a numbers game. Creative people tend to be prolific, and usually the misfires far outnumber the hits. "I recently went to a museum in Germany, and they had a Picasso exhibition," says Jung. "But the paintings were terrible. I think I saw every lousy Picasso out there. He created about 50,000 works, and not all of them were masterpieces."

It's a powerful lesson: accept failure. *Enjoy* it, even. Embrace the suck, for the suck is part of the process.

That night I spend 20 minutes cooking up ideas for my parents' 50th anniversary. I write down whatever absurd notion pops into my brain, then read my wife the list.

"It's their golden anniversary, so we could do a gold theme. Everyone could dress up in gold clothes."

"Sounds tacky," my wife responds. OK. No problem. Remember—Bach wrote some shoddy concertos.

"They have a total of 100 years of marriage between them. So we could do 'A Century of Marriage,'" I say.

"I'm worried that might make them feel old."

Embrace the suck, I tell myself.

"Maybe if we did a graph," I suggest. "On one end, we can have Kim Kardashian's 72-day marriage. And on the other end we could have my parents' 50-year marriage."

My wife pauses. "That could work," she says.

I feel my confidence swell just a bit.

Being a Kid Again

A couple of days later, I enroll in a creativity class. This seems like an oxymoron. Isn't it like taking a class in how to be tall or have a smaller nose? But I guess creative people are open-minded, so I want to give it a shot.

I arrive at the Creativity Workshop, in New York City, for my one-on-one training with the directors, a ponytailed artist named Alejandro Fogel and his partner, Shelley Berc, a novelist. Berc asks me to sit on the floor, as a kid would. She says I need to be more playful.

My problem is that I'm too logical, Berc tells me. I like to analyze and compartmentalize. "We're going to try to make you think less," she says in a soothing voice. "Logic is important. But if it comes in too early, it ruins things." Neuroscience backs her up: according to Jung, creative people know how to mute the volume on the frontal lobes (the buttoned-up, analytical portion of the brain), freeing the rest of the brain to make unexpected connections.

Fogel and Berc lead me through a series of exercises to help unburden me from linear, sensible thinking. I draw doodles with my eyes closed. I make up a story about 10 random objects, including a penny and a plastic lobster. (It's a love story in which the lobster is really a beautiful wizard.) I feel dorky, but that's my analytical side talking.

I pledge to try the techniques at home. The next night, I tell my wife that I can't watch *Downton Abbey*. I have a date. Fogel told me, "Make an appointment with your creativity." We can't wait for creativity to strike us like lightning, he says. We have to build it into our lives as a discipline.

My goal is to brainstorm article ideas about fatherhood. As my gurus instructed, I sit on the floor. I look around the room, at the towering lamps, at the underside of the table. *This is what the world looks like to my sons*, I think. *Hmm*. What if I wrote an article from the point of view of kids? Or, better yet, an article of kids' advice to dads? It's a lightbulb. Not the brightest bulb, but not bad.

Flipping the Problem Over

I'm in charge of my five-year-old twins, and they're about to come to blows because they both want to play with the lone plastic light saber. I need to engage in some creative parenting. "You guys can take turns," I say. "I'll flip a coin to see who goes first."

They agree. And then get in a fight over who is heads and who is tails. This could get ugly fast. I know I should remain calm. Research shows that a positive mood is most conducive to creative thinking; negativity inhibits ingenuity. I take some deep breaths. (Sniff the flower; blow out the candle, as I tell the kids.)

I think of a classic technique I read about in *Cracking Creativity*, by creativity expert Michael Michalko: reversal, in which you turn the problem on its head. Take Henry Ford. In the beginning, carmakers kept the vehicle stationary and had factory workers congregate around it to install parts. Ford's idea was to keep the workers stationary and move the car from worker to worker. Thus was born the assembly line. Maybe instead of discouraging my kids' argument, I should push it further.

"I know how we decide who gets heads," I say. "We need to roll a die. Who wants evens, and who wants odds?" As predicted, the twins get in a fight over evens and odds. To decide that fight, we use the spinner from Twister. To settle the Twister, we use dreidels. Then playing cards. The boys are having so much fun, they forget all about the light saber.

Crowdsourcing

I've been trying to become creative on my own, which has its advantages. According to writer Susan Cain in her book *Quiet: The Power of Introverts in a World That Can't Stop Talking*, some of the greatest innovations happen when people have the chance to sit with their thoughts. Steve Wozniak invented the Apple computer mostly by himself in that now legendary garage.

But a group's collective brainpower can also foster creativity. Wozniak got started only after he had been swapping ideas with other nerds. So I decide to hold my first salon: a gathering of people having an old-fashioned exchange of ideas. The more diverse the group, the better, so I invite a TV producer, a banker, a personal trainer, and a theater manager.

I start with a story about the creative power of groups. In his new book, *Imagine: How Creativity Works*, writer Jonah Lehrer tells how advertising executive Dan Wieden and his team were trying to brainstorm a new slogan for Nike in 1988 and coming up empty. But later that night Wieden found that the brainstorming had yielded something worth using: he remembered a colleague's comment on Norman Mailer, which made him think about Mailer's book on the serial killer Gary Gilmore. (Stay with me here.) Gilmore's last words before being executed were "Let's do it." Eureka! Wieden's version— "Just do it"—would be the new Nike slogan. Weird, but fascinating.

I ask my fellow thinkers for creative ideas on how to write my creativity article. The TV producer says, "You should just write it stream-of-consciousness." The theater manager says, "You should write it in orange crayon on a paper towel roll." Intriguing, although likely to result in being asked to return my paycheck.

The conversation takes some strange turns (we discuss klezmer music at length), but in the end no breakthroughs. And yet, the next day, one of the trainer's stray comments pops into my head. "When I'm trying to bulk up, I do everything I can. I lift weights, drink protein shakes, take supplements—all cylinders."

What if I fired on all cylinders? What if I tried all creativity enhancers at the same time? And that is the story of how I came up with the first paragraph of this article. Thanks, salon.

Playing the Fool

I save the truly painful experiment for last. I'm going to sign up for some public humiliation in the form of an improv class. As you probably know, improv is unscripted comedy in which performers make things up as they go along, letting one absurd situation build on the next. I'm terrified, but as adman Jim Riswold—another Nike mastermind, who created campaigns starring Michael Jordan and Spike Lee—told me, "You cannot be creative unless you're willing to walk around with your pants around your ankles." Isn't my creative growth more important than my dignity?

At the Magnet Theater, in New York City, on a dimly lit bare stage, there are 16 of us, ranging in age from 20s to 60s. We learn the first rule: it's not just OK to make a fool of yourself—it's encouraged. We do a series of exercises designed to maximize our foolishness. We make crazy body-building poses. We confess our most absurd pet peeves. (One woman says hers is when charities ask her for money. "I couldn't give less of a crap about other people," she says. I make a note to myself: maybe she's not the ideal partner for team exercises.)

Our teacher, Rick, tells us the next rule: "Yes, and . . . " Whatever your partner says, your job is to affirm it and add to it. If he says there's an arm coming out of your forehead, you say, "Yes, and isn't it wearing a nice glove?"

I'm paired with a guy from Boston. Rick gives us our assignment: we're drivers fighting over a parking space. Now go! Everyone is watching. My palms are sweaty.

"My wife's leg is broken," says the Boston guy.

I remember my "Yes, and . . . " How can I take his idea further?

"Yeah, so what?" I respond. "My kid has the runs."

I'm ashamed of myself for going lowbrow. But the audience laughs. I'm a genius!

The Finish Line

After all this schooling, I haven't created my magnum opus yet. I don't sit down to write in a sweaty Mozart-style flurry of fevered inspiration. (My workday still involves a lot of staring into space, followed by snacking—I imagine it looks more like Salieri's.) But I have to admit that writing this story felt less tortured than writing usually is for me; I even chuckled a little, which I rarely do when I'm working.

And, in fact, I have spent the last few days in a creative frenzy of sorts. I came up with a name for a friend's business, figured out novel ways to stop compulsively checking e-mail, and decorated my son's wall. Inspired by a trip to the Metropolitan Museum of Art, I hung my son's drawings and put plaques next to them: *Orange Man with Purple Car*, by Jasper Jacobs. We both think it's a masterpiece.

Analyze

1. According to Jacobs, what does a 2006 George Washington University study of three hundred senior citizens have to teach us about the value of creativity? What does Washington DC neurologist Richard Restak add to this point?
2. Why does Jacobs say you should "Embrace the suck!" What does he mean?
3. What does the Creativity Workshop in New York City teach Jacobs? What science backs it up?
4. How effective does Jacobs say his salon was in helping him write this article? How effective was the salon *really*?

Explore

1. How would you describe the tone of this article? How does it compare to that of other pieces in this book? In what way do you think tone is a creative choice a writer makes? How consciously do you decide on tone when you write?
2. What lessons emerge from the incident with the light saber? What would creativity expert Michael Michalko think about how Jacobs handled the issue? What other techniques might you have tried to overcome the challenge of two kids and one light saber?

3. How does Jacobs's improv experience connect with Hugh Hart's piece from Chapter 4: Collaboration and Creativity, which also talks about improv techniques? Where have you tried to be purposefully foolish? Applied the "Yes, and . . . ?" strategy? How might these techniques offer opportunities to improve your writing?

4. Create your own creative salon in the classroom. Break up into groups and instead of having a rigid agenda, simply discuss ideas and bat them around. Take turns. Contribute as much or as little as you choose, but actively listen to all that's being said. Talk about Big Ideas, small ideas, pop culture, writing, creativity, or the coolest smartphone app. Let the energy of the group take the conversation where it wants to go. After fifteen minutes, explore what happened. How many topics did you encounter? How deeply did you go into them? What did you learn? How creative do you feel now (do you have the "creative frenzy of sorts" that Jacobs experienced)? Consider making a salon experience a regular part of your creative life.

Scott Berkun
"Creative Thinking Hacks"

The author of six books, **Scott Berkun** (1961–) is a popular speaker on culture, business, philosophy, and creativity. He has been a regular commentator on CNBC, MSNBC, and National Public Radio. Berkun is also the director of the film project *We Make Seattle*. "Creative Thinking Hacks" first appeared in his book *The Myths of Innovation*.

Each one of us possesses everything necessary to be more creative. The problem is that schools, parents, and workplaces tend to reward us for following rules. It's something quite different to learn to ask our own questions and seek our own answers (which is one simple definition of creative thinking). This chapter is a high-speed, condensed version of a course I taught at the University of Washington on how anyone, with some honest effort, can easily become more creative at any task at any time.

Kill Creative Romance

L ike most media today, this chapter starts with violence—and an unnecessary exclamation point! Close your eyes, and imagine the most amazing sword ever made. Now, with it in hand, attack every creative legend
you've ever heard. (We've romanticized da Vinci, Mozart, and Einstein
into gods, minimizing the ordinary aspects of their lives so intensely that
their mothers wouldn't recognize them in the legends we tell.) Next, using
your sword's mint-scented flamethrower attachment, set fire to childhood
tales of Isaac Newton and the apple, Benjamin Franklin and the lightning
kite, and Edison and the lightbulb. Think of other similar legends you've
heard, even if they were not mentioned in this book. These popular tales of
creativity are deceptive at best, wild lies at worst. They're shaped to placate
the masses, not to inform or help people actually interested in doing creative
work. Slash each and every one with your sword, throw a dozen napalm-
coated hand grenades in for good measure, and watch your old, broken-
down view of creativity go up in flames. Dance around the smoldering ruins!
Roast marshmallows over the still-warm remains of your creative fulmina-
tions! The fun begins now: free yourself. Feel like you did when you were
young, without any preconceptions over what is or is not creative.

In this new landscape, plant the following simple definition: *an idea is a
combination of other ideas.* Say it five times out loud. Say it to your cat. Yell
it out your car window at strangers waiting for the bus. Every amazing creative thing you've ever seen or idea you've ever heard can be broken down
into smaller ideas that existed before. An automobile? An engine and
wheels. A telephone? Electricity and sound. Reese's Peanut Butter Cups?
Peanut butter and chocolate. All great creative ideas, inventions, and theories are composed of other ideas. Why should you care? Because if you want
to be a creator instead of a consumer, you must view existing ideas as fuel
for your mind. You must stop seeing them as objects or functional things—
they are combinations of ingredients waiting to be reused.

Combinations

C ooking is a brilliant analogy for creativity: a chef's talents hinge on his
ability to bring ingredients together to create things. Even the most
inspired chef in history did not make bacon appear by mere concentration,

nor suggest to the divine forces that a ripe tomato should be on the list of evolution's desired outcomes. Faith in the creativity-as-combinations view of the world helps creators in many ways. It means that if at any time you feel uncreative, the solution is to look more carefully at the combinations available to you, or to break apart something to see how it's made. Increasing creativeness doesn't require anything more than increasing your observations: become more aware of possible combinations. Here's a test: quickly pick two things in front of you, say, this book and your annoying, smelly friend Rupert. Now close your eyes and imagine different ways to combine them.

If you're stuck, here are three:

1. Rupert with a table of contents
2. An annoying, smelly book about innovation
3. Reading a book on, or making one out of, Rupert's face

Now while these combos might not be useful, good, or even practical, they're certainly creative (and if you think these are stupid and juvenile, you have confused bad taste with lack of creativity). Adding a third element, perhaps a gallon of cappuccino, might yield even more interesting combinations (a caffeine-overdosed, smelly book infused with Rupert's annoying personality).

Over time, creative masters learn to find, evaluate, and explore more combinations than other people. They get better at guessing which combinations will be more interesting, so their odds improve. They also learn there are reusable combinations, or patterns, that can be used again and again to develop new ideas or modify existing ones. For example, musicians throughout history have reused melodies, chord progressions, and even entire song structures. The national anthem of the United States was based on the tune of an old British drinking song.[1] The Disney film *The Lion King* is a retelling of Shakespeare's *Hamlet*. Shakespeare was likely influenced by the early Greek tragedies. Study any creative field, from comedy to cooking to writing, and you'll discover patterns of reuse and recombination everywhere. It's an illusion that when an artist makes a painting or an author writes a novel it appeared magically into her hands from out of nowhere. Everything comes from somewhere, no matter how amazing or wonderful the thing is. The *Mona Lisa* was not the first portrait any more than the Destiny's Child song "Survivor" was the first four-minute R&B hit.

I'm not suggesting you steal something someone else made and put your name on it. That's theft, and a fairly uncreative kind of theft at that. Instead, the goal is to recognize how much in the world there is to borrow from, reuse, reinterpret, use as inspiration, or recombine without breaking laws or violating trust. Every field has its own rules and limitations, but creative fields are more liberal than you'd expect.[2]

Inhibition

We're afraid. We're afraid of the dark, of our parents, and what our parents do in the dark. Our tiny, efficient brains do their best to keep us from thinking about things we fear or don't understand. This is good for survival but bad for combination making. We shut down the pursuit of many combinations because of predictions we make about what the result will be. But remember: we suck at prediction. Lewis Thomas mentioned the best sign of progress in his research lab was laughter, and laughter often comes from surprise.

Many of us who have the potential to be creative fail only because we struggle to turn off our filters and fears. We don't want to do anything that could yield an unexpected result. We seek external validation from our teachers, bosses, family, etc., but creativity usually depends on internal validation. We have to judge for ourselves whether our ideas are interesting or useful.

One way to think of creative people is that they have more control over their fears—or less fear of embarrassment. They're not necessarily smarter or more capable of coming up with good ideas, they simply filter out fewer ideas than the rest of us. Creativity has more to do with being fearless than intelligent or any other adjective superficially associated with it. This explains why many people feel more creative when drinking, on drugs, or late at night: these are all times when their inhibitions are lower, or at least altered, and they allow themselves to see more combinations of things than they do normally.

Environment

Creativity is personal. No book or expert can dictate how you can be more creative. You have to spend time paying attention to yourself:

when do ideas come easiest to you? Are you alone? With friends? In a bar? At the beach? Are there times of day when you're most relaxed? Is there music playing? Start paying attention to your rhythms and then construct your creative activities around them. To get all Emersonian on you, this is called self-knowledge:[3] you can't be productive as a creator if you're not paying attention to your own behavior and learning how best to cultivate the unique wonder in this universe that is you. Nothing is more counterintuitive than trying to be yourself by being like other people. It doesn't work that way—no book, course, or teacher can give this to you.

To help you figure this out, you need to experience different ways of working, and pay attention to which ones best suit you. They might be unexpected, not fitting into your framework (i.e., filters) for how creative work should be done, or what's appropriate for a 42-year-old middle manager to do. I learned that I tend to be most creative late at night. I don't find it convenient, and neither does my family, but I've recognized it to be true. If I want to maximize my creativity, I will spend hours working late at night. Each of us responds to environmental conditions differently. Half the challenge is experimenting to find out which ones work best; the other half is honoring them despite how inconvenient or unexpected they might be.

Persistence

Being creative for kicks is easy. But if you want to be creative on demand you must develop helpful habits, and that's about persistence. You won't always find interesting combinations for a problem right away, and identifying fears and working through them is rarely fun. At some point, all creative tasks become work. The interesting and fun challenges fade, and the ordinary, boring, inglorious work necessary to bring the idea to the world becomes the reality. Study the histories of great creators, and you'll find a common core of willpower and commitment as their driving force. Van Gogh, Michelangelo, and Mozart worked every day. Edison, Hemingway, and Beethoven, as well as most legendary talents, outworked their peers. Forget brilliance or genetics, the biggest difference between the greats and us was their dedication to their craft. Each of the names we know had peers who were just as talented, or more so, but twice as lazy. They consistently gave up before their projects were finished. Want to guess why we don't know their names? The world can only care about ideas that are shared.

When I give lectures on creative thinking, I often ask who in the audience has had an idea for a business, movie, or book. Most of the audience raises their hands. I then ask how many people have done any work at all on these ideas, and most of the audience drops their hands. That tells the whole story: ideas are lazy. They don't do anything on their own. If you aren't willing to do the ordinary work to make the idea real, the problem isn't about creativity at all.

When an idea is fully formed in your head, there's no escaping the fact that for the idea to change the world, it has to leave your brain—a journey that only happens with hard work and dedication. Writing proposals, sketching designs, pitching ideas: it's all work you know how to do. But how far are you actually willing to go to make your idea real?

Creative Thinking Hacks

Here are some clever tactics for applying this advice:

- **Start an idea journal.** Write down any idea that pops in your mind at any time. Don't be inhibited: anything goes. You will never have to show anyone else this journal, so there should be no filters—it's safe from judgment. This should help you find your own creative rhythms, as over time you can note what times of day you're more creative. I recommend a paper journal so you can doodle and write freely, but digital journals also work. Whenever you're stuck, flip through your journal. You're bound to find an old idea you've forgotten about that can be used toward the problem you're trying to solve.
- **Give your subconscious a chance.** The reason ideas come to you in the shower is that you're relaxed enough for your subconscious to surface ideas. Make this easier: find time to turn your mind off. Run, swim, bike, have sex, do something that's as far from your creative problem as possible. Afterward, you might just find that the problem you struggled with all morning isn't as hard, or that you have a new idea for approaching it.
- **Use your body to help your mind.** This is entirely counterintuitive to your logical mind, but that's exactly why it's so likely to work. In John Medina's *Brain Rules*, he explains how physical activity, even for people who don't like it, has positive effects on brain function. The theory is that for most of our evolutionary history, the acts of physical exertion

and maximum brain function were correlated (think how creative you have to be when being chased by tigers). If your body is active, your mind will follow. Einstein and Bohr used to debate physics while going for long walks—they both believed they thought better when moving around. This might be true for you.

- **Inversion.** If you're stuck, come up with ideas for the opposite of what you want. If your goal was to design the best website for your team, switch to designing the worst one you can imagine. Five minutes at an inverted problem will get your frustrations out, make you laugh, and likely get you past your fears. Odds are high you'll hit something so horribly bad that it's interesting, and in studying it, you'll discover good ideas you would never have found any other way.

- **Switch modes.** Everyone has a dominant way of expressing ideas: sketching, writing, talking. If you switch the mode you're working in, different ideas are easier to find, and your understanding of a particular problem will change. This is both a way to find new ideas and to explore an idea you're focused on. Working on paper, rather than computers, can make this easier because you can doodle in the margins (a form of mode switching), something you can't really do with a mouse and a keyboard. Or, try explaining your problem to a child, or to the smartest person you know, which will force you to describe and think about the problem differently.

- **Take an improvisational comedy class.** This will be easier and less painful than you think. These classes, offered for ordinary people by most improv comedy groups, are structured around simple games. You show up, play some games, and slowly each week you learn how to pay more attention to the situations the games put you in, as well as how to respond to them. You will eventually become more comfortable with investing in combinations without being sure of the outcome.

- **Find a partner.** Some people are most creative when they're with creative friends. Partnering up on a project, or even being around other creative people who are working on solo projects, keeps energy levels high. They will bring a new perspective to your ideas, and you will bring a new perspective to theirs. It also gives you a drinking buddy when things go sour.

- **Stop reading and start doing.** The word *create* is a verb. Be active. Go make things. Make dinner, make a drawing, make a fire, make some noise, but make. If all your attempts at being creative consist of passively consuming, no matter how brilliant what you consume is, you'll always be a consumer, not a creator. An entire culture of tinkerers and makers is out there, with projects and tools to help you get started. Check out *http://makezine.com* and *www.readymade.com,* two sites waiting to show you the way.

NOTES

1 *http://en.wikipedia.org/wiki/The_Star-Spangled_Banner.*

2 An interesting challenge to this claim is the issue of sampling in music. How much of one song can another artist sample and reuse? One second? Five? None? See the excellent film *Copyright Criminals,* which explores this question from many different perspectives (and there's lots of good music in the film, too): *http://www.pbs.org/independentlens/copyright-criminals/film.html.*

3 Read Ralph Waldo Emerson's essay "Self-Reliance" at *http://www.emersoncentral.com/selfreliance.htm.*

Analyze

1. In your own words, explain how Berkun sees cooking as a useful analogy for creativity. What other analogies for creativity can you come up with? Share these with a classmate.

2. What is self-knowledge? And why is it useful to think about in a conversation on creativity?

3. Why does Berkun say "ideas are lazy." What does he mean?

4. How can using your body help your mind? What does John Medina and his book *Brain Rules* have to say about it?

Explore

1. Berkun says creativity is taking what's out there and reusing, reshaping, resizing, recombining it to make something new. What do you think about how this plays out in the sampling of music? At what point does sampling become theft? Berkun suggests watching the film *Copyright Criminals.* Another good voice to add into this discussion is Lawrence Lessig—his TED talk "Laws That Choke Creativity" is quite interesting.

2. "Van Gogh, Michelangelo, and Mozart worked every day," writes Berkun. "Edison, Hemingway, and Beethoven, as well as most

legendary talents, outworked their peers. Forget brilliance or genetics, the biggest difference between the greats and us was their dedication to their craft." How much do you agree with this idea? How much do the other authors in this book agree? Do you think Berkun is being 100% serious or is simply making a provocative point?

3. Try out Berkun's idea of inversion. For the next three minutes, work with a classmate or two and come up with strategies for being uncreative. Have fun with it. Get it all out. Then revisit the idea of creating new strategies for being creative. Share those ideas and discuss the merits of each. How did inverting the problem first help?

4. Creative create is a verb, Berkun reminds us. So create something right now. As he says, "make dinner, make a drawing, make a fire, make some noise, but make!" Does the act of creating feel creative? Does it encourage more creativity? Keep being creative—make it part of your daily practice, and Berkun believes the results will come.

The Creative Group
"Innovation in the House: Creativity Lessons from Five Top In-House Creative Teams"

The Creative Group is a leading creative staffing agency that specializes in connecting interactive, design, marketing, advertising, and public relations talent with the best companies. They also conduct ongoing research on hiring and employment issues.

12 Insider Creativity Tips

1. **Be open to failure—from yourself and teammates.**
   It's often a critical step on the path to a big breakthrough. "We try to make it an environment where it's OK to fail," says Will Gay, creative director at Disney's Yellow Shoes Creative Group. "Walt Disney failed many times before he got it right with Mickey Mouse and was super successful. You have to fail in order to get to the good stuff."

2. **Show your work—and not just to other designers.**
   Hizam Haron, senior manager, visual identity at McKesson, a health-care services company, often hangs draft images or layouts on the wall. "When people walk past they're always very curious," he says. "They say, 'Oh what is this?'" Haron briefly explains the in-progress work and then asks for input. "Having that open, porous environment really helps because people [throughout the organization] like to see what you're working on. You don't have to follow everything they say." Instead, it's a great way to test new ideas, push past feeling stuck or simply broaden your perspective.

3. **Give clients what they should have requested.**
   Did your client ask for something you think is a bad idea? Or not the best solution? "I'll give them what they're asking for, and then I'll give them what they should be doing," says Allan Peters, associate creative director at Target. "And I'll keep giving them the second option every time to push the idea forward."

CREATIVITY CASE STORY
Target: Going to Work in the Garage

Creative teams of the future will actively invent new things. When James Dyson, inventor of the famous Dyson vacuum cleaner, came to speak at Target, someone asked him, "How do you innovate?" He replied, "That's easy. Find something that pisses you off and fix the problem." It's the philosophy behind Target's Garage program. Staff members identify something that bothers or irritates them about the company and then come up with ideas to fix it. The group picks out the best ideas and forms teams around them.

4. **Don't wait for a creative brief.**
   If you want to innovate, don't wait for the juicy projects to hit your desk. "You're not always going to get the brief you wanted," says Peters. "Identify the problem, and try and fix it. You have to put it on yourself to rock out some good ideas." Then sell those big ideas to your boss or team.

5. **Always create multiple solutions to the problem.**
True creativity means exploring more than one option to any design problem. "The more you push yourself to do three or four different versions, the more you're going to have to get creative," says Scott Kirkwood, editor in chief at *National Parks* magazine and senior director of publications at the National Parks Conservation Association.

6. **Distill your message or story down to its essence.**
Creative teams of the future will cut through the noise with concise communication. "Every story can be boiled down," says Kirkwood. "You can tell a story in one sentence or 10 sentences or 100 pages, but the more succinct you are, the more likely you are to get someone's attention."

CREATIVITY CASE STORY
National Parks **Magazine: Telling Better Stories**

Creative teams of the future will tell exceptional stories. "Every challenge we have must be told through a story," says Scott Kirkwood, editor in chief at *National Parks* magazine and senior director of publications at the National Parks Conservation Association. "We're not going to produce a boring fact sheet in the magazine. We always have to come up with a story and a person and a human angle." Good stories feature an element of surprise, a person to root for and the challenges that person faces. It also helps to add layers by including the perspective from the other side.

7. **Look for creative ways to bring the tactile into digital.**
Creative teams of the future will humanize digital experiences. "Digital concepts and designs are the future," Gay says. "But when we tie them into a real-world touch and feel, that's how the emotional connections are made." That might mean creating a hand-drawn map for a website or bringing old-school 2D animation into a banner ad.

8. **Make every project better than the last one.**
Moving into the future means always pushing your work. "If you can make it just a little bit better, you're going to be happier and everyone

else is going to be happier," Peters says. "Depending on the brand you're working on, that might not be a huge shift, but it's the little wins you should celebrate."

9. **Make it a point to truly listen to your customers.**
   Creative teams of the future will ask what their customers think. At Square, Chris Heimbuch, director of Square's Brand group, says the in-house team ran a "Let's Talk" program that involved a multicity tour. They rented venues and brought small business customers up on stage to talk about their entrepreneurial efforts and how their Square credit card readers factored into those risks and dreams. It reminded the creative team how much Square affects people's lives.

CREATIVITY CASE STORY
McKesson: Thinking B-to-P (Business to People)

Creative teams of the future will focus more on people and less on the distinctions between B-to-C or B-to-B. "People are people," says Hizam Haron, senior manager for visual identity at McKesson, a major healthcare services company. "People like to see beautiful things. People appreciate creativity. You don't have to dumb it down because it's B-to-B. The design still has to be smart and solve the challenge." Whatever company you're selling to, the audience is still ultimately the person who's actually hiring you or buying the product. Focus on appealing to the target audience's needs on a humanistic level.

10. **Don't spend your whole life at work.**
    Creative teams of the future know that more hours don't always mean better results. Before coming to Target, Peters worked 60 to 65 hours a week at agencies. Now he logs around 40 to 45. "I create more work," he says. "And I make better work, really the best work of my career, since coming to Target, and a lot of that is just having time away from the office and being inspired by life."

11. **Take a class about something other than design.**
    A little cross-pollination can kick-start your creativity. "I always encourage people to take classes," says Heimbuch. "If you're a photographer, that doesn't mean you take another level of photography. Think creative writing or painting. Break out from the familiar."

12. **Meet as many people as you possibly can.**
There's nothing better for your career and creative perspective than authentic networking. "I see creators running into issues when they operate a little bit too much in a vacuum," says Heimbuch. "Develop a healthy network around you so you don't end up being too isolated."

CREATIVITY CASE STORY
Square: Stepping Outside Your Discipline

Creative teams of the future will actively solve business problems. Once a quarter at Square, the entire company holds "Hack Week," where people are free to examine different parts of the business and take a hack at challenges outside their department. "It's really pretty liberating," says Chris Heimbuch, director of creative operations of Square's brand group. "It gets people out of their comfort zones. We tend to mix up teams that don't normally work with one another and foster a different way of looking at things."

Conclusion

In the end, creativity and innovation are all about pushing yourself forward. You need to be open to new ideas, relationships, working methods and feedback. It's not enough to keep doing what you've always done. Instead, you'll need to actively invent the future as you focus on building real relationships with real people—whether it's a colleague or someone in your target audience. The power of connection is a truth that applies across mediums, disciplines and industries.

To see the latest research from The Creative Team of the Future, visit the TCG Blog.

Expert Contributors
Thanks to the following INitiative advisory committee members who contributed to this project:

- Will Gay, Creative Director, Disney's Yellow Shoes Creative Group
- Hizam Haron, Senior Manager, Visual Identity, McKesson
- Chris Heimbuch, Director of Creative Operations of Square's Brand group

- Scott Kirkwood, Editor in Chief, *National Parks* magazine, and Senior Director of Publications, National Parks Conservation Association
- Allan Peters, Associate Creative Director, Target

CREATIVITY CASE STORY
Disney: Making Magic with a Cereal Bar

Creative teams of the future will be in touch with their inner child. When Will Gay, creative director at Disney's Yellow Shoes Creative Group, visited the company's Animation Studios in Burbank, Calif., he came around a corner and found himself face to face with an employee eating cereal at a breakfast cereal bar. He thought it was such a smart idea that he had one built outside his office in Orlando, Fla., and had it stocked with all kinds of milk and favorite childhood cereals, like Cap'n Crunch's Crunch Berries and Chocolate Lucky Charms. "It's just one more thing that keeps the creative team young," he says. "It's a little thing, but it goes a long way." Perks like free food have even been shown to enhance employee retention.

Analyze

1. What's the value of showing your work to other people beyond designers?
2. What does the Creative Group mean by "Don't wait for a creative brief"? How is this a creativity tip? How might this apply to the world of a college student?
3. What does it mean to "humanize digital experiences"? What's the danger in not doing that?
4. How might intellectual or artistic cross-pollination help your creativity? What are three specific things you might engage in that could impact your own creative efforts?

Explore

1. In the Creativity Case Story on *National Parks* magazine, editor in chief Scott Kirkwood says, "We're not going to produce a boring fact sheet in the magazine. We always have to come up with a person and a

human angle." Why? What's wrong with numbers, statistics, graphs, and charts? As a student, how might Kirkwood's idea lead you to a different way of completing your own fact-based assignments?

2. Why would a company like Square have Hack Week, where "people are free to examine different parts of the business and take a hack at challenges outside their department"? If you could take a hack at school, what would you do? How about taking a hack at work? In your own family? In the White House?

3. What's the real lesson in the Creativity Case Story about Disney and the cereal bar? What does Cap'n Crunch have to do with creativity? What other similarly unexpected ideas might bring a little energy to a work environment? A school environment? Come up with at least three options and share them with a classmate.

Ed Goodman and Dave Goodman
"The Spiral Thinking Guide"

The career of **Ed Goodman** (1954–) has spanned the fields of experience design, marketing, strategic planning, entertainment engineering, land planning, television/media production, and nonprofit think tank management. With Dave Goodman, he is coauthor of *Creating the New American Dream— The Spiral Renaissance Theory*. As a trumpet player, Goodman has performed with Dizzy Gillespie, Maynard Ferguson, Doc Severinsen, Olivia Newton John, Tony Bennett, and The Four Tops.

Former vice president and executive producer of Walt Disney Entertainment, **Dave Goodman** (1957–) has over thirty-five years of domestic and international entertainment and leadership experience. He is the award-winning executive producer of corporate and charity galas, parades, fireworks shows, music festivals, sporting events, award shows, movie premieres, animal shows, product launches, promotional tours, and events for US presidents, foreign royalty, heads, and heads of state. With Ed Goodman, he is coauthor of *Creating the New American Dream—The Spiral Renaissance Theory*.

Today's World . . . Discovery, Strategy and Innovation for the 21st Century

These are extraordinary times. The predictability of the past two hundred years has been obliterated by the use of technology, computers and all of the various forms of digital information, transfer and communication. As a nation and as individual organizations we simply cannot comprehend all of the changes that will take place in the near future.

In a world that is growing exponentially, we must think differently than ever before. We must find a way to get from Point "A" to Point "G" or "M" or even "Z" without the burdens of slow linear progress. We believe it is time for a new brand of thought . . . a renaissance of sorts but with a methodology, a process and a system to spiral upward, out of the current chaos and journey to an even better nation . . . and a better world. The world of business must also embrace the pace of change by providing its people with a 21st century capability for innovation through a new process called functional creativity.

Functional Creativity and the Spiral Thinking Theory

Introducing a new process of ideation and problem solving. We call it the spiral thinking theory or functional creativity. This process forms the framework to look at almost any challenge and construct a vision and action plan as a guide. It is perfectly suited to discovering the best and brightest ideas, mapping the course of the vision, designing the outcome, building the dream and living out the results. This is a thinking process that is uniquely suited to the 21st century challenge of strategy, creativity and innovation for a world where ideas are the currency of the future.

Many people have created processes and strategies to enable brainstorming, creativity and problem solving. From creativity guru Edward de Bono to Joey Reiman at BrightHouse, all have offered a great deal to the science and importance of ideas. We owe a debt of gratitude to these thinkers and more, who have sought to promote the value of ideas, creativity and imagination.

This functional creativity process extracts concepts that we developed working in the fields of entertainment, education, engineering, community development, business consulting and more. This is a process that is easy to follow and helps anyone feel comfortable creating their own dreams and mapping a course to realization. In business, it provides increased creativity, team engagement, activated learning and a deeper level of thinking... all leading to enhanced outcomes.

The Logarithmic Spiral Form . . . the Shape of Thinking for the 21st Century

Our concept of considering the spiral as a design for thinking methodology was forged from a collection of theories and studies on the thought process, particularly as it relates to creativity and problem solving. It is important to note that the study of thought has been around for centuries. Hundreds of books and theses have been written about how the human mind works. Labels for thinking paradigms include words like linear, vertical, lateral, abstract, creative, blue sky, and many more. The spiral thinking/functional creativity process provides a new, four-dimensional roadmap from which to enhance innovation, personalized learning activation and strategic problem solving. But first, let us discuss the power, flexibility and efficiency of spiral thinking.

Spiral thinking is a process designed to expand the patterns and rigors of our traditional learned linear thinking. It makes every attempt to extend beyond the routine, the obvious and the expected, not to be rebellious, but to become exponentially productive at the speed of the new century. It is however deeply rooted in the most basic of human characteristics such as trust, belief, hope and faith. These human characteristics are connected because of the engagement and personal connection to the learning challenge that stems from the process.

Spiral thinking allows us to assume that what we know to be true is in fact true.

It gives us the freedom to trust and believe in that which has already been proven and that which may still be unknown.

Spiral thinking has infinite potential yet it can produce specific, targeted results, especially as it relates to learning objectives.

The process of spiral thinking is motivated by growth and forward, upward momentum. It respects and incorporates the past as a historical foundation without getting bogged down in past precedent.

Spiral thinking incorporates all that we already know while catapulting us towards what we need. Spiral thinking involves several thinking styles;

however, its simplicity provides us with the opportunity to glance back at our most recent critical path of decisions to ensure that our course is valid. Spiral thinking involves the entire brain, draws upon the senses and is led by active engagement. It is not just a tool for problem solving or creating the next "big idea." It is a way of thinking and learning that can extend to all aspects of our business and personal lives.

How Spiraling Works

The concept of spiraling is really more of a process or method of approaching the challenges of problem solving, innovation, creativity and discovery. You could think of spiraling as an adventure or quest because it goes well beyond the typical methods of linear thinking. Spiraling can be applied to any issue, topic, subject or intention. It can also be applied to ever-larger spheres of influence such as dream-mapping individual lives, businesses, communities and more.

In the spiral thinking theory, logarithmic spirals are used to symbolize the process, incorporating five phases . . .

The logarithmic spiral begins simply and humbly in the center where ideas are born or discovered. As the process grows, ideas are studied, evaluated and enhanced. In the third phase, the best concepts are further defined, designed or delineated. Next, we put the ideas and preferred concepts into action. Lastly, we re-evaluate the effectiveness of the concepts as we live out these implemented dreams.

The process is both simple and comprehensive. You can use spiraling for a wide variety of applications:

discovery

enhanced learning

group and collaborative learning

strategizing

creative thinking

problem solving

brainstorming

innovating

There are many ways to think of this process of spiraling. The commonality is that logarithmic spiraling is a sequential, ever-growing phenomenon. Starting with a multitude of possibilities (phase 1), narrowing to the select few (phase 2), enhancing the ideas into designed realities (phase 3), putting them into practice (phase 4) and living the results (phase 5). Spiraling provides the self-directed answer to many needs. Here are a few examples of spiraling applications:

Phase	1	2	3	4	5
	imagination	ideation	illustration	implementation	invitation
	dream	create	design	construct	experience
	discover	define	strategize	activate	live

If you apply spiraling in larger spheres of influence you can approach concepts that have broad reach:

Phase	1	2	3	4	5
	individual lives	businesses	communities	America	The world

In each case, the power of the ideas grows from thoughts to selected concepts. It then progresses into definitive objectives that lead us to action plans and implementation. Lastly, we live the concepts, re-assess the dreams and enhance them further as they are fully realized. The dream is now a reality . . . it has come to fruition because we had a method to bring the intangible vision into a celebrated, living dream come true. It is obvious how this process can provide advanced thinking and innovation. It can be a vital process for preparing organizations and their people for their future roles in a 21st century world.

Let's look into the process at each phase. Once we select a topic, problem/challenge, or business need, we begin the spiraling process.

Phase 1: Imagination—Dream—Discover
Abstract Thinking

In phase 1, we use our creativity to discover as many ideas as possible. We jot down each idea we think of regardless of whether or not we think it is good or bad, feasible or unfeasible, fantastic or ridiculous. The goal is to imagine as many ideas and new concepts as we can. Sometimes a seemingly silly idea will trigger a new thought that would have never been considered unless the "silly" idea was exposed. Don't try to judge the ideas or new imaginings, simply bring every one forward and write them all down. Get as many as you can ... set them aside and let them percolate in your mind for a while.

Phase 2: Ideate—Create—Define
Convergent Thinking

Now is the time to review the ideas from phase 1. Here, we take some time to consider the merits of the ideas. We add a dose of common sense, conduct research on ideas that seem promising, look for connections and commonalities. Are there some themes that are emerging? Begin to narrow the long list down to the ideas that are the most significant and compelling. Sometimes we combine ideas to generate a new, stronger vision that resonates even more with the overall dream.

Choose the best of the best and create a vision for how this might look and feel. Do the selected ideas resonate with your intellectual intuition and the challenge at hand? Take some time to consider your discovery and imagine the results. Feel what it is like to be there. Does it feel great? If so, you're on the right track. Can you imagine a pathway to get you there, even if it seems distant? Regardless, if it feels right, if research points you there, if your intuition is strongly favorable, if it resonates positively when you think about it . . . you're on your way. You can see, feel and almost experience the result or challenge as if the solution is already here, right now.

The best ideas now are chosen and it feels great. You can see it and the experience is what you dreamed about. You're ready to make it happen.

Phase 3: Illustrate—Design—Strategize
Vertical Thinking

Next, we illustrate the preferred concepts and ideas. We can now create a design or strategy for how to move the ideas forward. If it is a smaller or more short-term concept, we can design the steps to get us to implementation. If the idea or concept is large and complex, we may only be able to see the first several steps and not the entire road ahead. That is just fine. We don't need to see the entire journey unfold. We simply must have faith that if we take the first few steps, the right path will be found. We take a few steps and the next few will be revealed and so on until we reach our final destination.

Many great leaders have believed in this strategy . . . Dr. Martin Luther King, Alexander Graham Bell, Albert Einstein. They made a great many dreams come true and inspired generations to follow, just by having a dream, seeing the vision and being dedicated to taking the first steps in good faith.

Create the design and illustrate the ideas with stories, drawings, or anything that make it seem real. Develop a solution strategy to move the challenge forward, as far as you can see right now, knowing what the end looks and feels like.

Phase 4: Implement—Construct—Activate
Linear Thinking

In phase 4, we activate the challenge. In many cases, you will be able to implement your strategy and immediately construct the solution. In larger examples, you may be implementing a series of steps that propel you to forward the designs and strategies, implementing as you go. Regardless, you are on the way to challenge/project realization. The seeing is becoming believing and a visible reality is coming forth. The phases of seeing, believing and feeling, now become actual experiences. By activating your designs and strategies, you have moved into a new phase where ideas, concepts and strategies become tangible. Your dreams now have life, due to your imagination and design.

Move forward, step-by-step, until the journey we call visioneering or spiraling has led you to the activation of your dream, your challenge, your innovation or business project.

Phase 5: Invitation—Experience—Live
Experiential Thinking

You are now invited to live the dream you had only imagined. You are here and it is time to experience the benefits of your spiral quest. Enjoy the journey. Live the dream. Feel your heart soar and experience the magic you have created, the challenge or innovation you have been able to accomplish.

Making Learning Fun and Our Dreams Come True

When we apply spiraling, the process is always building on the power of ideas. Spiraling is a positive energy exercise. It takes our dreams and provides the visualization and the accompanying feelings that this reality is not only possible, but it is likely. Spiraling creates the energy boost to keep you moving in the best direction. It creates the visualization you need to see the dream coming true and the ability to actually feel what it will be like to live out the dream or idea. This thinking . . . to seeing . . . to feeling . . . to experiencing phenomenon is what allows us to bring our dream from an idea to a living truth. Our learning challenge has become a fun, engaging, personal process that we feel confident in exploring.

Spiraling grows new possibilities into tangible visions that become actionable. It provides increased energy and direction and an ever-widening sphere of influence and reach. The ideas become brighter, better designed and more fulfilling. We are creating incremental momentum at every phase.

Today, we all need inspiration, hope and optimism to meet the challenges of life. Positive spiraling can keep us spinning forward and upward, reaching beyond today's momentary limitations toward a more boundless potential. Where could we go if we used the power of our brains to broaden our dreams into tangible realities? How could we enrich our lives and relationships? What would the future for our business look like if we engaged our people through functional creativity? How would we design the innovations of tomorrow if we really took the time to spiral think a better dream?

Human Potential

There is an inner genius in every human being. For some people, genius is discovered early in life and they become the model for all of us to study. For the rest of us, we may not be labeled as brilliant, talented or gifted, but we all have enormous potential. The genius within all of us may not be measured by master works of art or innovative life changing inventions. But we all have the potential for excellence. We all have the potential to make a significant difference . . . at home, work, schools, volunteer organizations, or in our local community and beyond.

Discovering one's true potential is more art than science. Spiral thinking can stimulate individual human potential beyond our current imaginations.

We All Have the Potential for Excellence
Examples of Spiral Thinking in Practice

Spiral thinking theory has been applied across a wide array of industries, businesses and civic and educational applications. Here is a brief summary:

Healthcare . . . Spiral thinking has been used to completely reimagine the healthcare experience and facility design for hospitals, clinics, cancer centers, medical campuses, internal education centers (experience universities), collaboratories and outreach opportunities. The results have been very promising and include increased business, reduced employee turnover, improved patient satisfaction, reduced complaints, higher morale and repurposing of outdated facilities into exceptional "story structures" with renewed purpose.

Corporations . . . A variety of companies and businesses have used this technique to improve, reimagine, and revitalize their strategic plans and futures. These businesses have included entertainment, hospitality, engineering, architecture, law, technology, computers, clean energy, beverage, media and real estate. New strategic plans, cultural enhancements, new products, new offerings and new facilities have all been created using Spiral Thinking approaches to innovation.

Cities . . . Spiral thinking was applied to a number of complex city needs including downtown revitalization, city planning, transportation, entertainment and cultural activation and land development planning. A variety of projects are underway to bring these visions to life.

Education . . . Colleges and universities have engaged in Spiral Experience Presentations and Thinkshops for leadership, innovation, engagement and experience design. An elementary school created an innovation plan to help their school increase its academic achievement. Spiral thinking was applied across the curriculum as a learning overlay and within one school year students reported an overall increase in test scores of as much as 46%. Grants are in review to expand this into more schools. In addition, private sector education producers are considering the adoption of spiral thinking and functional creativity models into their learning products/offerings.

Analyze

1. What are the five phases of spiral thinking? In which part of the spiral are ideas born?
2. If you apply spiraling to a larger sphere of influence, where do you end up? Why is that useful?
3. What type of leaders do Goodman and Goodman reference regarding phase 3? How do you envision those people being examples of illustrate—design—strategize? What other examples come to mind?

Explore

1. Pretend you were hired by Goodman and Goodman to take their Spiral Thinking Guide out into the world and find clients who would benefit from using it. You can see that they've already partnered with school, cities, corporations, and health care businesses. Where else might this way of thinking work well? Make a list of as many options as you can think of. Your "job," after all, is on the line!

2. This reading mentions how spiral thinking "goes well beyond the typical methods of linear thinking." What is linear thinking? What are some examples? When/where is linear thinking useful?

3. Spiral thinking promises to be useful for a wide variety of applications, such as discovery, enhanced learning, group and collaborative learning, strategizing, creative thinking, problem solving, brainstorming, and innovating. Let's suppose that you have a problem that needs solving—a roommate who drives you bonkers with his unexpected slovenliness (e.g., dishes left out, dirty clothes everywhere, etc.). Use spiral thinking to solve this challenge. Follow each step carefully and see if you can get to phase 5 where the problem will be resolved. Which step(s) was the most challenging? Why? How happy are you with the outcome of this hypothetical problem? How else might you use spiral thinking in your life?

Forging Connections

1. If you were to hire one of the authors from this chapter as a creativity guru for a week to help you out, who would you choose? Why? What do you think he could do for you? What do you think this person would say was your greatest strength? Your greatest challenge? What would you expect to pay for a full week of intense one-on-one coaching like this? How much would you expect to improve after the week?

2. What connections do you see between any of the texts in this chapter and that of Freeman and Rountree from Chapter 1: The Creative Process? Do they have a different idea of spirituality or the role it can play in creativity? Using a search engine or the library, locate another text that explores the role of spirituality, religion, or prayer in the creative process. In what way does this new text engage with the selections in this chapter? With Freeman and Rountree? What new possibilities do you now see for your own creative process?

Looking Further

1. In what ways would you like to be more creative? Give three specific examples. Explain why these three areas are important to you and how being creative in them would benefit you. What tips, tactics, strategies, or processes from the chapter would assist you in this?

2. Come up with four of your own creativity hacks, meaning specific tips, techniques, or strategies for increasing one's level of creativity. If you feel stuck, Google "creativity hacks for a few ideas," though don't just copy what you see—use it to inspire your own fresh contributions. Work with a partner if that seems like a good option for you both. Strive to not only come up with the tip or idea, but the reasoning behind it. Perhaps personal anecdotes might help. Share your creativity hacks with the class. Consider assigning each other hacks to use on your next writing assignment.

Researching and Writing about Creativity
Barbara Rockenbach and Aaron Ritzenberg

Research-based writing lies at the heart of the mission of higher education: to discover, transform, and share ideas. As a college student, it is through writing and research that you will become an active participant in an intellectual community. Doing research in college involves not only searching for information but also digesting, analyzing, and synthesizing what you find in order to create new knowledge. Your most successful efforts as a college writer will report on the latest and most important ideas in a field as well as make new arguments and offer fresh insights.

It may seem daunting to be asked to contribute new ideas to a field in which you are a novice. After all, creating new knowledge seems to be the realm of experts. In this guide, we offer strategies that demystify the research and writing process, breaking down some of the fundamental steps that scholars take when they do research and make arguments. You'll see that contributing to scholarship involves strategies that can be learned and practiced.

Throughout this guide we imagine doing research and writing as engaging in a scholarly conversation. When you read academic writing, you'll see that scholars reference the studies that came before them and allude to the studies that will grow out of their research. When you think of research as

Barbara Rockenbach, Director of Humanities & History Libraries, Columbia University; Aaron Ritzenberg, Associate Director of First-Year Writing, Columbia University.

engaging in a conversation, you quickly realize that scholarship always has a social aspect. Even if you like to find books in the darkest corners of the library, even if you like to draft your essays in deep solitude, you will always be awake to the voices that helped you form your ideas and to the audience who will receive your ideas. As if in a conversation at a party, scholars mingle: they listen to others and share their most recent ideas, learning and teaching at the same time. Strong scholars, like good conversationalists, will listen and speak with an open mind, letting their own thoughts evolve as they encounter new ideas.

You may be wondering, "What does it mean to have an open mind when I'm doing research? After all, aren't I supposed to find evidence that supports my thesis?" We'll be returning to this question soon, but the quick answer is: to have an open mind when you're doing research means that you'll be involved in the research process well before you have a thesis. We realize this may be a big change from the way you think about research. The fact is, though, that scholars do research well before they know any of the arguments they'll be making in their papers. Indeed, scholars do research even before they know what specific topic they'll be addressing and what questions they'll be asking.

When scholars do research they may not know exactly what they are hunting for, but they have techniques that help them define projects, identify strong interlocutors (people who take part in a dialogue), and ask important questions. This guide will help you move through the various kinds of research that you'll need at the different stages of your project. If writing a paper involves orchestrating a conversation within a scholarly community, there are a number of important questions you'll need to answer: How do I choose what to write about? How do I find a scholarly community? How do I orchestrate a conversation that involves this community? Whose voices should be most prominent? How do I enter the conversation? How do I use evidence to make a persuasive claim? How do I make sure that my claim is not just interesting but important?

GETTING STARTED

You have been asked to write a research paper. Whether this is your first research paper at the college level or not, you still face the same challenge: where do you start? The important thing when embarking on any kind of writing project that involves research is to find something that you are interested in learning more about. Writing and research are easier if you care about your topic. Your instructor may have given you a topic, but you can make that topic your own by finding something that appeals to you within the scope of the assignment.

Academic writing begins from a place of deep inquiry. When you are sincerely interested in a problem, researching can be a pleasure, since it will satisfy your own intellectual curiosity. More important, the intellectual problems that seem most difficult—the questions that appear to resist obvious answers—are the very problems that will often yield the most surprising and most rewarding results.

PRESEARCHING TO GENERATE IDEAS

When faced with a research project, your first instinct might be to go to Google or Wikipedia, or even to a social media site. This is not a bad instinct. In fact, Google, Wikipedia, and social media can be great places to start. Using Google, Wikipedia, and social media to help you discover a topic is what we call "presearch"—it is what you do to warm up before the more rigorous work of academic research. Academic research and writing will require you to go beyond these sites to find resources that will make the work of researching and writing both easier and more appropriate to an academic context.

Google

Let's start with Google. You use Google because you know you are going to find a simple search interface and that your search will produce many results. These results may not be completely relevant to your topic, but Google helps in the discovery phase of your work. For instance, let's say that you are asked to write about creativity and gender.

This Google search will produce articles from many diverse sources—magazines, government sites, and nonprofit organizations among them. It's not a bad start. Use these results to begin to hone in on a topic you are interested in pursuing. A quick look through these results may yield a more focused topic such as how creativity and gender is related to academic achievement. Another source takes an interdisciplinary approach to "issues of identity and its representation, examining intersections of age and gender in relation to music and musicians across a wide range of periods, places, and genres."

Figure A.1 Results of a Google search for "creativity and gender."

Wikipedia

A Wikipedia search on creativity will lead you to many articles that address creativity and gender as well as a variety of other possible subtopics and connection. The great thing about Wikipedia is that it is an easy way to gain access to a wealth of information about thousands of topics. However, it is crucial to realize that Wikipedia itself is not an authoritative source in a scholarly context. Even though you may see Wikipedia cited in mainstream newspapers and popular magazines, academic researchers do not consider Wikipedia a reliable source and do not consult or cite it in their own research. Wikipedia itself says that "Wikipedia is not considered a credible source . . . This is especially true considering that anyone can edit the information given at any time." For research papers in college, you should use Wikipedia only to find basic information about your topic and to point you toward scholarly sources. Wikipedia may be a great starting point for presearch, but it is not an adequate ending point for research. Use the References section at the bottom of the Wikipedia article to find other, more substantive and authoritative resources about your topic.

Using Social Media

Social media such as Facebook and Twitter can be useful in the presearch phase of your project, but you must start thinking about these tools in new ways. You may have a Facebook or Twitter account and use it to keep in touch with friends, family, and colleagues. These social networks are valuable, and

References [edit]

- Amabile, Teresa M.; Barsade, Sigal G; Mueller, Jennifer S; Staw, Barry M., "Affect and creativity at work," *Administrative Science Quarterly*, 2005, vol. 50, pp. 367–403.
- Amabile, T. M. (1998). "How to kill creativity". *Harvard Business Review* **76** (5).
- Amabile, T. M. (1996). *Creativity in context*. Westview Press.
- Balzac, Fred (2006). "Exploring the Brain's Role in Creativity". *NeuroPsychiatry Reviews* **7** (5): 1, 19–20.
- BCA (2006). *New Concepts in Innovation: The Keys to a Growing Australia*. Business Council of Australia 🔗.
- Brian, Denis, *Einstein: A Life* (John Wiley and Sons, 1996) ISBN 0-471-11459-6
- Byrne, R. M. J. (2005). *The Rational Imagination: How People Create Counterfactual Alternatives to Reality*. MIT Press.
- Carson, S. H.; Peterson, J. B.; Higgins, D. M. (2005). "Reliability, Validity, and Factor Structure of the Creative Achievement Questionnaire". *Creativity Research Journal* **17** (1): 37–50. doi:10.1207/s15326934crj1701_4 🔗.
- Craft, A. (2005). *Creativity in Schools: tensions and dilemmas*. Routledge. ISBN 0-415-32414-9.
- Dorst, K.; Cross, N. (2001). "Creativity in the design process: co-evolution of problem–solution". *Design Studies* **22** (5): 425–437. doi:10.1016/S0142-694X(01)00009-6 🔗.
- Feldman, D. H. (1999). "The Development of Creativity". In ed. Sternberg, R.J. *Handbook of Creativity*. Cambridge University Press.
- Finke, R.; Ward, T. B. & Smith, S. M. (1992). *Creative cognition: Theory, research, and applications*. MIT Press. ISBN 0-262-06150-3.

Figure A.2   List of references from a Wikipedia search on creativity. Use these links to further your research.

you may already use them to gather information to help you make decisions in your personal life and your workplace. Although social media is not generally useful to your academic research, both Facebook and Twitter have powerful search functions that can lead you to resources and help you refine your ideas.

After you log in to Facebook, use the "Search for people, places, and things" bar at the top of the page to begin. When you type search terms into this bar, Facebook will first search your own social network. To extend beyond your own network, try adding the word "research" after your search terms. For instance, a search on Facebook for "creativity research" will lead you to a Facebook page for the Centers for Research on Creativity. The posts on the page link to current news stories on creativity, links to other similar research centers, and topics of interest in the field of creativity research. You can use these search results as a way to see part of the conversation about a particular topic. This is not necessarily the scholarly conversation we referred to at the start of this guide, but it is a social conversation that can still be useful in helping you determine what you want to focus on in the research process.

Twitter is an information network where users can post short messages (or "tweets"). While many people use Twitter simply to update their friends ("I'm going to the mall" or "Can't believe it's snowing!"), more and more individuals and organizations use Twitter to comment on noteworthy events or link to interesting articles. You can use Twitter as a presearch tool because it aggregates links to sites, people in a field of research, and noteworthy sources. Communities, sometimes even scholarly communities, form around topics on Twitter. Users group posts together by using hashtags—words or phrases that follow the "#" sign. Users can respond to other users by using the @ sign followed by a user's twitter name. When searching for specific individuals or organizations on Twitter, you search using their handle (such as @barackobama or @whitehouse). You will retrieve tweets that were created either by the person or organization, or tweets that mention the person or organization. When searching for a topic to find discussions, you search using the hashtag symbol, #. For instance, a search on #creativity will take you to tweets and threaded discussions on the topic of creativity.

There are two ways to search Twitter. You can use the search book in the upper right-hand corner and enter either a @ or # search as described earlier. Once you retrieve results, you can search again by clicking on any of the words that are hyperlinked within your results such as #innovation.

If you consider a hashtag (the # sign) as an entry point into a community, you will begin to discover a conversation around topics. For instance, a search on Twitter for #creativity leads you to Creativity Magazine (@creativitymag), which the editor claims has "the best ideas in advertising and brand creativity—and a generous helping of inspiration." News agencies such as Reuters are also active in Twitter, so an article from a Reuters publication will be retrieved in a search. Evaluating information and sources found in social media is similar to how you evaluate any information you encounter during the research process. And, as with Wikipedia and Google searches, this is just a starting point to help you get a sense of the spectrum of topics. This is no substitute for using library resources. Do not cite Facebook, Twitter, or Wikipedia in a research paper; use them to find more credible, authoritative sources. We'll talk about evaluating sources in the sections that follow.

CREATE A CONCEPT MAP

Once you have settled on a topic that you find exciting and interesting, the next step is to generate search terms, or keywords, for effective searching. Keywords are the crucial terms or phrases that signal the content of any given source. Keywords are the building blocks of your search for information. We have already seen a few basic keywords such as "creativity" and "gender." One way to generate keywords is to tell a friend or classmate what you are interested in. What words are you using to describe your research project? You may not have a fully formed idea or claim, but you have a vague sense of your interest. A concept map exercise can help you generate more keywords and in many cases, narrow your topic to make it more manageable.

A concept map is a way to visualize the relationship between concepts or ideas. You can create a concept map on paper, or there are many free programs online that can help you do this (see, for instance http://vue.tufts. edu/, http://www.nchsoftware.com/chart/index.html, or http://freeplane. sourceforge.net). There are many concept mapping applications available for mobile devices; the concept map here was created using the app SimpleMind.

Here is how you use a concept map. First, begin with a term like creativity. Put that term in the first box. Then think of synonyms or related words to describe creativity such as "innovation," "psychology," "originality,"

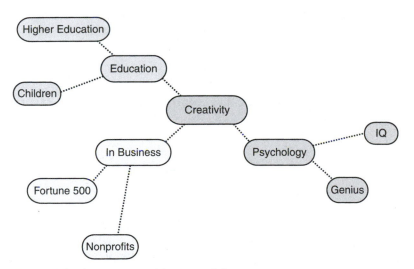

Figure A.3 A concept map about creativity.

"imagination," "right brain thinking," and "inventiveness." This brain-storming process will help you develop keywords for searching. Notice that keywords can also be short phrases.

After some practice, you'll discover that some phrases make for excellent keywords and others make for less effective search tools. The best keywords are precise enough to narrow your topic so that all of your results are relevant, but are not so specific that you might miss helpful results. Concept maps created using apps such as SimpleMind allow you to use templates, embed hyperlinks, and attach notes, among other useful functions.

KEYWORD SEARCH

One of the hardest parts of writing is coming up with something to write about. Too often, we make the mistake of waiting until we have a fully formed idea before we start writing. The process of writing can actually help you discover what your idea is, and most important, what is interesting about your idea.

Keyword searches are most effective at the beginning stages of your research. They generally produce the most number of results and can help you determine how much has been written on your topic. You want to use keyword searches to help you achieve a manageable number of results. What is manageable? This is a key question when beginning research. Our keyword search in Google on creativity and gender produced over 62 million results. The same search in JSTOR.org produces over 40,000 results. These are not manageable results sets. Let's see how we can narrow our search.

Keyword searches, in library resources or on Google, are most effective if you employ a few search strategies that will focus your results. Use AND when you are combining multiple keywords. We have used this search construction previously:

creativity AND gender

The AND ensures that all your results will contain both the term creativity and gender. Many search engines and databases will assume an AND search, meaning if you type

creativity definitions

the search will automatically look for both terms. However, in some cases the AND will not be assumed and creativity definitions will be treated as a phrase. This means that creativity will have to be immediately next to the word definitions to return results. Worse yet, sometimes the search automatically assumes an OR. That would mean that all your results would come back with either creativity or definitions. This will produce a large and mostly irrelevant set of results. Therefore, use AND whenever you want two or more words to appear in a result.

1. Using OR can be very effective when you want to use several terms to describe a concept such as:

creativity OR innovation OR right brain thinking

A search on creativity and gender can be broadened to find other possible avenues for exploration. The following search casts a broader net because results will come back with creativity and any of the other three terms:

globalization AND (gender OR sex OR identity)

Not all of these words will appear in each record. Note also that the parentheses set off the OR search indicating that creativity must appear in each record and then gender, sex, or identity needs to appear along with creativity.

2. Use quotation marks when looking for a phrase. For instance, if you are looking for information on creativity and gender in multinational corporations you can ensure that the search results will include all of these concepts and increase the relevance by using the following search construction:

creativity AND gender AND "multinational corporation"

This phrasing will return results that contain both the words "creativity" and "gender" and the phrase "multinational corporation."

3. Use NOT to exclude terms that will make your search less relevant. You may find that a term keeps appearing in your search that is not useful. Try this:

creativity NOT politics

If you are interested in the linguistic side of this debate, getting a lot of results that discuss the politics of creativity may be distracting. By excluding the keyword politics, you will retrieve far fewer sources, and hopefully more relevant results.

RESEARCHABLE QUESTION

In a college research paper, it is important that you make an argument, not just offer a report. In high school you may have found some success by merely listing or cataloging the data and information you found; you might have offered a series of findings to show your teacher that you investigated your topic. In college, however, your readers will not be interested in data or information merely for its own sake; your readers will want to know what you make of this data and why they should care.

In order to satisfy the requirements of a college paper, you'll need to distinguish between a topic and a research question. You will likely begin with a topic, but it is only when you move from a topic to a question that your research will begin to feel motivated and purposeful. A topic refers only to the general subject area that you'll be investigating. A researchable question, on the other hand, points toward a specific problem in the subject area that you'll be attempting to answer by making a claim about the evidence you examine.

"Creativity and gender" is a topic, but not a researchable question. It is important that you ask yourself, "What aspect of the topic is most interesting to me?" It is even more important that you ask, "What aspect of the topic is it most important that I illuminate for my audience?" Ideally, your presearch phase of the project will yield questions about creativity and gender that you'd like to investigate.

A strong researchable question will not lead to an easy answer, but rather will lead you into a scholarly conversation in which there are many competing claims. For instance, the question, "What are the official languages of the United Nations?" is not a strong research question, because there is only one correct answer and thus there is no scholarly debate surrounding the topic. It is an interesting question (the answer is: Arabic, Chinese, English, French, Russian, and Spanish), but it will not lead you into a scholarly conversation.

When you are interested in finding a scholarly debate, try using the words "why" and "how" rather than "what." Instead of leading to a definitive answer, the words "why" and "how" will often lead to complex, nuanced answers for which you'll need to marshal evidence in order to be convincing. "Why did Arabic become an official language of the UN in 1973?" is a question that has a number of complex and competing answers that might draw from a number of different disciplines (political science, history, economics, linguistics, and geography, among others). If you can imagine scholars having an interesting debate about your researchable question, it is likely that you've picked a good one.

Once you have come up with an interesting researchable question, your first task as a researcher is to figure out how scholars are discussing your question. Many novice writers think that the first thing they should do when beginning a research project is to articulate an argument, then find sources that confirm their argument. This is not how experienced scholars work. Instead, strong writers know that they cannot possibly come up with a strong central argument until they have done sufficient research. So, instead of looking for sources that confirm a preliminary claim you might want to make, look for the scholarly conversation.

Looking at the scholarly conversation is a strong way to figure out if you've found a research question that is suitable in scope for the kind of paper you're writing. Put another way, reading the scholarly conversation can tell you if your research question is too broad or too narrow. Most novice writers begin with research questions that are overly broad. If your question is so broad that there are thousands of books and articles participating in the scholarly conversation, it's a good idea for you to focus your question so that you are asking something more specific. If, on the other hand, you are asking a research question that is so obscure that you cannot find a corresponding scholarly conversation, you will want to broaden the scope of your project by asking a slightly less specific question.

Keep in mind the metaphor of a conversation. If you walk into a room and people are talking about creativity, it would be out of place for you to begin immediately by making a huge, vague claim such as "Creativity is more relevant today than ever before." It would be equally out of place for you to begin immediately by making an overly specific claim, such as "Women from the 1900s were inherently more creative than men thanks to differences in brain chemistry and key sociopolitical factors." Rather, you would gauge the scope of the conversation and figure out what seems like a reasonable contribution.

Your contribution to the conversation, at this point, will likely be a focused research question. This is the question you take with you to the library. In the next section, we'll discuss how best to make use of the library. Later, we'll explore how to turn your research question into an argument for your essay.

YOUR CAMPUS LIBRARY

You have probably used libraries all your life, checking out books from your local public library and studying in your high school library. The difference between your previous library experiences and your college library experience is one of scale. Your college library has more stuff. It may be real stuff like books, journals, and videos, or it may be virtual stuff, like online articles, e-books, and streaming video. Your library pays a lot of money every year to buy or license content for you to use for your research. By extension, your tuition dollars are buying a lot of really good research material. Resorting to Google and Wikipedia means you are not getting out all you can out of your college experience.

Not only will your college library have a much larger collection, it will have a more up-to-date and relevant collection than your high school or community public library. Academic librarians spend considerable time acquiring research materials based on classes being taught at your institution. You may not know it, but librarians carefully monitor what courses are being taught each year and are constantly trying to find research materials appropriate to those courses and your professor's research interests. In many cases, you will find that the librarians will know about your assignment and will already have ideas about the types of sources that will make you most successful.

Get To Know Your Librarians!

The most important thing to know during the research process is that there are people to help you. While you may not yet be in the habit of going to the library, there are still many ways in which librarians and library staff can be helpful. Most libraries now have an e-mail or chat service set up so you can ask questions without even setting foot in a library. No question is too basic or too specific. It's a librarian's job to help you find answers, and all questions are welcome. The librarian can even help you discover the right question to ask given the task you are trying to complete.

Help can also come in the form of consultations. Librarians will often make appointments to meet one-on-one with to offer in-depth help on a research paper or project. Chances are you will find a link on your library website for scheduling a consultation.

Among the many questions fielded by reference librarians, three stand out as the most often asked. Because librarians hear these questions with such regularity, we suggest that students ask these questions when they begin their research. You can go to the library and ask these questions in person, or you can ask vie e-mail or online chat.

1. How do I find a book relevant to my topic?

The answer to this question will vary from place to place, but the thing to remember is that finding a book can be either a physical process or a virtual process. Your library will have books on shelves somewhere, and the complexity of how those shelves are organized and accessed depends on factors of size, number of libraries, and the system of organization your library uses. You will find books by using your library's online catalog and carefully noting the call number and location of a book.

Your library is also increasingly likely to offer electronic books or e-books. These books are discoverable in your library's online catalog as well. When looking at the location of a book you will frequently see a link for e-book versions. You will not find an e-book in every search, but when you do the advantage is that e-book content is searchable, making your job of finding relevant material in the book easier.

If you find one book on your topic, use it as a jumping-off point for finding more books or articles on that topic. Most books will have bibliographies either at the end of each chapter or the end of the book in which the author has compiled all the sources he or she used. Consult these bibliographies to find other materials on your topic that will help support your claim.

Another efficient way to find more sources once you've identified a particularly authoritative and credible book is to go back to the book's listing in your library's online catalog. Once you find the book, look carefully at the record for links to subjects. By clicking on a subject link you are finding other items in your library on the same subject. For instance, a search on

creativity AND gender

will bring you to items with subjects such as

creative ability

creativity in advertising

creativity in old age

2. What sources can I use as evidence in my paper?

There are many types of resources out there to use as you orchestrate a scholarly conversation and support your paper's argument. Books, which we discussed earlier, are great sources if you can find them on your topic, but often your research question will be something that is either too new or too specific for a book to cover. Books are very good for historical questions and overviews of large topics. For current topics, you will want to explore articles from magazines, journals, and newspapers.

Magazines or **periodicals** (you will hear these terms interchangeably) are published on a weekly or monthly schedule and contain articles of popular interest. These sources can cover broad topics like the news in magazines such as *Newsweek, Time,* and *U.S. News and World Report.* They can also be more focused for particular groups like farmers—(*Dairy Farmer*—or photographers (*Creative Photography*). Articles in magazines or periodicals are by professional writers who may or may not be experts. Magazines typically are not considered scholarly and generally do not contain articles with bibliographies, endnotes, or footnotes. This does not mean they are not good sources for your research. In fact, there may be very good reasons to use a magazine article to help support your argument. Magazines capture the point of view of a particular group on a subject, like how farmers feel about increased globalization of food production. This point of view may offer support for your claim or an opposing viewpoint to counter. Additionally, magazines can also highlight aspects of a topic at a particular point in time. Comparing a *Newsweek* article from 1989 on Japan and globalization to an article on the same topic in 2009 allows you to draw conclusions about the changing relationship between the United States and Japan over that 20-year period.

Journals are intended for a scholarly audience of researchers, specialists, or students of a particular field. Journals such as *Globalization and Health, Modern Language Journal,* or *Anthropological Linguistics* are all examples of scholarly journals focused on a particular field or research topic. You may hear the term "peer-reviewed" or "referred" in reference to scholarly journals. This means that the articles contained in a journal have been reviewed by a group of scholars in the same field before the article is published in the journal. This ensures that the research has been vetted by a group of peers before it is published. Articles from scholarly journals can help provide some authority to your argument. By citing experts in a field you are bolstering your argument and entering into the scholarly conversation we talked about at the beginning of this guide.

Newspaper articles are found in newspapers that are generally published daily. There is a broad range of content in newspapers ranging from articles written by staff reporters, to editorials written by scholars, experts, and general readers, to reviews and commentary written by experts. Newspapers are published more frequently and locally than magazines or journals, making them excellent sources for very recent topics and events as well as those with regional significance. Newspaper articles can provide you with a point of view from a particular part of the country or world (e.g., How do Texans feel about globalization vs. New Yorkers?); or a strong opinion on a topic from an expert (e.g., an economist writing an editorial on the effects of globalization on the Chinese economy).

A good argument uses evidence from a variety of sources. Do not assume you have done a good job if your paper only cites newspaper articles. You need a broad range of sources to fill out your argument. Your instructor will provide you with guidelines about the number of sources you need, but it will be up to you to find a variety of sources. Finding two to three sources in each of the aforementioned categories will help you begin to build a strong argument.

3. Where should I look for articles on my topic?

The best way to locate journal, magazine, or newspaper articles is to use a database. A database is an online resource that organizes research material of a particular type or content area, For example, PsycINFO is a psychology database where you would look for journal articles (as well as other kinds of sources) in the discipline of psychology. Your library licenses or subscribes to databases on your behalf. Finding the right database for your topic will depend upon what is available at your college or university because every institution has a different set of resources. Many libraries will provide subject or research guides that can help you determine what database would be best for your topic. Look for these guides on your library website. Your library's website will have a way to search databases. Look for a section of the library website on databases and look for a search box in that section. For instance, if you type "language" in a database search box, you may find that your library licenses a database called *MLA International Bibliography* (Modern Language Association). A search for "history" in the database search box may yield *American History and Life* or *Historical Abstracts*. In most instances, your best bet is to ask a librarian which database or databases are most relevant to your research.

When using these databases that your library provides for you, you will know that you are starting to sufficiently narrow or broaden your topic when you begin to retrieve 30–50 sources during a search. This kind of narrow result field will rarely occur in Google, which is one of the reasons why using library databases is preferable to Google when doing academic research. Databases will help you determine when you have begun to ask a manageable question.

When you have gotten down to 30–50 sources in your result list, begin to look through those results to see what aspects of your topic are being written about. Are there lots of articles on creativity and gender? Creativity and the workplace? Creativity and mental illness? If so, those might be topics worth investigating since there is a lot of information for you to read. This is where you begin to discover where your voice might add to the ongoing conversation on the topic.

USING EVIDENCE

The quality of evidence and how you deploy the evidence is ultimately what will make your claims persuasive. You may think of evidence as that which will help prove your claim. But if you look at any scholarly book or article, you'll see that evidence can be used in a number of different ways. Evidence can be used to provide readers with crucial background information. It can be used to tell readers what scholars have commonly thought about a topic (but which you may disagree with). It can offer a theory that you use as a lens. It can offer a methodology or an approach that you would like to use. And finally, evidence can be used to back up the claim that you'll be making in your paper.

Novice researchers begin with a thesis and try to find all the evidence that will prove that their claim is valid or true. What if you come across evidence that doesn't help with the validity of your claim? A novice researcher might decide not to take this complicating evidence into account.

Indeed, when you come across complicating evidence, you might be tempted to pretend you never saw it! But rather than sweeping imperfect evidence under the rug, you should figure out how to use this evidence to complicate your own ideas.

The best scholarly conversations take into account a wide array of evidence, carefully considering all sides of a topic. As you probably know, often the most fruitful and productive conversations occur not just when you are talking to people who already agree with you, but when you are fully engaging with the people who might disagree with you.

Coming across unexpected, surprising, and contradictory evidence, then, is a good thing! It will force you to make a complex, nuanced argument and will ultimately allow you to write a more persuasive paper.

OTHER FORMS OF EVIDENCE

We've talked about finding evidence in books, magazines, journals, and newspapers. Here are a few other kinds of evidence you may want to use.

Interviews

Interviews can be a powerful form of evidence, especially if the person you are interviewing is an expert in the field that you're investigating. Interviewing can be intimidating, but it might help to know that many people (even experts!) will feel flattered when you ask them for an interview. Most scholars are deeply interested in spreading knowledge, so you should feel comfortable asking a scholar for his or her ideas. Even if the scholar doesn't know the specific answer to your question, he or she may be able to point you in the right direction.

Remember, of course, to be as courteous as possible when you are planning to interview someone. This means sending a polite e-mail that fully introduces yourself and your project before you begin asking questions. E-mail interviews may be convenient, but an in-person interview is best, because this allows for you and the interviewee to engage in a conversation that may take surprising and helpful turns.

It's a good idea to write down a number of questions before the interview. Make sure not just to get facts (which you can likely get somewhere else). Ask the interviewee to speculate about your topic. Remember that "why" and "how" questions often yield more interesting answers than "what" questions.

If you do conduct an in-person interview, act professionally. Be on time, dress respectfully, and show sincere interest and gratitude. Bring something to record the interview. Many reporters still use pens and a pad, since these feel unobtrusive and are very portable.

Write down the interviewee's name, the date, and the location of the interview, and have your list of questions ready. Don't be afraid, of course, to veer from your questions. The best questions might be the follow-up questions that couldn't have occurred to you before the conversation began. You're likely to get the interviewee to talk freely and openly if you show real intellectual curiosity. If you're not a fast writer, it's certainly OK to ask the interviewee to pause for a moment while you take notes. Some people like to record their interviews. Just make sure that you ask permission if you choose to do this. It's always nice to send a brief thank-you note or e-mail after the interview. This would be a good time to ask any brief follow-up questions.

Images

Because we live in a visual age, we tend to take images for granted. We see them in magazines, on TV, and on the Internet. We don't often think about them as critically as we think about words on a page. Yet a critical look at an image can uncover helpful evidence for a claim.

Images can add depth and variety to your argument, and they are generally easy to find on the Internet. Use Google Image search or flickr.com to find images using the same keywords you used to find books and articles. Ask your instructor for guidance on how to properly cite and acknowledge the source of any images you wish to use. If you want to present your research outside of a classroom project (for example, publish it on a blog or share it at a community event), ask a research librarian for guidance on avoiding any potential copyright violations.

Multimedia

Like images, multimedia such as video, audio, and animations are increasingly easy to find on the Internet and can strengthen your claim. For instance, if you are working on globalization and language, you could find audio or video news clips illustrating the effects of globalization on local languages. There are several audio and video search engines available such as Vimeo (vimeo.com) or Blinkx (blinkx.com), a search engine featuring audio and video from the BBC, Reuters, and the Associated Press, among others. As with images, ask your instructor for guidance on how to properly cite and acknowledge the source of any multimedia you wish to use. If you want to present your research outside of a classroom project (for example, publish it on a blog or share it at a community event), ask a research librarian for guidance on avoiding any potential copyright violations.

EVALUATING SOURCES

A common problem in research isn't a lack of sources, but an overload of information. Information is more accessible than ever. How many times have you done an online search and asked yourself the question: "How do I know what is good information?" Librarians can help. Evaluating online sources is more challenging than traditional sources because it is harder to make distinctions between good and bad online information than with print sources. It is easy to tell that *Newsweek* magazine is not as scholarly as an academic journal, but online everything may look the same. There are markers of credibility and authoritativeness when it comes to online information, and you can start to recognize them. We'll provide a few tips here, but be sure to ask a librarian or your professor for more guidance whenever you're uncertain about the reliability of a source.

1. **Domain**—The "domain" of a site is the last part of its URL. The domain indicates the type of website. Noting the web address can tell you a lot. A ".edu" site indicates that an educational organization created that content. This is no guarantee that the information is accurate, but it does suggest less bias than a ".com" site, which will be commercial in nature with a motive to sell you something, including ideas.
2. **Date**—Most websites include a date somewhere on the page. This date may indicate a copyright date, the date something was posted, or the date the site was last updated. These dates tell you when the content on the site was last changed or reviewed. Older sites might be outdated or contain information that is no longer relevant.
3. **Author or editor**—Does the online content indicate an author or editor? Like print materials, authority comes from the creator of the content. It is now easier than ever to investigate an author's credentials. A general Google search may lead you to a Wikipedia entry on the author, a Linked In page, or even an online resume. If an author is affiliated with an educational institution, try visiting the institution's website for more information.

MANAGING SOURCES

Now that you've found sources, you need to think about how you are going to keep track of the sources and prepare the bibliography that will accompany your paper. Managing your sources is called "bibliographic citation management," and you will sometimes see references to bibliographic citation management on your library's website. Don't let this complicated phrase deter you; managing your citations from the start of your research will make your life much easier during the research process and especially the night before your paper is due when you are compiling your bibliography.

EndNote and RefWorks

Chances are your college library provides software, such as *EndNote* or *RefWorks*, to help you manage citations. These are two commercially available citation management software packages that are not freely available to you unless your library has paid for a license. *EndNote* or *RefWorks* enables you to organize your sources in personal libraries. These libraries help you manage your sources and create bibliographies. Both *EndNote* and *RefWorks* also enable you to insert endnotes and footnotes directly into a Microsoft Word document.

Zotero

If your library does not provide *EndNote* or *RefWorks*, a freely available software called *Zotero* (Zotero.org) will help you manage your sources. *Zotero* helps you collect, organize, cite, and share your sources, and it lives right in your web browser where you do your research. As you are searching *Google*, your library catalog, or library database, *Zotero* enables you to add a book, article, or website to a personal library with one click. As you add items to your library, *Zotero* collects both the information you need for you bibliography and any full-text content. This means that the content of journal articles and e-books will be available to you right from your *Zotero* library.

To create a bibliography, simply select the items from your *Zotero* library you want to include, right click, and select "Create Bibliography from Selected Items . . . ," and chose the citation style your instructor has asked you to use for the paper. To get started, go to *Zotero.org* and download *Zotero* for the browser of your choice.

Taking Notes

It is crucial that you take good, careful notes while you are doing your research. Not only is careful note taking necessary to avoid plagiarism, careful note taking can help you think through your project while you are doing research.

While many researchers used to take notes on index cards, most people now use computers. If you're using your computer, open a new document for each source that you're considering using. The first step in taking notes is to make sure that you gather all the information you might need in your bibliography or works cited. If you're taking notes from a book, for instance, you'll need the author, the title, the place of publication, the press, and the year. Be sure to check the style guide assigned by your instructor to make sure you're gathering all the necessary information.

After you've recorded the bibliographic information, add one or two keywords that can help you sort this source. Next, write a one- or two-sentence summary of the source. Finally, have a section on your document that is reserved for specific places in the text that you might want to work with. When you write down a quote, remember to be extra careful that you are capturing the quote exactly as it is written—and that you enclose the quote in quotation marks. Do not use abbreviations or change the punctuation. Remember, too, to write down the exact page numbers from the source you are quoting. Being careful with small details at the beginning of your project can save you a lot of time in the long run.

WRITING ABOUT CREATIVITY

In your writing, as in your conversations, you should always be thinking about your audience. While your most obvious audience is the instructor, most college instructors will want you to write a paper that will be interesting and illuminating for other beginning scholars in the field. Many students are unsure of what kind of knowledge they can presume of their audience. A good rule of thumb is to write not only for your instructor but also for other students in your class and for other students in classes similar to yours. You can assume a reasonably informed audience that is curious but also skeptical.

Of course it is crucial that you keep your instructor in mind. After all, your instructor will be giving you feedback and evaluating your paper. The best way to keep your instructor in mind while you are writing is to periodically reread the assignment while you are writing. Are you answering the assignment's prompt? Are you adhering to the assignment's guidelines? Are you fulfilling the assignment's purpose? If your answer to any of these questions is uncertain, it's a good idea to ask the instructor.

FROM RESEARCH QUESTION TO THESIS STATEMENT

Many students like to begin the writing process by writing an introduction. Novice writers often use an early draft of their introduction to guide the shape of their paper. Experienced scholars, however, continually return to their introduction, reshaping it and revising it as their thoughts evolve. After all, since writing is thinking, it is impossible to anticipate the full thoughts of your paper before you have written it. Many writers, in fact, only realize the actual argument they are making after they have written a draft or two of the paper. Make sure not to let your introduction trap your thinking. Think of your introduction as a guide that will help your readers down the path of discovery—a path you can only fully know after you have written your paper.

A strong introduction will welcome readers to the scholarly conversation. You'll introduce your central interlocutors and pose the question or problem that you are all interested in resolving. Most introductions contain a thesis statement, which is a sentence or two that clearly states the main argument. Some introductions, you'll notice, do not contain the argument, but merely contain the promise of a resolution to the intellectual problem.

Is Your Thesis an Argument?

So far, we've discussed a number of steps for you to take when you begin to write a research paper. We started by strategizing about ways to use presearch to find a topic and ask a researchable question, then we looked at ways to find a scholarly conversation by using your library's resources. Now we'll discuss a crucial step in the writing process: coming up with a thesis.

Your thesis is the central claim of your paper—the main point that you'd like to argue. You may make a number of claims throughout the paper; when you make a claim, you are offering a small argument, usually about a piece of evidence that you've found. Your thesis is your governing claim, the central argument of the whole paper. Sometimes it is difficult to know if you have written a proper thesis. Ask yourself, "Can a reasonable person disagree with my thesis statement?" If the answer is no, then you likely you have written an observation rather than an argument. For instance, the statement, "There are six official languages of the UN" is not a thesis, since this is a fact. A reasonable person cannot disagree with this fact, so it is not an argument. The statement, "Arabic became an official language of the UN for economic reasons" is a thesis, since it is a debatable point. A reasonable person might disagree (by arguing, for instance, that "Arabic became an official language of the UN for political reasons"). Remember to keep returning to your thesis statement while you are writing. Not only will you be thus able to make sure that your writing remains on a clear path, but you'll also be able to keep refining your thesis so that it becomes clearer and more precise.

Make sure, too, that your thesis is a point of persuasion rather than one of belief or taste.

"Chinese food tastes delicious" is certainly an argument you could make to your friend, but it is not an adequate thesis for an academic paper, because there is no evidence that you could provide that might persuade a reader who doesn't already agree with you.

Organization

In order for your paper to feel organized, readers should know where they are headed and have a reasonable idea of how they are going to get there. An introduction will offer a strong sense of organization if it:

- introduces your central intellectual problem and explains why it is important,
- suggests who will be involved in the scholarly conversation,
- indicates what kind of evidence you'll be investigating, and
- offers a precise central argument.

Some readers describe well-organized papers as having a sense of flow. When readers praise a sense of flow, they mean that the argument moves easily from one sentence to the next and from one paragraph to the next. This allows your reader to follow your thoughts easily. When you begin writing a sentence, try using an idea, keyword, or phrase from the end of the previous sentence. The next sentence, then, will appear to have emerged smoothly from the previous sentence. This tip is especially important when you move between paragraphs. The beginning of a paragraph should feel like it has a clear relationship to the end of the previous paragraph.

Keep in mind, too, a sense of wholeness. A strong paragraph has a sense of flow and a sense of wholeness: not only will you allow your reader to trace your thoughts smoothly, but you will ensure that your reader understands how all your thoughts are connected to a large, central idea. Ask yourself, as you write a paragraph: what does this paragraph have to do with the central intellectual problem that I am investigating? If the relationship isn't clear to you, then your readers will likely be confused.

Novice writers often use the form of a five-paragraph essay. In this form, each paragraph offers an example that proves the validity of the central claim. The five-paragraph essay may have worked in high school, since it meets the minimum requirement for making an argument with evidence. You'll quickly notice, though, that experienced writers do not use the five-paragraph essay. Indeed, your college instructors will expect you to move beyond the five-paragraph essay. This is because a five-paragraph essay relies on static examples rather than fully engaging new evidence. A strong essay will grow in complexity and nuance as the writer brings in new evidence. Rather than thinking of an essay as something that offers many examples to back up the same static idea, think of an essay as the evolution of an idea that grows ever more complex and rich as the writer engages with scholars who view the idea from various angles.

Integrating Your Research

As we have seen, doing research involves finding an intellectual community by looking for scholars who are thinking through similar problems and may be in conversation with one another. When you write your paper, you will not merely be reporting what you found; you will be orchestrating the conversation that your research has uncovered. To orchestrate a conversation involves asking a few key questions: Whose voices should be most prominent? What is the relationship between one scholar's ideas and another scholar's ideas? How do these ideas contribute to the argument that your own paper is making? Is it important that your readers hear the exact words of the conversation, or can you give them the main ideas and important points of the conversation in your own words? Your answers to these questions will determine how you go about integrating your research into your paper.

Using evidence is a way of gaining authority. Even though you may not have known much about your topic before you started researching, the way you use evidence in your paper will allow you to establish a voice that is authoritative and trustworthy. You have three basic choices to decide how best you'd like to present the information from a source: summarize, paraphrase, or quote. Let's discuss each one briefly.

Summary   You should summarize a source when the source provides helpful background information for your research. Summaries do not make strong evidence, but they can be helpful if you need to chart the intellectual terrain of your project. Summaries can be an efficient way of capturing the main ideas of a source. Remember, when you are summarizing, to be fully sympathetic to the writer's point of view. Put yourself in the scholar's shoes. If you later disagree with the scholar's methods or conclusions, your disagreement will be convincing because your reader will know that you have given the scholar a fair hearing. A summary that is clearly biased is not only inaccurate and ethically suspect; it will make your writing less convincing because readers will be suspicious of your rigor.

Let's say you come across the following quote that you'd like to summarize. Here's an excerpt from *The Language Wars: A History of Proper English*, by Henry Hitchings:

> No language has spread as widely as English, and it continues to spread. Internationally the desire to learn it is insatiable. In the twenty-first century the world is becoming more urban and more middle class, and the adoption of English is a symptom of this, for increasingly English serves as the lingua franca of business and popular culture. It is dominant or at least very prominent in other areas such as shipping, diplomacy, computing, medicine and education. (300)

Consider this summary:

> In *The Language Wars*, Hitchings says that everyone wants to learn English because it is the best language in the world (300). I agree that English is the best.

If you compare this summary to what Hitchings actually said, you will see that this summary is a biased, distorted version of the actual quote. Hitchings did not make a universal claim about whether

English is better or worse than other languages. Rather, he made a claim about why English is becoming so widespread in an increasingly connected world.

Now let's look at another summary, taken from the sample paper at the end of this research guide:

> According to Hitchings, English has become the go-to choice for global communications and has spread quickly as the language of commerce and ideas. (300)

This is a much stronger summary than the previous example. The writer shortens Hitchings's original language, but she is fair to the writer's original meaning and intent.

Paraphrase   Paraphrasing involves putting a source's ideas into your own words. It's a good idea to paraphrase if you think you can state the idea more clearly or more directly than the original source does. Remember that if you paraphrase you need to put the entire idea into your own words. It is not enough for you to change one or two words. Indeed, if you only change a few words, you may put yourself at risk of plagiarizing.

Let's look at how we might paraphrase the Hitchings quote that we've been discussing. Consider this paraphrase:

> Internationally the desire to learn English is insatiable. In today's society, the world is becoming wealthier and more urban, and the use of English is a symptom of this. (Hitchings 300)

You will notice that the writer simply replaced some of Hitchings's original language with synonyms. Even with the parenthetical citation, this is unacceptable paraphrasing. Indeed, this is a form of plagiarism, because the writer suggests that the language is his or her own, when it is in fact an only slightly modified version of Hitchings's own phrasing.

Let's see how we might paraphrase Hitchings in an academically honest way.

> Because English is used so frequently in global communications, many people around the world want to learn English as they become members of the middle class. (Hitchings 300)

Here the writer has taken Hitchings's message but has used his or her own language to describe what Hitchings originally wrote. The writer offers Hitchings's ideas with fresh syntax and new vocabulary, and the writer is sure to give Hitchings credit for the idea in a parenthetical citation.

Quotation   The best way to show that you are in conversation with scholars is to quote them. Quoting involves capturing the exact wording and punctuation of a passage. Quotations make for powerful evidence, especially in humanities papers. If you come across evidence that you think will be helpful in your project, you should quote it. You may be tempted to quote only those passages that seem to agree with the claim that you are working with. But remember to write down the quotes of scholars who may not seem to agree with you. These are precisely the thoughts that will help you build a powerful scholarly conversation. Working with fresh ideas that you may not agree with can help you revise your claim to make it even more persuasive, since it will force you to take into account potential counterarguments. When your readers see that you are grappling with an intellectual problem from all sides and that you are giving all interlocutors a fair voice, they are more likely to be persuaded by your argument.

To make sure that you are properly integrating your sources into your paper, remember the acronym ICE: Introduce, Cite, and Explain. Let's imagine that you've found an idea that you'd like to incorporate into your paper. We'll use a quote from David Harvey's *A Brief History of Neoliberalism* as an example. On page 7, you find the following quote that you'd like to use: "The assumption that individual freedoms are guaranteed by freedom of the market and of trade is a cardinal feature of neoliberal thinking, and it has long dominated the US stance towards the rest of the world."

The first thing you need to do is *introduce* the quote ("introduce" gives us the "I" in ICE). To introduce a quote, provide context so that your readers know where it is coming from, and you must integrate the quote into your own sentence. Here are some examples of how you might do this:

> In his book *A Brief History of Neoliberalism*, David Harvey writes . . .
> One expert on the relationship between economics and politics claims . . .
> Professor of Anthropology David Harvey explains that . . .
> In a recent book by Harvey, he contends . . .

Notice that each of these introduces the quote in such a way that readers are likely to recognize it as an authoritative source.

The next step is to *cite* the quote (the C in ICE). Here is where you indicate the origin of the quotation so that your readers can easily look up the original source. Citing is a two-step process that varies slightly depending on the citation style that you're using. We'll offer an example using MLA style. The first step involves indicating the author and page number in the body of your essay. Here is an example of a parenthetical citation which gives the author and page number after the quote and before the period that ends the sentence:

> One expert on the relationship between economics and politics claims that neoliberal thinking has "long dominated the US stance towards the rest of the world." (Harvey 7)

Note that if it is already clear to readers which author you're quoting, you need only to give the page number:

> In *A Brief History of Neoliberalism*, David Harvey contends that neoliberal thinking has "long dominated the US stance towards the rest of the world." (7)

The second step of citing the quote is providing proper information in the works cited or bibliography of your paper. This list should include the complete bibliographical information of all the sources you have cited. An essay that includes the quote by David Harvey should also include the following entry in the Works Cited:

> Harvey, David. *A Brief History of Neoliberalism*. New York: Oxford UP, 2005. Print.

Finally, the most crucial part of integrating a quote is *explaining* it. The E in ICE is often overlooked, but a strong explanation is the most important step to involve yourself in the scholarly conversation. Here is where you will explain how you interpret the source you are citing, what aspect of the quote is most important for your readers to understand, and how the source pertains to your own project. For example:

David Harvey writes, "The assumption that individual freedoms are guaranteed by freedom of the market and of trade is a cardinal feature of neoliberal thinking, and it has long dominated the US stance towards the rest of the world" (7). As Harvey explains, neoliberalism suggests that free markets do not limit personal freedom but actually lead to free individuals.

Or:

David Harvey writes, "The assumption that individual freedoms are guaranteed by freedom of the market and of trade is a cardinal feature of neoliberal thinking, and it has long dominated the US stance towards the rest of the world" (7). For Harvey, before we understand the role of the United States in global politics, we must first understand the philosophy that binds personal freedom with market freedom.

Novice writers are sometimes tempted to end a paragraph with a quote that they feel is especially compelling or clear. But remember that you should never leave a quote to speak for itself (even if you love it!). After all, as the orchestrator of this scholarly conversation, you need to make sure that readers are receiving exactly what you'd like them to receive from each quote. Notice, in the earlier examples, that the first explanation suggests that the writer quoting Harvey is centrally concerned with neoliberal philosophy, while the second explanation suggests that the writer is centrally concerned with US politics. The explanation, in other words, is the crucial link between your source and the main idea of your paper.

Avoiding Plagiarism

Scholarly conversations are what drive knowledge in the world. Scholars using each other's ideas in open, honest ways form the bedrock of our intellectual communities and ensure that our contributions to the world of thought are important. It is crucial, then, that all writers do their part in maintaining the integrity and trustworthiness of scholarly conversations. It is crucial that you never claim someone else's ideas as your own, and that you always are extra careful to give the proper credit to someone else's thoughts. This is what we call responsible scholarship.

The best way to avoid plagiarism is to plan ahead and keep track careful notes as you read your sources. Remember the earlier advice on *Zotero* and taking notes: find the way that works best for you to keep track of what ideas are your own and what ideas come directly from the sources you are reading. Most acts of plagiarism are accidental. It is easy when you are drafting a paper to lose track of where a quote or idea came from; plan ahead and this won't happen. Here are a few tips for making sure that confusion doesn't happen to you.

1. Know what needs to be cited. You do not need to cite what is considered common knowledge such as facts (the day Lincoln was born), concepts (the earth orbits the sun), or events (the day Martin Luther King was shot). You do need to cite the ideas and words of others from the sources you are using in your paper.
2. Be conservative. If you are not sure if you should cite something, either ask your instructor or a librarian, or cite it. It is better to cite something you don't have to than not cite something you should.
3. Direct quotations from your sources need to be cited as well as anytime you paraphrase the ideas or words from your sources.
4. Finally, extensive citation not only helps you avoid plagiarism, but it also boosts your credibility and enables your reader to trace you scholarship.

Citation Styles

It is crucial that you adhere to the standards of a single citation style when you write your paper. The most common styles are MLA (Modern Language Association, generally used in the humanities), APA (American Psychological Association, generally used in the social sciences), and Chicago (*Chicago Manual of Style*). If you're not sure which style you should use, you must ask your instructor. Each style has its own guidelines regarding the format of the paper. While proper formatting within a given style may seem arbitrary, there are important reasons behind the guidelines of each style. For instance, while MLA citations tend to emphasize author's names, APA citations tend to emphasize the date of publications. This distinction makes sense, especially given that MLA standards are usually followed by departments in the humanities and APA standards are usually followed by departments in the social sciences. While papers in the humanities value original thinking about arguments and texts that are canonical and often old, papers in the social sciences tend to value arguments that take into account the most current thought and the latest research.

There are a number of helpful guidebooks that will tell you all the rules you need to know in order to follow the standards for various citation styles. If your instructor hasn't pointed you to a specific guidebook, try the following online resources:

Purdue Online Writing Lab: owl.english.purdue.edu/

Internet Public Library: www.ipl.org/div/farq/netciteFARQ.html/

Modern Language Association (for MLA style): www.mla.org/style/

American Psychological Association (for APA style): www.apastyle.org/

The Chicago Manual of Style Online: www.chicagomanualofstyle.org/tools_citationguide.html/

Answers to Puzzles and Games

CHAPTER 1
Edward De Bono "Creativity Workout"
Explore Question #1:

a. The baby fell out of a first-floor window.

b. The last person to take a loaf of bread takes the entire basket with the final loaf of bread still in it.

CHAPTER 2
Scott Berkun "Good Ideas Are Hard to Find"
Explore Question #2:

Bug squasher
Paperweight
Toilet paper
Back scratcher
Good posture practice (balance on head)
Makeshift baseball bat
Manual fan
Crooked table leg fixer
Booster seat
Place to hide loose $20 bills

CHAPTER 4
Keith Sawyer "Small Sparks"

Figure B.1 Solution to the "Nine Dots" problem.

The x-ray problem: Mount ten separate radiation guns around the patient's body, each of them set to deliver only one-tenth of the necessary radiation. Focus all ten on the tumor so that only at that point will the total radiation be high enough to destroy the malignant tissue.

The landscape gardener problem: One of the four trees must be planted on a hill (or in a deep pit) and the other three at the base, so that the four trees form the vertices of a pyramid.

The ten coins problem: Use the ten coins to form a five-pointed star shape; five coins form the five points, and the other five form the pentagon at the center of the star.

The RAT triplet solutions: ICE, BOAT, FIRE, DAY, BLOOD

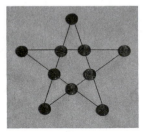

CHAPTER 6
Forging Connections

- Calculate $14 \times 8 - 11 \times 2$. (202)
- What is the official currency of Kenya? (Kenyan shilling)
- Which is the scientific name of the shinbone? (tibia)
- Spell "triskaidekaphobia."
- What is the order of bats called? (Chiroptera)
- What device did Trevor Baylis invent in 1991? (windup/clockwork radio)

credits

The Creative Process

"Isaac Asimov Asks, 'How Do People Get New Ideas?'" by Isaac Asimov, *MIT Technology Review* (October 2014). Copyright © MIT Technology Review, Inc. Reprinted with permission.

Abridged from "The Creative Personality" (pp. 51–76) from CREATIVITY: Flow and the Psychology of Discovery and Invention by Mihaly Csikszentmihalyi. Copyright © 1996 by Mihaly Csikszentmihalyi. Reprinted by permission of HarperCollins Publishers.

"The Adjacent Possible" (pp. 25–42) from WHERE GOOD IDEAS COME FROM: The Natural History of Innovation by Steven Johnson. Copyright © 2010 by Steven Johnson. Reprinted by permission of Riverhead, an imprint of Penguin Publishing Group, a division of Penguin Random House LLC.

Chapter 11, "Inside Out and Outside In" (pp. 183–201) from INGENIUS: A Crash Course on Creativity by Tina Seelig. Copyright © 2012 by Tina L. Seelig. Reprinted by permission of HarperCollins Publishers.

"Creativity Theory" by D. Anthony Miles, CEO and Founder, Miles Development Industries Corporation. Reprinted by permission of the author.

"Creativity from Beyond One's Natural Grasp: Finding Your Most Creative Ideas through Spirituality" by Stephanie Freeman and Wendy Rountree. Reprinted by permission of Stephanie Freeman.

"Creativity Workout" (pp. 1–8) from CREATIVITY WORKOUT: 62 Exercises to Unlock Your Most Creative Ideas by Edward de Bono. Copyright © 2008 by Edward de Bono. Reprinted by permission of Ulysses Press.

Creativity Myths

CALVIN AND HOBBES Copyright © 1992 Watterson. Reprinted with permission of UNIVERSAL UCLICK. All rights reserved.

DILBERT Copyright © 2013 Scott Adams. Used By permission of UNIVERSAL UCLICK. All rights reserved.

Figure 2.2: Copyright © SRI International. Reprinted courtesy of SRI International.

"Good Ideas are Hard to Find" (pp. 84–95) from THE MYTHS OF INNOVATION by Scott Berkun. Copyright © 2010 by Scott Berkun. Published by O'Reilly Media, Inc. All rights reserved. Used with permission.

The Creative Workplace

Collaboration and Creativity

Creativity and the Arts

"Creativity across the Domains" (pp. 359–390) from CREATING MINDS: An Anatomy of Creativity Seen through the Lives of Freud, Einstein, Picasso, Stravinsky, Eliot, Graham, and Gandhi by Howard Gardner. Copyright © 1993, 2011 by Howard Gardner. Reprinted by permission of Basic Books, a member of the Perseus Books Group.

"On Nonconformity" (pp. 73–91) from THE SHAPE OF CONTENT by Ben Shahn. Copyright © 1957 by the President and Fellows of Harvard College. Copyright renewed 1985 by Bernarda B. Shahn. Reprinted by permission of Harvard University Press, Cambridge, Mass.

Excerpt from pp. 181–191 from ON BECOMING AN ARTIST: Reinventing Yourself through Mindful Creativity by Ellen Langer, Ph.D. Copyright © 2005 by Ellen Langer, Ph.D. Used by permission of Ballantine Books, an imprint of Random House, a division of Penguin Random House LLC. All rights reserved.

Pp. 118–131 from WRITING ON BOTH SIDES OF THE BRAIN by Henriette Anne Klauser. Copyright © 1987 by Henriette Anne Klauser. Reprinted by permission of HarperCollins Publishers.

The Creative Genius

GARFIELD Copyright © 1981 Paws, Inc. Reprinted with permission of UNIVERSAL UCLICK. All rights reserved.

"Where Is Creativity?" (pp. 23–50) from CREATIVITY: Flow and the Psychology of Discovery and Invention by Mihaly Csikszentmihalyi. Copyright © 1996 by Mihaly Csikszentmihalyi. Reprinted by permission of HarperCollins Publishers.

"Secrets of the Creative Brain" by Nancy Andreasen, *The Atlantic* (July/August 2014). Copyright © 2014 by The Atlantic Media Co., as first published in *The Atlantic Magazine*. All rights reserved. Distributed by Tribune Content Agency, LLC.

"Chaos and Order" from CREATIVITY: The Perfect Crime by Philippe Petit. Copyright © 2014 by Departure Corp. Used by permission of Riverhead, an imprint of Penguin Publishing Group, a division of Penguin Random House LLC.

Creativity Strategies and Hacks

"How to Be More Creative" by A. J. Jacobs. http://www.realsimple.com/health/mind-mood/how-to-be-creative. Reprinted by permission of A. J. Jacobs.

"Creative Thinking Hacks" (pp. 168–174) from THE MYTHS OF INNOVATION by Scott Berkun. Copyright © 2010 by Scott Berkun. Published by O'Reilly Media, Inc. All rights reserved. Used with permission.

"Innovation in the House: Creativity Lesson from Five Top In-House Creative Teams" (pp. 4–8) by The Creative Group. Reprinted by permission of The Creative Group. http://www.creativegroup.com.

"The Spiral Thinking Guide" by Ed Goodman and Dave Goodman. Copyright © 2015 by Spiral Experiences, LLC. Reprinted by permission of Spiral Experiences, LLC. http://www.spiralexperiences.com.

index